Using Generic CADD

Using Generic CADD

Ray C. Freeman III

Osborne **McGraw-Hill**

Berkeley New York St. Louis San Francisco
Auckland Bogotá Hamburg London Madrid
Mexico City Milan Montreal New Delhi Panama City
Paris São Paulo Singapore Sydney
Tokyo Toronto

Osborne **McGraw-Hill**
2600 Tenth Street
Berkeley, California 94710
U.S.A.

For information on translations and book distributors outside of the
U.S.A., please write to Osborne **McGraw-Hill** at the above address.

A complete list of trademarks appears on page 453.

Using Generic CADD

1234567890 DOC 89

ISBN 0-07-881499-5

Contents

Acknowledgments

Thanks go to the following, for the following reasons: My wife, Amy, for not getting too upset about watching various versions of this book on TV at night and waking up with a mouse in the bed; My office, Workshop 3D, for putting up with my being otherwise useless during the writing of this book; Laurie Beaulieu, Associate Editor at Osborne/McGraw Hill, for putting up with my indignation and outbursts at her perfectly reasonable requests; The folks at Generic Software, for making a program worth spending the time to write about; Finally, Davis Straub, for getting me involved with CAD in the first place and Generic CADD in the second.

Introduction

This is a book about drawing.

Just as you use a word processor to *write,* and you use a spreadsheet to *analyze* or make projections, so it is that you use a CADD program to *draw.* Whether you are a new computer user or an experienced CADD veteran, this book will help you learn how to *draw* with Generic CADD, and to do it well, with ease, speed, accuracy, and efficiency.

As the title *Using Generic CADD* suggests, this book is organized to teach the user the concepts and skills required to master Generic CADD as a drawing tool. The ideas and techniques discussed in *Using Generic CADD* are the result of several years of experience and experimentation with Generic CADD in both professional and non-technical applications.

What is CAD?

This book begins with important conceptual ideas about Computer Aided Design (CAD). The first chapter discusses the philosophy behind CAD as a program type and as a drawing medium. This conceptual background will help you to understand exactly what a CAD program does best.

The second chapter deals with how these ideas are approached in Generic CADD. This chapter also examines the drawing screen and its cursor, the menu and its cursor, and the Generic CADD command structure and syntax.

Getting Started

Chapter 3 reviews installation, configuration, and data paths. Some time is spent in making sure that Generic CADD is configured to run exactly the way that you want it to, by selecting default colors, a unit system, and a drawing size.

Drawing

Chapters 4 through 12 are organized into a number of sample drawing tasks, arranged from the simplest drawings to those that require more complex techniques. Simple drawing commands are introduced in Chapter 4, while basic editing is covered in Chapter 5.

Drawing organization and special drawing aids are the subject of Chapters 6 and 7, and more complex drawing techniques that deal with more complicated tasks are covered in Chapters 8, 9, and 10. At this point, Level 2 and Level 3 users will be able to take advantage of the extended drawing and editing functions of these programs. You will also see that Level 1 users can accomplish many of the same tasks by introducing a little ingenuity where automated features are not available.

Automated Dimensioning, available in Levels 2 and 3, is the topic of Chapter 11. Special consideration is given to customizing the dimensioning functions to draw the way that *you* do, so that your drawing will look as though *you* drew them.

Saving and loading your drawings are covered in Chapter 12. Topics include all file input techniques such as moving information from one drawing to another, saving partial drawings, saving and loading your drawing as a screen image only, and saving and loading your drawing to and from ASCII text files to provide for interaction with other software.

Peripheral Devices: Printers, Plotters, and Digitizers

Chapter 13 focuses on getting the drawing from the screen (or, more accurately, the disk) to the paper. Whether you are using a dot matrix or laser printer with Levels 1 and 2, or a plotter with Level 3, many of the basic considerations are the same. The specifics of the various output devices are covered as well.

Chapter 14 explains the use of a digitizer with Level 3 including its use as a pointing device, a command generator, and a tracing tablet.

Beyond Drawing

The final chapters show how to take advantage of the Level programmable menu structure, Level 3's ability to communicate with other software through batch files, and the availability of utility software to take up where Generic CADD leaves off.

Appendixes

Three appendixes provide a summary of commands, a guide to available software that may be used with or interfaced to Generic CADD, and an extensive glossary.

Not everyone who reads this book will be trying to draw the same thing. A drawing program is in many ways more flexible, and the variety of possible applications wider, than most other application software.

By combining readily applicable techniques with explanations of their conceptual backgrounds, *Using Generic CADD* will lead you to discoveries that you can adapt to meet your own drawing needs and enhance your personal drawing style. This is not so much the nature of this book, or even Generic CADD, as it is the nature of drawing.

1 The Essence of CAD

Powerful, inexpensive CAD (an acronym for Computer Aided Design) for microcomputers is a fairly recent phenomenon. This chapter will provide a general overview of the basic nature of CAD for the personal computer environment. By taking the time to acquaint yourself with CAD's conceptual foundations, you will be able to apply the detailed information and applications contained in the following chapters. Generic CADD may be your first exposure to a CAD program, and you may find it to be quite different than you had imagined. If you have experience with more expensive CAD systems, you will be surprised that Generic CADD offers many capabilities that were difficult to find even on powerful mainframe systems only a few years ago. With the low price and easy-to-use features of Generic CADD, many more people can now take advantage of CAD's technical and creative features.

As you will see, drawing with CAD and drawing by hand are very different processes. If you assume that drawing with CAD is intended to simply mimic the hand drawing process, you will miss many of the conceptual and technical benefits of CAD. In general, the best approach is to pretend that you have never drawn before.

To get the most out of any CAD program, it is important to understand some of the conceptual differences between CAD programs and other types of drawing software. CAD has evolved principally as a technique for representing real objects on a computer. The storage and representation of real and accurate data make CAD an ideal tool for industrial, engineering, architectural, manufacturing, electronic, scientific, and many other applications.

The representational aspect of CAD introduces a refreshing rigor into the drawing process: Every object is defined by its location and geometric properties, and every entity in the drawing plays a representational role. A line, for example, might be the perimeter of an object, a fold line or corner, or a change of material, but it almost always represents *something*. A drawing medium that not only encourages a methodical way of thinking about drawing but also provides the means for doing so is an interesting and valuable tool indeed.

CAD can be classified as a drawing medium or as a type of software. Because CAD is a relatively new drawing process, its inherent characteristics have hardly been explored, much less technically or artistically exploited to their fullest potential. To use any CAD program effectively, however, you must first master it as a program, so that its use becomes second nature. Once you have done this, you will be able to utilize CAD as a drawing medium, which is more interesting and ultimately more useful.

CAD Program Characteristics

The term "Computer Aided Design" is rather broad and often stimulates confusion and controversy. Some people prefer words such as "Drawing" or "Drafting " to "Design." However, not every use of the computer for design, drawing, or drafting is considered to be CAD. Over the past several years, a specific technical definition of CAD as a type of computer program has evolved. To understand the characteristics that are unique to CAD, it is helpful to examine both what CAD is and what it is not, by comparing it to other computerized and manual drawing techniques.

Many properties of a CAD program are very different from another class of drawing programs, commonly referred to as *painting programs*. The distinction between these two types of programs does not necessarily make a CAD program better than a painting program, just different. A CAD program is better for certain uses, while a painting program is more useful for other functions. Understanding the difference between the two program types makes it easier to determine which would be more effective for your particular application.

The information that is input, stored, processed, and output by a CAD program is considered real geometric data, rather than graphic data. The data stored by a CAD program represents physical properties (such as an

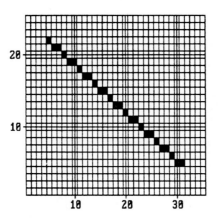

Line from 5,22 to 31,5
Layer 0
Color 1
Line type 1
Line Weight 1

Data stored in
a typical CADD program

Figure 1-1. *A line and its associated data in a CAD program*

object's actual location, size, edges, and shape) rather than the graphic depiction of those properties—that is, their appearance on the screen. In order to display, print, or otherwise make use of graphic depictions of objects, a CAD program creates these visual images from stored definitions. In contrast, painting programs store data as graphic depictions of these properties, in the form that they appear on the computer screen, as a number of dots called *pixels*.

The difference between the data actually stored when a line is drawn in a CAD program and when one is drawn in a painting program is shown in Figures 1-1 and 1-2. Although the user may input similar data in both types

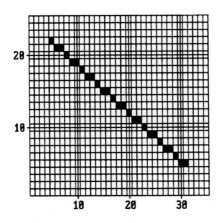

5,22;6,21;7,21;8,20;9,19;10,19;
11,18;12,17;13,17;14,16;15,15;
16,15;17,14;18,13;19,13;20,12;
21,11;22,11;23,13;24,9;25,9;
26,8;27,7;28,7;29,6;30,5;31,5;

Data stored in
a typical painting program

Figure 1-2. *A line and its associated data in a paint program*

of programs (in this example, the location of the two endpoints of a line), the data stored by a CAD program and a painting program are quite different.

A CAD program stores the location of the two endpoints that you have specified and derives the information regarding which pixels should be turned on each time the line is displayed. A painting program, on the other hand, actually stores only the locations of the pixels that represent the line on the screen. This means that a CAD program can calculate the length of a line, its angle, and its X and Y displacements, but a painting program can do none of these things, and in fact doesn't even remember the two endpoints that you specified originally. As you will notice from the illustrations, the CAD program also stores a number of other defining features of the line, including its color and thickness, which can be changed later if you like.

Real World Scale

The part of real world that you are trying to draw is usually larger or smaller than your computer screen. The standard technique for fitting a drawing onto a sheet of paper is a scale conversion factor. For example, building floor plans are typically drawn at scales of 1/4" = 1'-0", meaning that one-quarter inch on the drawing represents one foot in the real building. Certain types of manufacturing drawings are larger than real life. Scales like 4:1 mean that the drawing is four times larger than the actual object.

With a CAD program, this scaling is not necessary. If the object you are drawing is ten feet long, you can tell the CAD program to draw a line ten feet long. You needn't worry that the object must eventually be reduced to fit on a piece of paper or that the screen is only eight inches wide—that's the program's responsibility! You can draw objects in *real world scale* (actual size).

This is one way in which CAD is markedly different from drawing by hand. When you draw by hand, you must always be aware of your scale and either use a scale or conversion units as you draw. A CAD program almost never asks you to do the conversion yourself. Because the CAD program stores the actual sizes and dimensions of what you are drawing rather than its screen image, it can display or print the drawing at *any* scale.

CAD programs do not reduce dimensional data to the lowest common denominator of video resolution, plotter resolution, or any other limiting factor. Only the current display or print is affected by these hardware considerations. CAD software can work with any numbers that can be stored on your computer. Painting programs, on the other hand, are always limited to the *minimum* resolution available, that of the video display. The very premise of a painting program is based on manipulating pixels; CAD programs manipulate data.

To develop a high level of accuracy, CAD programs generally offer a number of methods of specifying numeric data. Most allow you to point to places on the screen, to trace drawings on a digitizer, or to enter coordinates manually by typing dimensions on the keyboard. Generic CADD offers all of these forms of data input, as well as others. Of these methods, typing on the keyboard is undoubtedly the most reliable. *Digitizing,* or tracing drawings into the CAD database from a specially designed tablet (called a *digitizer*) that sends coordinate information to the CAD program, can be useful when absolute accuracy is not important or when combined with other automated geometry-adjusting features of CAD software. Pointing on the screen is accurate only when combined with automatic incrementation techniques (definable tolerances or resolution-enforcing grids, for example), or when referencing existing geometry (such as the center of an existing circle or the end of an existing line).

Real Data Storage   In a CAD program, a line can be one inch long, 12 feet long, 225 feet long, or any other dimension because, as you have seen, a CAD program records the definition of the line rather than its graphic representation. Additional information can be derived from this data depending on your drawing needs.

The stored definition of any object is based on its geometric properties. In the case of a line, the properties are namely that it starts at one point and ends at another. For a circle, the locations of the center point and either the radius or one additional point on the circle are sufficient to generate not only the graphic representation of the circle, but all of its other physical properties as well. Figure 1-3 shows the data associated with and derived from the geometric properties of a circle.

Flexibility of Stored Data   Because CAD programs record geometric properties, you have considerable control over the way this data is displayed and used. You can view the same drawing in various sizes and can query the database for accurate dimensional information derived from the existing geometry of a single object, or from the relationships between objects. You will find that editing a CAD drawing is crucial to its eventual accuracy. When editing a line, for example, you can move either endpoint, changing the location, length, and angle of the line simultaneously. In addition, the color, thickness, type (solid or dashed), and other properties of the line are always adjustable. These editing capabilities make CAD exceptionally flexible as a drawing tool. When drawing by hand, you have to decide, for example, the thickness and color of a line before you draw it. With a CAD program, you can draw the line first, and then try various color and thickness alternatives.

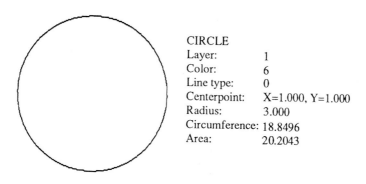

CIRCLE
Layer: 1
Color: 6
Line type: 0
Centerpoint: X=1.000, Y=1.000
Radius: 3.000
Circumference: 18.8496
Area: 20.2043

Figure 1-3. *The data associated with or derived from a circle*

Real Objects Versus Symbols Certain CAD drawing tasks seem to break the rule of real world scale. However, if you examine these tasks carefully (see Chapter 8), you will see that they are not actually exceptions.

Many drawings, especially those that will eventually be printed or plotted at other than real world scale, contain two distinct types of information. The lines, circles, arcs, and so on that represent actual objects make up the "real" portion of your drawing and follow the real world scale concept as you would expect. The second type of information, drawing symbols, such as text, arrows, dimensions, and other symbols, are not representations of objects but help to describe these objects. When such symbols are used, the concept of real world scale is irrelevant because the size of these objects is related to the reduced or enlarged scale of the final paper print or plot, not the size of the "real" objects in the drawing.

There is no specific agreement among CAD programs as to how the difference between "real" and "symbolic" information is handled. In Generic CADD, components are used for both real and symbolic information. Generally, it is left to the user to make the distinction and scale objects accordingly.

Scaled Output All CAD programs contain some method for obtaining proportionally correct scaled output of the drawing data. This provides the final reconciliation between the real world scale of the object and the size of the paper on which you are printing it. Most CAD programs provide a choice between a user-selected scale and automatic scaling. Generic CADD provides a number of automated and user-generated scaling functions as part of its printing and plotting routines.

Basic Drawing Elements

The geometric properties and dimensional data that we have been discussing are created and stored as a series of predefined elements, which are often referred to as *primitives*. So far, a line has been used as the primary example of a primitive. CAD programs include a variety of commands for actually placing a number of these primitives (including circles, arcs, and others) and additional commands for combining and editing these primitives once they are placed. These commands vary among CAD programs.

To understand the concept of primitives, compare the basic facets of a CAD program, which creates, edits, and processes drawing data, to a word processing program, which creates, edits, and processes written data. In a typical English-language word processor, letters, numbers, and punctuation symbols may be considered the primitives for that type of software. These primitives are placed into the document by moving a cursor to a desired location and typing the characters on a keyboard. These characters are then manipulated through combinations of editing keystrokes. Many times, the editing process adds no new characters, but merely manipulates existing ones. However, you can't edit a document until you have created at least part of it with a few characters.

In a CAD program, primitives take the form of lines, circles, arcs, points, ellipses, curves of various types, and other basic geometric shapes. Normally, a number of these primitives are placed into a drawing by moving a cursor to a desired location and then selecting commands, either from a menu or by typing them on a keyboard. Figure 1-4 shows a number of primitives common to most CAD programs.

Just as the writer is limited to the 26 letters of the alphabet, ten numeric digits, and a finite number of punctuation marks, the CAD drafter is limited to the primitives provided by a particular CAD program. As might be expected, CAD programs are less standard in regard to the number and type of primitives than word processors, which are based on an accepted standard that has been in use for centuries.

The writer conquers the 26-character limitation of the alphabet by combining these characters into words and then combining these words

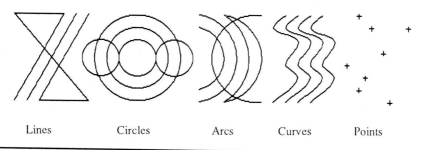

| Lines | Circles | Arcs | Curves | Points |

Figure 1-4. *Typical CAD primitives*

into sentences, poems, novels, and software user manuals. In a similar way, the CAD drafter combines various geometric primitives to form more complex shapes and to describe objects and then places these objects in relation to one another, creating everything from garage sale signs to circuit board diagrams, to building details, to conceptual layouts for space stations.

Grouping Primitives

In addition to providing an assortment of primitives, CAD programs typically provide a number of ways to organize them. At the most basic level, primitives are used to draw "things." These things must then be given identities, so that they can be referenced, replicated, and manipulated as objects.

Drawing Files   Although CAD programs identify these objects in a variety of ways, almost all CAD programs store a certain amount of drawing information as a *drawing file*. This is similar to the way in which a word processor stores a certain amount of text information as a document file. Working within the computer's operating system, which separates information into files stored on disk, this is a logical way to organize text information at the most basic level. Likewise, one drawing—a readily identifiable group of drawn elements—can also be placed into a file that is a nameable, storable, retrievable quantity of computer data.

Definable Objects   At the next "higher" level, small portions of the drawing are often called *symbols, components,* or *blocks,* depending on the CAD program you are using. These consist of a number of primitives that have been placed in such a way as to describe one object, usually an object that appears more than once in the drawing.

These objects can often be replicated within the drawing by referring to their name or number. They can also generally be placed in the drawing at other scales and orientations than those at which they were originally created. In some cases, they can be redefined after they have been placed in the drawing, allowing global editing commands to make changes throughout a drawing.

The rules that govern the use of defined objects vary among CAD programs. Some programs allow *nested definitions,* in which defined objects contain the definitions of others, and some programs do not. Some even allow a *recursive definition,* which is a definition that contains a definition of itself. Generic CADD allows both methods. Yet other programs provide a specific type of definition and set of rules for each nesting level. For instance, drawings might be made of parts that are, in turn, composed of symbols, which are composed of the most basic elements, the program's specific primitives.

The storage of these defined objects is another area in which CAD programs vary. Some store the definitions within the drawing file; others store them in separate definition files. In some cases, these definition files are treated exactly as if they were drawing files, allowing any drawing to be treated as a defined object with another file. Generic CADD allows a number of combinations of these storage schemes, depending on your needs, as explained in Chapter 8.

Associated Entities   Often, certain elements in a drawing do not create a specific object but instead share some other common characteristic. Most CAD programs provide an organizational device called a *layer,* a *level,* or an *overlay* that allows you to group entities. A layer is often visualized as a transparent sheet on which certain entities have been drawn. In CAD, this device provides a means of identifying certain entities that have something in common.

The characteristic that is shared by a group of entities varies depending on the application. A circuit board designer, for example, might group together all items that are to be etched in copper and separate into another group the items that are to be silkscreened onto the board. An architect might put a basic floor plan on one layer and place the wiring, plumbing, and heating systems onto separate layers.

Display and editing control are often associated with these groupings. The CAD user can usually choose to display certain groups of information while excluding others. In addition, the user sometimes has control over which layers can be edited and which are "display only." Generic CADD provides both display and editing control over layers.

The interaction between drawing files, definable objects, and related groups of information is one feature that defines the "personality" of a particular CAD program. The simple but effective way in which Generic CADD deals with these relationships is a major reason for the program's popularity and usefulness.

Hardware Independence

The storage of definitions (rather than images) means that CAD programs are essentially hardware-independent; that is, neither the program nor the data is bound to specific hardware configurations. Any graphics card can represent a line of specific length or a circle of a given diameter. The same is true for printers and plotters.

Hardware Support   In practice, the devices to be used with the CAD program (graphics card, printer, and so on) must be supported by that CAD program. The CAD program must contain or have access to instructions that make it compatible with your particular hardware devices. Currently, major CAD vendors such as Generic are making this part of their programs accessible to third-party developers and equipment manufacturers so that their programs can work with the latest technology on the market.

Resolution   Even though CAD programs are theoretically hardware-independent, the capability of the particular display or output device does determine the displayed resolution at any given time. Even when the defined data contains a great deal of information, the CAD program cannot create any more dots on the screen or paper than the hardware allows. Figure 1-5 shows a simple drawing displayed at different resolutions on different display devices.

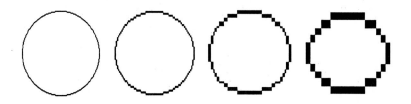

Figure 1-5. *The same circle on several different display devices*

Data Transferability Device independence means that drawings created on one system can often be transferred to another without losing important information or degrading data. Because the information stored by a CAD program is essentially geometric, not graphic, transfers can also be made between higher- and lower-resolution systems, systems with or without color, and even among machines that run on different operating systems.

Although no standard in the CAD world is as widely accepted as ASCII is in the text-oriented community, numerous CAD-specific data transfer formats have gained wide acceptance in a variety of disciplines in which CAD is used frequently. Among these are IGES, the Initial Graphics Exchange Standard, and DXF, a drawing exchange format developed and promoted by AutoDesk, Inc. Generic CADD data files can be exchanged with other CAD software through either of these popular formats.

CAD as a Drawing Medium

Once you have a general understanding of CAD's capabilities as a computer program, you can begin to understand CAD's advantages as a drawing tool. CAD is a surprisingly flexible drawing medium. Like every medium, CAD has certain physical limitations within which the artist or drafter works. The artistry lies in the user's ability to transcend the medium by blending personal expression with the inherent characteristics of the medium.

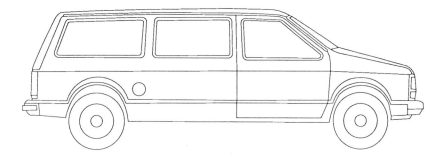

Figure 1-6. *CAD drawing of a minivan (Courtesy of Mobile Office Vehicle Engineering)*

Figures 1-6 through 1-9 show several different types of CAD drawings, ranging from more technically oriented drawings, which use real world scale and exact dimensions, to more purely creative uses of CAD. The more experimental drawings vary in their approach to scale, as they are not typical representations of reality.

Figure 1-7. *CAD elevation of a house*

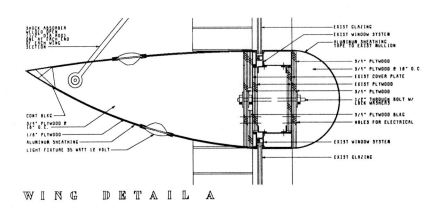

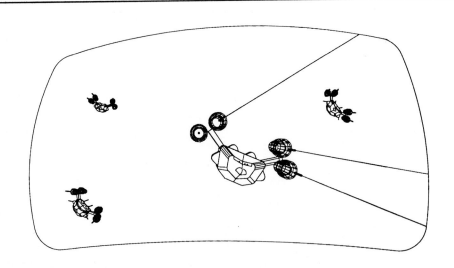

Figure 1-8. *Architectural detail drawn on a CAD program*

Figure 1-9. *Creative CAD drawing (courtesy of Del Saul)*

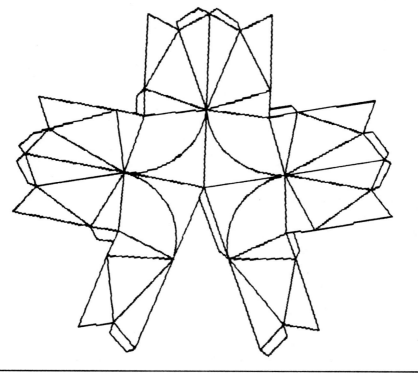

Figure 1-10.   *CAD used to create fold-up art (courtesy of Del Saul)*

As a tool for technical drawing, CAD offers precision, pure geometry, and subtlety of detail and technique. When considered as works of art or craftsmanship, CAD drawings differ from drawings done in other mediums in that they have several distinct physical forms. Created with drawing and editing commands, the CAD drawing first appears on the computer screen as an electronic image. In another form, the CAD drawing appears as hard copy printed on a mechanical device such as a printer or a plotter. A third and intermediate manifestation of the CAD drawing is in the form of a disk file, which has no visible attributes at all. Because you can think of any of these as the actual drawing, CAD offers a virtually infinite number of opportunities for artistic manipulation of the physical drawing process.

Figure 1-11. *Photo of finished piece folded from CAD drawing (courtesy of Del Saul)*

Figure 1-10 shows another example of a multiple-process artistic investigation with CAD—the design of a folded object. Figure 1-11 shows the finished product, a hybrid object that was first created electronically using the automated drawing capabilities of a CAD program, then plotted on paper, and finally folded by the human hand. As the capabilities of CAD become available to a wide audience through inexpensive easy-to-use programs like Generic CADD, inventive and artistic applications will continue to develop.

As you can see from this brief overview, Computer Aided Design is both a valuable electronic drawing tool and a creative artistic medium. In the following chapters, you will learn how to harness the versatility and efficiency of Generic CADD to accomplish your specific drawing tasks.

2 *The Generic Approach*

Generic CADD is in every sense a true CAD program of the type described in Chapter 1. This chapter first focuses on how Generic CADD specifically approaches the general issues discussed in Chapter 1. Then, the chapter introduces Generic CADD's user interface, including the basic screens that you will encounter and the structure of Generic CADD's menus and commands.

History

Generic CADD was introduced in 1985 as a low-cost alternative to the CAD software available for PCs at that time. Since that introduction of version 1.0, Generic Software has subscribed to the basic CAD concepts that are generally well accepted in the industry (see Chapter 1). The development of the product through versions 2.0 and 3.0 to the current Level has not changed the basic direction of the program in any way. The maturation of Generic CADD has, however, added speed, more sophisticated editing commands, and expanded capabilities, such as dimensioning, hatching and filling, and geometric referencing (snaps and trims), among several other enhancements.

Generic CADD Versus Generic CAD

Chapter 1 described CAD in general terms. The following sections refine some of these general definitions, making them more specific to Generic CADD, and introduce the terms and definitions used in Generic CADD to describe the basic features and functions of a CAD program.

The Generic CADD Drawing Database

Generic CADD stores drawing data as a collection of primitives or entities, which are referred to as *lines*. The term applies to all basic entities, whether they are circles, arcs, curves, points, or straight lines. This book, however, generally uses the term *entity* to avoid confusion with Generic's STRAIGHT LINE command. Occasionally, the term *line* is used when it helps to coordinate the discussion with Generic's own terminology in its menus and prompts.

Entities are described using a number of properties, attributes, and coordinates, which are organized according to predefined rules. Attributes, such as color, are stored for every entity, while coordinates are used to define specific geometric properties, such as the location of the center point of a circle. The use of coordinates is different for each entity type, as are properties such as roundness or straightness.

This drawing database is essentially the same for all versions of Generic CADD. With certain exceptions (such as entity types no longer in use), drawings made in Generic CADD 1.0 can be loaded into and edited by Level 3. To maintain a degree of downward compatibility, all versions of Generic CADD ignore data (such as new entity types) that cannot be recognized as entities. Figure 2-1 shows a drawing created with Generic CADD 1.0, and Figure 2-2 shows the same drawing loaded into Level 3.

Hardware Support

As part of a true CAD system, the Generic CADD drawing database is device-independent; that is, the same information is stored no matter which type of system you make your drawings on. A Generic CADD drawing made on a high-resolution color system can be displayed and edited on a lower resolution monochrome system without losing any

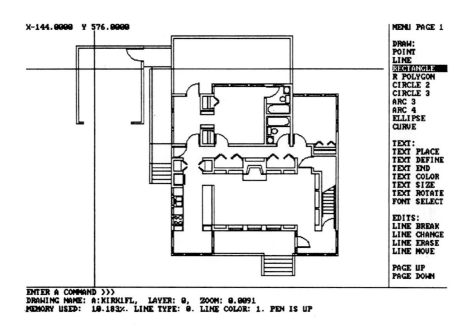

Figure 2-1. *A drawing made with Generic CADD 1.0*

information, and vice versa. Even monochrome systems can create drawings using color as an attribute of the entities for later color printing or display on a color system. These colors, of course, cannot be displayed on a monochrome monitor.

To take advantage of this device independence, Generic CADD utilizes a device "driver" system. Essentially, this means that the parts of the program that communicate with external devices are separate from the rest of the program. When you install and configure Generic CADD, you select the drivers you want to use for your particular computer setup. Figure 2-3 illustrates the relationship between Generic CADD, the device drivers, and the external devices.

Generic CADD uses drivers for three different external devices: (1) the graphics card, which controls display of the drawing on the monitor; (2) the pointing device or mouse, which controls the movement of the cursor

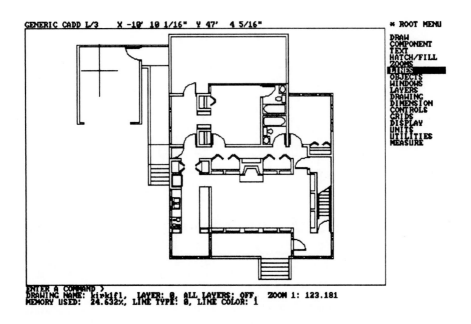

Figure 2-2.   *The same drawing in Generic CADD Level 3*

on the screen; and (3) the printer or plotter, which prints hard copy of your drawing. Formerly, the program code for controlling all of these devices was imbedded in the main Generic CADD program, and the driver merely provided certain parameters. In the Levels products, however, much of the code for running the video card has been moved from the main Generic CADD program to the driver. This modification saves space toward an even more device-independent program in the main program and allows individual board manufacturers and third-party developers to write drivers for boards that Generic Software has not tested.

Coordinates

Generic CADD stores all numeric data as X and Y coordinates, relative to an origin, which is considered to be 0,0. This process allows every object in

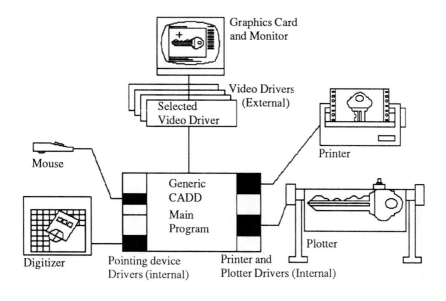

Figure 2-3. *The relationship among Generic CADD, the drivers, and the external devices*

the drawing to be accurately located and sized in relation to every other object.

When you are placing a point (the endpoint of a line, the center of a circle, and so on), its coordinates can be typed manually by specifying an X and Y value. These values can be the actual X and Y values of the point relative to the origin, or they can be relative to a selected basepoint or the last point entered.

Coordinates can also be specified by pointing to a location on the screen. Generic CADD displays the current coordinates of the cursor on the screen. This coordinate display, like manual entry of coordinates, is relative to the origin or to another point that you have selected.

Movement of the cursor can be adjusted to any increment or level of resolution or accuracy that you like, which is reflected in the coordinate display and the points actually selected. This incrementation can be overridden at any time by manually typing coordinate data.

Because you can choose the units of these coordinates, you should use them to specify the actual size of the object you are drawing, rather than scaling your input to fit the screen, a sheet, or any other arbitrary format—that's the computer's job. Several metric formats are available, as are a number of different combinations of feet and inch coordinates. The number of decimal places or smallest fractional value are also user-controlled.

Hard Copy Output

Generic CADD provides printer support in Levels 1 and 2 as well as plotter support in Level 3. Printer and plotter support are available separately if your version does not provide them in Generic's DotPlot and PenPlot products.

Many different devices are supported, using the driver system discussed under "Hardware Support." Generic's printing and plotting routines allow you to fit any drawing to any sized sheet automatically or to define a specific printing or plotting scale. Drawings can be rotated 90 degrees with respect to the paper, and any portion of the drawing can be printed. Drawings may be printed in sections if they are too big to fit on one sheet of paper.

Printing and plotting are proportionately accurate, whether the drawing is scaled automatically or according to a specified scale factor. Various levels of resolution are available for most supported printers, allowing the user to select the most appropriate tradeoff between quality and speed. Plotter support allows the use of multiple pens, even on single-pen plotters, selective plotting of individual layers, and plotting to a file, for manipulation by other software at a later time.

Simple Entities

As you have seen, Generic CADD's basic building block is the line or entity. Every item in the drawing is an entity of some kind. Primitives of the type discussed in Chapter 1 are called *simple entities,* while defined objects are called *complex entities.*

Simple entities in all versions of Generic CADD include the Point, Line, Circle, Arc, Ellipse, and Curve. Level 3 adds the Bezier Curve to this list. Earlier versions (1.0 and 2.0) supported two other simple entities, the Rectangle and the Regular Polygon. The previous version, Generic CADD 3.0, converted these Rectangle and Polygon entities to Lines when a drawing was loaded, while the current Levels products discard them.

Every simple entity in Generic CADD is defined by a certain number of definition points or *construction points*. Even though numerous methods may be used to create a particular entity type, the definition of that type of entity is always stored in the same way. A Line, for instance, is always defined by the location of its endpoints, as X and Y coordinates relative to the origin. As noted in Chapter 1, this information is enough to recreate the line on the screen or on the plotter or to determine its length, angle, and horizontal and vertical displacements.

A Circle is defined by two points: its center and one point on its perimeter. An Arc is defined by three points: its two endpoints and any point on the Arc in between. A Point requires only one definition point: the location of the Point itself. An Ellipse requires four points: the endpoints of the two axes of the Ellipse. A Curve can be defined by any number of points that form it, but at least three are required. The Bezier Curve uses four definition points: the two endpoints of the curve and two "control points" that determine its direction and curvature. (The obsolete entities, Rectangle and Regular Polygon, stored, respectively, the four corners of the Rectangle and the center and any vertex of the Regular Polygon. The number of points on the Polygon was also stored, but as an integer rather than as a coordinate.) Figure 2-4 shows the simple entity types and the definition points that are used to describe them.

Everything in the drawing, including the definitions of complex entities, is made from these simple entities. The process of drawing, as you will see, consists of placing these simple entities into the drawing with certain commands and then manipulating them with others.

Complex Entities

As described in Chapter 1, a CAD program generally includes methods for defining and placing certain objects or figures that are composed of other, simpler objects. Generic CADD currently provides four such complex entities, as listed on the next page.

■ *Components* are groups of entities that can be collected, given a name, and placed into a drawing at any scale or rotation.

■ *Characters* are similar to Components but are stored in different files called "Fonts" and behave in special ways due to their particular requirements as part of Generic CADD Text functions.

■ *Hatches* are composed of a number of simple entities that form an enclosed area, into which a specified pattern of Lines is inserted.

■ *Fills* are similar to Hatches but, as their name implies, they are filled with a solid pattern rather than a pattern of Lines.

See Figure 2-5 for examples of complex entities. Note that complex entities do not have construction points but instead often have a single "reference point."

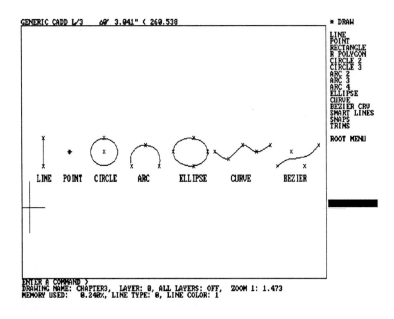

Figure 2-4.   *Simple entities and their definition points*

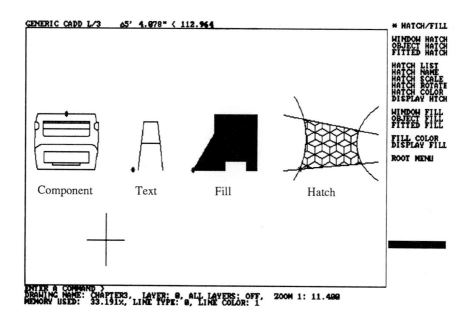

Figure 2-5. *Complex entities and their reference points*

Some Generic CADD commands produce more that one simple entity at a time, but do not produce a defined object or a combination of simple and complex entities. These combinations are called "multiple entities" to differentiate them from complex entities.

Layers

CAD programs generally provide a method for keeping track of objects that might be associated with one another in some way. Generic CADD provides the "layer" concept for this purpose.

You can understand the concept of layers by imagining each layer as a piece of very thin, very transparent tracing paper, each laid over the next. Generic CADD offers 256 layers. Any number of these layers can be viewed simultaneously, or any individual layer can be turned off or *hidden,* as if

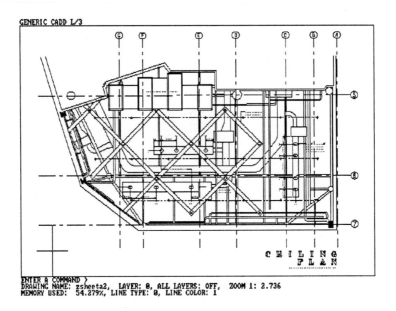

Figure 2-6.   *A sample drawing, courtesy Workshop 3D*

particular sheets were removed from the stack. Figure 2-6 shows a sample Generic CADD drawing composed of several layers. Figure 2-7 shows the same drawing with a single layer (layer 1) turned on. Figure 2-8 shows the same drawing again, with all layers turned on except layer 1. Layers, as you can see, provide a great deal of display flexibility.

Another way of picturing layers is simply as an attribute of each entity. Each entity in the drawing, simple or complex, is located on a layer or has that layer number as an attribute. In fact, this is close to the way that layer information is actually stored in the drawing database.

Both ways of thinking about layers can be useful, depending on the application. Generic CADD does not stipulate how layers are to be used; that is up to you. You will explore several ways of using layers later in this book.

All layers in Generic CADD are either displayed or hidden, that is, visible or invisible. One layer is considered the "current" layer, and all new

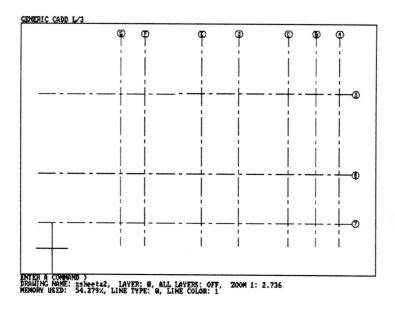

Figure 2-7. *The sample drawing with only layer 1 turned on*

entities are created on this layer. Editing can be done on the current layer, or on any visible layer. Different colors are often used on different layers to distinguish them. If you are using a color monitor, you can see which entities are on each layer without turning layers on and off. Color-coding of layers can also be useful when you want to plot some layers with one pen and some with another.

Drawing Files

The largest organizational structure for Generic CADD data is the drawing file itself. Again, it is up to the user to determine how much information goes into a single drawing file, but "one drawing, one file" is common practice.

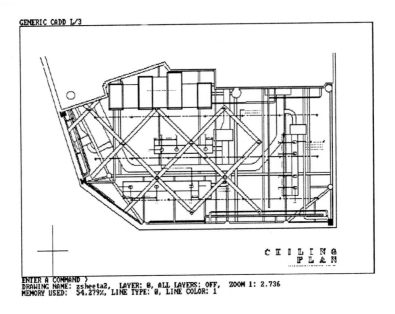

GENERIC CADD L/3

ENTER A COMMAND >
DRAWING NAME: zsheeta2,   LAYER: 0, ALL LAYERS: OFF,   ZOOM 1: 2.736
MEMORY USED: 54.279%, LINE TYPE: 0, LINE COLOR: 1

CEILING
PLAN

Figure 2-8.   *The sample drawing with layer 1 turned off*

Each drawing file contains the definitions and placements of all of the complex entities, including Components, Text Characters, Hatches, and Fills, and all of the simple entities. The definition of a complex entity is stored only once in each file, even though it might be placed in the drawing several times. As a result, the use of components, where appropriate, can save drawing file space.

Drawing file space is valuable and worth conserving. Smaller files take up less space on your disk, load and save faster, and allow Generic CADD to run faster for many tasks. Besides, the size of the drawing that Generic CADD can work with depends on the memory available in your computer, so you don't want to exceed this maximum. (The available drawing memory is shown on the opening screen when you load Generic CADD.) For certain applications you may want to break up a sheet of drawings into several drawing files; this strategy will let you stay under the maximum drawing size and run Generic CADD faster and more efficiently.

Generic CADD uses standard DOS filenames, with the extension .DWG for drawing files. This means that you can use up to eight characters (not including the extension) for a filename. Drawing files are stored in directories, which can be organized any way you like. Other extensions used by Generic CADD are .CMP for components files, .FNT for font files, and .GX2 for screen image files, which are designed primarily for compatibility with the GENERIC PRESENTATION package but have some interesting uses in CADD itself.

Modeling Reality

Generic CADD is ideally suited for simulations of real world objects. Simple entities are adequate to describe almost any physical object, and these entities can then be combined to define repeatable components that represent actual parts of an object or symbols used to describe an object; these complex entities and symbols can then be inserted by name at any scale or rotation. Layers can be used to organize your drawing data to simulate the real object or to impose a strictly imaginary hierarchy, as you see fit.

The Look and Feel of Generic CADD

Several aspects of Generic CADD contribute to the overall look and feel of the program, including the organization and operation of the screen, the way that text menus and the cursor are implemented, and the methods for giving instructions to the program. These facets of Generic CADD are investigated in the remainder of this chapter.

The Generic CADD Screen

If you have not yet installed and configured Generic CADD as described in the Generic CADD manual, do so now. (If you are having trouble, see Chapter 3 of this book for help.) Go to the directory where you have installed Generic CADD, type **CADD**, and press ENTER. If you are using a

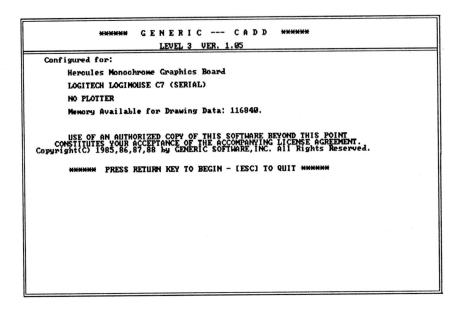

Figure 2-9.   *The configuration and copyright screen*

floppy drive system, insert the CADD disk and type the letter of the drive first.

The first screen that appears is the copyright and configuration screen (see Figure 2-9). This screen shows you which version of Generic CADD you have loaded, which device drivers have been selected, how much memory you have available for your drawing, and the Generic Software copyright notice. To move on to the next screen, press ENTER. Note that when you first typed **CADD** at the DOS prompt, you could have pressed ENTER twice, which would take you right past this screen automatically.

Next, a prompt asks you for the name of the drawing. If you do not see this prompt, you have probably configured your graphics card improperly. You must either return to Generic's CONFIG program and select a different graphics card or adjust hardware or software switches on your graphics card. See the instructions that came with your card to make sure that it is

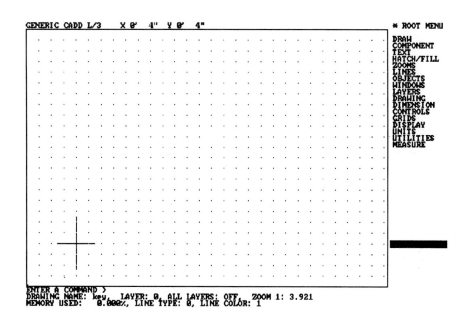

Figure 2-10. *The main Generic CADD screen*

set up properly. When you see the prompt, type in a name for your drawing of not more than eight characters. Then press ENTER. Unless you type the name of an existing drawing, Generic CADD asks you if this is a new file. If this is the case (which it probably is), type **Y**.

You now arrive at the main Generic CADD screen, which should look similar to the one shown in Figure 2-10. (There may be some variation in the size of the text and the proportion of the screen due to the graphics card in your computer.) This screen is displayed most of the time while you are running Generic CADD. Let's examine this screen in detail, so that you always know where to find important information as you draw with Generic CADD.

Drawing Area   By far the largest area on the screen is the *drawing area* (now blank except for the drawing cursor and possibly a grid of dots), as

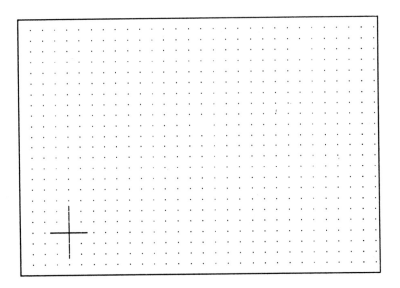

Figure 2-11.   *The drawing area*

shown in Figure 2-11. The drawing area is like a viewport to your drawing. Since we currently have a blank drawing, the viewport shows nothing.

More about the grid later, but let's take a look at the cursor. When you move the pointing device (mouse, roller ball, digitizer, or the like), the cursor moves around the drawing area. Move the pointing device to the right, and the cursor moves to the right; move the pointing device forward (away from you), and the cursor moves up the screen, and so on. Notice that you cannot move the drawing cursor beyond the boundaries of the current drawing area. Keep in mind that as the drawing area is only a viewport to your drawing, the drawing might actually be larger than the portion currently shown on the screen. In order to move the cursor to another part of the drawing, you must change the location or size of viewport by using one of the ZOOM commands. More about these commands later.

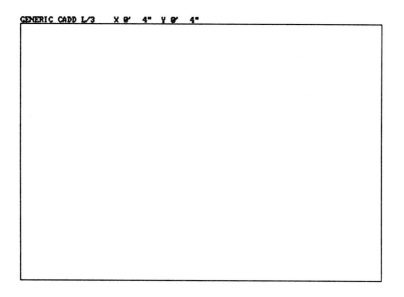

Figure 2-12. *The coordinate area*

Coordinate Area   At the top of the screen is the *coordinate area*—a single line of text that starts in the upper-left corner of the screen and begins with the name of the program. As shown in Figure 2-12, you should see the words GENERIC CADD, followed by L /1, L /2, or L /3, indicating the Level number. Following this, you may see more text in the form of X and Y coordinates. These coordinates indicate the location of the drawing cursor. Depending on your Generic CADD configuration, you may see *absolute coordinates* (the distance the cursor is to the right (X) and above (Y) the lower-left corner (origin) of the drawing; *relative coordinates,* the distance from the cursor to the last point entered (if no point has been entered, they will be relative to the origin); *polar coordinates,* shown as a distance and angle; or no coordinates at all—they may be turned off and not visible. All

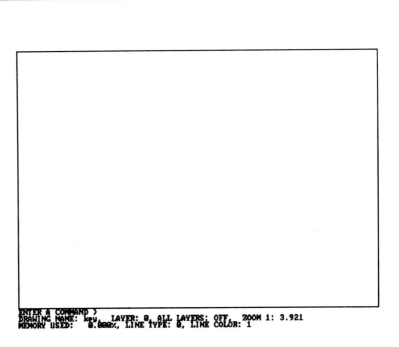

Figure 2-13. *The prompt area*

not visible. All that's really important now is to know where to find them, and to notice that they change as you move the drawing cursor around the drawing area.

Prompt Area At the bottom of the screen, there is space for three lines of text. This space is the *prompt area,* also called the *message area,* and is shown in Figure 2-13. This is where Generic CADD asks (prompts) you for information and where your typed responses will appear. Similarly, Generic CADD uses this area to display information that you request. Again, depending on your configuration, the information in the prompt area may

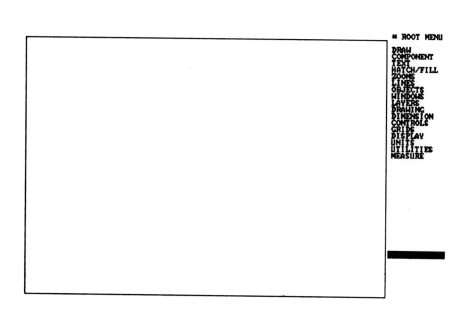

Figure 2-14.   *The menu area*

vary, but at the very least you should see the current prompt, which reads
"ENTER A COMMAND >." This prompt tells you that Generic CADD is
waiting for instructions.

Video Menu Area   Along the right side of the screen is the *Video menu,*
as illustrated in Figure 2-14. This area lists commands that you can select
with the pointing device. Notice that a highlighted bar moves up and down
the menu as you move the pointing device forward and back. This bar is
called the *menu cursor,* and it moves simultaneously with the movement
of the drawing cursor (though it does not move from side to side). Like the
drawing cursor, its movement is restricted to its own area of the screen.

Two Cursors Are Better Than One If you are unfamiliar with Generic CADD, you may wonder how two cursors can be active on the screen at the same time. The drawing cursor, which looks like cross hairs, is used for pointing in the drawing area, and the menu cursor is used for selecting items from the video menu—but how can they be used simultaneously?

When the program asks you for the location of a point, you will probably use the drawing cursor to point to a location on the screen; when you see the prompt "ENTER A COMMAND >" you generally use the menu cursor to select it. However, you may want to use a menu item to do something like turning on a grid before specifying the point. There are also times when you will be asked to "ENTER A COMMAND >" and you will start a Line command by placing a point on the screen rather than by selecting a menu item.

So you need quick access to both cursors almost all the time. It is relatively easy to keep track of which cursor you want to use. First, you can ignore the one that you are not using. If you want to select a point on the screen, for example, don't worry about the menu cursor; its location is irrelevant. Similarly, if you are selecting a menu item, use only the menu cursor and pay no attention to the location of the drawing cursor. Second, if you are selecting a point on the screen, press the first button (the one farthest to the left) on your pointing device. If you are selecting a menu item, press the second button. (On a two-button mouse this is the right button; on a three-button mouse this is the middle button. On a multi-button digitizer puck, it is the button with the second-lowest number.) If you are not using a mouse or digitizer, press the ENTER key to select points on the screen and the HOME key to select menu items.

When you consider these two buttons for a moment, the graphic connection between the two cursors and the two buttons becomes quite clear. The drawing cursor is activated by the left button, and the menu cursor is activated by the right button. See Figure 2-15 for a diagram of how this works. This cursor control scheme is extremely efficient. Most CAD programs make you move your cursor into the menu area before you can use it to select menu items, and all of the pull-down menu schemes require you to move to the top of the screen before you can pull down a menu. This simple cursor control feature contributes significantly to the ease and fluidity with which Generic CADD can be handled by the practiced user.

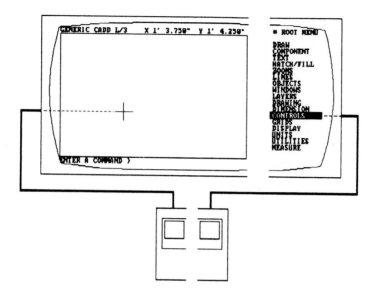

Figure 2-15. *How the mouse controls two cursors*

Menu Structure

At the top of the video menu are the words "ROOT MENU," which means that the menu is hierarchical. In fact, selecting any item on this ROOT menu takes you to a submenu, where you will find a list of menu items, including ROOT menu at the bottom. Selecting this item takes you back to the ROOT menu (see Figure 2-16).

Each submenu contains a group of commands that are related in some way. The name of the submenu provides a clue to the type of commands that you will find there. Some submenus include items that give access to another level of submenus. Briefly, the menus that appear on the Level 3 ROOT menu are arranged as follows (see Appendix A for a summary of which commands are included in Levels 1 and 2).

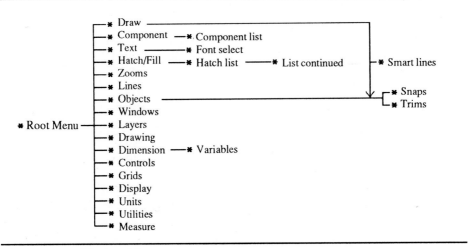

Figure 2-16. *The Level 3 menu structure*

The DRAW Menu   The DRAW menu consists of commands used for placing simple entities into a drawing. It also includes access to two submenus (SNAPS and TRIMS) that are often useful when placing entities and to a menu (SMART LINES) for placing multiple entities.

The COMPONENT Menu   The COMPONENT menu lists commands for creating and working with Components, the primary Generic CADD means of defining objects for replication. It also includes access to the COMPONENT LIST menu, from which Components can be selected.

The TEXT Menu   Text placement and editing commands are found on the TEXT menu. Also included are commands for selecting a font, defining your own text characters, and text display control.

The HATCH/FILL Menu   This menu includes commands for hatching and filling enclosed areas, using a number of methods. It also provides access to the HATCH LIST menu, from which a hatch pattern can be selected.

The ZOOMS Menu   The commands on this menu control the relationship between the viewport (the drawing area) and the drawing as a whole. It includes commands for zooming in (UP) and out (BACK), fitting the whole drawing to the screen (ALL), as well as a number of other ZOOM commands.

The LINES Menu   The first three commands control the LINE COLOR, LINE WIDTH, and LINE TYPE of all new entities that are placed into the drawing. This information is stored with each entity. The fourth command, LINE TYPE SCALE, is a global parameter that controls all entities in the drawing; this information is not stored with each entity. Don't worry too much about these commands now, except for remembering that COLOR, WIDTH, and TYPE affect *only new entities* placed in the drawing, and SCALE affects *all entities*—those already in the drawing and those yet to be placed. The video menu will show you examples of choices you have for the COLOR, WIDTH, and TYPE commands.

The OBJECTS Menu   The OBJECTS menu contains the simplest editing commands. Editing commands are listed on several menus, depending on what, or how much, you are editing. The clue to what you can edit from this menu is the word "objects," meaning "entities." The commands on this menu allow you to ERASE, MOVE, COPY, and CHANGE only one entity at a time, or to move one of the definition points of a single simple entity.

The WINDOWS Menu   The WINDOWS menu lists the next level of editing commands. The commands on this menu allow you to select the entities that you wish to edit by drawing a rectangle, called a "window," around them. Any number of entities can be selected this way. Note that more commands are available for editing on the WINDOWS menu than on the OBJECTS menu. Any WINDOW command can be used on a single entity by simply placing the window around only that entity.

The LAYERS Menu   There are two different types of commands on the LAYERS menu. One type, editing commands, allows you to select objects for editing by indicating the layer on which they are located (instead of by placing a window around them or by pointing to them on the screen). Another type, "layer management" commands, selects the CURRENT layer, allows you to HIDE and DISPLAY layers, and determines whether editing should take place on ALL LAYERS or just the current layer.

The DRAWING Menu   This menu also contains two types of commands. Like the LAYERS menu, the DRAWING menu includes editing commands, which allow you to edit all entities in a drawing at one time. The others, such as SAVE, LOAD, and PLOT, deal with drawing file management.

The DIMENSION Menu   The DIMENSION menu includes commands for placing dimensions into a drawing. It also provides access to a submenu for setting a number of VARIABLES that control the way in which these dimensions are placed.

The CONTROLS Menu   These commands are a miscellaneous group of general-purpose commands for controlling the way other commands work. Generally, they set parameters that are used by other commands. Digitizer users can turn TRACE MODE on and off and select a digitizing SCALE. Commands controlling the DISPLAY of text and arcs are included here, and a group of PATH commands determine where on the disk Generic CADD looks for your files.

The GRIDS Menu   This menu lists commands controlling a grid of dots that can be overlaid onto your drawing for the purpose of visualization or controlling accuracy. The grid can be turned on and off from this menu, and the spacing of its dots can be changed, either by selecting from a list of typical spacings or by typing your own specification.

The DISPLAY Menu   Most of the features of the video display—other than the setting of the drawing area viewport, which is controlled by the ZOOM command—can be found on this menu. These commands control the display of several types of points, the coordinates, the amount of information that appears in the prompt area, and various other display attributes, including the display of the video menu itself. If the display function that you want isn't here, try the CONTROLS menu. For some reason, the FLIP SCREEN command, available only in Level 3, is located on the DISPLAY menu as well, instead of the UTILITIES menu, where you might expect to find it.

The UNITS Menu   This menu contains commands that allow you to select systems of linear and angular measurements and to set the display resolution of both. Several variations on both English and metric systems are available.

The UTILITIES Menu   On this menu the MANUAL ENTRY (M.E.) commands control how manually typed coordinates are interpreted, and the QUIT and PACK DATA commands have to do with drawing management. A number of UTILITIES commands allow loading and canceling of various Video and Digitizer menus, while others permit the saving and loading of both BATCH files (the drawing as an ASCII file of commands and points) and IMAGE files (the current display as a set of pixels, for use with painting and publishing programs).

The MEASURE Menu   Three commands on this menu allow you to ask Generic CADD for information. You can request the DISTANCE between two points, the ANGLE between two lines, or the AREA enclosed within any space that can be defined by tracing its perimeter.

Two-Character Commands

In addition to the video menu, Generic CADD provides a second means of selecting commands—the keyboard. Every Generic CADD command can be activated by a simple two-character code. These codes can be used in place of or in combination with the video menu.

The two-character codes are, for the most part, mnemonic. One-word commands usually use two letters of the word, often the first two, such as *LI* for LINE and *PO* for POINT. Two-word commands often use the initials of the two words, such as *ZA* for ZOOM ALL and *DL* for DRAWING LOAD. A complete list of the two-character codes is shown in Appendix A, along with a note indicating the Level(s) of Generic CADD that includes the command. This list also classifies the commands into a number of types, which may help you to understand when each can or should be used.

Standard Abbreviations

To avoid confusion, Generic CADD uses certain characters to mean the same thing in different commands. The position of these characters (first or second keystroke) is also relatively consistent for certain types of commands.

First Character   In many cases, there is a direct relationship between the first character of the two-character command and the submenu on which the command is found. For example, all of the ZOOM commands start with start with the letter *Z*. As noted above, the abbreviation for ZOOM ALL is *ZA*. ZOOM UP is *ZU*, ZOOM BACK is *ZB*, and so on. The only exception is the code for PAN, which is *PA* (because *ZP* is already used for ZOOM PREVIOUS). PAN is a borderline ZOOM command anyway, because it goes sideways instead of going in and out.

All COMPONENT command codes begin with *C*, except for COMPONENT SNAPS, which is *GC*. Again, the exception is little different in function from the rest because it could be considered a CONTROL command (it controls whether or not construction points inside placed components can be accessed by other commands). The letters *GC* come from Generic's original working name for the command, which was GHOST COMPONENTS.

Similarly, the TEXT commands begin with the letter *T*, with the exception of the FONT SELECT command. True to form, the exception in this case is quite different from the rest of the TEXT commands, and has its own distinct initials, *FS*.

The OBJECT commands begin with *O*, except for MOVE POINT, which is abbreviated *MP*. The WINDOW commands begin with *W*, the LAYER commands start with *Y*, and the DRAWING commands all use a *D* as their first character. Similarly, most of the SNAP commands begin with *S*, and all three MEASURE commands begin with *M* (as do the three MANUAL ENTRY commands). Finally, the commands governing the display of various types of POINTS all start with the letter *P*.

Second Character   The second character is often used to distinguish among the commands of a certain family that share a common first character. There are quite a few commonalities between many of these second-character codes.

The letter *K* in the second position, for example, signifies a command that involves COLOR. The letters *L* and *S* in this position stand for LOAD and SAVE, respectively.

The actions of the editing commands are somewhat standardized by letter as well. ROTATE commands use *R* as the second character. MOVE is indicated by an *M* as the second character, and COPY is signified by a *C* in the second position. The letter *Z* always relates to SIZE or SCALE, while a *G* in the second slot indicates a CHANGE. The letters *E* and *X* usually indicate ERASE when found in this position, although there are some exceptions: TEXT DELETE, for example, is *TD*.

As for nonediting examples, a command with the second character *B* is a BATCH command. The three COORDINATE commands both end in *C*.

Non-Position-Specific Characters   Several characters may appear in either the first or second spot but mean the same thing wherever they appear. The HATCH commands, for example, sometimes start and sometimes end with an *H*. Similarly, the FILL commands start with an *F* in some commands and end with an *F* in others.

The letter *I* usually indicates an IMAGE, although this may have different meanings in different commands. The exception is *WI*, meaning WINDOW MIRROR. (To remember this code, you might think of the command as "MIRROR IMAGE.") The letter *V* in any position indicates the Video menu. A *W* in either position usually means a window is involved in the command.

Editing Command Syntax

The editing commands, such as MOVE, COPY, and ERASE, form an interesting pattern in this alphabet soup. They have a logical construction that makes them very easy to remember, so that they will most likely be the two-character codes you learn first. This is fortunate because they are typically the most-used commands.

Nouns and Verbs   There are four different ways of selecting what you want to edit: OBJECT, WINDOW, LAYER, or the whole DRAWING. In the two-character code format, each one is represented by a first-position character, standing for a *noun*: *O* for OBJECT, *W* for WINDOW, *Y* for LAYER, and *D* for DRAWING. A number of different actions, or *verbs,* can be combined with these nouns to create a command. These include *E* or *X* for ERASE, *M* for MOVE, *C* for COPY, *R* for ROTATE, *Z* for SCALE, *I* for MIRROR, and two nonediting actions, *L* for LOAD and *S* for SAVE.

Combinations   From these four nouns and eight verbs, you can theoretically construct 32 different commands. Not all of the combinations are valid commands, but a majority of them are, particularly in Level 3. See Table 2-1 for a complete matrix of the possibilities. This noun-verb construction of the editing commands means that you don't have to memorize the codes but can, in most cases, create them extemporaneously by knowing what you want to edit and what you want to do to it.

How Shall I Command Thee?
Let Me Count the Ways...

The two-character codes are really the heart of Generic's command structure, even though they appear to be quite separate from the Video menu. In fact, when you select an item from the Video menu, Generic CADD simply types the corresponding two-character code for you, even though you don't see the two-character code on the screen. Actually, commands can be issued in a number of ways.

Two-Character Commands   The two-character codes are constant for any version of Generic CADD, and cannot be changed by the user. They are, for the most part, consistent among the Levels, with only a few exceptions. Turn to Appendix A for a complete list of commands and two-character codes.

The numbers in the table indicate which Level(s) of Generic CADD supports the command shown.

		nouns			
		OBJECT	WINDOW	LAYER	DRAWING
verbs	chars	O	W	Y	D
ERASE	E X	1 2 3 OE	1 2 3 WE	2 3 YX	3 DX
BREAK	B	1 2 3 OB	.	.	.
COPY	C	1 2 3 OC	1 2 3 WC	.	.
MOVE	M	1 2 3 OM	1 2 3 WM	.	a2a3 DO
MIRROR	I	.	2 3 WI	.	.
CHANGE	G	1 2 3 OG	1 2 3 WG	3 YG	3 DG
ROTATE	R	.	2 3 WR	3 YR	3 DR
RE-SCALE	Z	.	2 3 WZ	3 YZ	3 DZ
LOAD b	L	.	.	3 YL	1 2 3 DL
SAVE b	S	.	3 WS	3 YS	1 2 3 DS

Notes: a) The DRAWING RE-ORIGIN (DO) command performs the
                same function as would a DRAWING MOVE

             b) LOAD and SAVE are not editing commands, but this table
                still applies

Table 2-1.   Generic CADD Editing Commands

Video Menu   The video menu is really just a list of words that appear on the screen, with each word followed by a two-character command that is typed automatically when you select that word. This list is in an ASCII file, called LEVEL1.MNU, LEVEL2.MNU, or LEVEL3.MNU. This file can be rearranged if you like, and the words that appear on the menu can be changed. In Level 3, more than one command can be issued by a single selection from the menu and can be combined with user input. For example, the GRIDS menu, which allows you to select typical grid sizes, can be used to type more than one command. These commands are followed by a number which sets the grid size. See the user manual and Chapter 15 of this book for more information on the video menu.

Digitizer Menu   For Level 3 users who have a digitizer, the tablet can be set up to issue commands in much the same way as the video menu. As a digitizer has no display, a grid of rectangles is defined on the tablet, and each rectangle is assigned a line of text, with a format similar to that of video menus. Several different gridded areas can be assigned simultaneously on the same tablet, and each can be activated independently. See the user manual, as well as Chapters 14 and 15 of this book for more information.

Function Keys   Using the CONFIG program, which comes with all versions of Generic CADD, a single two-character command can be assigned to each of the first 10 function keys. This can be an effective way to gain quick access to some of your most-used commands.

Pointing Device Buttons   Level 3 users who have a pointing device with more than two buttons can use the CONFIG program to assign a single two-character command to each button beyond the first two. For users of Levels 1 and 2, the third button of a three-button mouse is automatically assigned the NP (Nearest Point) function.

Batch Files   Level 3 users can create ASCII files full of Generic CADD two-character commands, intermixed with pauses for user input, to be loaded into any Generic CADD drawing and executed at any time. These commands can be used for automating certain procedures that occur regularly or for programming other software to produce batch files as output, allowing a method for Generic CADD drawings to be generated by nongraphic software. For more information see the user manual and Chapter 16 of this book.

Other Software   Many Generic Software products and third-party programs can perform certain functions or manipulations on Generic CADD drawing files, create Generic CADD format drawing files from a different user interface, or provide other forms of input or transformations of Generic CADD drawings. These programs provide functions not otherwise available in Generic CADD or provide more automated ways of performing certain tasks.

Together with Chapter 1, this chapter gives you a good idea of what Generic CADD does and how it compares conceptually with other drawing software that you may have used. You should now be able to recognize the various items on the Generic CADD screen and the various Generic CADD menus and commands.

3 *Preliminary Considerations*

Before you begin drawing, you still have several decisions to make: how you will set up the hardware and software, where your drawings are going to be stored, what type of unit system you are going to be using, how much area you are going to need for your drawing and others.

Installing Generic CADD

All levels of Generic CADD come with an installation program that installs Generic CADD on your computer. You can install Generic CADD on your system by putting the main program disk in drive A, typing **GO**, and pressing ENTER.

The installation program copies the Generic CADD files onto your hard disk or onto a floppy disk, depending on how you respond to the installation program prompts. The Generic CADD program contains a number of files, including files for fonts, hatch patterns, and other auxiliary files. If you are trying to minimize the amount of space that Generic CADD occupies on your disk after you have installed it, the following list includes the very minimum files that you need to run Generic CADD:

CADD.EXE	The main Generic CADD program
CONFIG.FIL	Your configuration choices
LEVEL?.MNU	A video menu for Level 1, 2, or 3
MESSAGE	A list of messages or prompts

*.VGD	The video driver that you have selected
*.TPR	The printer driver that you have selected (Levels 1 and 2 only)

Additionally, the following files are required to set up Generic CADD, or change the configuration:

CONFIG.EXE	The configuration program
POINTERS.TDG	The pointing device driver (Level 3)
PLOTTERS.TPL	The plotter drivers (Level 3)
MESSAGE2	A list of messages or prompts for CONFIG.EXE
*.DIG	Pointing device drivers (Levels 1 and 2)
*.TPR	Printer drivers (Levels 1 and 2)
*.VGD	Video drivers

The following files are required to take advantage of certain features of Generic CADD:

*.HCH	Hatch patterns for use with Level 3
*.FNT	Font files; may be in any directory

Finally, these files are created as you use Generic CADD:

*.DWG	Drawing files
*.CMP	Component files
*.TXT	Batch files
*.GX2	Image files

Setting Up CADD to Run on Your Computer

When you install Generic CADD, all of the files are automatically placed in the same directory on your hard disk or on a single "working" floppy disk. Note that running Level 3 from floppy disks requires a 1.2 MB 5 1/4-inch drive or a 720K 3 1/2-inch drive to keep all of these files available at one time.

Certain files, however, can be stored in subdirectories, or even in directories that are not below the Generic CADD directory. There are three types of files that can be stored separately from the main program: fonts (.FNT), components (.CMP), and drawings (.DWG). CADD can find these files through the "default paths," which can be set in the CONFIG program or from within CADD.

Suppose, for example, that your Generic CADD program files are in a directory called CADD. You might want to keep your font files in a subdirectory called FNT, your components in CMP, and your drawings in DWG. To do this, you need to create these three directories, place the files where they belong, and configure Generic CADD to look in the right directories for these files.

Creating Subdirectories To create the directories, at the DOS prompt type **CD \CADD** and press ENTER (use the name of your Generic CADD directory). When you see the DOS prompt again, type

MD DWG and press ENTER

MD CMP and press ENTER

MD FNT and press ENTER.

These commands create the subdirectories within the current directory (CADD) that you will use to store the individual files.

Copying Files If you have already installed Generic CADD, all of the font files will be in the main Generic CADD directory. If you wish to keep them separate, as suggested above, stay in the Generic CADD directory and type **COPY *.FNT FNT** and press ENTER. When all of the fonts have been copied to the FNT subdirectory, type **DEL *.FNT** and press ENTER.

This last command removes the fonts from your main Generic CADD directory so that you do not end up with duplicates. If you have already made some drawings with Generic CADD, you probably saved them in the main Generic CADD directory. It is good practice to keep these files separate as well. To separate them from the program and copy them into their own directory, type **COPY *.DWG DWG** and press ENTER.

Any drawings that you have created, or that may have come as sample drawings on the Generic CADD distribution disks, are now copied into the DWG subdirectory. To eliminate the duplicates in the current directory, type **DEL *.DWG** and press ENTER.

Similarly, to move any components that you may have made into their own directory, type **COPY *.CMP CMP** and press ENTER. When this has been completed, type **DEL *.CMP** and press ENTER.

These maneuvers should clear the main Generic CADD directory of any extraneous files that are not needed to run the program. Though the program will run satisfactorily even with these extra files, separating these files creates a cleaner environment for troubleshooting if something goes wrong.

AutoConvert Users' Note   If you use older versions of Generic Auto-Convert, you may have noticed that AutoConvert requires the fonts to be in the same directory as AutoConvert. For this reason, it is often a good idea to keep all of your font files in your AutoConvert directory, and to use them from there, even for Generic CADD. This practice avoids having to store multiple copies of the fonts on your hard disk, which takes up valuable space. If your version of AutoConvert supports paths, you can put your fonts wherever you like.

Configuring to Use Subdirectories   To tell Generic CADD where you have stored these font, drawing, and component files so that the program can find them, you must use the configuration program to set the "default paths" for these various file types.

While you are in the Generic CADD directory, at the DOS prompt, type **CONFIG** and press ENTER. The current configuration screen will appear. Press ENTER to get to the CONFIGURATION menu. From there, select "Set Default Paths for Files." In Level 3, this item can be found under "Other Options" rather than on the main menu. The Level 3 CONFIGU-RATION menu is shown in Figure 3-1.

Three separate paths can be set for access to the Drawing files, Component files, and Text Font files. If these files are going to be located in subdirectories of your Generic CADD directory, you can just show the subdirectory name, followed by a backslash (\). For instance, if your Generic CADD directory is titled C:\CADD, and your drawing directory is called C:\CADD\DWG, you can specify a drawing path of DWG\ (don't forget the backslash).

If you want to keep your drawings, components, and fonts in completely separate directories, you must specify the whole pathname. If the directory is on the same disk, you can start with the backslash, such as \CONVERT\ for fonts you are storing in the CONVERT directory. If you plan to save and load files to and from disk, you can use the disk drive designator, such

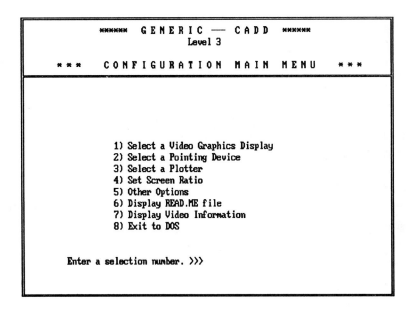

```
       ****** G E N E R I C — C A D D  ******
                     Level 3

   * * *   C O N F I G U R A T I O N   M A I N   M E N U   * * *




          1) Select a Video Graphics Display
          2) Select a Pointing Device
          3) Select a Plotter
          4) Set Screen Ratio
          5) Other Options
          6) Display READ.ME file
          7) Display Video Information
          8) Exit to DOS


    Enter a selection number. >>>
```

Figure 3-1. *Level 3 configuration screen*

as A:\ for a default component path when you are saving and loading components from drive A. Figure 3-2 shows a typical setup for paths.

Other Configuration Options The only really important configuration options are Video Graphics Card, Pointing Device, and Printer or Plotter. You must select the proper option for each of these, or Generic CADD won't work.

If you haven't tried some of the options that might work with your system, don't be afraid to experiment. If you have an EGA clone, for instance, try the VEGA Deluxe driver. Your card might work at a higher

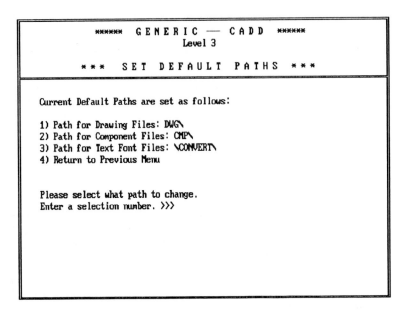

Figure 3-2. *Typical configuration for paths*

resolution than you think. If you are having trouble with your printer, try various Epson and IBM drivers, which work with many printers that aren't made by these companies. Several pointing device drivers work with the Logitech mouse, and the MOUSE.COM drivers let you set the sensitivity. If you are having trouble with your mouse, try unplugging it from the computer and then plugging it back in again. Your mouse might have a memory that gets programmed by the driver and can't forget what you told it until you turn off the power.

Don't spend much time thinking about the other configurable options now, though it might be helpful to get an idea of your options. After you have made a few drawings, you will have a better idea about what changes to make in your configuration.

Starting Generic CADD

As you discovered in Chapter 2, Generic CADD is not a program in which you work your way through various menu screens. For the most part, the program looks the same the entire time you are running it. Of course, there are a few exceptions, such as the copyright and configuration screen that appears when you first start up and the inquiry screens that are available for looking up files.

Loading a Drawing

Starting Generic CADD and loading a drawing file are almost identical processes. You cannot really start Generic CADD without specifying a new or existing drawing file. It is logical, therefore, that when you start Generic CADD, the first and only choice that you are asked to make before beginning work is the name of the drawing file. It is as if when you say "CADD," the computer asks "CADD what?"

If you want to avoid this little conversation, you can simply follow the word CADD with the name of the drawing file that you want to load. For example, typing **CADD BOOKCASE** loads Generic CADD and brings up the drawing called BOOKCASE.DWG. You don't have to type .DWG because Generic CADD can only load files that have the extension .DWG, so it is therefore assumed.

If the file BOOKCASE does not exist, Generic CADD asks if you want to start a new drawing with this name. If not, you will be given another chance to type the name of the file correctly. The current drawing path will be shown (in Level 3, at least), so that you can see if Generic CADD is looking for the file where you think it should be.

Loading from Other Than the Default Directory Since Generic CADD uses a "default directory" to look for drawing files, it sometimes cannot find the drawing that you are trying to load. This may happen when you want to load a drawing from a disk, or any time your drawing is located on a drive or directory that is not on the default drawing path. In these instances, you will need to type the full pathname of the drawing file that you are trying to load. For example, typing **A:CHAIR** is the proper way to identify a drawing that is called CHAIR.DWG on the A drive, and **\CADD\HOUSE\PLAN1** is the required pathname for a drawing called

PLAN1.DWG that is in the subdirectory HOUSE under the CADD directory, when DWG\ is the default drawing path.

Another way to go about loading these files is to use the CONFIG program to change the default drawing path before attempting to load these drawings. It pays to remember that you can run CONFIG as often as you like, not just during the installation process. CONFIG can be used to alter the way that Generic CADD runs whenever you use it. Changing default drawing paths with CONFIG can save a lot of needless typing if you frequently work on drawings from the same directory.

Beginning a New Drawing   Even when you start from scratch with a blank screen, you must specify a *filename*—the name of the file in which the drawing will be stored if you elect to keep it. Filenames can be up to eight characters and must not include any spaces, or certain other characters, such as * or ?. An underscore is a good substitute for a space if you really need one. Think of a name that has significance to the drawing that you are making. If nothing else comes to mind, type **TRY1**, so that you can distinguish it from your next one, which you might call TRY2, and so on.

Notice that if you try to start a new drawing using the same filename as an existing one, the existing drawing is simply called up instead. You must erase the existing file either before starting the drawing or when it is loaded by Generic CADD.

First Things First

You probably want to start drawing right away, which is natural, but you still have a few more tasks; doing these tasks before you start will make drawing a lot easier later.

Many of the topics that we cover in this section are configurable options, which can be set with the CONFIG program once you know how you want them set when you start a drawing.

Selecting a Unit System

The unit system controls how coordinates are displayed at the top of the screen, as well as how they are interpreted when you type them as dimensions in response to Generic CADD prompts for information.

Two primary unit systems are available, and several variations within these. All of the units commands are "parameter settings" (see Appendix A for a complete list of all the units commands and an explanation of how they might be divided into types). A *parameter* is a variable value that controls how other commands work. In the case of the units commands, selecting a specific command sets the parameter to a specific value or setting. These parameter settings are distinct from toggles, which turn something on when you select them the first time, and then turn it off when you select them again. These parameter settings might be considered "one-way toggles," or "mode" settings; that is, they only switch on, and they stay on unless you select contradictary settings. If you select MM, for example, you are choosing millimeters as your unit system. If you select MM again, you are still working in millimeters. If you select IN, you are switching to inches. As many times as you select IN, you can never return to millimeters unless you select MM. When we come to the discussion of toggles in the next chapter, you'll understand the importance of these rules.

For your primary unit system, you can choose one of the following commands from the UNITS menu:

METERS	(MT)
CENTIMETERS	(MC)
MILLIMETERS	(MM)
FEET	(FT)
FEET/INCHES	(FI)
INCHES	(IN)

Position the menu cursor over the word UNITS on the ROOT menu and press the second pointing device button. Then move the menu cursor over the command that you wish to select and press the second button again. An alternative method is to type the two-character command code shown in parenthesis on the keyboard (you do not need to press ENTER).

If you do not choose a unit system, whichever system is configured will be used by default. If you have never configured for any particular unit system, you will use whatever parameter was configured on the factory-release disk, probably FEET/INCHES. To follow along with the examples in this chapter, select FEET/INCHES for your unit system now.

It is important to notice that you can change unit systems whenever you like, and that changing your units does not change the size of your drawing or the scale of your objects in any way. Objects are always drawn at real size, even though the units that you use to measure or describe them may change. It is not a problem, then, to create your drawing using Feet and

Inches, and later change to one of the metric formats for dimensioning; this is one of Generic CADD's convenient features.

You can also control the level of accuracy of the units. If you use a unit system that involves inches, you can choose to display fractional parts of an inch as fractions or as decimals. The commands FRACTIONS (FR) and DECIMALS (DE) are one-way toggles or parameter settings. When you choose either one, inches are displayed in that mode from then on. Repeatedly selecting the same command has no effect.

If you use FEET, or any of the metric settings, all dimensions less than one unit are shown as decimals. You can control the number of displayed decimal places with the DEC.VALUE (DV) command, or the largest denominator in fractions with the FRACT. VALUE (FV) command. Obviously, the fractional value has no effect if you are using decimals, and vice versa.

Finally, on the UNITS menu, you have the option of displaying partial angles in decimal degrees or in minutes and seconds. Like the other unit settings, these two commands are one-way toggles. ARC DEGREES (AD) selects decimal degrees (the number of places is controlled by DEC. VALUE (DV)), while ARC MINUTES (AM) selects a display of minutes and seconds. The choice is yours and depends on your drawing and the form of your information. If you are not working with angle displays, don't worry about selecting either of these commands now. You can use the UNITS commands any time you are drawing, and you can always select the proper format at a later time.

When you finish making selections from the UNITS menu, select the last option, ROOT MENU, to take you back to the Root Menu.

Defining the Drawing Space

Next on the agenda is the question of how much drawing space you need. This is in some ways a meaningless question, because Generic CADD can handle both very large and very small numbers; you can draw objects almost any size. In addition, Generic CADD has built-in features to adjust both the display and the printed image of the objects in the drawing.

However, you might be a bit uneasy about looking at a blank screen and wondering how much space is represented there. Once you have drawn an object of a certain size, however, the amount of space on the screen will become clear, by comparison to the object that you have drawn. But where do you start?

Generic CADD uses a concept called "limits" to determine the size of the drawing area. The idea of limits is to make drawing more convenient, and does not impose any special constraints on the use of Generic CADD. You are free to draw outside the limits, if you like, with no penalty or undue hardship. Defining the limits of the drawing area is like creating an imaginary dotted line around a certain amount of space, and saying, "This is about how much room I need for this drawing." The limits are defined by two numbers—the height and the width—and can be changed as often as you like.

In some ways, setting the limits for your drawing can be compared to choosing the paper size when you are drawing by hand. This comparison is somewhat strained, however, and can often be misleading. The limits are measured in the units of the objects that you are drawing, not in the scaled units of the final output. In other words, your limits can be measured in hundreds or even thousands of feet, while the piece of paper on which the drawing is printed might be only 24 inches × 36 inches. Also, the paper analogy implies that the limits are more restrictive than they actually are. In the hand drawing process, if you run off the edge of the paper, you end up drawing on the desk. With Generic CADD, drawing outside the limits has no similar repercussions.

A good rule of thumb for setting limits is to make them a little larger (perhaps 25 to 50 percent larger) than the object in the drawing. If you are going to draw a typical office workstation, for example, with a desk, chair, and work table, you might set the limits at 12 feet × 12 feet, allowing plenty of work space. You would do this by selecting LIMITS from the CONTROLS menu or by typing **LS** on the keyboard. Generic CADD will show the defaults for the height and width and ask you for new values. When asked for each, type **12′** and press ENTER. Notice that if you just typed **12** and pressed ENTER, your input would be interpreted as 12 inches, so you must add the foot mark (′). Also note that the lower-left corner of the limits is assumed to be located at the origin, 0,0, and that your values become not only the height and width of the limits, but the upper limits of the coordinates as well.

Adjusting the Display

While we have set the drawing limits as 12 feet × 12 feet, the screen has not changed. Generic CADD now knows your drawing limits but hasn't been asked to do anything about it.

The commands that control how much of the drawing is displayed on the screen are the ZOOM commands. You will learn these in detail later, once you have a drawing on the screen, but for now one command is particularly useful—the ZOOM LIMITS (ZL) command. This command adjusts the display so that the LIMITS you have set with the previous command are shown on the screen.

You can execute this command by selecting LIMITS from the ZOOM menu or by typing **ZL** on the keyboard. Apart from a flash of the display, which may happen so quickly that you don't see it, the screen shows no apparent change, even though, in fact, it has changed. If you move the drawing cursor around now and look at the coordinate area, you notice that the Y coordinate ranges between 0 at the bottom of the screen and 12′ 0″ at the top of the screen (approximately). If you do not see these coordinates, type **AC** on the keyboard to activate absolute coordinates, or select ABS COORDS from the DISPLAY menu.

You might wonder why the X coordinates are not constrained by the same range. The reason is that your monitor probably has greater width than height. Generic CADD simply adds the "leftover" space on the right side of the screen to the drawing area.

You now know that the height shown on the screen represents 12 feet, and the width a little more than 12 feet. Now you need only do a few more things before you start drawing.

Turning on the Grid

Generic CADD provides a grid that is similar to the graph paper often used in the hand drawing process. The grid allows you to visualize the size of a unit easier, and can be used to provide a certain level of accuracy.

To try this feature, type **GS** or select GRID SIZE from the GRIDS menu. You are shown the current (default) grid size and asked to specify a new one. Type **12** (for 12 inches) or **1′**, press ENTER, and you will see a grid displayed on the screen, in which the dots are 12 inches apart in both the horizontal (X) and vertical (Y) directions. You now have an additional visual cue to use when making your drawing. The screen should be divided into 12 spaces vertically and about 15 spaces horizontally, depending on the proportional resolution of your video card and monitor. Whenever you change the grid size, the grid is automatically turned on, whether it was on before you changed the size or not. Figure 3-3 shows the Generic CADD screen with the 12-inch grid.

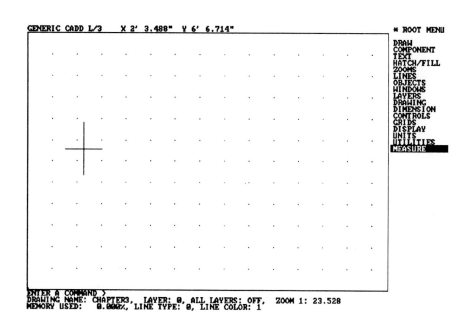

Figure 3-3. *The grid appears as equally spaced dots*

If you like, you can show the grid spacing on the screen, rather than typing the value. When asked for the new GRID SIZE, type **D** (for Distance) on the keyboard instead of typing a number. You will be asked to place two points. The distance between the two points will be measured and used as the new GRID SIZE. If you want to know what the GRID SIZE has been set to, simply use the same command again, from the menu, the keyboard, or by pressing the SPACEBAR. You will be asked for the new GRID SIZE and shown the default, which will be the value that you have just shown on the screen. If you are just checking, press either ESCAPE or ENTER.

You can use this same technique with many of the commands that ask for a size or distance. If you are unsure, try typing **D** on the keyboard. If nothing happens, you cannot show a distance but must type a value instead.

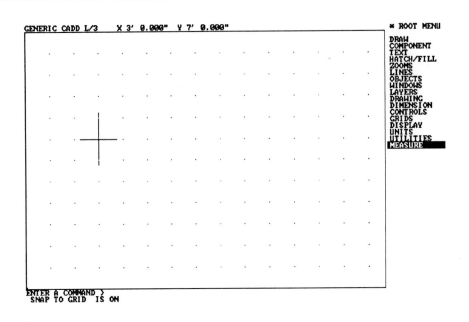

Figure 3-4.   *With SNAP GRID on, the cursor "sticks" to the grid*

Using the Grid   The grid can be used simply as a visual device, or it can be used to control the actual points that are input with the pointing device. Move the drawing cursor around the screen, and you will see that the grid is just like a transparent overlay: It has no effect on cursor movement or the coordinates that appear at the top of the screen. However, if you type **SG** or select SNAP TO GRID from the GRIDS menu, you see that the movement of the cursor is now tied to the grid, as shown in Figure 3-4. Each time you move the cursor, it jumps to the next grid point. The coordinate display at the top of the screen reflects this condition: Both X and Y are shown in even feet, with no inches and no fractions.

If you type **SG** or select SNAP TO GRID again, cursor movement is "freed" from the grid, and the coordinates again begin to show all of the inches and fractions of inches between grid points. The SNAP TO GRID (SG) command is, as we can see, a "toggle": Selecting it once creates one condition; selecting it again creates the opposite condition. Many of the toggles turn something on or off. SNAP TO GRID is an example of this type of toggle. If SNAP TO GRID is on, selecting the command will turn it off. If it is off, selecting SNAP TO GRID will turn it on.

For now, turn SNAP TO GRID on so you can see how it is used. Change the grid size to 6 (select GRID SIZE or type **GS**, type **6**, and press ENTER). The cursor now jumps six inches in both horizontal and vertical directions. The grid then, together with SNAP TO GRID, can be used to control the level of accuracy of cursor movement and entry of point data. SNAP TO GRID continues to work even if the grid itself is not displayed, which you can verify by selecting GRID ON/OFF or by typing **GR** from the GRIDS menu.

You may think of SNAP TO GRID as being an option that you turn on only when you need it. On the contrary, to preserve the precision of your drawing (and CADD drawings are always precise, whether they are accurate or not), you should leave SNAP TO GRID turned on most of the time, and turned off only when it gets in the way. Chances are, if the point you want to select is not on the grid, the spacing of the grid is just too large. Rather than turning off SNAP TO GRID, make the grid size smaller. The Level 3 GRIDS menu contains a number of commonly used grid sizes that can be selected directly from the menu. If you use other grid sizes frequently, these can be added to the menu (see Appendix A of the Generic CADD manual and Chapter 14 of this book for instructions).

Setting the Current Drawing Parameters

Numerous commands set parameters that determine the attributes of new entities placed into the drawing. For example, if the current line color is 2, all new entities drawn will be color 2. The current line color is set by the LINE COLOR command, which is selected from the LINES menu or by typing the two-character code LK.

Other similar parameter-setting commands include the LINE TYPE (LT) and LINE WIDTH (LW) commands, also listed on the LINES menu. Each of these commands sets attributes that are picked up by all new entities created. Each of these commands also activates a special display in the video menu area that shows examples of these attributes that you can select. See Figures 3-5 and 3-6 for illustrations of the LINE WIDTH and LINE TYPE menus. Again, your display might be slightly different, depending on your graphics card. If you are configured for a color system, the LINE COLOR command will also bring up a similar special menu display. None of these special menu displays will be shown if the video menu is currently turned off.

Figure 3-5. *The LINE TYPE menu*

You may set any of these three parameters by choosing from the examples shown using the menu cursor and the second pointing device button, or you may type a number and press ENTER. The range of allowable values for these parameters is shown in the prompt area at the bottom of the screen. For LINE COLOR, values from 0 to 255 are available, no matter how many colors can actually be generated by your graphics card. If you have, for example, 16 colors, colors 0 through 15 will be as shown on the LINE COLOR menu, and these same 16 colors repeat for numbers 16 to 31, 32 to 47, and so on.

LINE TYPES vary from 0 to 255 as well, and the first 10 (0 to 9) are shown on the special video menu display when you select the command. However, these LINE TYPES do not repeat in the same way as the colors. LINE TYPES 0 to 9 always look the same, no matter how much you zoom in or out or at what scale you print or plot your drawing. These might be considered "hardware" line types, that is, the length of the dashes is tied to the display or printed output rather than the real size of the drawing.

Figure 3-6. *The LINE WIDTH menu*

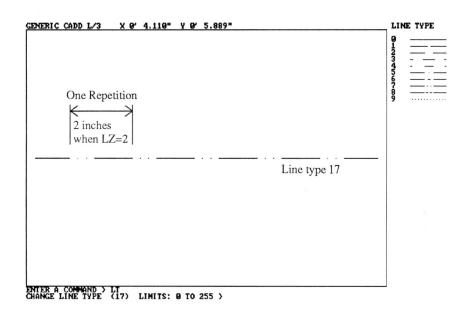

Figure 3-7. *One repetition of any scaled line type is one unit long*

LINE TYPES 10 to 19, on the other hand, can be scaled to the objects that you are drawing. The distance from the start of one dash to the start of the next dash is controlled by the LINE SCALE (LZ) command, also listed on the LINES menu. The default value for LINE SCALE is 1, or one dash per inch, unless you change the LINE SCALE.

When you change the LINE SCALE, the space between the dashes in LINE TYPES 10 to 19 changes as well. A LINE SCALE of 2 means one dash every two inches. More complex LINE TYPES, such as number 17 (which looks like number 7, but is scalable), may be composed of more than one size of dash. In these cases, the entire pattern of dashes repeats according to the module specified by the LINE SCALE. With the LINE SCALE set at 2 and LINE TYPE at 17, one long dash and two short ones would appear every two inches, as shown in Figure 3-7.

You may want to use lines that have the same pattern at different scales. LINE TYPES 20 to 255 are provided for this purpose. LINE TYPES 20 to 29 are the same as 10 to 19, but twice as long, while LINE TYPES 30 to

39 are three times as long. In other words, with a line scale of 1, the dash interval within a line of line type 22 will be 2 units, while the interval for line type 32 will be 3 units. If the LINE SCALE is changed to 2, the line will consist of one dash every four inches in line type 22 and one dash every six inches in a line of type 32. Lines that use types 0 to 9 will not be affected by the LINE SCALE.

Fortunately, LINE WIDTH is not nearly as complex because only the ten options shown on the screen are available. However, the actual width does vary with your display or output device because the width of the line is measured in dots. On the screen, this means pixels, while on the printer it translates to print elements (pins). On a plotter, each incremental LINE WIDTH adds another stroke of the pen. LINE WIDTHS are similar to LINE TYPES 0 to 9 in that they look the same no matter how far you zoom in or out, and they are plotted the same no matter which plot scale you use. A LINE WIDTH of 3 translates to three strokes of the plotter pen, side by side, no matter what the scale of the drawing.

Choosing the Layer for Drawing

Just as you set the LINE COLOR, LINE TYPE, and LINE WIDTH before you draw anything, you also select the layer on which you want to draw. The default is layer 0, but you have another 255 from which to choose.

To draw on any layer other than 0, use the CURRENT LAYER (or LAYER CURRENT) command from the LAYERS menu, or type **YC** on the keyboard. (Users of certain early versions of Level 1 may need to use YS instead, for LAYER SELECT.) Generic CADD indicates the current layer and asks you to type the new current layer. Type a number between **0** and **255** and press ENTER. Any new entities that you create will then appear on this layer.

The current layer has one quality that the other current drawing parameters don't have: editing can be limited to this layer as well. Generic CADD allows you to edit either on the current layer only, or on all visible layers, using the ALL LAYERS command (AL) from the LAYERS menu. ALL LAYERS is a true toggle—each time you select it, it reverses its status, from EDIT ALL LAYERS OFF to EDIT ALL LAYERS ON and back again.

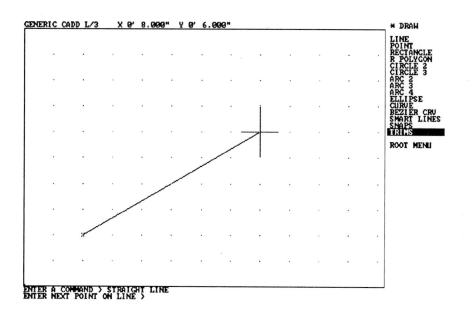

Figure 3-8. *Drawing a line using absolute coordinates*

Coordinate Display Modes

The coordinates at the top of the screen, as you have seen, are in the format specified by the current UNIT system. You can also control where they are measured from, and how they are measured.

Coordinates can be displayed as absolute, that is, as measured from the origin, 0,0. This means that the X and Y numbers displayed on the screen are just like Cartesian coordinates on a graph. This mode is selected by choosing the ABS COORDS command from the DISPLAY menu or by typing **AC** on the keyboard. An example of a line that is drawn by using absolute coordinates is shown in Figure 3-8.

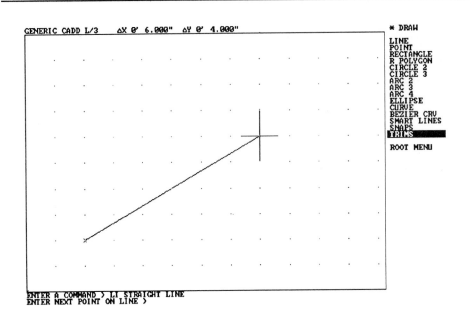

GENERIC CADD L/3   ΔX 0' 6.000" ΔY 0' 4.000"   * DRAW

LINE
POINT
RECTANGLE
R POLYGON
CIRCLE 2
CIRCLE 3
ARC 2
ARC 3
ARC 4
ELLIPSE
CURVE
BEZIER CRU
SMART LINES
SNAPS
TRIMS

ROOT MENU

ENTER A COMMAND > LI STRAIGHT LINE
ENTER NEXT POINT ON LINE >

Figure 3-9. *Drawing a line using delta coordinates*

Alternatively, coordinates can be displayed as relative to the last point entered. This method allows you to use the coordinates to determine, for example, the actual horizontal and vertical distances between the endpoints of a line as you draw it. This mode is selected by typing **DC** or by choosing DEL COORDS (short for delta coordinates) from the DISPLAY menu. Once you execute this command, the coordinates refer to the distance that the cursor travels from the last point placed rather than from the origin. Figure 3-9 shows a line drawn with relative coordinates.

A further refinement, if you wish, allows you to display the actual distance between the last point and the cursor, together with the angle between them. This mode, available only if you are using DEL COORDS, is selected by typing **PT** or by choosing the POLAR COORDS command from the DISPLAY menu. Figure 3-10 shows a line drawn using polar coordinates.

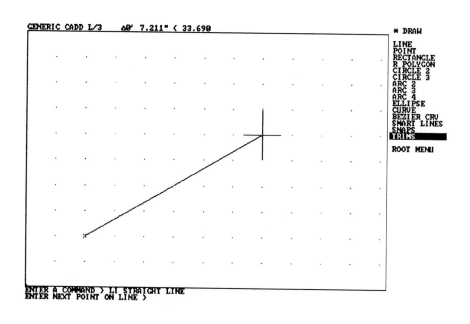

Figure 3-10. *Drawing a line using polar coordinates*

These three commands are all toggles and may appear to behave strangely if you use them one after another. If you simply type **AC** or choose ABS COORDS repeatedly, you turn absolute coordinates on and off. When they are on, you can see the coordinates, and when they are off, you can see nothing. However, if you type **DC** or choose DEL COORDS while ABS COORDS is on, the absolute coordinates are replaced by delta coordinates. Now if you turn DEL COORDS off, no coordinates appear at all. The absolute coordinates are not hiding "underneath," waiting to be displayed when the delta coordinates are turned off. Whenever you select the command for the coordinates that are currently displayed, all coordinate display is turned off until selection of the next coordinate command, ABS COORDS or DEL COORDS (AC or DC). Polar coordinate format remains in effect even when delta coordinates are turned off, so that when they are turned back on, delta coordinates will still be in polar format, until POLAR COORDS (PT) is selected again.

You will find that different types of coordinates have different uses, and you may want to change back and forth between these types fairly frequently. Whichever you use most often, especially at the beginning of a drawing session, can be configured with the CONFIG program to be in effect automatically every time you load Generic CADD. As you begin to draw, it will be important to be aware of which coordinate display is currently on. The delta coordinates are marked with small triangles (resembling the Greek letter delta) in front of the X and Y at the top of the screen.

Manual Entry of Coordinates

Just as the display of coordinates can be set relative to the origin or the last point, so can the keyboard or manual entry of coordinates.

You can type absolute coordinates of points by selecting the MANUAL ENTRY ORIGIN command on the UTILITIES menu, or by typing **MO** on the keyboard. This is the default mode for manual entry of coordinate data. Whenever you type a set of X and Y coordinates, it is assumed that you mean them to be measured from the origin, 0,0.

Many times, however, it is much more convenient to type the distance from the last point entered (because you happen to know it), rather than bothering to figure out how far it is from the origin. This mode of manual entry can be selected with the M.E. RELATIV command on the UTILITIES menu, or by typing **MR** on the keyboard. Now, whenever you type coordinate data, your X and Y values are assumed to be measured from the last point entered. This method is appropriate for situations when you know the length of a line or the distance that you want to move or copy something. If you are just starting your drawing and there is no last point, the first point specified in this mode will be relative to the origin, 0,0.

One more manual entry mode is available. Sometimes you may want to measure entities from a particular point in the drawing, other than the origin. You can place the basepoint at this location (with the BASEPOINT (BP) command on the CONTROLS menu), and then select M.E. BASEPNT from the UTILITIES menu, or type **MB** on the keyboard. All subsequent manual entry will use this basepoint as its reference.

All MANUAL ENTRY commands are one-way toggles, or, in other words, parameter-setting commands. Each one forces all manual entry to be in its own mode, no matter what mode was previously active. There is no state in which all modes are off, as there is no way to turn off a particular manual entry mode other than selecting a different one.

Once again, each mode has a variety of uses, and you will use these commands frequently as you draw and edit. When you start your first line, M.E. ORIGIN works well because there is no last point from which to measure. As you develop the drawing, M.E. RELATIV and M.E. BASEPNT become more valuable, although M.E. ORIGIN may still be used. M.E. RELATIVE is particularly useful with the editing commands, such as MOVE and COPY. For now, leave manual entry set to ORIGIN.

Other Drawing Aids

Generic CADD offers a number of other drawing aids, such as RUBBER BANDING and CONSTRUCTION POINTS, which will be discussed in the next chapter as you begin your first drawing.

4 *Basic Drawing Tasks*

This chapter introduces Generic CADD's entity drawing commands and a number of basic drawing techniques through several simple drawing examples. If you do these examples on your computer, you will better learn the commands and also end up with some simple drawing files for use in later chapters. You will also be able to try some of the parameters and drawing aids that were discussed in previous chapters, as well as a few new ones.

If you are following along with Generic CADD, just pick up where you left off in the last chapter. If you are starting from scratch, call up CADD and start a new drawing, select FEET/INCHES for your units, set your LIMITS at 12′ × 12′, and turn on a 12″ grid. Make sure that SNAP GRID is on by typing **SG**. If you get the message "SNAP TO GRID IS OFF," type **SG** again. If you get "SNAP TO GRID IS ON," make sure that you have absolute coordinates on, too. If you are uncertain, select ABS COORDS from the DISPLAY menu or type **AC**. Since this is a one-way toggle, it won't matter whether it is already on; this will make sure that it is.

Your First Drawing: A Room

Your first drawing will be the floor plan of an eight-by-ten-foot room, as shown in Figure 4-1. Drawing floor plans may not be exactly what you have

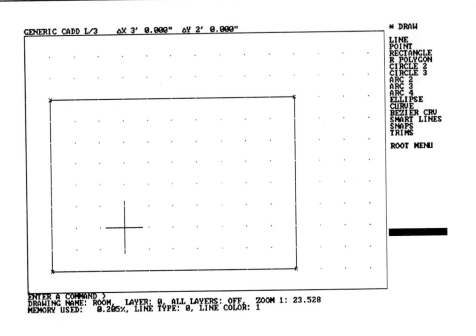

GENERIC CADD L/3   ΔX 3' 0.000"   ΔY 2' 0.000"

* DRAW

LINE
POINT
RECTANGLE
R POLYGON
CIRCLE 2
CIRCLE 3
ARC 2
ARC 3
ARC 4
ELLIPSE
CURVE
BEZIER CRV
SMART LINES
SNAPS
TRIMS

ROOT MENU

ENTER A COMMAND >
DRAWING NAME: ROOM,   LAYER: 0, ALL LAYERS: OFF,   ZOOM 1: 23.528
MEMORY USED: 0.205%, LINE TYPE: 0, LINE COLOR: 1

Figure 4-1.   *First drawing: an eight-by-ten-foot room*

in mind for Generic CADD, but this kind of practical example acts as a reminder that CADD drawing data represents real information.

Several methods are used for this drawing task to illustrate the flexibility of Generic CADD input techniques. It doesn't really matter which method you use for similar drawings in the future, as long as it works and you are comfortable with it. Sometimes one method may be faster than another in a particular situation.

Drawing a Rectangle

The simplest way to draw a rectangle is with the RECTANGLE command. From the ROOT menu, go to the DRAW menu by positioning the menu cursor over the word DRAW and pressing the second button on the pointing device. From the DRAW menu, select the RECTANGLE command, using the same technique.

Notice that moving from the ROOT menu to the DRAW menu causes no change in the prompt area, but selecting RECTANGLE initiates a series of prompts that are associated with this command. The first prompt asks you to enter the first corner of the rectangle.

The First Corner   As discussed, there are a number of ways to enter points. In this case, specify the first corner by moving the drawing cursor to the lower-left corner of the screen (it really doesn't matter where you start, as long as you leave enough space to draw the eight-by-ten room). When the cursor is in the right place, say one grid point up from the bottom and two or three in from the left, press the first pointing device button.

Preferences for Drawing Aids   As Generic CADD is a highly configurable program, you might see a number of things at this point. A small "x" may appear at the location that you have just selected. If this happens, it is because you have CONSTRUCTION POINTS turned on; if not, CONSTRUCTION POINTS is off. Construction points, which let you see the points that you have already chosen, can be very useful devices for visualizing the object you are drawing. However, they are optional. You may prefer other visualizing devices, and you can customize Generic CADD to fit these preferences.

You might see a rectangle that changes size as you move the cursor. (Move the cursor around to see if this is the case.) Like construction points, this "rubber band" rectangle aids in visualizing as you draw. If such a rubber band rectangle appears on the screen, you have RUBBER BANDING turned on; if no such line is displayed, RUBBER BANDING is off.

To change the way that Generic CADD is currently handling construction points and rubber banding, you must first cancel the RECTANGLE command by pressing the escape key (ESC). To toggle CONSTRUCTION POINTS on or off, select CON.POINTS from the DISPLAY menu or type **PC**. To toggle RUBBER BANDING on or off, select RUBBER BAND from the same DISPLAY menu, or type **RB**.

In order to see what you are drawing, it is usually a good idea to have one of these commands turned on. If you have a relatively fast computer (286 or 386) or a math coprocessor, rubber banding is a great help for most drawing tasks. If you have a slow computer (8086 or 8088) or no math coprocessor, rubber banding can be slow. If this is the case, use construction points instead. It is easier to work with the examples in this book if they are both turned on. Later, as you do more drawings, you will learn which method works best for you.

If you have interrupted the RECTANGLE command to change either of these toggles, select it again from the DRAW menu or type **RE** on the keyboard, and place your first point again, near the lower-left corner of the screen.

The Opposite Corner   Now you are ready to select the second point—the upper-right corner of the RECTANGLE. Because you intend to draw a room of specified dimensions, eight by ten feet, you need to be precise about the location of the second point. The second point should be exactly ten feet to the right and eight feet above the first point.

Counting grid points as you move the cursor would, of course, work just fine. In fact, when you are only moving a few grid points, and the grid is composed of a round number of dots, such as 12, this can be the best way. However, Generic CADD provides several other means that are not as tedious as counting grid dots.

Using Coordinates   One of these methods is provided by the coordinates, which show the location of the cursor. When ABSOLUTE COORDINATES are turned on, they change by one foot every time you move the cursor one grid point in any direction. If you note the location of your first point, you can simply add ten feet in the X direction (to the right) and eight feet in the Y direction (toward the top of the screen), and move the cursor until these values appear.

You *can* improve on this technique. If you type **DC** or select DEL COORDS from the DISPLAY menu, you will activate DELTA or RELA-TIVE COORDINATES, which refer to the last point selected. For this example, that is exactly the information you need to select the second corner of the rectangle accurately. Now, you can move the cursor until the X coordinate reads "10'" and the Y coordinate reads "8'," as you can see in Figure 4-2.

When you have the cursor in the right place, press the first pointing device button to select the point. Your rectangle will be drawn, the prompt will read "ENTER A COMMAND >," and the cursor will float freely from dot to dot with no rubber band. Notice that you did not have to interrupt the RECTANGLE command to change the coordinate display. The ABS COORDS (AC), DEL COORDS (DC), and POLAR COORDS (PT) commands are all "transparent" toggles, meaning that you can use them anytime, even in the middle of another command. CON. POINTS (PC) and

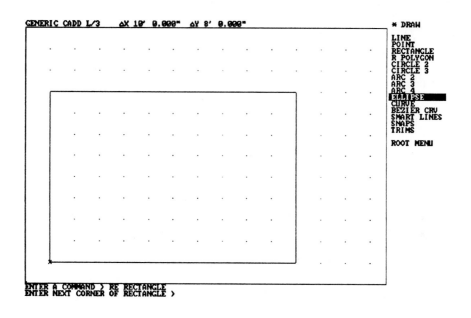

Figure 4-2. *Finishing the rectangle using delta coordinates*

RUBBER BAND (RB), on the other hand, are not transparent toggles: the prompt "ENTER A COMMAND >" must be displayed in order to use one of them.

Drawing Another Rectangle

For the next task, let's assume that you want to place an exterior wall six inches around the outside of the room to represent wall thickness, as shown in Figure 4-3. Because the grid spacing is too big (12 inches), you may be tempted to turn SNAP TO GRID off in order to draw off the grid. Resist this impulse! Instead, change the GRID to six inches and leave SNAP TO GRID turned on. Use the GRID SIZE command from the GRIDS menu, or type **GS**. Then, go back to the DRAW menu and select the RECTANGLE command, or type **RE**. Show the first point of the outside wall by going to

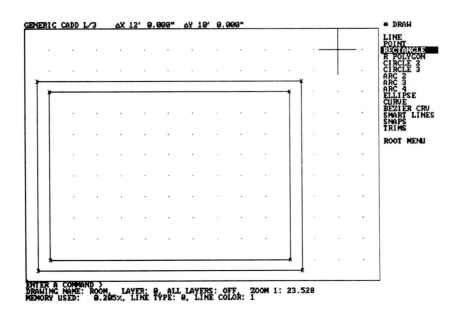

GENERIC CADD L/3   ΔX 12' 0.000" ΔY 10' 0.000"   ✳ DRAW

LINE
POINT
RECTANGLE
R POLYGON
CIRCLE 2
CIRCLE 3
ARC 2
ARC 3
ARC 4
ELLIPSE
CURVE
BEZIER CRV
SMART LINES
SNAPS
TRIMS

ROOT MENU

ENTER A COMMAND >
DRAWING NAME: ROOM,   LAYER: 0, ALL LAYERS: OFF,   ZOOM 1: 23.528
MEMORY USED: 0.205%, LINE TYPE: 0, LINE COLOR: 1

Figure 4-3.   *The room with six-inch-thick walls*

one corner of the existing rectangle, moving toward the outside by one grid point in each direction, and then pressing the first pointing device button. (Even though you started in the lower-left corner to draw the room, you can start with any corner for the exterior wall.) Notice that all of the grid points might not be represented by visible dots, depending on your graphics card, but that you are still able to snap to these invisible grid points.

Move the cursor until it is one grid point outside the opposite corner, and press the first pointing device button to select the point. Note that the coordinates show X to be 11 feet and Y to be 9 feet, until the point is selected. Once you select the second corner of the rectangle, it becomes the last point selected, and the coordinates change to 0, 0.

Erasing the Drawing

Let's try another method of drawing an eight-by-ten-foot box. First, erase what you've drawn so far. The fastest, most powerful erasing command is DRAWING ERASE, which, as it sounds, removes all entities from the current drawing. However, it does leave the GRID SIZE, the LIMITS, and all of the toggles as currently set, so that even though your drawing is erased, you don't have to start completely from scratch. Select ERASE from the DRAWING menu, or type **DX** on the keyboard. Since this command is not reversible, Generic CADD asks you if you are sure that you want to do this. To go ahead, type **Y**. (If you had selected the ERASE command by mistake, you would now have a chance to cancel it by typing **N**.) After you type **Y**, the screen and the current drawing will be cleared of all entities.

Using Lines

The second way to create the eight-by-ten-foot room is with the LINE command. With the LINE command, you draw each side of the box, starting in one corner and working your way around until you get back to the same point. Notice that the DRAWING ERASE command did not clear the 6-inch grid from the screen. Before you start drawing lines, change the GRID SIZE (GS) back to 12 inches.

The First Line To start a line, you can either use the LINE command by selecting it from the DRAW menu or by typing **LI** on the keyboard, or you can select a starting point of the line. Whenever the "ENTER A COMMAND >" prompt is displayed and you select a point, Generic CADD assumes that you are initiating a LINE command. Therefore, using the LINE command itself is optional, though under certain conditions it might be preferable to use the command instead of selecting points, as you will see later. So, either execute the command or choose a point. If you use the LINE command or type **LI**, you are asked for the starting point of the line. Pick a point near the lower-left corner of the screen, just as you did when you were using the RECTANGLE command. (If CONSTRUCTION POINTS is turned on, you will see a small "x" appear at the location you selected; if RUBBER BANDING is on, a rubber band line will stretch from this first point to the current cursor location.) Move the cursor to the right,

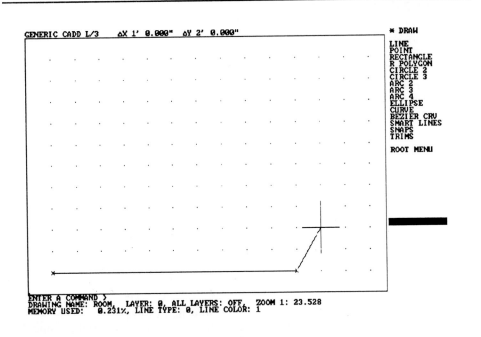

GENERIC CADD L/3   ΔX 1' 0.000"   ΔY 2' 0.000"   * DRAW

LINE
POINT
RECTANGLE
R POLYGON
CIRCLE 2
CIRCLE 3
ARC 2
ARC 3
ARC 4
ELLIPSE
CURVE
BEZIER CRV
SMART LINES
SNAPS
TRIMS

ROOT MENU

ENTER A COMMAND >
DRAWING NAME: ROOM, LAYER: 0, ALL LAYERS: OFF, ZOOM 1: 23.528
MEMORY USED: 0.231%, LINE TYPE: 0, LINE COLOR: 1

Figure 4-4. *One side of the room drawn with the LINE command*

watching the coordinates at the top of the screen. When the X coordinate reads 10′ (and the Y coordinate reads 0), select the second point. The first side of the box and a new rubber band line appear, as shown in Figure 4-4.

Continuing Around   Now, even though the prompt reads "ENTER A COMMAND >," you can continue selecting points to draw the rest of the box. Move the cursor until Y is 8′, making sure that this time X stays at 0. Select this point. Continuing on, move the cursor to the left until X reads −10′. Notice that the coordinate is negative because you are moving to the left instead of to the right. For X (horizontal) movement, positive is to the right and negative is to the left. For Y (vertical) movement, up (toward the top of the screen) is positive and down (toward the bottom of the screen) is negative.

More Drawing Aids Before you select this fourth point, the upper-left corner of the box, you might want to add one more helpful command to your arsenal, SNAP ORTHO or ORTHO MODE. Select this command from the CONTROLS menu, or type **OR** on the keyboard (Level 1 users type **SO**). You don't have to interrupt the LINE command, as this is another transparent toggle that can be used whenever you want. When ORTHO MODE is on, you can only move directly to the right or left, or straight up and down. This means that one of the coordinates will always stay at 0, so you only have to watch the other one. When you are moving directly to the left, as you are now, for example, you can ignore the Y coordinate, because it stays at 0. The advantage of this command is that you can retain your accuracy without having to be quite as careful, so you can draw faster. Go ahead and select the fourth point, and then continue on to the beginning point at the lower-left corner. After you have selected this final point, press ESC to end the LINE command. If you have been using RUBBER BAND-ING, the rubber band line disappears when you end the LINE command. The box is now complete.

Notice that the LINE command is not as quick for this simple figure as the RECTANGLE command, as it requires that you place all four corners, instead of just two. The LINE command is, however, significantly more flexible. With the LINE command you can create a box, for example, with a two-foot-square notch cut out of one corner or any other shape that you want. As you will see later when you begin to edit your drawings, using the RECTANGLE command or drawing four lines individually produces exactly the same result. Remember, the Generic CADD primitives do not include a simple entity called a Rectangle. The RECTANGLE command is really just a quick way of drawing this simple shape when you do not need anything more complex.

Typing the Dimensions

One last method for drawing a box requires typing the coordinates of points rather than selecting them on the screen. This method can be used with either the LINE or RECTANGLE command, but for illustration purposes, continue with the LINE command.

Manual entry requires that you select a point of reference. Generic CADD offers the options Origin, Basepoint, or the last point entered (Relative). In this case, relative coordinates are the most useful. Notice that relative manual entry and relative coordinates are each activated by their own commands. Just because you have relative coordinates on the screen doesn't mean that the coordinates you type will be interpreted in the same way. To select RELATIVE mode for manual entry, select M.E.RELATIV from the UTILITIES menu or type **MR** on the keyboard.

Describing a Box with Coordinates   To practice this method, let's draw the same outer box six inches outside the one that you have on the screen now. Since you won't be showing points on the screen, you don't need to change the grid. Either start an implicit LINE command by typing the coordinates of the first point, or by using a LINE command selected from the DRAW menu, or by typing **LI**. Since the last point that was entered was the lower-left corner of the existing box, you can specify your first point by typing **–6,–6** and pressing ENTER. This indicates a point 6 inches to the left and six inches below the last point placed. To place the next point, moving horizontally to the right, type **11′,0** and press ENTER, indicating 11 feet to the right and zero feet vertically. Don't forget the foot mark (′), or you will only move 11 inches. The coordinates of the next point are **0,9′**, and then **–11′,0** (remember, negative numbers indicate movement to the left), and finally **0,–9′** (down nine feet) to get back to your starting point. After selecting this last point, press ESC to end the LINE command.

Notice that manual entry can be used to specify exact lengths of lines, or exact cursor movements, regardless of the current grid and regardless of the setting of ORTHO MODE. By its nature, manual entry is more accurate than pointing on the screen, and so it overrides any toggles or drawing aids that you have set to help with cursor movement and point selection.

Saving the Drawing

If you want to edit this drawing later, you must save it. This process sends the drawing from the computer's temporary memory, where it is now, to a file on a hard or floppy disk. If you don't save your drawing before you end Generic CADD or turn off the computer, you will have to start from scratch the next time you want to work on it.

One of the easiest ways of saving the drawing is by selecting the QUIT command from the UTILITIES menu, or by typing **QU** on the keyboard. Although the QUIT command has a number of different functions, one of the most important options of the QUIT command is the option to SAVE the drawing.

When you issue the QUIT command, you are asked if you want to save the drawing. For the purpose of this example, type **Y**. The filename of the drawing is shown, together with the default drawing path where the file will be saved. If the path and the filename are correct, you can just press ENTER. If you want to make a change, type the new drawing name (not including the extension .DWG) and press ENTER. In fact, you can save this drawing in a new file called ROOM by typing **ROOM** now. (If you want to save the drawing somewhere other than the default path, type the new pathname, including the drawing name without the .DWG extension, and press ENTER.) The drawing will be saved on disk. If the file already exists, you will be asked if you want to Overwrite or Rename the existing file.

Overwrite or Rename?   At this point you have three options: (1) You can type **O** to Overwrite, which will replace the old file with the new one. (2) You can type **R** to Rename the old file. The old file will be renamed with the same name, except for the extension, which will be changed to .BAK (for backup). This allows you to have two versions of the drawing on the disk at the same time: the current version, which will have the extension .DWG, and an older version (as it was before the current drawing session) with the extension .BAK. (3) You can press ESC and start the process over again with a different filename altogether.

Quit or Continue?   After the file is saved, you will be asked if you want to quit or continue. If you type **Q**, you automatically exit to DOS. From here, if you want to work on another drawing, you must start up Generic CADD again by typing **CADD** and pressing ENTER or by typing **CADD** and the filename and pressing ENTER. If you type **C**, you can continue working on your drawing just as you were before.

You should quit this drawing now so that you can start a new one. Even if you are not finished with the drawing, it is a good idea to save the drawing after coming to the end of some specific task, in case you need to retrieve the file from disk.

Your Second Drawing: A Musical Staff

In the previous example of the room, you were able to use a continuous series of lines because the basic box could be drawn without stopping. This is rather like drawing a figure without lifting the pencil from the paper. You will, of course, want to draw more complex objects.

In the next example, you will draw a series of parallel lines that represent a musical staff, as shown in Figure 4-5, to illustrate the repeated use of the LINE command in a noncontinuous mode. At the DOS prompt, start up CADD and the new drawing by typing **CADD MUSIC** and pressing ENTER. Press ENTER when you come to the configuration screen, and type **Y** when asked if this is a new drawing.

The Drawing Setup

Whenever you start a new drawing, you need to ask yourself the same questions: What units will I use? How much space do I need? What size grid is appropriate? Do I want to use other settings than the default line color, type, width, or layer?

For units, select INCHES from the UNITS menu, or type **IN** on the keyboard. For drawing space, set the LIMITS (by choosing the command from the CONTROLS menu or by typing **LS** on the keyboard) to 6 inches high by 9 inches wide. Don't forget to ZOOM ALL (choose ALL from the ZOOMS menu, or type **ZA**) after setting the limits. Set your GRID SIZE, from the GRIDS menu or GS on the keyboard, to 1/8 inch. (You can either type **1/8** or **.125** and press ENTER, it doesn't matter which.) Turn on SNAP TO GRID, also on the GRIDS menu, or **SG** on the keyboard. When you select the command, note whether it goes on or off. If it turns off, select it again to turn it on. Turn on RELATIVE COORDINATES by selecting DEL COORDS from the DISPLAY menu or by typing **DC** on the keyboard. All

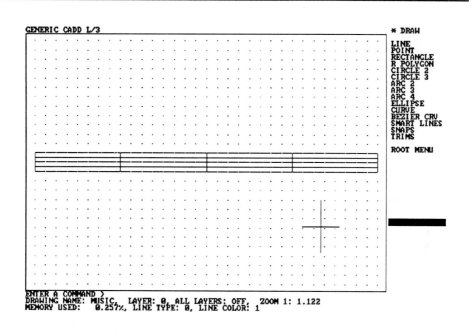

GENERIC CADD L/3 * DRAW

LINE
POINT
RECTANGLE
R POLYGON
CIRCLE 2
CIRCLE 3
ARC 2
ARC 3
ARC 4
ELLIPSE
CURVE
BEZIER CRV
SMART LINES
SNAPS
TRIMS

ROOT MENU

ENTER A COMMAND >
DRAWING NAME: MUSIC, LAYER: 0, ALL LAYERS: OFF, ZOOM 1: 1.122
MEMORY USED: 0.25%, LINE TYPE: 0, LINE COLOR: 1

Figure 4-5. *Second drawing: a musical staff*

of the default drawing attributes (color, type, width, and layer) are fine the way they are.

The First Line

You can start the staff the same way you did the box in the previous drawing. Pick the LINE command from the DRAW menu or type **LI** on the keyboard. When asked for the first point, select a point near the upper-left corner of the screen, a few grid dots down from the top and in from the left. Move the cursor eight inches to the right (watch the coordinates), and select the second point. If you have trouble moving the cursor in a straight horizontal line because the grid is relatively small, select ORTHO MODE from the CONTROLS menu or type **OR** (**SO** for Level 1).

Repeating the LINE Command

To draw the next line, you need to stop the previous LINE command and start a new one. You could use the same technique that you used for the box drawing—pressing ESC and starting a new line with another LINE command—but there is a faster way. Most Generic CADD commands can be repeated by pressing SPACEBAR (the long horizontal bar at the bottom of the keyboard). If you have just drawn one line using the LINE command, you can start a new one by simply pressing SPACEBAR. The rubber band line, if you are using rubber banding, will be ended, and you will get a prompt asking you for the first point of the line.

With this method, complete the four remaining horizontal lines of the musical staff. Place two points, each of which is one grid point (visible or invisible) below the starting points and endpoints of the last line drawn, and press SPACEBAR. Do the same three more times. When you have finished the last line, press ESC instead of SPACEBAR, so that you don't get another LINE command. You should end up with five eight-inch lines, 1/8 inch apart. Notice that this technique does not work if you start the first line by simply picking a point instead of using the LINE command, because there will be no LINE command to repeat. Instead, whatever command you issued before starting the line will be repeated.

Also note that toggles that are used during another command cannot be repeated with the SPACEBAR. This means that even if you use a toggle command while doing a line, when you press SPACEBAR it will be the LINE command that will be repeated rather than the toggle.

Distance Between Lines

So far, you have been using the relative coordinates to show the actual length of lines as you draw. These coordinates can also be used to determine the distance between lines as well. Select another LINE command by pressing SPACEBAR. Note that you can repeat the LINE command even though you ended it with ESC. Draw the first vertical line at the far left end of the musical staff. It will be 1/2 inch long. Notice that as you choose the second point, the relative coordinates return to 0,0.

To draw the next vertical line, press SPACEBAR again and move the cursor to the right, noticing that the coordinates show how far the cursor has moved from the end of the last line. Move exactly two inches to the right, and draw the second line. Press SPACEBAR again, and draw three more lines the same way. Then press ESC to end the last LINE command.

Notice that if you drew your first line with an upstroke (second point above the first), your second line will be drawn with a downstroke, the third up, fourth down, and so on. If you started with a downstroke, the order is reversed. This is a good technique for drawing a series of lines when you know the horizontal or vertical distances between their endpoints.

Save the Drawing

To save this drawing for later use, select QUIT from the UTILITIES menu, or type **QU** on the keyboard. Type **Y** when asked if you want to save the drawing, press ENTER when shown the default drawing name (MUSIC.DWG), and then type **Q** when asked if you want to Quit or Continue. After some time, you will become very familiar with this series of keystrokes.

Your Third Drawing: A Key

The third drawing, the key shown in Figure 4-6, is more complex. You should feel comfortable with the LINE command by this time, so it will be used freely from now on. It will also be assumed that you now know how to select a UNIT system, set the LIMITS and the GRID SIZE, and how to turn on and off RELATIVE COORDINATES, SNAP TO GRID, and ORTHO MODE.

Starting Out

Start the key by typing **CADD KEY** and pressing ENTER at the DOS prompt. It can be drawn using INCHES (IN) and FRACTIONS (FR), with FRACTION VALUE (FV) set to 1/16 as the units in a drawing space (LIMITS) of 3 inches high by 4 inches wide (don't forget to ZOOM ALL). The GRID SIZE should be set for 1/16 inch, and SNAP TO GRID should be on.

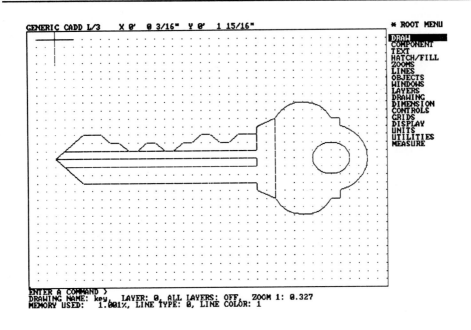

Figure 4-6. *Third drawing: a key*

A good way to start a complex drawing is with a *reference line*. This key happens to have a center line that passes through both the tip of the key and the center of the hole at the other end. The exact length of this key is 2 1/8 inches. So the first entity to draw is this horizontal line. Start on the left of the screen, using manual entry in the relative mode (M.E. RELATIV on the CONTROLS menu or **MR** on the keyboard) to select the second point, which should be typed as **2 1/8,0** or **2.125,0**. (Note that the X coordinate would be negative if you had started on the right.)

A vertical reference line will also come in handy. Use another LINE command to draw this line starting at −7/16,7/16 (relative to the last point placed on the right end of the line) and going down to 0,−7/8. This line will help you to construct the head of the key later.

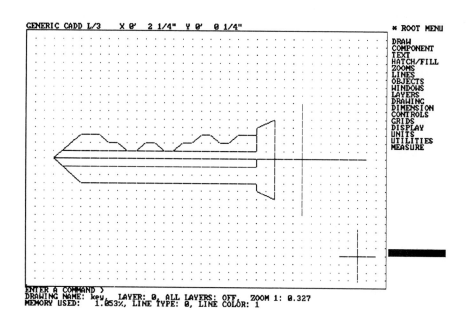

Figure 4-7. *A portion of the key, drawn entirely with LINES*

The Easy Part

The left side of the key is made entirely from lines and should be relatively easy to draw by this time. This portion is 1 1/2 inches long, measured from the tip to the point where the rounded portion begins. At this point, the key is 5/8 inch wide. All points required to draw the key are on a grid snap point. Using Figure 4-7 as a guide, draw this portion of the key. If you compare Figure 4-6 with Figure 4-7, you notice that you need to draw a horizontal line on top of the horizontal reference line. This line will be obscured on your screen, but you should draw it nonetheless.

The Round Parts

Drawing the rest of the key requires two new entity types, a Circle and a number of Arcs. Several commands are used to create these two entities: you see ARC 2, ARC 3, ARC 4, CIRCLE 2, and CIRCLE 3 on the DRAW menu. These commands provide three ways of drawing an arc and two methods for circles. For the key drawing, you can use the ARC 3 and CIRCLE 2 commands and explore the others later.

Three-Point Arcs   The name "ARC 3" means that you are going to draw an arc by specifying three points: the two endpoints and a third point located somewhere on the arc. Generic CADD defines the term *arc* as a circle segment, that is, part of a circle with the same center point as the circle. As all points on the arc are an equal distance from that center, a unique arc can be drawn for any three such points. All arcs in Generic CADD, regardless of the command used to create them, are stored in this three-point format.

Drawing Arcs   To draw a three-point arc, select the command ARC 3 from the DRAW menu or type **A3** on the keyboard. The arc and circle two-character codes are particularly easy to remember. As shown in Figure 4-8, note that the second point of each arc is located exactly on the end of one of your reference lines. With this in mind, draw the three arcs that appear on the head of the key. The locations of the first and last points for each arc should be easy to locate on the grid. After you select the ARC 3 command, you are prompted for each point in turn. With SNAP TO GRID turned on, move the cursor to the proper location and press the first pointing device button. If you place any of the points in the wrong place, simply press ESC and issue the ARC 3 command again. When you have completed each of the first two arcs, press SPACEBAR to get another ARC 3 command. When you have finished with the arcs, draw the four short lines that connect them at the corners.

Two-Point Circles   Again, the name of this command, CIRCLE 2, provides a significant clue to its operation. The two points required are the center point of the circle and any point on the circle itself. This is a good command to use when you know the location of the center and the radius of the circle, as the distance between the two points is the radius. After showing or specifying the first point, use relative mode for manual entry,

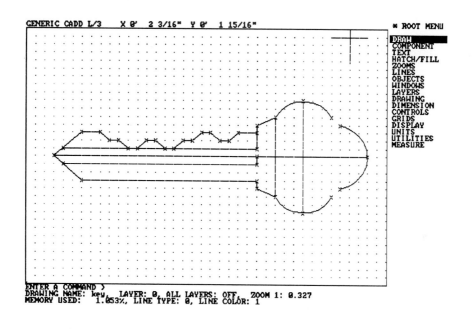

Figure 4-8.   *Arcs added to the key, with CONSTRUCTION POINTS on*

and type a second coordinate that has the length of the radius as X and zero as Y. All Generic CADD circles are stored using the center and one point, regardless of the command that is used to create them.

Drawing Circles   The key drawing contains one circle, which you can draw by selecting CIRCLE 2 from the DRAW menu or by typing **C2** on the keyboard. You will be asked for the center point. Position the cursor, using Figure 4-6 as a guide. Note that the center point is on the horizontal reference line, so you can locate it by counting grid points. Select the point by pressing the first pointing device button. You will next be prompted for a point on the circle. Move the cursor to the desired point, again using Figure 4-6 as a guide, noticing that the radius will be displayed as one coordinate of the relative coordinate display if you move either vertically or horizontally. In addition, if RUBBER BANDING is turned on, a rubber band circle helps you to visualize the circle as you draw it. Press the first pointing device button once you have the cursor properly located, and the circle will be drawn.

A Less Powerful ERASE Command

Now that the key is complete, you need to erase your reference lines. Obviously, the DRAWING ERASE command that you used earlier is too wide-ranging for this task, so something simpler is needed. A number of editing commands on the OBJECTS menu work on only one entity or object at a time. The name of the Generic CADD menu is intended to signify the relative strength of its editing commands: Other menus include commands that can edit all entities in a window, all entities on a selected layer, or all entities in a drawing.

To erase a single line, select ERASE from the OBJECTS menu or type **OE** (for OBJECT ERASE) on the keyboard. A prompt asks you to select the object to be erased. Position the drawing cursor near the lines that you want to erase, preferably near the middle of the line and not near another entity. The important criteria is that the object you want to erase is the closest object to the cursor. When you press the first pointing device button, the object nearest to the cursor will be erased. To erase another object, press SPACEBAR to repeat the command, and select this line in the same way. When you are finished erasing, you may want to do a REDRAW (RD) to clean up the screen.

Oops! If you make a mistake and erase the wrong entity, use the UNERASE command from the OBJECTS menu, or type **UE** on the keyboard, to reverse the action of the ERASE command. The UNERASE command returns to the screen whatever was erased in the last ERASE command. In this case, since the OBJECT ERASE command erases only one entity at a time, the UNERASE command brings back only one object when it is chosen. If you are using a command that erases more than one object at a time, the UNERASE command brings back the same number of objects. The UNERASE command has certain limitations, which will be investigated later. Among other things, it cannot reverse the action of a DRAWING ERASE command.

Save and Exit to DOS

Once the reference lines have been erased, save the drawing by selecting QUIT from the UTILITIES menu or typing **QU** on the keyboard. Type **Y** and press ENTER, and then type **Q** to save the drawing under the default name (the one you used to start the drawing) and exit to DOS. If you have previously saved the drawing, you will be asked if you want to Rename or Overwrite it. In this case, type the letter **O** to update the file.

Your Fourth Drawing: A Star

With this drawing, you will get a chance to use two more commands, REGULAR POLYGON and SNAP TO NEAREST POINT. By combining Generic CADD's ability to create a figure with any number of equal sides and its ability to snap new points exactly onto the location of points already in the drawing, you will find it quite easy to draw a star-shaped figure, as shown in Figure 4-9.

The Drawing Setup

Begin a new drawing called STAR, by typing **CADD STAR** at the DOS prompt and starting Generic CADD in the usual way. The star is going to be two inches high, so use INCHES (IN) for your UNITS, and set your LIMITS (LS) to 5 inches high by 7 inches wide. Follow the setting of the limits, as usual, with a ZOOM ALL (ZA). Set your GRID (GS) to 1 inch, and turn on RELATIVE COORDINATES and SNAP TO GRID. The choice of RUBBER BAND (RB) or CONSTRUCTION POINTS (PC) is up to you.

A Five-Sided Figure

The easiest way to draw a star is to use Generic CADD's ability to create a figure with any number of sides, in this case, five. You can then use this five-sided figure as a construction aid to draw the star.

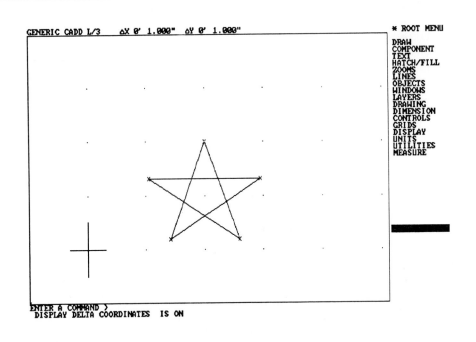

Figure 4-9. *Fourth drawing: a star*

Select the REGULAR POLYGON command from the DRAW menu or type **RP** on the keyboard. When you are asked for the center of the polygon, select a point right in the middle of the screen. When you are asked for a point on the polygon—one of the five vertices or "corners" of the polygon and also the top point of the star—move the cursor up one inch to the next grid point, and select that point. The last bit of required information is the number of sides of the polygon. Type **5**, press ENTER, and the regular polygon appears, as shown in Figure 4-10.

Like the RECTANGLE command, the REGULAR POLYGON command is really a drawing aid that helps you to draw a specific type of figure using lines. There is no such primitive entity as a "regular polygon." In this case, you have just placed five lines into the drawing, and will be able to take advantage of the fact that each line has its own endpoints as you draw the star.

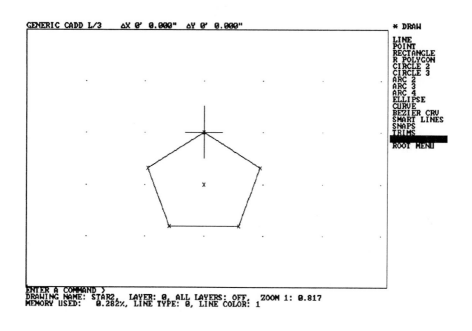

Figure 4-10.   *A five-sided regular polygon*

Snapping to an Existing Endpoint

The SNAP TO NEAREST POINT (NP) command is unusual in that it does not appear on any menu and does not display prompts when you use it. You will find, however, that you will probably use this command more than any other, with the possible exception of the automatic LINE command. If you have a three-button mouse and are using Level 1 or Level 2, the SNAP TO NEAREST POINT command is hard-wired onto the third button of the mouse. Whenever you press the third button, you get an NP command. Level 3 can also be configured to respond in the same way and is so configured when shipped. If you have not changed the configuration of the pointing device buttons using the CONFIG program, your mouse or other pointing device should be set up to use the third button as NP as well.

Because no prompts are associated with the SNAP TO NEAREST POINT command, you must position the drawing cursor before issuing the command. Since you will be snapping to the nearest point, you no longer need to snap to the grid. In fact, if SNAP TO GRID is on, you will have trouble getting near enough to the points that you want to snap to. Turn off SNAP TO GRID by selecting it from the GRIDS menu or by typing **SG** on the keyboard.

Start an implicit LINE command by positioning the cursor near the top of the five-sided figure on the screen and pressing the third button on the pointing device or typing **NP**. You should try to be within 1/4 inch or so from the point that you are trying to select. What really matters is that the desired point is closer to the cursor than any other point. For this reason, selecting a cursor location slightly above the top of the figure ensures that the top point will be selected.

Do not use the first pointing device button to select the point. When using the NP command, pressing the third button or typing **NP** on the keyboard replaces the normal point selection process. As soon as you issue the NP command, the cursor jumps to the nearest point, and places a construction point or connects a rubber band if you have turned on either of these features.

Continuing with the NP Command

Now that you have started the LINE command, cross to one of the opposite sides of the figure on the screen and select another corner with the NP command: Use the third button on the pointing device or type **NP**. The first Line will be placed. Continue adding more lines by criss-crossing the figure and snapping from corner to corner of the five-sided figure. When you have drawn five lines and have returned to the starting point, press ESC to end the automatic LINE command. Your drawing should resemble Figure 4-11.

Erasing the Construction Lines

Erase the construction lines of the original five-sided figure by using the ERASE command from the OBJECTS menu, or by typing **OE** on the keyboard. The command asks you to select an object to erase. Position the cursor near one of the original five lines, and press the first button on the

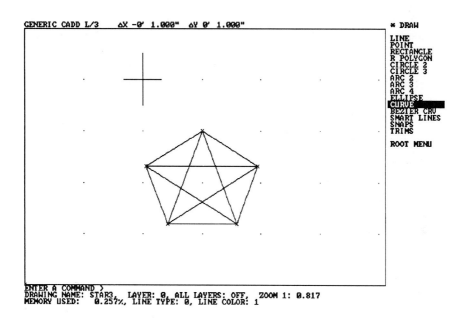

Figure 4-11.   *The star drawn by snapping to the existing points*

pointing device. Just make sure the line that you want to erase is closest to the cursor before you press the button.

To erase another Line, issue another OBJECT ERASE command by pressing the SPACEBAR and then selecting the Line. Continue this process until all five construction Lines have been removed.

Save and Exit

To save the drawing, select QUIT from the UTILITIES menu or type **QU**. Type **Y** to indicate that you want to save the drawing, and press ENTER to verify the filename, STAR.DWG. When asked if you want to Quit or Continue, type **Q**.

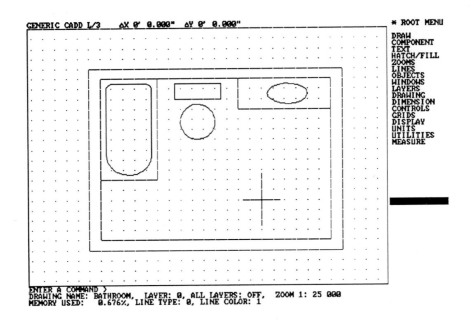

GENERIC CADD L/3   ΔX 0' 0.000"   ΔY 0' 0.000"

* ROOT MENU

DRAW
COMPONENT
TEXT
HATCH/FILL
ZOOMS
LINES
OBJECTS
WINDOWS
LAYERS
DRAWING
DIMENSION
CONTROLS
GRIDS
DISPLAY
UNITS
UTILITIES
MEASURE

ENTER A COMMAND >
DRAWING NAME: BATHROOM, LAYER: 0, ALL LAYERS: OFF,   ZOOM 1: 25 000
MEMORY USED: 0.676%, LINE TYPE: 0, LINE COLOR: 1

Figure 4-12.   *The ROOM drawing with bathroom fixtures added*

Adding to Your First Drawing: A Bathroom

For this drawing task, you will see how to return to a previously saved drawing and change it. You will use the eight-by-ten-foot room, which is stored in the drawing file ROOM.DWG. You will turn this room into a bathroom by adding a number of typical bathroom fixtures as shown in Figure 4-12, and learn some new DRAW commands and another ZOOM command at the same time.

To return to the ROOM drawing, type **CADD ROOM** at the DOS prompt. Press ENTER when you get the configuration and copyright screen. The drawing will be loaded automatically. Alternatively, you could just type **CADD** at the DOS prompt, and wait for Generic CADD to ask you for the drawing name after the configuration screen. Some operating systems do not recognize the drawing name after the CADD command, so you may be asked for the drawing name even if you type it at the DOS prompt.

Reviewing the Room

Notice that when Generic CADD loads an existing drawing, it automatically does a ZOOM ALL, so that the entire drawing is shown on the screen. In addition, you should notice that none of the toggles or settings are saved with the drawing file. The UNITS, LIMITS, and GRID SIZE settings, together with the SNAP TO GRID, ORTHO MODE, RUBBER BAND, CONSTRUCTION POINTS and COORDINATES toggles always start out the way that they are specified in the CONFIG program. If you find that you would like to retain typical values for any of these each time you call up a drawing, use CONFIG to set them.

Getting Ready to Draw

Before you start drawing again, set UNITS to FEET/INCHES (FI). Don't worry about the LIMITS, because you won't be drawing anything beyond the area that is already displayed on the screen. Set GRID SIZE (GS) to 6 inches. Turn on SNAP TO GRID (SG), ORTHO MODE (OR or SO), and DELTA COORDINATES (DC), and set CONSTRUCTION POINTS (PC) and RUBBER BAND (RB) to your own preferences.

Adding Lines and Rectangles

Using the LINE and RECTANGLE commands add the counter top, the back of the toilet, and the tub surround. Figure 4-13 will serve as a guide. The counter top and the tub surround should be drawn first, as they fit onto the six-inch grid. Make the counter 1 1/2 feet deep by four feet using two Lines, and the tub 2 1/2 feet wide by five feet long with another two Lines. To draw the back of the toilet, reduce the GRID SIZE (GS) to 3 inches, and then use a Rectangle to create it. The three-inch grid allows you to place the back of the toilet three inches from the wall. Make the Rectangle 24 inches wide by 9 inches deep.

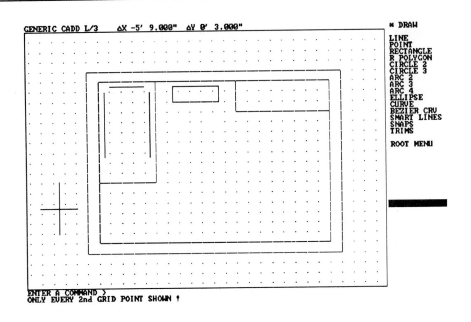

Figure 4-13.   *Lines and rectangles provide the basic layout*

Zooming in Closer

You will be using an ellipse to complete the toilet, on a 1 1/2-inch grid. When you set the GRID SIZE (GS) to 1.5, you might notice that it is a little difficult to position the cursor accurately. SNAP TO GRID works well when the grid is large, but when it is small, it can be hard to tell how far you are moving, and the cursor tends to jump around.

The solution to this problem is to zoom in closer on the area that you want to work on, so that 1 1/2 inches appears larger on the screen. Once you do this, cursor movement will be back to normal.

To zoom in closer to a specific area, select UP from the ZOOMS menu, or type **ZU** on the keyboard. Generic CADD asks you to indicate the new center of the screen. Use the drawing cursor and the first pointing device button to select a point about where the middle of the toilet will be drawn, a little below the back, which you have already drawn. As soon as you select this point, the display will be adjusted, and objects will appear exactly twice as large as they did a moment ago. To fit this part of the drawing on the screen at the larger size, Generic CADD must drop some of the drawing around the edges. Don't worry, this part of the drawing isn't lost, it just isn't displayed at the moment. Each time you use the ZOOM UP command, the apparent size of objects on the screen is doubled, and the display is recentered around an area that you select. As you will see later, ZOOM BACK (ZB) has exactly the opposite effect.

Drawing an Ellipse

An ellipse is defined by the locations of the endpoints of one axis and the length of the other axis. It is important to notice the distinction between *location* and *length*. The first two points position the location of the ellipse, while the second two points merely specify its width, which is the length of the second axis. Therefore, the ellipse actually passes through the first two points, but it might not pass through the next two.

The Major Axis   To draw an ellipse, select the ELLIPSE command from the DRAW menu or type **EP**. Generic CADD asks you for the first endpoint of the major axis, usually defined as the longer axis. In Generic CADD, however, the major axis can be the longer or shorter one, depending on which is placed first. It is also considered major because the ellipse actually passes through its endpoints.

Position the first endpoint carefully, 1 1/2 inches or one grid point below the back of the toilet, centered below the back. For the other endpoint, move the drawing cursor straight down until the Y coordinate reads –21.

The Minor Axis   As discussed, the points that you pick for the minor axis are simply used to specify the width of the ellipse. The distance between these two points is calculated, and the ellipse drawn. However, to visualize this width, it is often helpful to place the two points about where the ellipse should pass. Besides, construction points should not be placed too far away from the ellipse itself, as they can cause you trouble later if you forget where you put them.

For the two endpoints of the minor axis then, visualize an imaginary ellipse where you think you want it, and place the two points 18 inches apart, nine inches to each side of center. Again, don't worry too much if

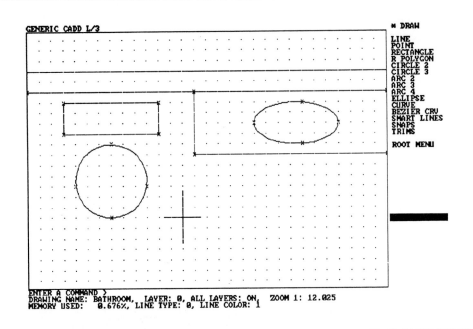

Figure 4-14. *Ellipses added with CONSTRUCTION POINTS on*

these two points are not placed exactly in the right location; it is important, however, that they be 18 inches apart.

True or Construction Ellipse? The ELLIPSE command is capable of producing two different types of primitives: a single ellipse, defined by the four points that you just specified, or four arcs that are fit into the same ellipse shape, each defined by three points, just like any other arc.

Once you have located the four points required to construct the ellipse, you are asked if you want a True or a Construction Ellipse. Typing **T** produces the single ellipse entity, while typing **C** creates four arcs. You will find that the two different types, True and Construction, have different uses. If the ellipse can stand alone (you will not have to edit it later or use it to edit other entities) the single entity is best, as it uses less space in the database. If you will need to edit the ellipse, break it into segments, or fill or hatch inside or around it, the four arcs are required. You can't break, fill, or hatch the Ellipse entity, or extend or trim Lines to it. The difference will become clear when you begin editing your drawings. In this case, choose a Construction Ellipse by typing **C**, so that you can later put a pattern on the bathroom floor.

Another Ellipse: The Sink

Use the ZOOM ALL (ZA) command to return to the full drawing, and then ZOOM UP (ZU) on the area around the bathroom sink, and draw another ellipse. Use the 1 1/2-inch grid and Figure 4-12 as a guide. This time, after you have selected the four points, specify a True Ellipse, as you will not need to do any more work on this one. ZOOM ALL when you are done, and then ZOOM UP on the bathtub area.

More Arcs

To round the corners of the bathtub, you should use arcs. Remember, you must place three points to define an arc with the ARC 3 command. For the large arc at the foot of the tub, you can use a three-point arc, because you can place the two endpoints and a point on the arc fairly easily. For the smaller arcs at the two corners of the tub, the point between the two endpoints is not so easy to locate. For these arcs, you have two more commands, ARC 2 and ARC 4, both of which allow you to construct an arc, rather than placing one with three points.

The ARC 4 Command As you might expect, the ARC 4 command requires four points: (1) the center point of the arc, (2) one endpoint, (3) a point indicating the direction of the arc from the endpoint, and (4) the final endpoint.

Of these four points, only the second point (one of the endpoints) is necessarily on the arc. The center is not on the arc by definition. The third point, which specifies the direction, might be on the arc, but only if you are really lucky, and the final point, which specifies the second endpoint, might also be on the arc, especially if SNAP TO GRID is turned on and the point is on the grid. On the other hand, because the center point is already located, and the radius has been determined by the location of the first point, the last point doesn't have to be on the arc. An imaginary line is projected between the center of the arc and the last point you select, and the arc is cut along this line.

This command is activated by selecting ARC 4 from the DRAW menu or by typing **A4** on the keyboard. Try it out on the upper-left corner of the bathtub. You might even ZOOM UP (ZU) a little closer if you desire. How far you need to zoom is determined by personal preference and the resolution of your graphics card. With higher-resolution hardware, you don't have to zoom as much.

After you select the command, you are asked for the center point of the arc. Starting with the arc on the left corner, select a point directly below the end of the horizontal line, and directly to the right of the vertical line. When you are asked for the first endpoint, select the left end of the existing horizontal line. When asked for the midpoint, select a point that is located approximately on the arc that you are creating, somewhat to the left of the point you just selected. You need not be too precise with this last point, as it is only used to tell Generic CADD which direction you want to go from the previous point. You might want to temporarily turn SNAP TO GRID off by typing **SG**. After you have selected the (approximate) midpoint, turn SG back on again. Finally, select the top of the vertical line for the other endpoint. See Figure 4-15 for the locations of all four points.

The arc will be drawn after you indicate the last point. If you have turned on CONSTRUCTION POINTS, you might notice an extra point or two appear as the arc is drawn. These are due to the fact that even though you specified this arc using four points, it is defined and stored by Generic CADD using three points on the arc, just like an ARC 3. All arcs created by Generic CADD are stored in this same format.

The ARC 2 Command The ARC 2 command is quite similar to ARC 4. The name may lead you to assume that this arc is created by selecting only two points, but three are required. (ARC 2 was chosen to fit into this naming convention because ARC 3 and ARC 4 already existed, and because ARC 2 is simpler in many ways than the other two.)

Use the ARC 2 command to draw the upper-right corner of the bathtub. First, ZOOM BACK (ZB) and then ZOOM UP (ZU) to move this corner to the center of the screen. Then select the ARC 2 command from the DRAW menu or type **A2** on the keyboard.

Specify the center and the first endpoint in the same way that you did with the ARC 4 command. After specifying these two points, turn off SNAP TO GRID by typing **SG**. If you don't have RUBBER BANDING turned on, activate it by typing **RB**. You will immediately see why ARC 2 is called a

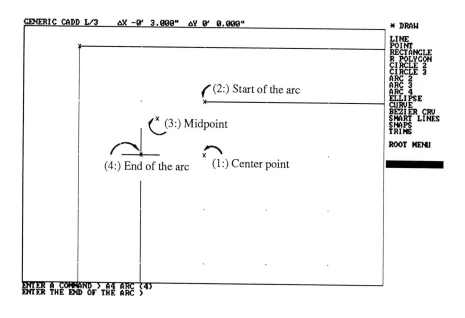

Figure 4-15.   *Constructing a four-point arc*

"rubber arc." As you move the cursor clockwise around the center point, the arc will be "rubber banded" in that direction as shown in Figure 4-16. When you move the other way, the rubber arc follows. Instead of turning SNAP TO GRID back on, use the SNAP TO NEAREST POINT command to select the final endpoint. Drag the arc to approximately where you want it and type **NP** on the keyboard, or press the third button on the pointing device, if you have three buttons. The arc will be drawn.

One Last Arc: Your Choice   To complete this drawing, draw the final arc at the foot of the bathtub. ZOOM BACK (ZB) until you can see this area, and then ZOOM UP (ZU) on it. Place the arc using any of the three commands. (Be sure to turn SNAP TO GRID back on before you start.) When you have finished, ZOOM ALL (ZA) to examine your work, and then save the drawing by using the QUIT (QU) command.

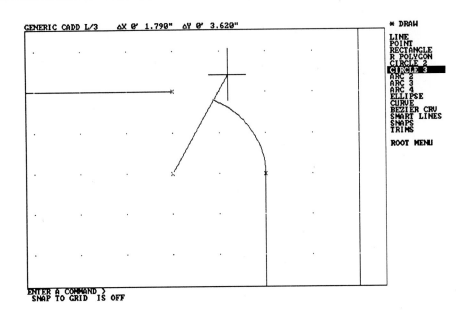

GENERIC CADD L/3   ΔX 0' 1.790"   ΔY 0' 3.620"

* DRAW

LINE
POINT
RECTANGLE
R POLYGON
CIRCLE 2
CIRCLE 3
ARC 2
ARC 3
ARC 4
ELLIPSE
CURVE
BEZIER CRV
SMART LINES
SNAPS
TRIMS

ROOT MENU

ENTER A COMMAND >
SNAP TO GRID IS OFF

Figure 4-16.   *Constructing a two-point rubber arc*

Your Fifth Drawing: A Site Plan

The last example in this chapter, the site plan shown in Figure 4-17, is more ambitious than the drawings you have made so far. The 50-by-100-foot site includes a sidewalk, house, driveway, walk, patio, swimming pool, and some trees. This drawing illustrates several new DRAW commands and a few new drawing techniques and reinforces the fact that you can easily draw objects that are much larger than the drawing screen.

Starting Up

To start this drawing, type **CADD SITEPLAN** at the DOS prompt, or type **CADD**, wait until you are asked for a drawing name, and then type

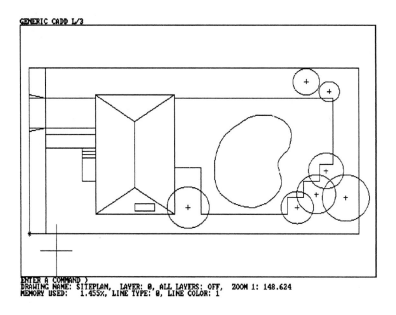

Figure 4-17. *The site plan drawing*

SITEPLAN. When you get Generic CADD running, set your UNITS to FEET (FT), your LIMITS (LS) to 60' high by 120' wide, and your GRID SIZE (GS) to 10 feet. Also turn on SNAP TO GRID (SG), ABSOLUTE COORDINATES (AC) rather than RELATIVE, and ORTHO MODE (OR or SO). CONSTRUCTION POINTS (PC) and RUBBER BAND (RB) should be turned on for illustrative purposes.

The REFERENCE POINT Command One more drawing aid will be useful as you start this drawing—REF. POINTS from the DISPLAY menu, or **PR** on the keyboard. This command toggles the display of reference points on or off. If the message in the prompt area tells you that it is turned off when you give the command, issue it again to turn it back on. Reference points have several uses, but one in particular will help with this drawing. When REFERENCE POINTS is turned on, a reference point is displayed at the origin, 0,0. Sometimes it is a good idea to start your drawing at the origin, so that if you ever want to combine drawings, you have a common reference.

Drawing the Lines and Rectangles

As with the key example, it is often easiest to start a drawing with the basic entities, Lines and Rectangles, that set up the overall configuration and then add the other entities that fill out the detail.

Start this drawing with a rectangle (RE), which will represent the boundary of the site. For the first point, move the cursor to the reference point at the origin. (It may be just barely peeking out of the lower-left corner of the screen.) When the cursor is at this point, the ABSOLUTE COORDINATES at the top of the screen should read exactly 0,0. It should be easy to move to this point with a ten-foot grid turned on. Once you have the cursor located, select the point with the first pointing device button and drag the other corner of the rectangle to 100',50'. In this case, because you started at the origin, the absolute coordinates give you the actual size of the rectangle.

After you select these points, change the GRID SIZE (GS) to 5 feet and place a Line for the sidewalk, which is exactly 5 feet in from the left side of the site boundary. You can see how easy it is to be accurate by adjusting the GRID SIZE to your current needs. Next, change the GRID SIZE to 1 foot, and draw the house, 15 feet from the sidewalk and 5 feet from the lower site boundary.

Use ESC to Reset the Coordinates   Whenever you want to draw one object (the house) a certain distance from another object (the sidewalk), the RELATIVE COORDINATES command can be useful. Select DEL COORDS from the DISPLAY menu or type **DC**. Your coordinates will now be measured from the last point entered instead of from the origin. But what if the point that you want to measure from (in this case, the lower end of the sidewalk line) is not the last point that you entered?

In this situation, the relative coordinates must be reset so that the point you want to measure from is, in fact, the last point entered. Do this simply by moving the drawing cursor to the point that you want to reference from and typing **NP** or pressing the third pointing device button. This point is selected, the coordinates are reset to 0,0, and a rubber-band line is attached to this point, as Generic CADD thinks that you want to start drawing a line. Since you don't, press ESC. The point that you just selected is now the last point entered, and the coordinates will now be measured from there.

The Rest of the Lines and Rectangles   Now you should be able to construct the house 15 feet from the sidewalk and 5 feet from the site boundary. Use the RECTANGLE (RE) command, positioning the cursor at 15′,5′, as displayed by the relative coordinates for the first point, and then at 24′,36′, the dimensions of the house.

Using the same technique, draw the driveway, which is 9 feet wide; the walk, 4 feet wide and 2 feet away from the driveway; and the patio, which extends 48 feet from the back of the house. The notches in the corner of the patio are 5 feet on a side. Any other dimensions you can make up. Change the GRID SIZE according to your needs, and use ESC to reset the coordinates if that becomes necessary. When you are finished, your drawing should resemble Figure 4-18.

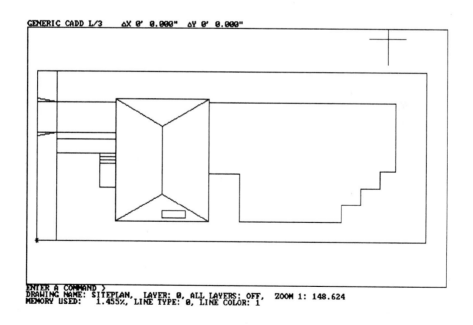

Figure 4-18.   *The site plan Lines and Rectangles*

A Curved Pool

The next task is to construct the curved pool. Before starting, ZOOM UP (ZU) to get a little closer. When you are ready to draw, use the CURVE command by selecting it from the DRAW menu, or by typing **CV** on the keyboard. Messages in the prompt area explain how the CURVE command works. At the bottom of the screen you will read: "ENTER A POINT ON CURVE >." You must specify a series of points through which the curve is to be constructed. Above this message is the message "ENTER A PEN UP TO END >." This means that when you are finished selecting points, you must type **PU** to draw the curve. An alternate method of "entering a PEN UP" is to select a blank line from the video menu. As soon as you do either, the curve will be drawn.

Because the pool is a free-form object, which doesn't necessarily pass through the grid points, you might want to turn off SNAP TO GRID before you begin selecting points. Starting with the second point, each time you indicate a new point, a temporary line is placed between the two points to help you visualize the curve. See Figure 4-19 for an example of what the curve should look like as you are drawing it. If you want to cancel the command after a number of points have been selected, press ESC.

When you are ready to close the kidney-shaped figure, use the NEAR-EST POINT snap to choose the same point that you started with by typing **NP** or pressing the third button on the pointing device. Once you have returned to the first point, type **PU** or move the menu cursor to a blank line and press the second button on the pointing device. The temporary lines will be removed, and the curve will be drawn.

Notice that because the last point was snapped onto the first point, the curve passes smoothly through this point in the same way as it goes through the others, as if it was one seamless loop. If these points were not quite in the same place, you might get a slight "dent" in the pool at this point. Whether you want a continuous loop depends on what you are trying to draw.

One last note about the CURVES command: You must specify at least three points before issuing PEN UP, or Generic CADD will not be able to construct a curve. If you want a short curve, place your points closer together. When you are done with the pool, ZOOM ALL (ZA) to see the entire drawing.

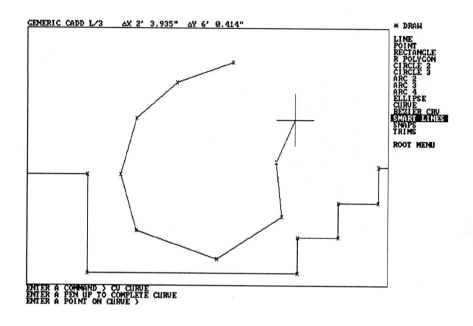

Figure 4-19.   *Constructing the curve*

Three-Point Circles

The trees in this drawing could be drawn with two-point circles, but you can use these trees to experiment with the other circle command, CIRCLE 3. Like a three-point arc, these circles are constructed using three points. In this case, the first and last points are not endpoints, of course, and the second point has no special significance. The three points can be given in any order, as only one circle can be defined that passes through any three specified points. Any one of the three points can be thought of as being between the other two.

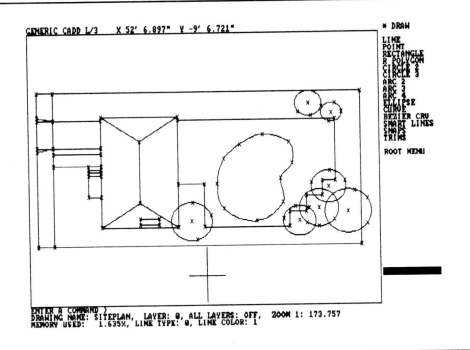

GENERIC CADD L/3   X 52' 6.897" Y -9' 6.721"

* DRAW

LINE
POINT
RECTANGLE
R POLYGON
CIRCLE 2
CIRCLE 3
ARC 2
ARC 3
ARC 4
ELLIPSE
CURVE
BEZIER CRV
SMART LINES
SNAPS
TRIMS

ROOT MENU

ENTER A COMMAND)
DRAWING NAME: SITEPLAN, LAYER: 0, ALL LAYERS: OFF, ZOOM 1: 173.757
MEMORY USED: 1.635%, LINE TYPE: 0, LINE COLOR: 1

Figure 4-20.   *The site plan with three-point circles for trees*

As you specify each point, a construction point appears. When you select the last point, a construction point appears not only at the cursor location, but at the center of the circle as well, because all circles, no matter how they are created, are actually defined by the location of the center and one point on the circle. When you use a three-point circle, the center and the first point that you specify are the ones that are actually stored. You can verify this with the REDRAW command from the ZOOMS menu, or by typing **RD** on the keyboard. When you issue this command, the screen will be redrawn, with the construction points shown at the actual definition points of the circles rather than at the locations that you used to create the circles. Compare Figure 4-20, shown with the construction points in the locations where they are placed, with Figure 4-21, showing the actual locations of the definition points.

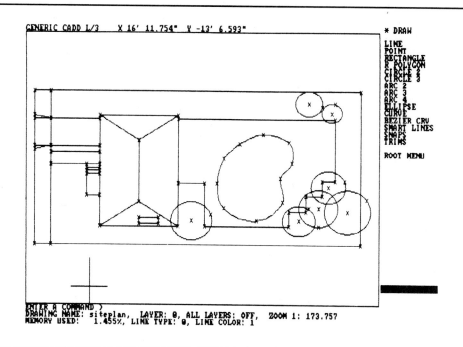

Figure 4-21. *The actual definition points*

Use Figure 4-20 as a guide for placing your three-point circles. You might try CIRCLE 2 (C2) to review the difference between the two commands.

Standard Points

Another Generic CADD primitive called a *standard point* can be used to mark the locations of the trunks of these trees. These are useful if you want to mark a location visibly, and have it show up when you print or plot your drawing. Standard points can be printed, while construction points and reference points cannot.

To draw a standard point, select POINT from the DRAW menu or type **PO** on the keyboard. Move the cursor to where you want to put the point, and press the first pointing device button. In the case of the trees in your drawing, you can place these POINTS exactly onto the centers by using the NEAREST POINT snap instead of the first button. When the cursor is near the center of a circle, type **NP** or press the third button on the pointing device. This will snap the point exactly where you want it. To draw another standard point, simply press SPACEBAR, and then move the cursor and snap onto the center of another circle. Continue until you have placed points in the center of every tree, and your drawing will be complete.

Display Without Construction Points

To see what your drawing really looks like, turn off CONSTRUCTION POINTS (PC) and REFERENCE POINTS (PR), and execute the REDRAW (RD) command. You will notice that a command on the DISPLAY menu also controls the display of Standard Points. If you turn off the display of STANDARD POINTS, they will not show up on the screen and they will not be printed, either. Finally, save the drawing and exit to DOS by using the QUIT (QU) command.

Through the examples provided in this chapter, you have tried out all of the basic DRAW commands, including POINT (PO), LINE (LI) or implicit by picking points, ARC 2 (A2), ARC 3 (A3), ARC 4 (A4), CIRCLE 2 (C2), CIRCLE 3 (C3), RECTANGLE (RE), REGULAR POLYGON (RP), EL-LIPSE (True and Construction) (EP), and CURVE (CV). The only DRAW command you have not tried, BEZIER, will be explored in a later chapter.

Also, you have used some of the ZOOM commands, ZOOM LIMITS (ZL), ZOOM ALL (ZA), ZOOM UP (ZU), and ZOOM BACK (ZB). In addition, you have used many of the drawing aids, such as the GRID (GR), GRID SIZE (GS), SNAP TO GRID (SG), ORTHO MODE (OR or SO), and SNAP TO NEAREST POINT (NP or third pointing device button).

You have seen how to use ABSOLUTE (AC) and RELATIVE (DC) COORDINATES, including how to reset the relative coordinates with ESC, and how to use manual entry of coordinates to type actual dimensions rather than showing points on the screen. You have used the DRAWING ERASE (DX) command to erase the entire drawing, and the OBJECT ERASE (OE) command to erase one entity at a time. You have repeated commands using the SPACEBAR, and have used construction lines and temporary entities to construct more complex objects.

You have created and saved several drawings, and in one case called up a previously saved drawing and added more information to it. You have saved the files ROOM.DWG, MUSIC.DWG, KEY.DWG, STAR.DWG, and SITEPLAN.DWG on your disk, and will return to some of these files in later chapters. All told, you have come a long way toward being a productive user of Generic CADD.

5 *Basic Editing Tasks*

This chapter provides a counterpoint to Chapter 4, which covered the creation of new drawings and the addition of new entities into the drawing database. This chapter, in contrast, examines the editing commands.

For the most part, you will use existing drawings to experiment with these commands. However, you will see that the editing commands are also an integral part of the drawing process and that editing need not be reserved for "fixing mistakes." In fact, in many cases you will find that the editing commands as well as the drawing commands can be used to create a brand new drawing.

Editing Command Organization

Unlike the entity-creating commands, which are primarily on the DRAW menu, the entity-editing commands are distributed across several menus. These menus are organized according to the type of entity to be edited rather than by function of the editing command.

The OBJECTS, WINDOWS, LAYERS, and DRAWING menus all contain editing commands in Level 3. Levels 1 and 2 include only the OBJECTS and WINDOWS editing commands. Users of these programs will find that some of the commands in this chapter do not exist. Levels 1 and 2 still have LAYERS and DRAWING menus, but these commands are used for other purposes.

Some commands, such as ERASE and CHANGE, appear on all four menus. This means that you can choose to erase one object, the entities in a window, the entities on a selected layer, or all of the entities in a drawing. You have seen the difference between the OBJECT ERASE and the DRAWING ERASE commands in the previous chapter. You will learn more about the WINDOWS and LAYERS commands in this chapter.

Other commands only appear on selected menus—for example, the BREAK command appears only on the OBJECTS menu, as you can only break one entity at a time. The MOVE command appears on the OBJECTS and the WINDOWS menus, so you can choose to move a single object, or all of the entities in a window. You cannot move a layer or an entire drawing.

Selection Types

The four editing menus, OBJECTS, WINDOWS, LAYERS, and DRAW-ING, represent the four different ways of selecting objects. As explained in Chapter 2, when combined with the actual objects which are selected, these four menus can be thought of as nouns—for instance, "this object," "the entities in this window," "layer four," "the whole drawing," and so forth. Each command on these four menus makes its specific entity selections in a different way. In the headings below, the two letters in parentheses show the format for the accompanying editing command. The lowercase *x* is replaced with the letter representing the actual function of the editing command.

The OBJECTS Menu (Ox)   All of the OBJECT editing commands first ask you to select the object that you want to edit. This is usually done by pointing to it with the drawing cursor and pressing the first button on the pointing device. The object closest to the cursor will be selected for editing. Although each OBJECT command affects only one entity at a time (the words "object" and "entity" are interchangeable in this context), you can always select the command again by pressing SPACEBAR and selecting another entity to edit.

The two-character commands for most of the OBJECT commands start with the letter *O*. The second letter indicates the type of editing operation you want to perform on the selected object.

One exception is the MOVE POINT command, which is activated by the two-character command MP. Because you can only move points on one object at a time, you do not really need the letter *O* to indicate that you want to select an object. The fact that you must select an object is implied by the nature of the command. The MOVE POINT command, like the other OBJECT commands, asks you to select an object, and then asks for the point on the object that you want to move and where you want to move it. You will get a chance to try this command later in this chapter.

Another exception is ERASE LAST (EL), which erases the last entity drawn. This abbreviation is logical in that, unlike the other OBJECT commands, this command does not ask you to select which object you want to edit. Generic CADD already knows the last object you drew, so it can select and erase the object with no further information.

Another exception on the OBJECTS menu, the UNERASE (UE) command, is unusual. This command, found on several menus, reverses the action of the last ERASE command, whether you erased one object, objects selected with a window, or an entire layer. The only ERASE command that it cannot reverse is the DRAWING ERASE command, which actually clears the portion of memory where the drawing is stored so that it cannot be retrieved.

Level 3 users will notice another exception, BEZIER EDIT (BE), which is limited to moving points on multiple Bezier Curves. This command is covered in Chapter 9.

Finally, Level 2 and Level 3 users will notice two additional menu items on the OBJECTS menu, SNAPS and TRIMS. These are not commands at all, but take you to other menus for working with objects. These are covered in Chapter 9 as well.

The WINDOWS Menu (Wx) The editing commands on the WINDOWS menu affect all of the objects that are selected by placing a window. When you select any of these commands, you are prompted to "PLACE A WIN-DOW." To do this, move the drawing cursor to one corner of the area in which the objects that you wish to edit are located, and press the first pointing device button. A rubber band rectangle will appear attached to the cursor. Stretch this cursor around the entities that you want to edit, and press the first button again once you surround them. If your first point proves to be in the wrong place and you can't get the window around the objects, press ESC to cancel the command and start over.

For an entity to be considered inside a window, all of the definition points of the entity must be inside the window. If the centerpoint of a circle, for instance, is inside the window, but the point on the circle is outside, the circle will not be selected. If a line passes through the window, but either endpoint is outside the window, the line will not be selected, and so on. In regard to complex entities which have no construction or definition point but only one reference point each, only the reference point need be included in the window for the entire complex object (such as a text character) to be selected.

Almost all of the two-letter WINDOW editing commands start with the letter *W* and end with a letter representing the type of editing to be done: WINDOW ERASE (WE), WINDOW COPY (WC), and so on. Of course, UNERASE (UE), which is not strictly a WINDOW command but appears on this menu for convenience, does not follow this format.

A few nonediting commands may appear on your WINDOWS menu, depending on which Level you are using. WINDOW TEXT can be used to create text characters (see Chapter 8), WINDOW COMPONENT (CC) is used to create components (see Chapter 8), and WINDOW SAVE is used to save a portion of the drawing into a file (see Chapter 12). Like the editing commands, these commands all ask you to place a window to select a number of entities.

The one true exception to the two-letter coding for WINDOW commands is the RADIAL COPY command, which is activated by typing **RC**. This Level 3 command was added after the rest of the commands had already been in use for some time. Because WR was already used for WINDOW ROTATE and WC used for WINDOW COPY, the code RC was chosen.

The LAYERS Menu (Yx)   In the drawings you have made so far, all of the entities have been created on a single layer, called layer 0 (zero). The number of the layer is stored as part of that entity's data. Every entity that you have created so far includes this information. As you move on to more complex drawings, you may want to keep different types of information on different layers. You will have a chance to try layers in some of the examples to come. The simplest way to visualize a layer is to imagine a transparent overlay which contains certain entities. Up to 256 of these overlays can be combined in a single drawing file. If you store entities on different layers, the editing commands on the LAYERS menu can be used to edit selected data on a chosen layer.

When selected, each of the LAYER editing commands asks you for the number of the layer on which you want to perform editing. You reply by typing a number (0 to 255) and pressing ENTER. The command then continues with its specific editing function.

The two-character LAYER commands all start with the letter *Y*, including the editing commands and the commands for selecting, displaying, and hiding layers as well. The only exception is the ALL LAYERS EDIT (AL) toggle, in which a three-letter command was shortened to the two-character format by dropping the last character.

The command ALL LAYERS EDIT, which appears on several menus as ALL LAYERS, toggles between two different modes of on-screen editing. When ALL LAYERS EDIT is on, you can use any editing command to edit any entity that is visible on the screen. When ALL LAYERS EDIT is off, you can only edit the entities that are on the current layer. Even with ALL LAYERS EDIT turned off, you can still *use* any of the editing commands; they just won't work on entities that are not on the current layer. The current layer is selected with the LAYER CURRENT (YC) command. You will soon have a chance to try the layer selection and display commands in Chapter 6.

The DRAWING Menu (Dx)   The DRAWING editing commands edit every entity in the drawing. They are, of course, the most powerful editing commands, but at the same time they are the least discriminating.

The DRAWING two-character commands—not only the editing commands, but also a number of other commands that perform operations on the drawing as a whole, such as DRAWING SAVE (DS) and DRAWING PLOT (DP)—start with the letter *D*.

Editing Functions

Just as the various objects and entities to be edited can be thought of as nouns, the editing functions can be thought of as verbs. They are found in one or more of the editing menus and represent certain operations or actions that are performed on or with the selected entities.

In general, a command that appears on more than one menu works in the same way on each. When you select OBJECT ERASE (OE), for example, as you did in Chapter 4, you are asked to select an object. Once you have selected it, it is erased. If you select WINDOW ERASE (WE), you are asked to place a window. Once you place the window, the objects within it are erased. When you select LAYER ERASE (YX), you are asked to choose a layer. After typing the number of the layer and pressing ENTER, the selected layer is erased. When you execute DRAWING ERASE (DX), the entire drawing is erased.

The main difference in these four commands is the way in which the entities are selected.

Certain basic editing commands are illustrated in this chapter, and numerous others are covered in Chapter 9. Again, the lowercase *x* in the two-character code represents the selection type, as discussed in the previous sections.

The ERASE Command (xE or xX) You have already seen this command in action. Once the entities have been selected by object, window, layer, or drawing, these entities are erased, that is, removed from the display. In the case of the OBJECT ERASE, WINDOW ERASE, and LAYER ERASE commands, they are not actually removed from the computer's memory, but marked as erased, so that Generic CADD knows not to display or save them any longer. Because they are not actually removed from memory, they can be rescued with the UNERASE (UE) command. Any number of entities that have been erased with the ERASE command can be resurrected with the UNERASE command. If you erased one object, UNERASE will retrieve the last object erased. If you erased an entire layer before that, the next UNERASE command would revive that layer, and so on. You can continue using UNERASE to reverse the effects of ERASE commands until no more entities that are marked as erased remain in the database. The UNERASE command does not work after a DRAWING ERASE (DX) command, as this command clears drawing memory rather than marking all of the objects as erased.

The COPY Command (xC) This command, which can be used on either a single object or on many within a window, makes exact copies of entities in your drawing. The two-character command is composed of either the letter *O* or *W* followed by a *C*. Of course, you must first specify which entity or entities you want to copy. This is done either by pointing to an object in the case of an OBJECT COPY command, or by placing a window in the case of a WINDOW COPY command.

After the selection has been made, you are asked for a reference point—usually some point on the object or set of objects that you want to copy. Then, you are asked for a new reference point or offset—the location where you want the copy to appear. As you will see, the first reference point does not have to be on the objects that you are trying to copy. What really matters is the distance between the first and second points, or the "offset." The object(s) will be copied at a location equal to the distance between the two points. If the first point *is* actually on the object(s), it can help to visualize where the copy is going to end up.

If MANUAL ENTRY is set to RELATIVE (MR) mode, the new reference point or offset can be typed in coordinate form. In this case, it doesn't matter where you put the first reference point. Because the coordinates of the second point are relative to the last point specified, they will equal the offset. If you want to copy, for example, two inches to the right and six inches up, you can enter anything for the first reference point (just press the first mouse button), and then type **2,6** for the second reference point.

Once the offset has been shown or typed, you will be asked how many copies you want to make. Type a number and press ENTER. The number of copies does not include the original. Each copy is copied from the last copy, so that if you copy one object two times, you end up with three objects, all equally spaced. The first copy is made at the specified distance from the original, and then the second copy is made at the specified distance from the first copy.

If you are making several copies of a complex part of the drawing, and none of these copies will need to be edited, you might consider defining and using a COMPONENT instead, to conserve drawing memory and file space. See Chapter 8 and your Generic CADD User's Manual.

The MOVE Command (xM)   Like the COPY commands, the MOVE commands are also available on the OBJECTS and WINDOWS menus. The two-character commands end with the letter *M*. You select the object if you are using OBJECT MOVE, or place a window if you are using WINDOW MOVE. Then, you show a reference point and a new reference point or offset. These points have exactly the same meaning as in the COPY command: You want to move from somewhere to somewhere else.

As with the COPY command, the two reference points do not have to be located on, or even near, the object(s) being moved. Again, what really matters is the distance between the two points, and you can use manual entry to indicate the exact distance that you want to move object(s).

The WINDOW MOVE command has one additional prompt before you specify the offset "STRETCH STRAIGHT LINES (Y,N) >." You may remember that if all of an entity's definition points were not in the window, that entity would not be selected. This prompt allows you to make an exception for lines only. If you type N, the window will work as usual. If you answer Y, lines that have one endpoint inside the window and one outside will be stretched. What this means is that the endpoint inside the window will be moved, while the endpoint outside the window will stay where it is. The term *stretch* simply means that the length of these lines will be changed by this action. They may, in fact, compress rather than stretch if you move the endpoint inside the window closer to the one outside the window.

The ability to allow straight lines to stretch makes editing certain types of drawings much simpler than without it. You can make a rectangle shorter, for example, by using the WINDOW MOVE command, specifying YES for "STRETCH STRAIGHT LINES," putting the window around one side of the box, and moving it closer to the other side. Both the line in the window and the line perpendicular to it will be adjusted so that the box still has squared-off corners, with no overlapping lines.

The ROTATE Command (xR)   Both windows and the entire drawing can be rotated. The WINDOW ROTATE command first asks you to place a window. Next, both commands ask for an *axis point*—the point around which the selected items will be rotated. (You might imagine the drawing or the window as a pinwheel and the axis point as the pin in the center.) Then, you are asked for the *rotation angle*. This angle is measured in degrees, counterclockwise. For example, 90 degrees will tip a straight-up-and-down drawing on its side, 180 degrees will turn it upside down, and 360 degrees will have no net effect.

You can also elect to show the angle on the screen rather than typing it if you like. When asked for the angle, you may type **A** or **V** to show the angle in two different ways. If you type **A**, you will be asked to show two points. The angle between these points will be measured, and will be entered as the rotation angle. The angle between the points is measured assuming that horizontal is zero. That is, if you pick the second point directly to the right of the first, you will specify a zero rotation; if the second point is directly above the first, you will get 90 degrees, and so on.

If you type **V** instead, you will be asked for three points, the first of which is considered the vertex of an angle. The second point specifies an endpoint of an imaginary line projected from the vertex, while the third point specifies an endpoint of another imaginary line, projected from the same vertex. The angle between the lines is measured and used as the rotation angle.

This same technique can be used with most commands which ask you to specify an angle. If you are unsure, type **V** or **A**. If nothing happens, you must type the angle rather than showing it on the screen.

If you like, the axis point may be selected by snapping onto an existing definition point using SNAP TO NEAREST POINT (NP or the third pointing device button). Angles do not have to be in full degrees, and negative angles will produce clockwise rotations.

The RE-SCALE Command (xZ)   As with the ROTATE command, you can issue the RE-SCALE command from either the WINDOWS or DRAWING menus, or type a two-letter editing command ending in *Z*. As usual, the WINDOW RE-SCALE command asks you to place a window by using something similar to an axis point, called a *reference point*. When a selected entity is rescaled (changed in size), the location of some point has to remain stationary, and all other points are repositioned in relation to this stationary reference point. For a growing child, the reference point is the floor. The reference point for an icicle that is being rescaled because of an accumulation of frozen water or warmer weather is the roof edge from which it hangs.

WINDOW RE-SCALE asks you to select a reference point, while DRAWING RE-SCALE assumes that the reference point is at the origin, 0,0. In both cases, you must then specify the X and Y scale factors. The entities selected can be rescaled both horizontally and vertically. In both cases, a scale factor of 1 indicates no change, 2 means twice as large, and .5 means half the current size. Generic CADD assumes that you want to scale the entities at the same scale factors for X and Y unless you type a different number in each case. You will notice that after you type the X scale factor, the default value for Y will be the same as X, and you can just press ENTER.

You should be aware that certain primitives do not rescale well in two directions, namely circle and arcs. No matter what you do to a circle, it is still defined by a center point and a point on the circle. When you rescale it, it gets smaller or larger, but it does not squash. The same is true for arcs, which are really just partial circles and follow the same rules. How a circle responds to a two-direction rescale depends on the location of the point on the circle. It will act differently if the point is above the center point than it will if the point is to the left or right.

The basic rule for rescaling (and rotating and moving, too), is that definition points are actually affected by the command, and that the objects themselves retain their basic geometric properties no matter what you do to them. There is no way to make a Line that is not straight or a Circle that is not round.

The MIRROR Command (WI) Generic CADD's MIRROR command makes a mirror image copy of the selected objects as shown in Figure 5-1. As you can see, much drawing time can be served when you need a reverse image of part or all of your drawing.

To make the mirrored copy, Generic CADD must know where the imaginary mirror is located, and in which direction you want to reflect the image. Four individual mirror directions and four double reflections are available. You can reflect to the right, left, up or down, across perfectly horizontal or vertical mirrors. Generic CADD does not support true diagonal reflections. If you attempt to reflect to the upper right, for instance, your objects are reflected upwards, and then to the right.

Because this command appears only on the WINDOWS menu, you must start by placing a window; after placing it you will be asked to locate the

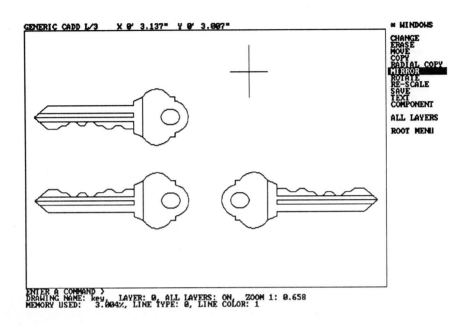

Figure 5-1. *Mirroring a portion of a drawing*

mirror, and then show the direction. The mirror can be located anywhere, including within the selected window. It is even possible to place a mirror right on top of the object. Sometimes this is desirable, but more often it is not. Usually, you will want to put your mirror to the right, left, above, or below the entities that you have selected, and reflect them in the same direction.

The MOVE POINT Command (MP) This command works on one entity at a time and is therefore available only on the OBJECTS menu. Like other OBJECT editing commands, the MOVE POINT command first asks which object you want to edit. In this case, you are going to move one of the definition points of a simple object, or the reference point of a complex object. Point to the object that you want to edit.

Next, select the point that you want to move. Obviously, the point must be one of the definition points of the entity that you have selected in the previous step. It helps if you have CONSTRUCTION POINTS turned on, so that you can see where the definition points are located. If you are trying to move the reference point of a complex object, it helps to have REFERENCE POINTS turned on. If you need to change the status of either of these, press ESC, use the appropriate toggle (PC or PR), do a REDRAW (RD), and start the MOVE POINT (MP) again.

Finally, indicate the new location of the point which you are moving. If you have RUBBER BANDING turned on, Lines, Arcs, and Circles will rubber band as you move the cursor, to show what the edited entity will look like. When you pick the point, the entity is redrawn. Like many others, this command can be repeated by pressing SPACEBAR.

The BREAK Command (OB)   You can break only one entity at a time also, so this command is found only on the OBJECTS menu. Typical of the OBJECT commands, you first select the entity that you want to break. You can break Lines, Circles, Arcs, and Curves. You cannot break True Ellipses (although you can break Construction Ellipses, which are really made of Arcs), Bezier Curves, or Standard Points.

After you have selected the entity to be broken, specify the first break point and the second break point. The gap will be created between these two points. With Arcs and Lines, the gap will be created between the two points, no matter what order you place them in. With Circles, the smaller portion of the circle will be removed.

If either of the selected break points is beyond the end of a Line or Arc, you will get some unusual results. The gap will appear between the first break point and the endpoint, and then a new segment of the Line or Arc will appear from the endpoint to the second break point. See Figure 5-2 for examples of Lines, Arcs, and Circles broken in the normal fashion and in this nonstandard way.

The CHANGE Command (xG)   Appearing on all four editing menus, the CHANGE commands allow you to change the line type, line width, line color, and layer of selected entities. If you are using OBJECT CHANGE (OG), you will simply be prompted for the new value for each of these four parameters. If your video menu is turned on, you will be shown video menu selections for "LINE TYPE," "LINE WIDTH," and "LINE COLOR" (if your video driver is currently configured for more than two colors). You can either type a number or select from the video menu for each of these options. For the new value of "LAYER," you must type a number. For each of these parameters, you will be shown the default value. If you do not want

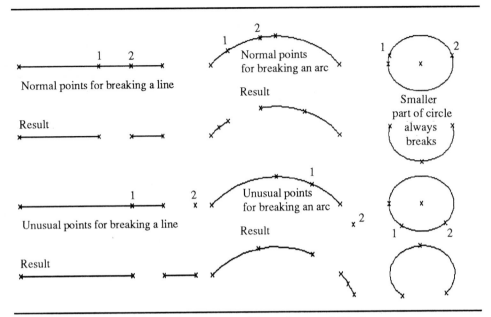

Figure 5-2. *Examples of breaking entities: Lines, Arcs, and Circles*

to change a particular value, simply press ENTER. When you have gone through all four prompts, the entity will be redrawn to reflect the new settings.

If you are using the WINDOW, LAYER, or DRAWING CHANGE command, you will first be asked for the specifications of the entities that you want to change: The first five prompts will ask for the existing settings, and the next four prompts will ask for the new value. Therefore, you can change only those entities that are currently a particular LINE TYPE, LINE WIDTH, LINE COLOR, and LAYER, or all entities currently selected, or any combination. To select all entities for any of the first five prompts, simply press ENTER. A typical specification might be ALL ENTITY TYPES, ALL LINE TYPES, ALL LINE WIDTHS, LINE COLOR 3, ALL LAYERS. This CHANGE command would change any entities in the current selection that are color 3, no matter which line type, line width, or layer. In response to the next four prompts you would specify the new LINE TYPE, LINE WIDTH, LINE COLOR, and LAYER for those entities that are currently COLOR 3.

Two-Character Commands

The two-character codes for each of the editing commands are formed by combining the character of the selection type with the character which represents the editing function. Some of these combinations do not make sense and therefore do not work. Others are simply not active at this time.

Editing Example: ROOM

You can try several editing commands on the existing drawing ROOM. Call up this drawing either by typing **CADD ROOM** at the DOS prompt, or by typing **CADD** at the DOS prompt and typing **ROOM** when asked for the drawing name. When this file is loaded, the display will automatically be set at ZOOM ALL.

Changing the Shape

Assume that you want to change the width of the bathroom from eight feet to six feet. First, change the GRID SIZE (GS) to 12 (inches), and turn on SNAP TO GRID (SG), and RELATIVE COORDINATES (DC). You might want to ZOOM BACK (ZB) to get a little more space around the edge of the room, which is probably crowding the edges of the screen.

To change the width of the room, use the WINDOW MOVE (WM) command. Place the window around the lower wall of the bathroom as shown in Figure 5-3. When asked about stretching straight lines, type **Y** to answer "Yes."

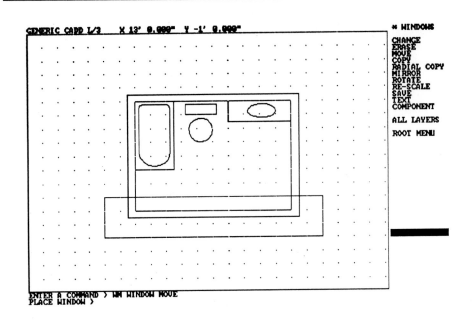

Figure 5-3.   *Placing a window to move the bathroom wall*

For a reference point, select one corner of the room. For the new reference point, move the cursor two feet upwards, until the Y coordinate reads 2' or 24". The X coordinate should stay at 0. If you are having trouble keeping the X coordinate at 0, turn on ORTHO MODE by typing **OR** or **SO**. After showing the new reference point, the two lower horizontal lines will be moved, and the four vertical lines will be shortened as required. Your drawing will look approximately like Figure 5-4.

You can also type coordinates to move this wall if you like. This time, make the length of the room six inches shorter. First, turn on MANUAL ENTRY RELATIVE (MR) so that you can type the exact distance that you want to move the wall. Then, issue the WINDOW MOVE (WM) command,

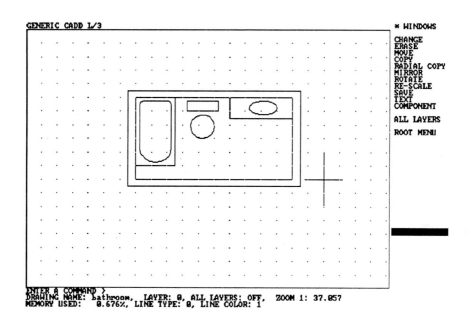

Figure 5-4. *The six-foot-wide bathroom*

and place a vertical window around the right wall, as shown in Figure 5-5.
(Don't worry about the window going through part of the sink, as the sink
won't move unless it is entirely in the window. If you *want* to move the sink
at the same time, make sure that it is entirely within the window.) Again,
specify Y for stretching straight lines. For a reference point, it doesn't
matter what you choose, since the second point will give the actual distance
of the move. Just pick a point or press ENTER. For the new reference point
or offset, type the coordinates – **6,0**, specifying six inches to the left. When
you press ENTER, the move will be completed, and the dimensions of the
room will now be 6′ × 9′6″.

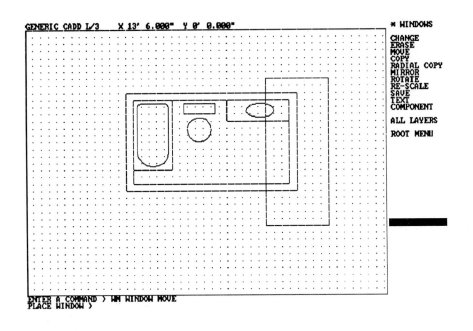

Figure 5-5. *Placing a window to move another bathroom wall*

Rotating the Fixtures

For this exercise, suppose that you want to move the toilet to the right wall. First, you must turn the toilet on its side with the WINDOW ROTATE (WR) command. If you place the axis point carefully, you should be able to rotate the toilet to the middle of the room and then move it against this wall.

Select ROTATE from the WINDOWS menu or type **WR** on the keyboard. Place a window around the toilet. You will probably need to turn off SNAP TO GRID (SG) temporarily to make sure that you don't include any other objects by mistake. After you have placed the window, turn SNAP TO GRID (SG) back on.

For an axis point, select a point directly below the toilet, exactly four feet into the room. In other words, with the grid set to 12 inches, and the room six feet wide, pick a point four feet (four grid points) from the top

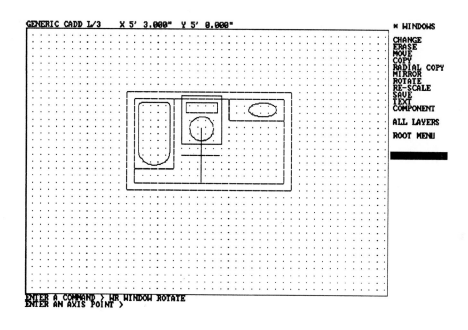

Figure 5-6. *The window and axis point used to rotate the toilet*

interior wall, as shown in Figure 5-6. For a rotation angle, type – **90** (for 90 degrees clockwise) and press ENTER. The toilet will be turned on its side, and will end up in the middle of the room, between the wall and the sink. You now need to use the WINDOW MOVE (WM) command to slide it into position against the right wall as shown in Figure 5-7. Again, you may need to turn off SNAP TO GRID (SG) temporarily to place the window. You may also need to reduce the GRID SIZE (GS) or use manual entry to move the toilet on a smaller module than 12 inches.

Reversing the Plan

To experiment with the WINDOW MIRROR (WI) command, imagine that you want to reverse the bathroom plan. You want the bathtub on the right

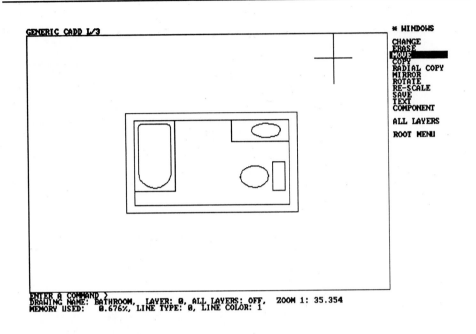

GENERIC CADD L/3

* WINDOWS

CHANGE
ERASE
MOVE
COPY
RADIAL COPY
MIRROR
ROTATE
RE-SCALE
SAVE
TEXT
COMPONENT

ALL LAYERS

ROOT MENU

ENTER A COMMAND >
DRAWING NAME: BATHROOM,   LAYER: 0, ALL LAYERS: OFF,   ZOOM 1: 35.354
MEMORY USED: 0.676%, LINE TYPE: 0, LINE COLOR: 1

Figure 5-7.   *The bathroom plan with the toilet rotated and moved*

wall instead of the left, and the toilet and sink on the left wall instead of
the right.

After selecting the command, put a window around the entire bathroom,
including the six-inch exterior wall. For a mirror location, select a point
just outside the window to the right of the bathroom. For a direction, choose
a point a little farther to the right (essentially you are telling Generic
CADD to "put it right here"). The mirror image of the bathroom will be
created next to the present one. The new bathroom may be partially off the
screen. If so, use the ZOOM ALL (ZA) command to see the whole drawing,
which will now include the two bathrooms. Erase the original bathroom by
using the WINDOW ERASE (WE) command. Place a window around the
whole drawing. As soon as you select the second corner of the window, all
entities inside the window will be erased. Use ZOOM ALL (ZA) again to
readjust the display to the new drawing contents. Your drawing should
now look much like the one shown in Figure 5-8.

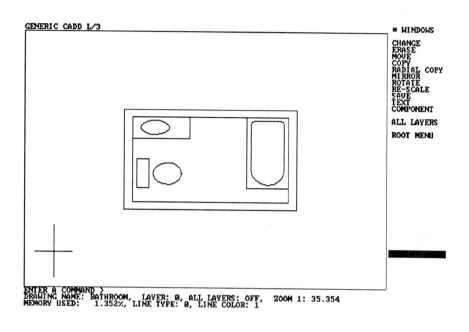

Figure 5-8.   *The mirrored bathroom plan*

Cutting a Doorway

To put a doorway into this room, you will need to break some of the existing lines (walls). Set your GRID SIZE (GS) to 6 inches before you start, and make sure that SNAP TO GRID (SG) is turned on.

Select BREAK from the OBJECTS menu or type **OB** on the keyboard. You will be asked for an object to break. Select one of the two horizontal lines at the bottom of the drawing. For the first break point, select a point somewhere on this line where you want to start the doorway. Use Figure 5-9 as a guide. For the next break point, move the cursor to the right or left until the X coordinate reads 2′6″, negative or positive. The Y coordinate should remain at 0. When you select this point, the line will be broken. Note that this is not really a line with a hole in it, but two lines, separated by 2 feet 6 inches of space. Each line has its own endpoints and its own definition in the database. Break the other horizontal line in the same way.

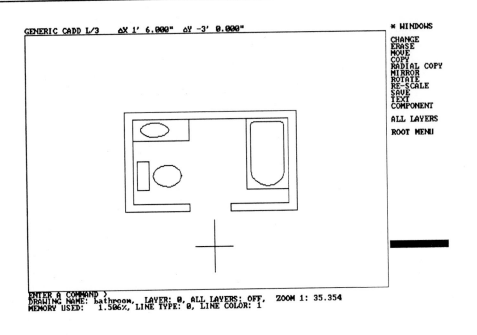

Figure 5-9.   *A doorway created by breaking and adding lines*

Issue another BREAK command by pressing the SPACEBAR and then choose points that are directly in line with the new endpoints of the lines above.

To finish off the doorway, simply snap onto one of these new endpoints with a SNAP TO NEAREST POINT (NP or third pointing device button) to start an implicit LINE command. Snap onto the opposite side of the wall with another NP, and then press ESC to end the command. Repeat this process on the other wall end. Your drawing will now approximate the one shown in Figure 5-9.

Adding Another Sink

Assume now that you want to add another bowl to the sink fixture. You will first need to make the room longer. Use the WINDOW MOVE (WM) command, place a window around the left wall, and stretch the straight lines. Pick your second reference point two feet to the left of the first one, and the room will be longer.

To create another sink, you can use the OBJECT COPY command because the sink is only one entity, a True Ellipse. If the sink were more than one entity (such as a Construction Ellipse, which is really four Arcs), you would need to use WINDOW COPY. Note that you can always use WINDOW COPY, even if copying only one object.

Before you start, make sure that GRID SIZE (GS) is set to 3 inches. Select COPY from the OBJECTS menu or type **OC** on the keyboard. Select a point on the sink. For the reference points, select a point on one end of the sink, and for the second point select a new point to the right or left of where the second sink would go. It may require a little practice to get a feeling for how to select these two reference points. For the number of copies, type **1** and press ENTER. If the second sink doesn't end up exactly where you want it, use the OBJECT MOVE (OM) command, which works almost exactly the same way as the OBJECT COPY command, except that you do not specify a number of copies at the end, and the object to be moved is erased when the new one is created. You may have to move both sinks to get the spacing right.

If you want to experiment more with this drawing, go ahead. When you are done, save it into the same file, ROOM, with the QUIT command. When asked if you want to Overwrite or Rename, type **O** to overwrite the old file.

Editing While Drawing: MUSIC Revisited

As noted previously, the editing commands are not just for fixing mistakes or changing your mind; they can be just as useful when you are creating your drawing. The musical staff example from Chapter 4 is a good illustration of how the editing commands can speed up the drawing process tremendously.

Two Lines Are Sometimes All You Need

Many drawings can be created by drawing only two lines, a vertical and a horizontal, and then copying, moving, rotating, breaking, and otherwise manipulating these two lines until you have the complete drawing. If you

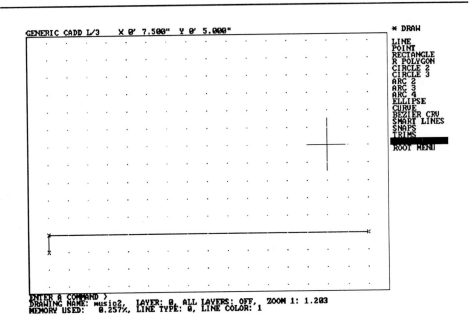

Figure 5-10.   *The first two lines of MUSIC2*

have a good deal of hand drawing experience, you may not recognize this as an advantage at first, but it can contribute much to your speed and efficiency.

Start a new drawing called **MUSIC2**. Set the UNITS to INCHES (IN), the LIMITS (LS) to 6 by 9, and ZOOM ALL (ZA). Specify a 1/2-inch GRID SIZE (GS .5), and turn on SNAP TO GRID (SG), RELATIVE COORDINATES (DC), ORTHO MODE (OR or SO), and MANUAL ENTRY RELATIVE (MR).

As in the previous MUSIC drawing, start by drawing an eight-inch line from left to right. You should be able to read this dimension from the coordinate display as you draw. When you have drawn one horizontal line, press ESC and draw a vertical line, starting at the left endpoint of the existing line, and going downward one-half inch. The Y coordinate should read "– .5" as you select this point. Your drawing should resemble the one shown in Figure 5-10.

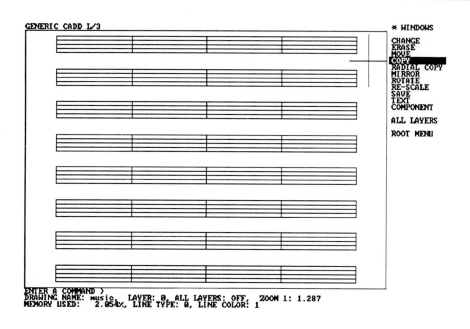

Figure 5-11.   *An entire music page created with the WINDOW COPY command*

Editing the Rest of
the Drawing into Existence

This time, instead of drawing the rest of the lines, you can create them with the OBJECT COPY (OC) command. Before you do this, change the GRID SIZE to 1/8 inch (GS .125). When you copy the object, select the horizontal line first, and pick the reference point on the line. For the new reference point, select a point exactly one grid point (visible or invisible) below the previous one. Specify **4** for the number of copies. You should now see all horizontal lines of the musical staff.

   To replicate the vertical line, press SPACEBAR to get another OBJECT COPY command. To select the vertical line, turn off SNAP TO GRID by typing **SG**. You won't need to turn it back on. After selecting the line, pick any point for a reference point. For a new reference point or offset, type **2,0** and press ENTER. For the number of copies, specify **4** again, and all of the vertical lines will be drawn.

Creating a Manuscript Page

You can quickly turn this one musical staff into an entire page of staffs with the WINDOW COPY command. Select COPY from the WINDOWS menu or type **WC**. Put the window around the whole drawing. Select any reference point, and type **0,1** and press ENTER for the new reference point or offset. Make 7 copies, and you wind up with a drawing similar to the one shown in Figure 5-11 after you ZOOM ALL (ZA). Save the new drawing and exit to DOS with the QUIT (QU) command.

This chapter has covered the structure behind the basic editing commands, including how entities are selected for editing and what each editing function does.

In the next few chapters, you will make use of many of these editing commands as you move on to more complex tasks. The remaining editing commands are addressed in Chapter 9.

6 *Drawing Aids and Controls*

This chapter does not explore any new DRAWING editing commands, but instead focuses on Generic CADD features that can help you use the commands that you already know to draw and edit better. The commands covered in this chapter are used with the drawing and editing commands and often affect the way that these commands work; alone, however, they perform no actual work and for the most part have no direct permanent effect on the drawing database. Once you exit Generic CADD, values that are set with these commands are not stored and will not reappear even if you call up the same drawing file. The only way that any of these values can be stored is by using the CONFIG program, which sets the values and toggle states of many of the drawing aids and controls.

The ZOOM Commands

The commands on the ZOOMS menu, almost all of which are represented by two-character codes that start with the letter *Z*, are used for adjusting the portion of the drawing that is shown on the screen. If you think of the screen as a viewport to the drawing, the ZOOM commands allow you to control the way the viewport works. They let you move closer to see more detail, or move further away to see more area. They allow you to see the full drawing, or any selected portion. They also allow you to return to the portion of the drawing on which you were previously working, and in Level

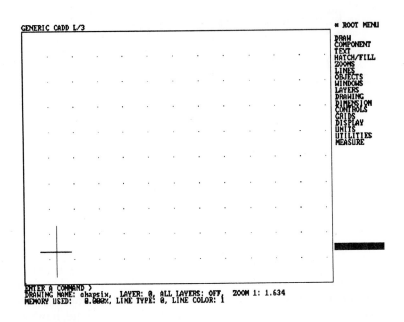

GENERIC CADD L/3

ENTER A COMMAND >
DRAWING NAME: chapsix, LAYER: 0, ALL LAYERS: OFF, ZOOM 1: 1.634
MEMORY USED: 0.000%, LINE TYPE: 0, LINE COLOR: 1

Figure 6-1. *Using a one-inch grid with 10-by-10-inch limits, ZOOM LIMITS or ZOOM ALL give the same results*

3, allow you to store certain settings of the viewport under names of your own choice, and to return to these views as often as you like.

Displaying the Entire Drawing

Two commands are used to display the entire drawing on the screen. Their functions differ depending on your definition of "the whole drawing." ZOOM ALL (ZA) displays every entity in the drawing; ZOOM LIMITS (ZL) displays the area that lies between the origin and the upper-right corner of the drawing, as specified by the LIMITS (LS) command.

When there is no object on the screen (for example, at the beginning of a drawing session when you have just created a new file and set the LIMITS), these two commands have approximately the same effect, and you can use them interchangeably for the purpose of simply showing the

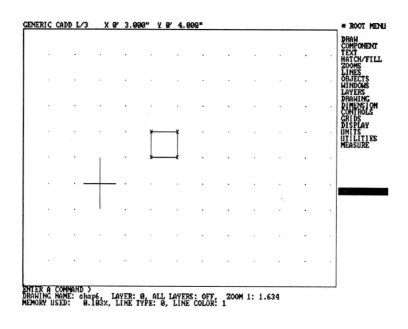

Figure 6-2. *ZOOM LIMITS after drawing a one-inch square*

entire drawing area on the screen before beginning to draw. If you make a new drawing and set its LIMITS (LS) to 10 × 10, you will see that ZOOM ALL (ZA) and ZOOM LIMITS (ZL) give you the same results. It helps to have a one-inch GRID on the screen to see that this is true, as shown in Figure 6-1.

When you have placed entities in the drawing, however, these two commands perform two very different functions. If you draw a one-inch-square rectangle in the middle of the screen, you will quickly see the difference between these two commands. ZOOM LIMITS continues to show the entire 10 × 10 area (plus a bit more in the horizontal direction), as illustrated in Figure 6-2. ZOOM ALL, now that it has something specific to zoom *to,* shows only the rectangle, plus a little extra space all around. This extra space ensures that the edges of the rectangle are not covered by the border of the drawing area, and that you can place a window around

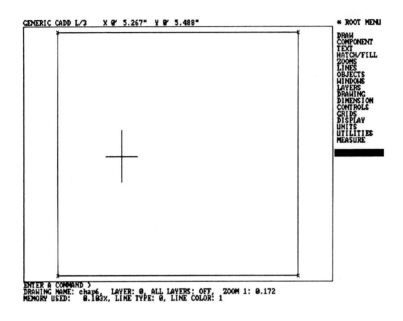

Figure 6-3.   *ZOOM ALL after drawing a one-inch square*

this object if you decide to select it. This phenomenon is illustrated in Figure 6-3.

You can see, then, that the ZOOM ALL command adjusts the display to show everything in the drawing—no more, no less—regardless of the set limits. When there is nothing in the drawing, it defaults to acting like ZOOM LIMITS, in order to have something reasonable to do. The ZOOM LIMITS command, on the other hand, always shows the set limits, whether the actual objects in the drawing are smaller or larger than these limits.

Generic CADD does not constrain you from drawing outside the area specified by the LIMITS command. The limits are simply a convenient way for you to view a known amount of area on the screen before you draw anything.

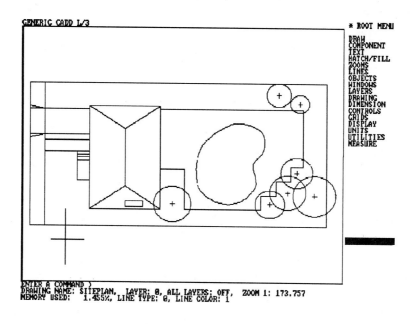

Figure 6-4. *ZOOM ALL is automatic when you first load a drawing*

Zooming In and Out

You have used the ZOOM UP and ZOOM BACK commands in previous chapters. These two reciprocal commands display, respectively, exactly half as much and twice as much area of the drawing on the screen. When you execute ZOOM UP, the drawing looks larger on the screen, as if you are getting closer to it, and you may be able to see more detail. Because the drawing is enlarged, some of it may be off the edges of the screen (not lost, just not currently displayed). ZOOM BACK does exactly the opposite, causing the screen to react as if you have taken a step back. Every object in the drawing looks smaller, some detail may not be visible, and you should see exactly twice as much area as you could a moment ago.

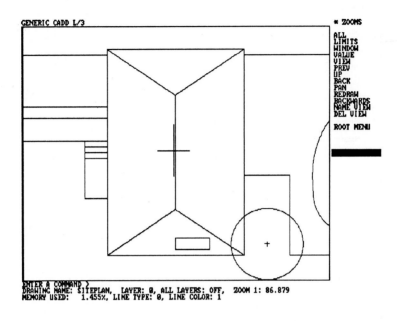

GENERIC CADD L/3   * ZOOMS

ALL
LIMITS
WINDOW
VALUE
VIEW
PREV
UP
BACK
PAN
REDRAW
BACKWARDS
NAME VIEW
DEL VIEW

ROOT MENU

ENTER A COMMAND >
DRAWING NAME: SITEPLAN,   LAYER: 0, ALL LAYERS: OFF,   ZOOM 1: 86.879
MEMORY USED: 1.455%, LINE TYPE: 0, LINE COLOR: 1

Figure 6-5.   *The display after one ZOOM ALL and then one ZOOM UP*

Call up an existing drawing, like SITEPLAN, and try these commands. When you first load it, SITEPLAN will be displayed as if you had issued ZOOM ALL, as shown in Figure 6-4. Both ZOOM UP (ZU) and ZOOM BACK (ZB) ask you to specify a new center of the screen, which allows you to move up or back in a specific direction, rather than just focusing in on the center of the screen. Pick a point that you want to use as the middle of the screen. Figure 6-5 shows the result of a ZOOM UP on the SITEPLAN drawing, using a point on the roof as the center. Figure 6-6 shows the effect of a ZOOM BACK after a ZOOM ALL.

Zooming to a Specified Area

Like ZOOM UP, the ZOOM WINDOW command lets you zoom in on a portion of the drawing, except that the portion is selected with a window.

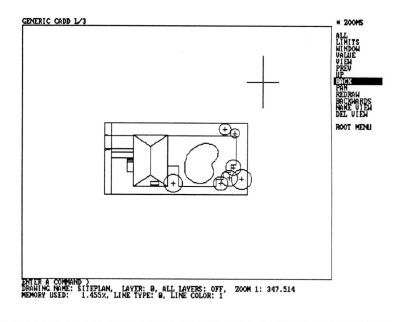

Figure 6-6. *The display after one ZOOM ALL and then one ZOOM BACK*

After selecting WINDOW from the ZOOMS menu or typing **ZW** on the keyboard, you will be asked to place a window. Put the window around the area that you want to display on the screen. Like all other windows, this window is specified by first selecting one corner with the drawing cursor, and then dragging a rubber band rectangle around the area that you want to select. If you place your first point in the wrong location, press ESC, and try the command again.

The window that you select should be about the same proportions as your screen display. The window you describe should be about the same shape as the border around the Generic CADD display area. Figure 6-7 shows the placement of a window for zooming into a portion of the SITEPLAN drawing. If you don't get the window the exact shape of the drawing area, Generic CADD will add a little space to the top and bottom or sides. After you have specified the window, the display will be adjusted

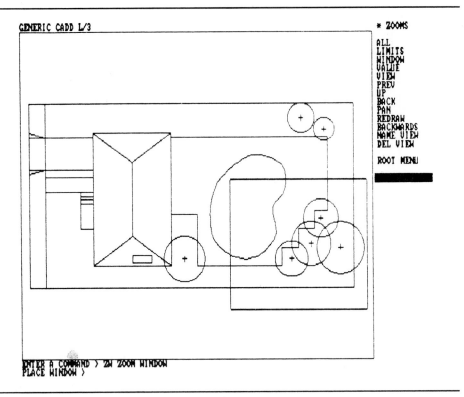

Figure 6-7. *Placing a window for a ZOOM WINDOW*

and redrawn. Figure 6-8 shows the display after zooming to the window placed in Figure 6-7.

Returning to the Last Screen

The ZOOM PREVIOUS (ZP) command returns to the view that you had before the last ZOOM command. This command can save time and effort. For example, if you ZOOM WINDOW and then ZOOM WINDOW again, but end up with the wrong view, you can use ZOOM PREVIOUS and try the ZOOM WINDOW again as opposed to issuing ZOOM ALL and then issuing ZOOM WINDOW twice to obtain the desired view.

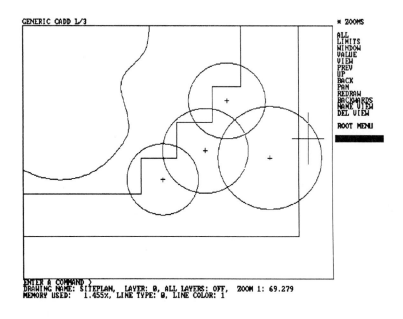

Figure 6-8. *The display after the ZOOM WINDOW*

If you execute one ZOOM PREVIOUS after another, you simply zoom back and forth between two views. Each ZOOM PREVIOUS will be previous to the next, so you will end up in a loop. This is a good way to go back and forth between two views when you need to move in and out repeatedly and quickly, but can be confusing if you are not expecting it. The logic behind this command is that only one previous view is stored, so it is not possible to ZOOM WINDOW three times and ZOOM PREVIOUS three times to get back to where you started. Instead, you will end up at the second window to which you zoomed, as follows:

ZOOM WINDOW   (ZW) (first window)

ZOOM WINDOW   (ZW) (second window)

ZOOM WINDOW   (ZW) (third window)

ZOOM PREVIOUS (ZP) (second window)

ZOOM PREVIOUS (ZP) (third window)

ZOOM PREVIOUS (ZP) (second window)

As you can see, the ZOOM PREVIOUS command takes its name literally. It always returns you to the view that you were looking at before the last ZOOM command, even if the view is the last ZOOM PREVIOUS.

Named Views

A group of commands (NAME VIEW, ZOOM VIEW, and DELETE NAMED VIEW) allows Level 3 users to give a name to a particular view so you can return to it later. Named views are useful for moving from one part of the drawing to another without having to ZOOM ALL (ZA) or ZOOM BACK (ZB) in between. It can be very useful to give names to the various areas of the drawing that you zoom to often. Whenever you have a view that you want to name, select the NAME VIEW command or type **NV**. You will be prompted for a name, which can be up to 12 characters long. Type the name and press ENTER. To check it, ZOOM ALL (ZA) and then ZOOM UP (ZU) or ZOOM WINDOW (ZW) to a different part of the drawing. Now select VIEW from the ZOOMS menu or type **ZV** and type the same name. The view that was on screen when you created the named view will be restored. Of course, you can now move easily between these two views with ZOOM PREVIOUS, which will take you back and forth.

Named views are saved in the drawing file with the rest of the drawing entities, so that you do not have to NAME VIEW all over again every time you edit the drawing. Named views can build up in the database, however; you may end up with many that you don't need, or you may want to change the definition of a view stored under a particular name. In these cases, you can use the DELETE NAMED VIEW command, which is called "DEL VIEW" on the ZOOMS menu and is invoked with **NX** on the keyboard (Name Erase?). You will be asked to type the name of the view that you want to delete. Once a named view is deleted, it is no longer saved with the drawing file, and the name can be used over again.

Notice that zooms and views only affect the way that the entities are displayed on the screen. None of these commands actually change the size or location of any drawing entities in the database, only the way that they appear on the screen. Stored named views do not keep track of what is on the screen in that view; they only keep track of where that view is in relation to the drawing as a whole. If you change something in the interim, your view may look different when you return to it than it did when you created it. If you move entities while zoomed out to the whole drawing, you may find that there is nothing on the screen when you zoom to a particular view!

What is actually stored in the database when you create a named view is the *name* of the view, and the absolute coordinates of the window that would be required to re-create that view with a ZOOM WINDOW. For this reason, be very careful with commands that alter the entire database. If none of your named views seem to go anywhere, you have probably RE-ORIGINED your drawing. (See Chapter 10 for more information on RE-ORIGIN.)

Getting a Scaled View

You might notice a message at the bottom of the screen from time to time that says "ZOOM 1:x," where x is some number. This ZOOM FACTOR or ZOOM VALUE stands for the relationship between real world scale and the drawing as displayed on the monitor. If the drawing is displayed at a ZOOM VALUE of 1, it is shown at its actual size. Although any drawing can be viewed at this ZOOM VALUE, it only makes sense for drawings of objects that are smaller than the display screen. If you try to display a house floor plan at a ZOOM SCALE of 1, for example, you may see at most a line or two because the house will not fit on the screen at this ZOOM VALUE.

When you use the other ZOOM commands, Generic CADD calculates the ZOOM VALUE automatically, which is a lot easier than doing the calculation yourself. However, if you wish to see the drawing displayed at a specific ZOOM VALUE, you can select VALUE from the ZOOMS menu or type **ZM** on the keyboard. You will be asked to type a number and to select a point that will be used for the center of the screen.

You should keep in mind that even if the object can fit on the screen, and you display it at a ZOOM VALUE of 1, the drawing that you see on the screen is not exactly what you will get when you print it at 1:1. Because the resolution of your printer or plotter is probably higher than your monitor's resolution, the printout will show more definition on circles and arcs, and there will be less visible stepping on diagonal lines, due to smaller steps. In general, your output will be crisper than what you see on the screen, unless you have a very high-resolution video card. Also, it is important to note that the accuracy of the ZOOM VALUE depends on an accurately specified SCREEN RATIO. The SCREEN RATIO, specified in the CONFIG program, requires that you measure a box that is displayed on the screen and tell CONFIG the dimensions, so that it can calculate the exact length of one inch on your screen.

Moving Around Without Changing Scale

The PAN (PA) command is an unusual ZOOM command in that it does not adjust the apparent size of the objects on the screen; it merely changes the portion of the drawing that is displayed. This command allows you to move the viewport around on the drawing without changing the ZOOM VALUE. After you issue this command, you simply select a new center of the screen, and the display is redrawn to reflect the newly selected center. Since the current center is, by definition, half way from any edge of the screen, you can move up, down, right, or left a maximum of about one-half the width of the screen at one time. (If you move on the diagonal, you can go a little farther than that.) The PAN command is useful when you use another ZOOM command, such as ZOOM UP, and what you want to edit ends up just off the edge of the screen. Rather than zooming back, and then up again, you can simply pan to one side to find the objects.

On the other hand, repeated panning is not really a fast way to get from one part of the drawing to another, as the screen must be redrawn each time you pan. You can speed up the process by pressing any key to stop the screen from redrawing after the first PAN and then the SPACEBAR to get another, if you know how many PANS it will take to get the object in view.

Refreshing the Screen

Though the REDRAW (RD) command is on the ZOOM menu, it is even less of a true ZOOM command than PAN. The REDRAW command simply refreshes the screen display to show the currently selected area on the screen, using all of the current display parameters.

This command is often used in conjunction with the DISPLAY toggles, such as CONSTRUCTION POINTS. Turning on CONSTRUCTION POINTS has no immediate effect on the display. It doesn't come into play until the next time you activate a ZOOM command. The REDRAW command provides a ZOOM command so you can see the changes in the display parameters (such as the display of construction points), without having to go anywhere. As you will see in the next section, many toggles are not activated after switching until REDRAW is used.

The REDRAW command may also be used when you want to see if anything is lying underneath an erased object. If you draw one line on top of another, for example, and then OBJECT ERASE (OE) one of them, both will disappear, as Generic CADD removes the pixels of one line without realizing that another line sits in the same place. Situations like this are automatically corrected whenever any ZOOM is executed. Once again, REDRAW can be used to refresh the display quickly without moving the viewport. You will find the REDRAW command to be very useful while editing. Sometimes a window or even the cursor can interfere with editing and cause distorted screen displays. The REDRAW command corrects any of these situations.

Changing the Order of Display

The last command on the ZOOMS menu, BACKWARDS, is not an active ZOOM command, but a ZOOM toggle. When any other ZOOM command (except NAME VIEW) is used, the entities in the drawing are redrawn on the screen, appearing (by default) in the order that they were drawn unless you have used certain editing commands, such as OBJECT BREAK that can change the order of entities. This can make an edited entity seem as if it were drawn more recently than unedited entities nearby. However, when the entities that you want to edit have just been drawn, it can be quicker to have the screen redraw from the opposite end of the database. The BACKWARDS command, chosen from the ZOOMS menu or issued by typing **BR** on the keyboard, reverses the display order of the database. After you have executed the command, when you ZOOM WINDOW (ZW) or ZOOM UP (ZU) to a certain area, the most recently created entities are displayed first. If you don't need to see the whole drawing in order to edit it, you can press any key as soon as the screen shows enough information. This will stop the current redraw, which happens implicitly as a part of every ZOOM command (except NAME VIEW), and you can immediately start editing.

To toggle BACKWARDS REDRAW off, that is, to redraw in the normal order, simply select BACKWARDS from the ZOOMS menu or type **BR** again. Like any other toggle, if it is on, it will be turned off; if it is off, it will be turned on. When you first start a drawing, BACKWARDS REDRAW is off.

The DISPLAY Commands

Many of the commands on the DISPLAY menu are toggles. For the most part, they control the display of the items on the screen which are not really part of your drawing. You have already used a few of these, such as RUBBER BANDING and CONSTRUCTION POINTS. There are no general rules regarding the two-character keystrokes that activate these commands. A few subgroups occasionally share a character, and these commands will be discussed in the text to follow.

Display of Points

The display of Generic CADD's three types of points is controlled by three toggles on the DISPLAY menu. Each of the two-character codes for these commands starts with the letter *P,* for Points, and ends with the first letter of the type of point. These DISPLAY toggles only affect the visibility of the points, not their function. Even when CONSTRUCTION POINTS is turned off, for example, you can still snap onto them with SNAP TO NEAREST POINT if you know where they are. Certain construction points are easy to identify, such as the endpoints of lines, while others, such as the points on a curve, are difficult to identify without displaying them. The diagram in Figure 6-9 includes all three types of points, with all three turned off.

Construction Points Display of construction points is toggled on and off by the CON. POINTS toggle on the DISPLAY menu, or by typing **PC** on the keyboard. When this toggle is on, construction points are shown at the definition points of all entities, such as the endpoints of lines, and the center and one point on a circle. They also appear when marking the offset on COPY and MOVE commands, and are used by many of the other DRAW and EDIT commands to show various points that you select.

Construction points do not magically appear or disappear as soon as this command is given. This command, as well as the rest of the point display toggles, enables or disables the display of points starting from the time that you toggle it. Construction points will appear or disappear the next time you do a ZOOM or any other command that causes the screen to be redrawn. Also, all DRAW commands and EDIT commands that use construction points will reflect the change as well. The quickest way to see the results of the CONSTRUCTION POINTS toggle without changing any-

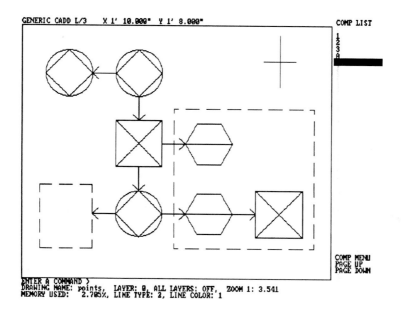

Figure 6-9.   *A sample drawing with all points turned off*

thing else in the drawing or on the screen is to issue a REDRAW (RD) command.

Construction points do not plot or print, and are saved with the drawing only to the extent that every definition point of every entity in the drawing is represented by a construction point when the toggle is turned on. The status of this toggle is not saved with the drawing file, but can be configured to a default value in the CONFIG program. The size of construction points is scaled to the screen, not to your drawing, so that they always appear to be the same size (a few pixels in each direction) no matter how far you zoom in on them. Construction points are always displayed in white on color systems, or in whatever color your monochrome system uses.

The principle function of construction points is to provide visual feedback when you are drawing new entities or editing old ones. For example, it is helpful to see where you put the first point on an arc when you try to place the second one. It helps to see the initial reference point of a MOVE

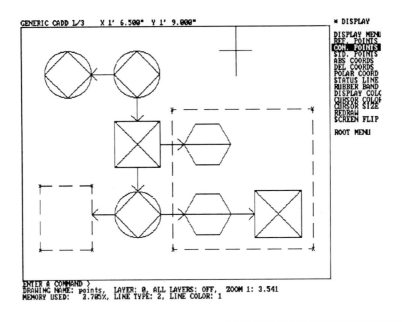

Figure 6-10. *Sample drawing with CONSTRUCTION POINTS turned on*

or COPY command marked on the screen when you try to select the new reference point. You can also use construction points to see where the definition points of entities are located for editing purposes. It is difficult to do a MOVE POINT on a curve, for instance, when you are not sure where the definition points are located. When placing windows, the only points on simple entities that you really have to get inside the window are the definition points, which are marked by construction points. Figure 6-10 shows the same diagram as shown in Figure 6-9, but with construction points turned on. You can see them at the corners of the large boxes, indicating the endpoints of the lines that form the boxes.

Reference Points   Display of reference points is controlled by this toggle, found on the DISPLAY menu as REF. POINTS, or toggled by typing **PR** on the keyboard. Reference points are the origin points for complex entities,

entities which include Components, Text Characters, Hatches, and Fills. These entities do not have individual construction points to accompany the simple entities that compose them, so the reference point is the only point that you can display. It becomes a sort of "handle" for the complex entity, which can be selected for the MOVE POINT and other commands. It is also the point that determines whether a complex entity is inside a window: If the reference point is within the window, the entire entity is within the window as well.

Like construction points, reference points do not automatically appear as soon as you toggle on their display, nor do they ever print or plot. They *will* appear on all new complex entities and on existing ones whenever the screen is redrawn. Their primary purpose is for editing, so it makes no difference whether or not they are displayed.

One reference point is always located at 0,0, to help you see where the origin is, especially when you first start a drawing. This reference point cannot be removed, but as with all other reference points, its display is controlled by the REFERENCE POINTS toggle. For reasons of visibility, the reference points of text characters are never displayed, even when the toggle is on. The reference points of text characters are in the lower-left corner of the letter, and you should be able to locate them easily enough by snapping onto them with the SNAP TO NEAREST POINT (NP) command, or with the third pointing device button.

The default status of this toggle is not saved with the drawing file, but can be set using the CONFIG program. Like construction points, reference points are scaled to the screen rather than to your drawing, so that they always seem the same size, no matter how far you zoom in on them, and they are always white or your monochrome color. Figure 6-11 shows the diagram drawing with reference points turned on, in addition to the construction points already on. You can see the reference points at the insertion points of the various symbols on the diagram, which have been drawn using predefined components. Note that the components do not have construction points.

Standard Points   This command, represented by the abbreviation STD. POINTS on the DISPLAY menu and typed **PS** on the keyboard, toggles on and off the display of points that you place in the drawing with the POINT command on the DRAW menu.

As is the case with the other types of points, standard points do not appear or disappear when you select the toggle; they appear when the screen is redrawn or when you use the POINT command. Points are always the same size, but have their own colors, which are determined by the

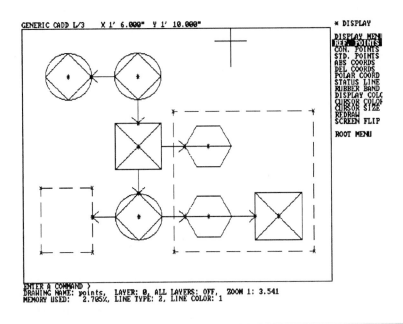

Figure 6-11.   *Sample drawing with REFERENCE POINTS turned on*

current LINE COLOR when the point is originally placed, or by the color to which it is changed by using any of the CHANGE commands. Standard points *will be* printed or plotted if they are currently displayed. Figure 6-12 shows the diagram drawing with standard points turned on. Compare this to the previous two figures. The points in this drawing are part of the components, so the construction points, which would normally be at the center of each point, do not appear.

The only time that you will find standard points that you didn't put into the drawing yourself is when the FAST TEXT toggle (TF) is turned on. The effect of this command is that text is replaced, for display purposes, with standard points. This causes the screen to regenerate much more quickly, and you can still tell where the text is, even though you can't read it. However, if DISPLAY STANDARD POINTS (PS) is turned off, you won't see anything at all where your text is supposed to be. If you turn FAST TEXT on and your text disappears, type **PS** to turn on standard points,

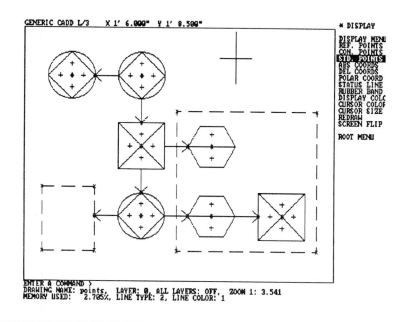

Figure 6-12. *Sample drawing with STANDARD POINTS turned on*

and then REDRAW (RD) the screen. Don't worry if this isn't clear right now; there will be more about FAST TEXT in Chapter 8.

Rubber Banding

As you have seen in previous chapters, rubber banding is toggled on and off by selecting the RUBBER BAND command on the DISPLAY menu, or by typing **RB** on the keyboard. You have seen rubber banding at work in the drawing of lines (LI), two-point circles (C2), and rubber arcs (A2). You may have also experimented with it when you used the MOVE POINT command on lines, arcs, circles, and curves.

Rubber banding displays the entity as it is being drawn during certain DRAW and OBJECT commands. At any given time, it shows you what the entity will look like if you select the point where the cursor is located.

Rubber banding can be very useful, particularly on fast computers. If you have a slow computer or one without a math coprocessor, rubber banding can create difficulties with the point selection while you wait for the object to redraw and try to press the button on the pointing device at just the right moment. In these cases, it is best to turn rubber banding off and use construction points as your main visual feedback. One of Generic CADD's best features is its ability to be optimized to run on your specific equipment, for your particular application. The status of the rubber banding feature may be established as a default in the CONFIG program.

Display of Coordinates

As you have seen, three different modes of coordinate display are possible (four, if you count no coordinates at all). Coordinates display the location of the cursor in relation to some point. The coordinates may be (1) ABSO-LUTE or AC, that is, measured from the origin, 0,0; (2) RELATIVE (also known as DELTA or DC), in which case they are measured from the last point entered; or (3) POLAR or PT (explanation follows).

Coordinates are displayed as X and Y values the horizontal distance (X) and vertical distance (Y) from the point of reference. Positive X values mean "to the right," while negative X values indicate "to the left." For Y values, positive is toward the top of the screen or drawing, and negative is toward the bottom. Relative coordinates are differentiated by the small triangle (Greek letter *delta*) that appears in front of the X and Y. Relative coordinates are used when it is more important to know the distances between points rather than their X and Y coordinates.

Polar coordinates show both distance and direction from the last point entered. The direction is measured in degrees above a horizontal line passing through the last point. Therefore, a point directly to the right of the last point entered would be at zero degrees, a point directly above would be at 90 degrees, and a point directly to the left would be at 180 degrees.

Because these commands are all toggles, if all coordinate display is turned off, there will be no coordinates at all. Turning off the coordinate display when you don't need it can make the drawing cursor move more smoothly, especially on slower machines.

It is worth noting that coordinate display is actually triggered by movement of the drawing cursor. Occasionally, you will not see any coordinates after a ZOOM or some other command that causes the screen to redraw, even when you have RELATIVE or ABSOLUTE COORDI-NATES turned on. This is because you have not moved the cursor since the redraw. If you move the pointing device a little, the coordinates will appear. This is particularly likely to occur when you have SNAP TO GRID (SG) turned on with a large GRID SIZE (GS).

Absolute Coordinates   The display of absolute coordinates is toggled on and off by choosing the ABS COORDS command on the DISPLAY menu, or by typing **AC** on the keyboard. Absolute coordinates track and display the location of the cursor using the currently selected unit system, as specified by the commands on the UNITS menu. The number of decimal places is controlled by the DECIMAL VALUE (DV) command, and the smallest fraction displayed when using fractions is controlled by the FRACTION VALUE (FV) command. These are also found on the UNITS menu.

When absolute coordinates are displayed, the numbers at the top of the screen will be labeled X and Y, as was illustrated in Figure 3-8. These values represent the actual horizontal and vertical distances between the cursor and the origin, 0,0. These values are rounded to the decimal or fractional value that you have indicated, and can be affected by pixel resolution of your graphics card. If you are at a ZOOM ALL (ZA) in the SITEPLAN drawing, for example, your cursor will probably jump a few inches at a time, even without having SNAP TO GRID (SG) turned on. These large jumps are simply due to the fact that there are no locations in between for the cursor to stop at. If you ZOOM UP (ZU) a few times, or ZOOM WINDOW (ZW) to a smaller area of the drawing, your cursor will move in smaller and smaller increments. When you zoom way in to a ZOOM VALUE (ZM) of one, your cursor will display every last bit of resolution that you have allowed with the UNITS commands. Don't forget, you can always override the cursor position with manual entry if you need to specify a dimension to the nearest 1/8 inch when zoomed out further.

Relative Coordinates   The display of relative (or delta) coordinates is toggled with the DEL COORDS command on the DISPLAY menu or the two-character code DC. Relative coordinates track and display the location of the cursor relative to the last point selected (see Figure 3-9). As with absolute coordinates, the format and precision of these coordinates is controlled by the UNITS commands, and how far you are zoomed in to the drawing.

It should be noted that absolute and relative coordinates cannot be turned on at the same time. While it is true that you can turn on relative coordinates, and then turn on absolute coordinates, you will not get relative coordinates back when you turn off absolute coordinates. Turning on a second mode of coordinate display turns off the first mode automatically, so that they will not be displayed on top of one another. Any time you turn off either system of coordinates, you end up with no coordinates at all until you turn one of them back on again.

Remember that the "last point entered" does not have to be an endpoint of a line, construction point, or definition point. You can simply select a point on the screen, using SNAP TO NEAREST POINT (NP) if you like, and then press ESC to cancel the implicit LINE command that will start as a result. This point is now the last point entered, even though the LINE command was canceled. When executing a MOVE or a COPY command, the first reference point that you select becomes the last point entered when you are selecting the new reference point, so that you can see how far you are moving or copying the object. When you issue the OBJECT ERASE or OBJECT CHANGE command, the point that you use to select the object becomes the last point entered. Almost any point selected on the screen becomes the last point entered and causes relative coordinates to be reset to 0,0.

Polar Coordinates   Polar coordinates are toggled with the POLAR COORDS command on the DISPLAY menu or **PT** on the keyboard. (PC is already tied up by CONSTRUCTION POINTS, and PO is used for STANDARD POINT. PT probably stands for "polar tracking;" as a mnemonic device, it's as good as anything else.)

Polar coordinates are actually a form of relative coordinates, so relative coordinates must be turned on before polar coordinates will work. Turning polar coordinates on or off while absolute coordinates are displayed, or while no coordinates are displayed at all, has no visible effect, but will be noticed the next time that relative coordinates are displayed. Relative coordinates "remember" whether polar coordinates are on, so polar coordinates do not have to be turned on every time you turn on relative coordinates.

Polar coordinates display the distance from the cursor to the last point entered, and also the angle between these two points, measured counterclockwise from an imaginary horizontal line passing through the last point, as illustrated in Figure 3-10. They can be useful if you want to draw a line of a particular length, or copy or move an object in a direction that is not

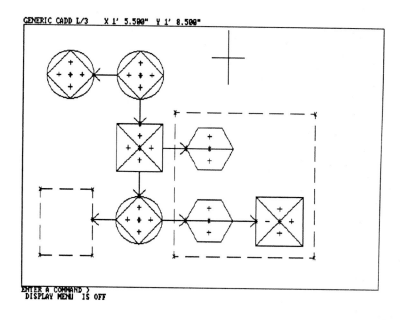

Figure 6-13. The display when the video menu is first turned off

strictly horizontal or vertical. Like the other coordinate displays, the format and accuracy of polar coordinates is controlled by the UNITS commands and how much drawing space is represented on the screen at the time.

Making More Room on the Screen

You can maximize the amount of display space for your drawing by eliminating the video menu. Although this means that you will have to use two-character commands to run Generic CADD, many users find they can learn these commands fairly quickly.

Display of the video menu is toggled with the DISPLAY MENU command on the DISPLAY menu, or by typing **VM** on the keyboard. The menu vanishes, and the box around the edge of the drawing screen expands so

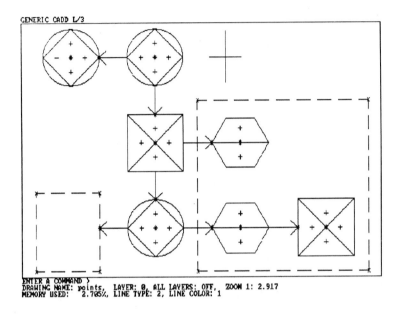

Figure 6-14.   *The display without a video menu after a ZOOM ALL*

that this area is now available for drawing, as shown in Figure 6-13. If you are zoomed in to a portion of the drawing, the area that was covered by the video menu will be blank at first, but you can remedy this situation by issuing the REDRAW (RD) command from the ZOOMS menu.

To turn the video menu back on, simply select the command or type **VM** again. The box around the drawing area returns to its normal size, and the menu reappears. A portion of the drawing display will no longer be visible, of course, but nothing in the drawing has actually been lost—it is just hidden "under" the video menu. Whenever you turn on the video menu, it always starts with the ROOT menu, rather than the menu that you had on the screen when you turned it off.

You can see the advantage of a larger screen when you examine the diagram drawing. Compare Figure 6-14, which shows the same drawing with no video menu at a ZOOM ALL, with Figure 6-13, before the new larger area was utilized. With the video menu off, you get a little more detail, and do not have to ZOOM UP quite as much, because the objects have a little better resolution. This technique will have a greater impact on more complicated drawings because there will be more detail to view and you will need to zoom more. If the drawing was more vertically oriented, turning off the video menu would not make as much difference, because all of the gain in drawing space is in the horizontal direction.

There is no way to gain more space in the vertical direction. When you turn off the coordinates, the drawing area does not expand; the coordinates just do not appear. The same is true with the three lines below the drawing area. The drawing area is not expandable into this space.

Cursor and Screen Text Display

Two commands control the display of the drawing cursor and one handles the screen text. These commands are designed to adapt to your personal preferences and also have some functional uses.

The CURSOR SIZE Commands   The size of the drawing cursor (in pixels or dots), is determined by the CURSOR SIZE command on the DISPLAY menu; the command is also activated by typing **CU** (for CUrsor). The default size (not configurable) is 32. The smallest cursor available is 1 pixel. You can specify zero. Instead of no cursor at all, with this selection you get a cursor that goes to all four edges of the drawing screen, as shown in Figure 6-15. This type of cursor can be very useful for checking to see if objects are aligned correctly from one side of the screen to the other, especially if you are using a small grid. However, you would still be wise to use the grid; just because objects *appear* to be aligned on the screen does not mean that they really are. The screen-size cursor should be used only as a tool for checking alignment when it is difficult to follow the grid dots all the way across the screen.

All other cursors contain the specified number of pixels on each of the four arms of the cursor. Actually, this is not exactly true. The left and top arms have the specified number, but the right and bottom arm have one less than the specified number. The missing pixel is actually the one in the middle of the cursor, which is blank, so that the cursor is slightly off-balance to the top-left. You will notice this only when you have a very small cursor. If you try a CURSOR SIZE (CU) of one, you will see two dots, one for the top arm and one for the left. The actual center of the cursor, where your points are actually selected, is the blank pixel between these two dots

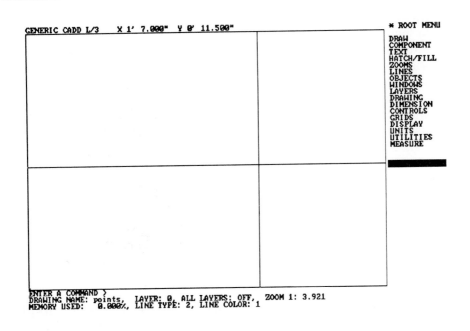

Figure 6-15.   *The cursor with CURSOR SIZE set at zero*

to the lower right. See Figure 6-16 for an enlarged view of several small cursors.

The CURSOR COLOR Command   You can also customize cursor color with the CURSOR COLOR command on the DISPLAY menu, or **CK** on the keyboard. (The letter *K* is almost always used to signify color in two-letter commands.)

When you select this command, if the video menu is on and more than two colors are available, you will get the special video menu color selection bars (see Chapter 3 for discussion of these bars in relation to LINE COLOR). You can either select from this menu, using the second pointing device button, or type a number. If the menu is off or if you are working on a monochrome system, the color bars will not appear, so you must type a number. The current color will be shown in the prompt. If you decide not

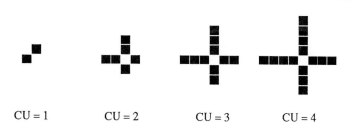

Figure 6-16. *Enlarged view of different-sized cursors*

to change it, just press ENTER. The initial cursor color is configurable in the CONFIG program, if you find one you particularly like.

This command also controls the color of the box around the drawing area. Both the cursor and the box change color immediately upon your selection of a new color. You won't need to do a REDRAW to see the effects of the change.

With the CURSOR COLOR command, you can also eliminate the cursor altogether. You might want to do this to save an IMAGE with no box for use with Generic PRESENT or Generic PAINT, or use some other screen-grabbing software for importing into other programs. If you select a color of zero, the cursor and the box around the drawing area both disappear. This even works on some monochrome systems; on others, the box vanishes, but the cursor remains. In this case, the closest you can get to getting rid of the cursor is to change the CURSOR SIZE to one.

The DISPLAY COLOR Command   This command, activated by choosing DISPLAY COLOR on the DISPLAY menu or typing **DK** on the keyboard, controls the color of the text in the menu area, the prompt area, and the coordinate area. It also controls the color of the grid dots. It can be selected from menu color bars or by typing a number. As with the CURSOR COLOR command, the default value is determined in the CONFIG program and it can be set to zero to get rid of the items whose color it controls. Unfortunately, this last function is not available with certain monochrome configurations, where all colors, even color zero, are defined as simply being in contrast to the background.

On most systems, the best way to display a Generic CADD drawing on the screen all by itself, just as it will be printed on a sheet of paper, is to

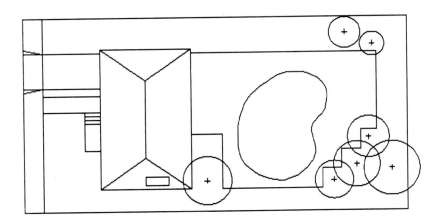

Figure 6-17.   *The display when the CURSOR COLOR and DISPLAY COLOR are set to zero with the ZOOM ALL issued*

set CURSOR COLOR to zero, set DISPLAY COLOR to zero, and issue the ZOOM ALL (ZA) command. This is the biggest, cleanest, drawing-only display you can get. You may find this display difficult to draw in and edit, but it may serve other purposes. Figure 6-17 shows the SITEPLAN drawing displayed in a manner that is ideal for on-screen presentations and capturing screen images.

The LAYERS Commands

The commands on the LAYERS menu fall into two groups, those for *editing* layers and those for *managing* layers. The LAYER editing commands were explained in Chapter 5. This section will concentrate on the LAYER management commands. Once you have a drawing with a few layers in it, you can try some of the editing commands.

In many applications, it is a good idea to set up a standard system of layers, so that you always know where to find certain types of information. If you use DIMENSIONING, you can use a special command to specify the layer for creating these dimensions. Drawings can be plotted a layer at a time if you like, layers can be saved in a drawing file, and entire drawings can be inserted onto a specified layer in your current drawing.

Layers are one of the more powerful data-organizing devices in Generic CADD, particularly for deterimining exactly what information should be displayed on the screen at a given time. All LAYER commands, except one, start with the letter Y (the middle letter in the word laYer).

The CURRENT LAYER Command

To take full advantage of the management capabilities of layers, you should assign each entity in the drawing to a specific layer. So far, all of the examples in this book have used only one layer—layer 0 (zero). All new entities are created on the current layer, and layer 0 is the default for all new drawings. To create entities on other layers, the current layer must be changed with the CURRENT LAYER command on the LAYERS menu, or by typing **YC** on the keyboard. (Certain Generic CADD versions that do not have LAYER SAVE and LAYER LOAD capabilities use YS for LAYER SELECT.)

When you use this command, you are shown the current layer and asked to type a number for the new current layer. Allowable values are from 0 to 255, which means you can have up to 256 layers in your drawing. Type a number and press ENTER. From this point on, until you change the current layer, all entities created will be placed on this new current layer. Note that the current layer is shown on the Status Line, so that you always know which layer you are working on. The ability to specify a CURRENT LAYER can also make your editing a little easier.

Editing on the Current Layer   In previous editing examples, whenever you chose an entity with an OBJECT command or selected entities with a WINDOW command, all entities on the screen were available because they were all located on one layer, which also happened to be the current layer, layer 0.

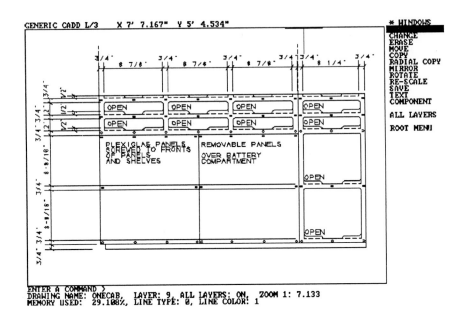

Figure 6-18.   *A drawing made with several layers (courtesy Mobile Office Vehicle Engineering)*

Layers, however, can be used to refine the selection process. You have a choice of selecting from all entities visible on the screen or only those entities residing on the current layer. The default condition when you start up Generic CADD and begin working on a drawing is that you can edit on only the current layer.

To change from editing only the current layer to editing all layers, use the ALL LAYERS EDIT command, shown as ALL LAYERS on the LAYERS menu, and abbreviated AL for the keyboard command. This toggle switches the layer editing mode back and forth between CURRENT-ONLY and ALL LAYERS. Whenever you use this command, a message in the prompt area will inform you of the new status of the EDIT ALL LAYERS toggle. If it was previously on, the message will state "EDIT ALL LAYERS OFF," meaning that you can only edit on the current layer now. If it was already off, you will get the message "EDIT ALL LAYERS ON," meaning that you can now edit all entities visible on the screen. If you have STATUS

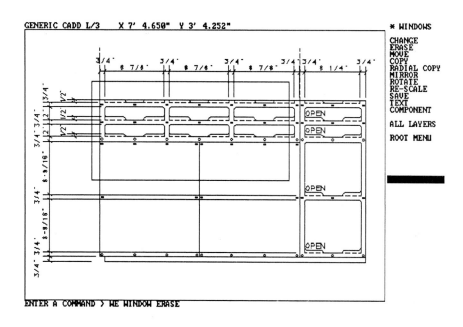

Figure 6-19. *A WINDOW ERASE with ALL LAYERS EDIT turned off*

LINE (SL) turned on, the status of the EDIT ALL LAYERS toggle is shown whenever the Status Line is displayed.

Figures 6-18 through 6-20 illustrate the difference between editing with the EDIT ALL LAYERS toggle on and off. Figure 6-18 shows a drawing that has been constructed on several layers. The basic drawing is on one layer, the text is on another, the dimension lines on another, and so on. Figure 6-19 shows what happens with a WINDOW ERASE when the layer that contains the text is the CURRENT LAYER and EDIT ALL LAYERS is off. Only the text is erased, even though many other entities are in the window. Figure 6-20 shows the same command with approximately the same window, but with EDIT ALL LAYERS turned on. All entities visible on the screen that are defined entirely within the window are erased. A few lines passing through the window are not erased, because one or the other or both of their endpoints are not in the window.

No matter what the status of the ALL LAYERS EDIT toggle, layers that are not currently displayed cannot be edited with the OBJECTS and WINDOWS editing commands.

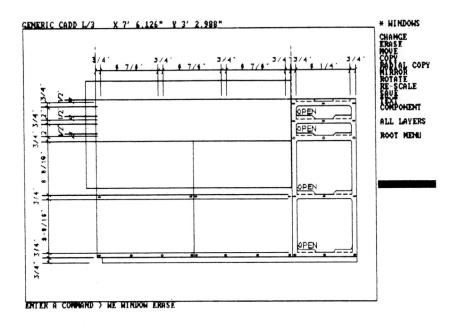

Figure 6-20. A WINDOW ERASE *with* ALL LAYERS EDIT *turned on*

Selecting Which Layers to Display

One of the advantages of using more that one layer is having the choice to make all of the entities on a certain layer or layers temporarily invisible. This process is called *hiding* layers. One typical reason for hiding layers is to temporarily get rid of information that has no bearing on the task at hand or is obscuring the entities that you want to edit.

Layers can be used to try different variations on a portion of your drawing. Then you can incorporate one of them into the final drawing by using one of the CHANGE commands to move certain entities onto your final layers, and the LAYER ERASE command to get rid of the extras. Construction lines can be placed on their own layer, and hidden when it's time to print. You might even designate one layer strictly for notes to yourself.

Entities on hidden layers cannot be edited with OBJECT or WINDOW editing commands. The CURRENT LAYER cannot be hidden. Entities that are moved to a hidden layer using the CHANGE command vanish from the screen, as if they had been erased, but will reappear when the hidden layers are displayed again.

The LAYER HIDE Command   Because all 256 layers are displayed when you first start Generic CADD, if you want to display layers selectively, the first thing to do is to hide the one(s) that you don't want to see. This is done with the HIDE command on the LAYERS menu, or with the two-character keyboard command **YH**. The prompt will simply ask which layer to hide. Type a number between 0 and 255, followed by ENTER. On the next ZOOM or REDRAW, any entities on the selected layer will not appear. If you want to hide more than one layer, don't REDRAW yet. Press the SPACEBAR to give another LAYER HIDE command, and select another layer. Repeat this process until you have specified all of the layers to be hidden, and then execute REDRAW (RD).

The LAYER HIDE (YH) command itself does not automatically execute a REDRAW, so you can select several layers to hide, one after the other, without waiting for the screen to redraw after each one. With this feature you can turn off some layers and then zoom to a location in the drawing. In this case, the ZOOM command automatically activates the redraw, so you do not even need to issue the REDRAW command.

If you want to hide all the layers (except for the CURRENT LAYER, which can't be hidden), type **256** when prompted for the layer to hide. In this case, a REDRAW will occur automatically, because Generic CADD realizes that you are not selecting one layer at a time. Actually, if you want to display less than half of the layers that contain entities, you are better off to hide all of the layers first, then select the layers that you want to display individually.

The LAYER DISPLAY Command   If you have hidden one or more layers and you want to see them again, use the DISPLAY command on the LAYERS menu, or **YD** on the keyboard. If you are not sure which layers are currently displayed, look on the second screen of the Show Layer Status option of the FLIP SCREEN (SF) command on the DISPLAY menu to find out. When you first start Generic CADD, all layers are displayed, so there won't be any hidden layers unless you have previously used the HIDE command.

When you use the LAYER DISPLAY (YD) command, you will get a prompt asking you to type the number of the layer that you want to display.

Type a number and then press ENTER. As with LAYER HIDE, selecting the layer does not automatically trigger a redraw, unless you type **256** to display all layers. You can specify more than one layer to display by pressing SPACEBAR and typing another number. When you have finished specifying layers, execute a REDRAW (RD) or ZOOM command to see these layers displayed.

If you try to display a layer that is already displayed or hide a layer that is already hidden, the drawing screen will show no change. The same thing happens if you change the status of a layer to hidden and back to displayed before a redraw occurs. The reverse is also true. In fact, you can change the display/hidden status of a layer as many times as you want before the redraw. Generic CADD keeps track of which layers are hidden and which are displayed even if this information has not yet been reflected on the screen.

The LINES Commands

These commands set a number of entity attributes that become part of the definitions of all new entities placed into the drawing. All new entities are created on the layer currently selected and are also created in the current LINE COLOR, using the current LINE TYPE and the current LINE WIDTH. The two-character codes for each of these commands start with the letter *L,* for Line.

Even though these commands establish the initial color, line type, and line width of new entities, these properties can be changed with any of the CHANGE commands. Note that these commands control the properties of all new entities created, not just Straight Lines. In Generic CADD, when you see the word "LINE" in the prompt or on the menu, it often applies to all simple entities.

The LINE COLOR Command

The color of all new entities created is controlled by the LINE COLOR command on the LINES menu, or by typing **LK** on the keyboard. When you select this command, you will be shown the current LINE COLOR, and asked to select a new one. This can be done by typing a number between 0 and 255, or by selecting a color from the colors bars shown in the video menu area (assuming that the video menu is active and more than two colors are available). If your video card displays less than 256 colors, the same colors repeat over and over again. On a 16-color system, for example, colors 0, 16, 32, and so on are all the same.

If you are working on a monchrome system, only two colors are available—the background color and a contrasting color. Generic CADD recognizes the background color as color 0 (zero), and the contrasting color as color 1. On some monochrome systems, notably Hercules-compatible graphics cards and the Toshiba 3100, entities always appear in color 1 no matter what color you select. On other monochrome systems, such as CGA compatibles, entities drawn using color 0 are displayed in the same color as the background, that is to say, they do not show up at all. If DISPLAY CONSTRUCTION POINTS is turned on, you will see construction points, as the entities actually exist, even though you can't see them.

The LINE WIDTH Command

The initial width of all new entities is controlled by the LINE WIDTH command on the LINES menu, or by **LW** on the keyboard. If the video menu is active, a menu of examples numbered 0 through 10 will be shown. You can either select from the menu using the second pointing device button, or type a number and press ENTER.

The units of line width are measured in whatever increment is available on the device used to display, print, or plot the drawing. On the video screen, each unit represents one pixel, or dot, no matter how far you ZOOM UP or ZOOM BACK. On the printer, the units are also one dot, so the actual thickness of the lines depends on the resolution of your printer. On a plotter, each unit represents one pen width. The width of the pen is controlled by a variable within the plotting command, rather than being the physical width of the pen, which Generic CADD doesn't know.

Line width, therefore, is not an absolute measurement. It always depends on the resolution of the display or output device, and the scale at which the drawing is displayed, printed, or plotted. LINE WIDTHS 2 through 10 are most useful for emphasizing certain entities. LINE WIDTHS 0 and 1 are both defined as being one unit wide, in order to avoid objects with Line Width zero not showing up. Figure 6-21 shows a drawing that has been created using three different line widths, 0, 2, and 4.

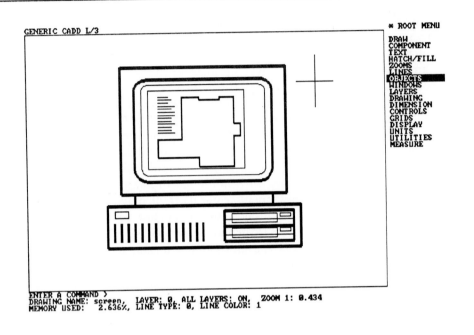

GENERIC CADD L/3

* ROOT MENU

DRAW
COMPONENT
TEXT
HATCH/FILL
ZOOMS
LINES
OBJECTS
WINDOWS
LAYERS
DRAWING
DIMENSION
CONTROLS
GRIDS
DISPLAY
UNITS
UTILITIES
MEASURE

ENTER A COMMAND >
DRAWING NAME: screen,   LAYER: 0, ALL LAYERS: ON,   ZOOM 1: 0.434
MEMORY USED: 2.636%, LINE TYPE: 0, LINE COLOR: 1

Figure 6-21.   *A drawing that uses a variety of LINE WIDTHS*

The LINE TYPE Command

The initial type of all new entities created in the drawing is controlled by the LINE TYPE command on the LINES menu, or by typing **LT** on the keyboard. LINE TYPE can be selected from a special video menu display if the video menu is turned on, or by typing a number from 0 through 255. LINE TYPES 1 through 9 are scaled to the output device, while the length of the dashes that make up types 11 through 255 is controlled by the LINE SCALE command. These are broken into groups of ten which are arranged in the same dash patterns as types 1 through 9, but at increasing scale factors. The dashes in types 21 through 29 are twice as long as in 11 through 19, while the dashes in types 31 through 39 are three times as long, and so on. Any Line Type value evenly divisible by 10 (0, 10, 20, 30, and so on) represents continuous lines. Figure 6-22 shows a drawing composed of a variety of line types. (For a complete discussion of LINE TYPES, see Chapter 3.)

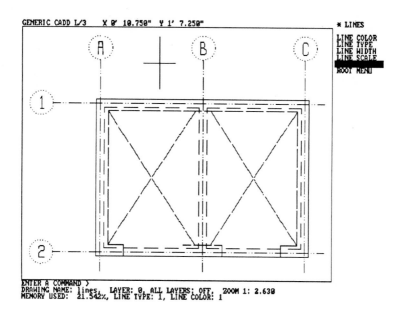

Figure 6-22. *A drawing that uses a variety of LINE TYPES*

The LINE SCALE Command

The LINE SCALE command on the LINES menu or the two-character keyboard command **LZ** controls the length of the dash patterns in the scalable LINE TYPES 10 through 255. The value of the Line Scale variable specifies the actual length of one repetition of any of LINE TYPES 11 through 19. (For a complete discussion of LINE SCALE, see Chapter 3.)

Unlike the other commands on the LINES menu, LINE TYPE does not set a parameter that becomes imbedded as part of the definition of the entities created. Instead it specifies an overall variable that affects *all* entities in the drawing, the next time that they are displayed. It may seem to apply only to new entities until you execute a REDRAW or any other ZOOM command.

Learning the material in this chapter should give you much greater control over your drawings and the way that they are displayed on the screen. Your drawing and editing should now be easier, more efficient, and more accurate. In addition, you should be able to organize the information in your drawings more efficiently and access that information for editing and for use in future drawings.

7 *Information and Inquiries*

This chapter focuses on the information that Generic CADD can provide about your drawing as you work on it. This information ranges from the status of certain toggles and drawing parameters to real data that can be calculated from the entities you have created. Several commands provide these different types of information. Two of these appear on the DISPLAY menu, three on the MEASURE menu, and two are not listed on the video menu.

The Status Lines

The simplest form of on-screen feedback available while running Generic CADD, beyond the coordinates (see Chapter 6), is the Status Lines—the two lines of text that appear below the "ENTER A COMMAND >" prompt if the STATUS LINE toggle is on (see Figure 7-1). Information provided on the first Status Line includes the name of the drawing on which you are working, the current layer, the status of the ALL LAYERS toggle (discussed later in this chapter), and the current zoom value. The second Status Line shows the percentage of available memory used by the drawing and the current line type and line color.

The Status Lines are only displayed while the "ENTER A COMMAND >" prompt is on the screen, that is, when you are not performing a command operation. The rest of the time the prompt area is used for command prompts. The Status Line area is regenerated at the end of every command.

```
ENTER A COMMAND >
DRAWING NAME: lines,  LAYER: 0, ALL LAYERS: OFF,  ZOOM 1: 3.921
MEMORY USED:   0.000%, LINE TYPE: 1, LINE COLOR: 1
```

Figure 7-1. *The Status Lines*

If the current command causes change in any information shown in the Status Line, it is reflected there immediately upon exiting the command.

In some situations the Status Line is not shown, even when you are not executing a command, such as after invoking a toggle command. After a toggle, Generic CADD flashes a message, such as "SNAP TO GRID IS ON," which stays on the screen until the next command is issued. Strangely enough, even when you turn on the Status Line with the STATUS LINE command from the DISPLAY menu or by typing **SL** on the keyboard, instead of the Status Line you get the message "STATUS LINE IS ON." Generic CADD is not giving you a hard time, it is just indicating that it has received the command, and it will show you the Status Line the next time it has a chance. If the Status Line was already on, the message would have read "STATUS LINE IS OFF," to let you know which way you have switched it. These messages are provided because sometimes you don't remember if a toggle is on or off, so you issue the command just to find out. If you get a message that you don't like, issue it again to return to the desired status.

Another time that you might not see the Status Line is when you have a small grid size (relative to the area currently shown on the screen). Generic CADD refuses to put the dots so close together that your drawing is difficult to see, so it leaves out some of them. You might get a message like "ONLY EVERY 4TH GRID POINT SHOWN" when you execute a redraw, indicating that for each visible grid dot, there are three invisible ones between, which you notice if you turn on SNAP TO GRID.

Anytime that both the "ENTER A COMMAND >" prompt and a message cause the disappearance of the Status Lines, you can clear the message by pressing ESC. When the message is cleared, the Status Lines appear.

More Information:
The FLIP SCREEN Command

More information is available to users of Level 3 and earlier versions of Generic CADD (2.0 and 3.0) with the FLIP SCREEN command on the DISPLAY menu. The two-character command code, SF, is easier to remember if you think of it as "SCREEN FLIP." As you will see, FS stands for FONT SELECT and is a TEXT command.

Generic CADD 2.0 and 3.0 users will be interested to learn that the FLIP SCREEN command in these versions was actually a text screen, rather than a graphics screen like the rest of the program. This screen provided a place to run memory-resident software that required a text screen in order to be activated. In Level 3, the FLIP SCREEN is on a graphics screen like the rest of the program, in order to run faster and minimize program size.

The FLIP SCREEN command offers options that provide information requiring more than the three lines at the bottom of the screen. Select an option by pressing the number alongside it (see Figure 7-2).

Display Drawing Status

This option provides some of the same information shown on the Status Lines (the drawing name and the zoom value), plus the number of points, lines, text characters, and components in the drawing. The memory usage is described in actual bytes instead of a percentage, and many more of the current drawing parameters are shown in addition to the line type and line color that you get on the Status Line. The status of some of the more important toggles is shown, as are the default paths for drawings, compo-

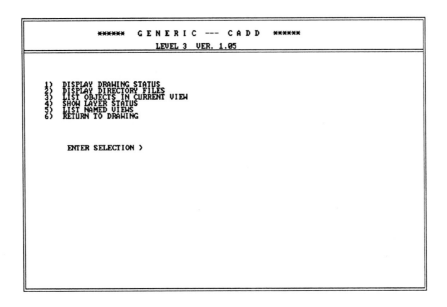

****** G E N E R I C --- C A D D ******
LEVEL 3 VER. 1.05

1) DISPLAY DRAWING STATUS
2) DISPLAY DIRECTORY FILES
3) LIST OBJECTS IN CURRENT VIEW
4) SHOW LAYER STATUS
5) LIST NAMED VIEWS
6) RETURN TO DRAWING

ENTER SELECTION >

Figure 7-2.   *The FLIP SCREEN menu*

nents, and fonts. Figure 7-3 shows the status screen for the SITEPLAN
drawing.

Even though the prompt at the bottom of the screen tells you to press
RETURN to exit the screen, you will be returned to the FLIP SCREEN menu
if you press any key.

Display Directory Files

This option lets you see the list of the filenames on any disk without leaving
Generic CADD. You might need to use this function before loading a file,
if you forget the name, or before loading a font, to determine which ones
are available.

When you select this option, you will be prompted to type a search
specification, which must be a complete pathname, with DOS wildcards if

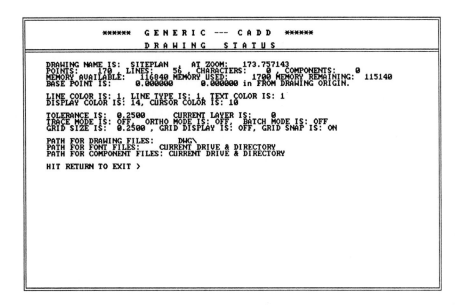

Figure 7-3. *The DRAWING STATUS screen*

you are looking for more than one file. If you want to see a list of all drawing files on a disk in the A drive, for example, you would type: **A:*.DWG**.

This instruction would tell Generic CADD to look for all files (the * is a DOS wildcard character meaning "anything") with the extension .DWG. Since all drawing files end with the extension .DWG, this instruction would tell Generic CADD to list all of the drawing files on the A drive.

If you simply press ENTER at the prompt rather than typing a search specification, you will see a directory of the drawings (*.DWG) in the currently logged directory, the one from which you started Generic CADD. Figure 7-4 shows an example of a directory of drawing files.

If the directory contains more files that fit your specification than fit on the screen, you will be prompted to press RETURN to move to the next screen or ESC to return to the menu. Again, pressing any key but ESC will move you to the next screen. When you get to the last screen, pressing any key returns you to the FLIP SCREEN menu.

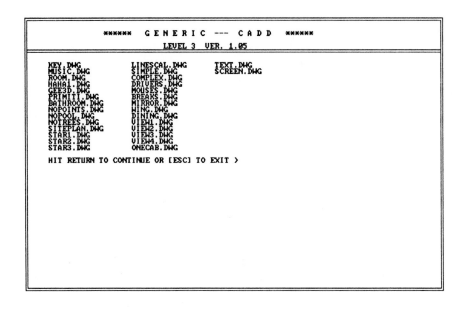

Figure 7-4. *The DISPLAY DIRECTORY screen*

List Objects in Current View

This option gives you a list of the visible and editable objects on the current Generic CADD screen. The type of entity is shown, along with its line type, width, color, and layer.

Note that if ALL LAYERS EDIT (discussed later in this chapter) is off, only the entities on the current layer will be listed, as shown in Figure 7-5.

If the entities run over onto a second screen, you can press any key to go to the next screen and continue the list, or press ESC to return to the FLIP SCREEN menu. At the last screen, pressing any key returns you to the menu.

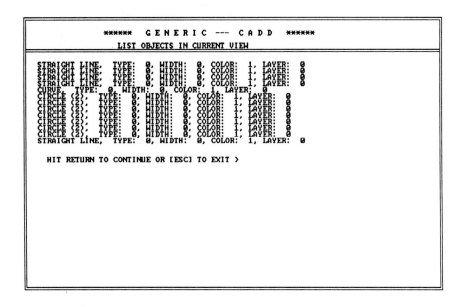

Figure 7-5.   *The LIST OBJECTS IN CURRENT VIEW screen*

Show Layer Status

Two separate screens of information are displayed here. The first shows
which layers presently contain entities. The layers are listed in order, with
a blank space left for the layers that do not contain any entities, so you will
probably only see the number zero in the upper-left corner. Unless you
change layers, all of your entities are created on layer zero. After you start
using more layers, you may see layer numbers sprinkled all over the
screen. Figure 7-6 shows the SHOW LAYER STATUS screen for a drawing
created on several layers.

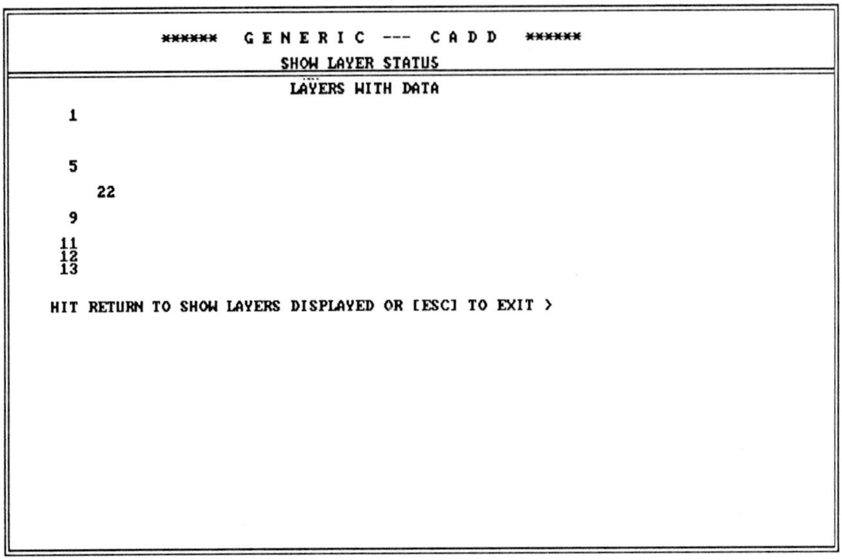

```
       ****** G E N E R I C  ---  C A D D  ******
                   SHOW LAYER STATUS
                   LAYERS WITH DATA

     1

     5
          22
     9
    11
    12
    13

HIT RETURN TO SHOW LAYERS DISPLAYED OR [ESC] TO EXIT >
```

Figure 7-6.   *The first SHOW LAYER STATUS screen, LAYERS WITH DATA*

When you press any key (other than ESC, which returns you to the FLIP SCREEN menu), the second screen appears, showing a list of the layers that are currently displayed, as shown in Figure 7-7. Unless you have turned off any layers (which you probably have not done because the appropriate commands have not been discussed yet), you will see all of the layer numbers listed. When you first load a drawing, all layers are displayed, even if they do not contain any data. If any layer is hidden, you will see a blank spot where that layer number should be. Pressing any key at this point returns you to the FLIP SCREEN menu.

List Named Views

This option allows you to review a list of the named views that you have created with the NAME VIEW (NV) command. A sample screen listing

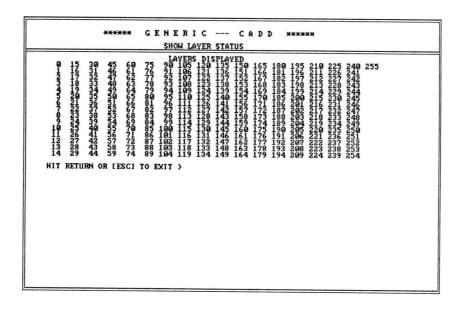

Figure 7-7. *The second SHOW LAYER STATUS screen, LAYERS DISPLAYED*

named views is shown in Figure 7-8. If you use named views regularly, it is a good idea to check this list occasionally to see if there are any that could be deleted with the DELETE NAMED VIEW (NX) command. Although superfluous named views do not really do any harm, they take up space on the disk and cause each SAVE and LOAD to take a little longer.

As usual, if the named views occupy more than one screen, you can press any key to see the next screen or ESC to return to the FLIP SCREEN menu. At the last screen, pressing any key returns you to this menu.

Return to Drawing

This last option simply restores the main Generic CADD screen so that you can continue working on your drawing.

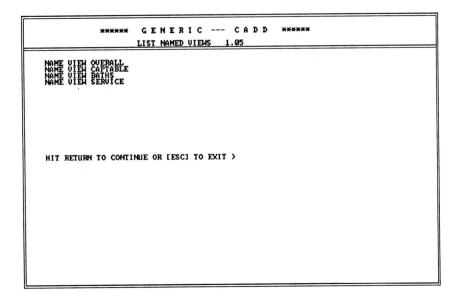

Figure 7-8.   *The LIST NAMED VIEWS screen*

The MEASURE Commands

The commands on the MEASURE menu provide access to information concerning the numeric data and geometric properties of the drawing. The information available includes distances, areas, and angles. All of the MEASURE command two-character codes begin with the letter *M*.

In addition to the MEASURE commands, there are two additional commands, not on the menu or in the Level 3 manual, which serve a similar function. These commands are included in Level 3 for transferring information to Generic Estimator, but they can be used without Estimator. These additional commands include a command that reports perimeter length as well as area, and a command for counting the number of times a component appears in the drawing.

The MEASURE DISTANCE Command

The DISTANCE command on the MEASURE menu, represented by MD on the keyboard, lets you obtain the distance between any two points, or the cumulative distance between a number of points.

When you select this command, you are asked to specify the first point. If you want to measure the distance between the endpoints of two lines, for example, you can use the SNAP TO NEAREST POINT command to locate the first endpoint by using the third button on the pointing device or by typing **NP** when you have positioned the cursor near the point that you want to select. You can use the same method to choose the second point. Once you have selected two points, the distance between these points is shown in the prompt area. Figure 7-9 shows the results of measuring the top line in the SITEPLAN drawing. When you have finished the MEASURE command, press ESC, type **PU**, or choose a blank menu line with the second pointing device button to return to the "ENTER A COMMAND >" prompt.

If you want to know the cumulative distance between a number of points, simply select more points. As you select each point, the cumulative distance will be shown. When you specify the last point, you will see the total distance. You must press ESC, type **PU**, or select a blank menu line with the pointing device to stop entering points and return to the "ENTER A COMMAND >" prompt. If you forget to do this, your next command will not work.

The MEASURE AREA Command

The AREA command on the MEASURE menu is activated by the keyboard command MV. Though the letter *V* stands for Volume, it does not imply that the MEASURE AREA command measures cubic volume; it measures flat area in any unit system you happen to be using. (The command code MA is used for Measure Angle.) If the units are inches, you will get square inches; if you are using feet, your area measurements will be in square feet. Similarly, the metric unit systems can provide square meters, centimeters, or millimeters.

When you select the MEASURE AREA command, you will be asked to select points. You simply pick points at each corner of the shape as if you

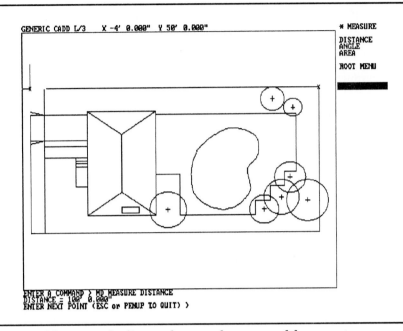

GENERIC CADD L/3   X -4' 0.000"   Y 50' 0.000"

* MEASURE

DISTANCE
ANGLE
AREA

ROOT MENU

ENTER A COMMAND > MD MEASURE DISTANCE
DISTANCE = 100' 0.000"
ENTER NEXT POINT (ESC or PENUP TO QUIT) >

Figure 7-9.   *Measuring the distance between the corners of the property*

were drawing lines around the perimeter until you get back to the beginning point. When you press ESC, the area will be shown. You can use SNAP TO THE NEAREST POINT while picking points, to get a more accurate area measurement. Figure 7-10 shows the result of measuring the area of the roof of the house in the SITEPLAN drawing.

The area that you are trying to measure must be closed. In other words, you must return to the starting point before pressing ESC. If you do not, Generic CADD assumes that the boundary of the area that you are trying to measure is a straight line between the last point entered back to the beginning point.

An undocumented feature of the MEASURE AREA command allows you to measure more than one area in the same command and get a cumulative total. You can do this by typing **PU** (for Pen Up) instead of ESC when you get back to the beginning point of the first area. You will remain in the MEASURE AREA command, but the calculation of the area will be

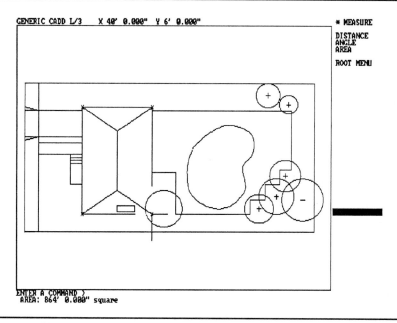

Figure 7-10.   *Measuring the area of a roof*

temporarily suspended. Move the cursor to a corner of the next area to be measured and begin choosing points again. When you return to the starting point of the second area, press ESC. The area shown will be the combined area of the two figures. This technique can be extended to combine as may figures as you like into one area calculation.

Users of early versions of Generic CADD will be interested to note that if you go around a figure clockwise, you will get a positive number for the area, and if you go around counterclockwise, you will get a negative result. On certain versions, if you combine this technique with the method of combining multiple areas, you can calculate the area of a shape that has a hole in it. First, go clockwise around the entire figure, type **PU**, and then go counterclockwise around the hole. The result will be the area of the first shape minus the area of the second shape. Some versions with positive and negative area calculations do not allow multiple areas, and the Levels products always calculate positive areas.

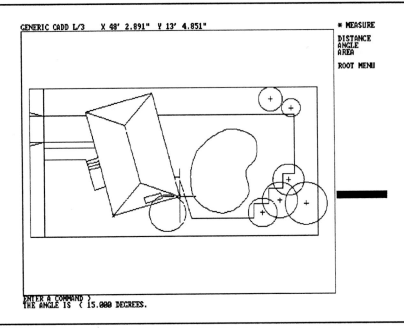

GENERIC CADD L/3   X 48' 2.891"   Y 13' 4.851"

* MEASURE

DISTANCE
ANGLE
AREA

ROOT MENU

ENTER A COMMAND >
THE ANGLE IS < 15.000 DEGREES.

Figure 7-11.   *Measuring the angle of the SITEPLAN house after it is rotated*

The MEASURE ANGLE Command

The ANGLE command on the MEASURE menu, shortened to MA for the keyboard, provides a display of the angle between two selected points. The angle is displayed in the currently selected unit system for angles.

When you select this command, you are asked to select two points. As with all of the MEASURE commands, these can be selected as free-floating points, snapped onto existing points, or specified by manual entry. After you select the second point, the angle is shown in the prompt area. Figure 7-11 illustrates the MEASURE ANGLE command used on the wall of the house in a modified version of the SITEPLAN drawing. The convention for angle displays is that a horizontal line from left to right is considered to be zero, and angles are measured counterclockwise from the following position: straight up from bottom to top is 90 degrees; horizontal right to left is 180 degrees; straight down is 270 degrees. In this command, there are no negative angles. The angle between any two points is always calculated as a positive angle between zero and 360 degrees.

The ESTIMATE BOUNDARY Command

This command, activated by EB on the keyboard only, is not found on the standard video menu. Don't let the name "estimate" fool you. This command provides just as exact a calculation as any of the measure commands. The name "estimate" is derived from its original purpose of interfacing with the Generic Estimator. ESTIMATE BOUNDARY works much like MEASURE AREA except that, in addition to calculating the area of a shape, it also calculates, on a running basis, the length of the perimeter of the same shape, as if you were using MEASURE DISTANCE at the same time.

Each time you pick a point (except for the first point), a new cumulative distance is shown. When you get to the final point and press ESC, both the area and the perimeter length are shown, and you are asked to verify sending this information to the Estimator. It doesn't really matter if you say Yes or No, unless you are actually using the Generic Estimator. If you answer Yes, you simply get a message telling you that the "message space" is not installed. This is the area that is set aside for transferring the data to the Estimator. If you answer No, you get no such prompt. In either case, you have already obtained the information that you sought.

The ESTIMATE COMPONENTS Command

This command is also provided to send information to the Generic Estimator and does not appear on the video menu. However, you can use the two-character command EC to activate the ESTIMATE COMPONENTS command even if you are not using the Estimator.

A component is simply a named symbol that you have previously drawn and may have inserted into the drawing any number of times. A typical example for floor plan drawings is a door swing, a sink, or a piece of furniture, such as a chair.

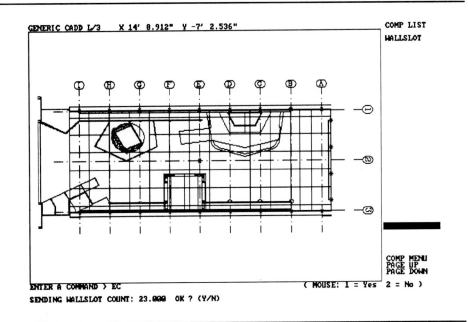

GENERIC CADD L/3   X 14' 8.912"   Y -7' 2.536"   COMP LIST
                                                                 WALLSLOT

ENTER A COMMAND > EC   (MOUSE: 1 = Yes 2 = No)
SENDING WALLSLOT COUNT: 23.000 OK ? (Y/N)

COMP MENU
PAGE UP
PAGE DOWN

Figure 7-12. *Using ESTIMATE COMPONENTS to count wallslots*

The ESTIMATE COMPONENTS command instructs Generic CADD to count the number of times a certain component appears in an area of the drawing, specified by placing a window. When you use this command, you are asked to type the name of the component, and then to place the window. When you have done this, a message in the prompt area informs you of how many there are. As with the ESTIMATE BOUNDARY command, you are asked if you want to send this data to the Estimator. Again, it does not matter whether you type Y or N, unless you are using the Generic Estimator.

Figure 7-12 shows the use of the ESTIMATE COMPONENTS command to count the number of times that the WALLSLOT component was used in the floor plan shown.

As you have seen in this chapter, Generic CADD keeps track of the information that you put into the drawing, but can also provide additional information about it. As a graphic model of reality that contains accurate data, Generic CADD can be used as a tool both to store existing information and to extrapolate additional information as required.

8 *Complex Entities*

Until now, you have been creating and editing only simple entities. These simple entities, Points, Lines, Circles, Arcs, Ellipses, and Curves, are the basic building blocks from which all drawings in Generic CADD are created. In this chapter you will explore how simple entities can be combined to create complex entities.

What Are Complex Entities?

Complex entities are composed of one or more other entities, usually simple entities, though complex entities can also be created from other complex entities already in the drawing. In some cases, you define complex entities; in other cases, you may use predefined complex entities, such as Text Characters. Still other complex entities, such as Hatches and Fills, are created automatically by Generic CADD.

Generic CADD has four types of complex entities, Components, Text Characters, Hatches, and Fills, all of which have certain features in common.

They May Be Complex,
But They Are Still Entities

Like a simple entity, each complex entity can be thought of as one distinct item. Each has only one reference point that is used for the editing commands, such as ERASE, MOVE, and COPY. Each complex entity is described in the database by the location of its reference point, the number of the layer on which it is located, its color, and so on. Each entity is placed with a single command that asks for points, just like the simple-entity DRAW commands. When you request a list of the items in the current window from the FLIP SCREEN (SF) command, each complex entity appears as one line item. The individual entities that make up a complex entity are not normally selectable, for editing or other purposes. However, there are some exceptions to this general rule, as you will see.

Complex Entities Are Defined Once

One of the obvious advantages of a complex entity is that once you draw it, you do not have to draw it again. This aspect is usually the most useful for Components and Text Characters. Another advantage, which is less evident, is that each complex entity is defined one time and then *placed* each time it appears. The main benefit of this feature is its space-saving capability. Compare the effect on the database of drawing a figure composed of 20 Lines and then copying it three times, to defining a complex entity and placing it four times. In the first case, you end up with a total of 80 entities (20 originals and 60 copies), each occupying space in memory and eventually on a disk. In the second instance, you have a total of 24 entities—the 20 original entities, plus one additional entity each time the complex entity is placed. (The second example actually contains 26 entities if you include the beginning and ending of the definition.) In reality, while complex entities take up a little more space than simple entities, they certainly do not take up the space of 80 simple entities. You never really see these extra entities, but they are stored in the database. In this example, if the simple entities were all Lines, these two drawings would take up 2410 bytes and 910 bytes, respectively, which illustrates the space-saving advantage of complex entities.

Even copying a complex entity does not cause the definition to be repeated in the computer memory or the disk file. The *placement* of the complex entity is copied, not the definition itself.

Placement Parameters

Each of the four types of complex entities has its own set of *placement parameters*—values or conditions that are set before placing the complex entity. These placement parameters greatly speed up the placement of complex entities, because you do not have to select them every time you place an entity. These placement parameters are comparable to the simple entity placement parameters—which are line color, line type, line width, and current layer. In fact, current layer is used by complex entities as well.

Components have two parameters that are set before a component is placed: (1) scale, which allows you to place the predefined component in a size different from the original size, and (2) rotation, which lets you turn a complex entity on any angle. These parameters rule all components that you place until the parameters are changed. When you change these parameters, only new component placements are affected. Once a component is placed, the parameters become part of that particular complex entity placement and can only be changed with the editing commands.

Text Characters have several parameters, including size and rotation, which are similar to the component parameter's scale and rotation. Text uses "size" instead of "scale" because characters are defined to be one unit tall. For example, when scaled by a factor of two, a Text Character will actually be two units tall. This is not necessarily true with components, which can be defined at any size. Text Character placement parameters also include color, aspect ratio (ratio of width to height), slant, and font. While components are placed by typing or selecting their name and showing a location, Text Characters are selected by combining the currently selected font and the characters that you type when you place the text. Several fonts are provided with Generic CADD.

Hatch placement parameters include the name of the Hatch that you are using, the rotation, scale, and color. Fill placements require only the rotation, scale, and color parameters, as there is only one type of fill: solid. Otherwise, Hatches and Fills are placed in a very similar manner, by selecting the objects to be hatched or filled.

Predefined Versus "On the Fly"

Complex entities can be divided into two distinct groups. One group includes Components and Text Characters; the commands for these entities are found on the COMPONENTS menu and TEXT menu, respectively.

Hatches and Fills, the other group, are located together on one menu, HATCH/FILL. COMPONENTS and TEXT commands are available in all three Levels of Generic CADD, while HATCH and FILL commands are available only in Level 3. Users of Generic CADD 3.0 should note that HATCH and FILL are part of *Drafting Enhancements 2.*

The first group (Components and Text Characters) may be called *pre-defined complex entities,* meaning that someone must draw the complex entity before it can be placed. In the case of Components, you can draw your own or purchase components in the form of *symbols libraries* from Generic Software or third-party developers. Each Component in a drawing has a unique name assigned to it when it is created. In the case of Text Characters, several fonts are included with Generic CADD, and others are available from Generic Software and third-party developers. Each font generally includes the upper- and lowercase alphabet, numerals, and punctuation marks. The name of a particular Text Character is a combination of the font and the character itself. You can also create your own fonts with Generic CADD or with software available from Generic and third parties.

The second group (Hatches and Fills) is defined *on the fly,* that is, instead of predefining a particular hatched or filled area and then placing it, the area to be hatched or filled is selected each time you use the HATCH or FILL command. A specific hatched or filled area has no particular name that you can use to place another of the same description. Generally, a hatched or filled area is a unique condition. If you need to place the same hatched or filled figure repeatedly, you can make a Component that includes the hatched or filled area, or you can copy a hatched or filled area already existing in the drawing.

As you will see in the following sections, the four types of complex entities differ in other ways, depending on their intended uses.

Components

The use of components is Generic CADD's primary method for creating repeating objects or symbols and placing them into your drawing. Components may be repeated within one drawing or throughout several drawings. Components are what people typically mean when they say, "With CAD, once you've drawn something you never have to draw it again."

Components are made by first drawing the repeatable object, and then defining it as a component. This process consists of giving the component a name and a reference point, and selecting the objects that make up the component with a window. A number of commands specifically for dealing with components are found on the COMPONENTS menu. All but one of these commands use a two-character command code that starts with the letter *C*. The one exception uses *C* for its second letter.

Creating a Component

To create a component, start up Generic CADD and create a new drawing called DINNER. Set units to INCHES (IN), LIMITS (LS) to 18 inches × 24 inches, and GRID (GS) to 1/2 inch. The other toggles may be set to your own preferences. Use any color(s) that you like.

Draw the Object   First, draw the place setting shown in Figure 8-1. Use the DRAW and EDIT commands that you already know, and make the grid smaller or turn on SNAP TO GRID (SG) as necessary. The plate shown in the figure is 11 inches in diameter, but you need not copy the drawing precisely. If you want, draw your own silverware and dishes instead of the ones in the example.

When making a drawing that will become a component, you can use any commands that you need; there are no restrictions on what can or cannot be part of a component. In fact, you can return to previous drawings and select either the whole drawing or portions of it to become a component, no matter which commands were used to create it.

Once you have completed the drawing, use the CREATE command on the COMPONENTS menu or type **CC** on the keyboard to turn it into a component. This command actually defines a component with a specified name and insertion point that looks exactly like the drawing that you have just made. In fact, the entities that you have just drawn remain unchanged and stay as individual entities in the database, unless you erase them when you have finished creating the component. When you use COMPONENT CREATE, you are asked to perform three tasks, as explained in the following sections.

Select the Entities   The COMPONENT CREATE command first asks you to select the objects that compose the component. You do this by placing

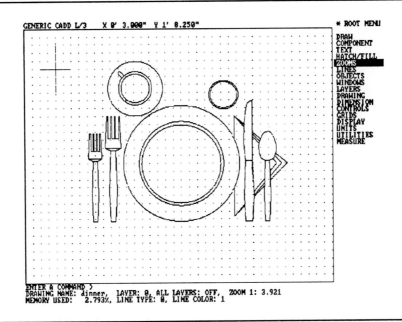

GENERIC CADD L/3   X 0' 3.000" Y 1' 8.250"   * ROOT MENU

DRAW
COMPONENT
TEXT
HATCH/FILL
ZOOMS
LINES
OBJECTS
WINDOWS
LAYERS
DRAWING
DIMENSION
CONTROLS
GRIDS
DISPLAY
UNITS
UTILITIES
MEASURE

ENTER A COMMAND >
DRAWING NAME: dinner, LAYER: 0, ALL LAYERS: OFF,   ZOOM 1: 3.921
MEMORY USED: 2.793%, LINE TYPE: 0, LINE COLOR: 1

Figure 8-1. *A drawing of a place setting*

a window, in the same way you used the WINDOW commands in previous chapters. The window may be started in any corner and dragged to the opposite corner. Only objects whose definition points are all within the window will be selected to become part of the component definition. If EDIT ALL LAYERS is off, only entities on the current layer will be selected; if it is on, any objects visible on the screen are available. Because you must be able to put a window around them, all entities that are to become part of the component definition must be visible on the screen at the time you use the COMPONENT CREATE command. In the case of your DINNER drawing, you can place a window around the entire drawing. Make sure that you surround the entire drawing, as shown in Figure 8-2. If you place your first window corner incorrectly, press ESC and use the CC command again.

Assign a Name Every component definition must be given a name, which can include up to 12 characters. The name should be descriptive. If

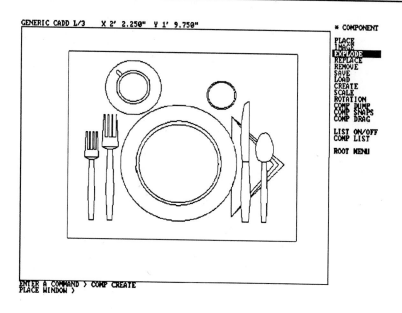

Figure 8-2.   *Placing a window to define a component*

you use many components, you may need to invent some sort of naming system that allows you to keep track of your components easily. Consider using a system that includes only eight characters—the maximum allowed by the operating system for saving individual files—even though Generic CADD allows 12 characters internally.

Component names cannot include spaces, commas, periods, or several other punctuation marks. Dashes and underlines are allowable both in Generic CADD component names and DOS filenames, but you should stay away from asterisks and question marks, to avoid confusion when you want to save your components to disk. For the current drawing, type the name **PLACESET**, and press ENTER. This name works as both a component name and a disk filename, and is relatively descriptive for identifying the component in the future.

Select a Reference Point   Later, when you are ready to place a copy of this component into the drawing, you will need to specify where you want to put it. This will be done by selecting the *reference point* of the component. If you choose a reference point near the lower-right corner of the drawing, the component will always appear to the upper right of the point you select (assuming that you place it with a rotation of zero). If you pick a reference point in the center, the component will always be drawn around this point.

Sometimes you might want to pick a point that is not on the component itself, but in a location that will be easier to select when it comes time to place the component. In the case of PLACESET, for example, it might be wise to place the reference point just below the bottom of the plate. This way, whenever you use PLACESET, you can choose a point on the edge of the table, and the component will always be placed the same distance from the edge. Figure 8-3 shows the selection of a reference point in this location.

What Really Happened?

If you have created the component successfully, you will see no message, just the "ENTER A COMMAND >" prompt and the Status Lines if

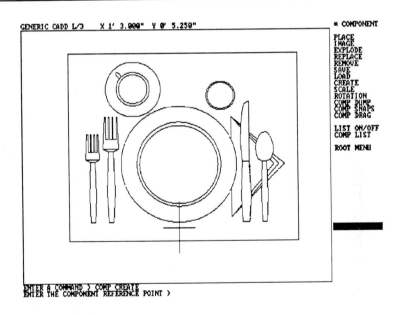

Figure 8-3.   *Selecting a reference point*

STATUS LINES (SL) is turned on. If you made a mistake, however, you will see a prompt such as "COMPONENT ALREADY EXISTS." Remember, each component in the drawing must have a unique name. You may use the same name for different components in separate drawings, but watch out for potential conflicts if you plan to move components around between drawings.

When you created the PLACESET component, the entities that you surrounded with the window were copied into another area of memory, where they were combined with the name of the component and the location of the reference point to form a *definition* for this component. At the present time, these entities occur twice in the drawing—once in their original form on the screen, and once in the computer memory only as part of the component definition.

It is very important to notice that if you never *place* the component into the drawing, the definition is removed when the drawing is saved as a file. Generic CADD only saves definitions of components that are actually used in the drawing. This is a very convenient way of making sure that old components, which are no longer being used, are not clogging up memory or disk space. However, this process can lead to big trouble if you are not aware of it. If you want to make sure that the component that you have just created will be saved, make sure that you either *place* one in the drawing or *save* the component individually as a component file. See "Placing Your First Component" later in this chapter.

The first clue that your component actually exists comes from the Component List, accessible from the COMP LIST command on the COMPONENTS menu. When you select this command, you get a list of components that are currently defined in the drawing. These components were already in the drawing when you loaded it, have been defined since you started the drawing session, or have been loaded specifically for use in this drawing. This command must be called from the video menu; it has no two-character command.

If more components exist than will fit in the menu area, you can select the PAGE UP and PAGE DOWN items at the bottom of the menu or press the PGUP and PGDN keys on the keyboard to move through the list of component names. As you will see, the Component List can be used for placing components, as well as checking to see which components are in the drawing. In some applications, you may not want the Component List to appear when you press the PGUP and PGDN keys to move through the rest of the video menu. In these cases, the display of the Component List may be toggled off with the CO keyboard command or by selecting LIST

ON/OFF from the COMPONENTS menu. Selecting the same command again reactivates the Component List.

Setting the Table

To make use of the PLACESET component, draw a table on which you can place these dishes and silverware. Before drawing the table, erase the drawing that was used to create the component definition with the WINDOW ERASE (WE) command. You do not need this drawing anymore, as it is now stored in memory as a component definition. Do not use the DRAWING ERASE (DX) command, as it erases not only what you see on the screen but also the area of memory where the definitions are stored.

Figure 8-4 shows a drawing of a table that might be used to place the new component. Your table need not be an exact duplicate of the one shown; just make sure that it is large enough for some place settings to fit on it.

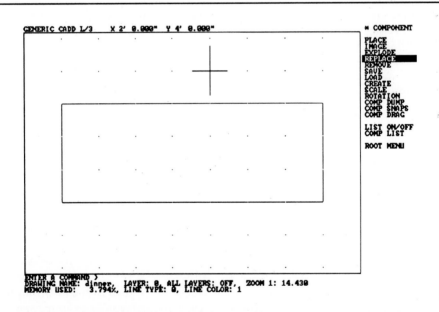

Figure 8-4. *A table ready to be set*

Placing Your First Component   There are two different ways to place a component into the drawing. The first is using the PLACE command from the COMPONENTS menu or typing **CP** on the keyboard. This command asks you to type the name of the component and then to specify the location where you want to place the component. The other method, using the Component List, works much the same way, except that you select the name of the component from the video menu instead of typing it. When you pick a component name from the Component List on the video menu by using the second button on the pointing device, you automatically issue a PLACE command, with the name of the component already typed for you.

From this point on, the two methods are the same. You are prompted to place the component reference point. In Level 3, a ghosted image of the component is dragged along with your cursor to aid in placing the component, as shown in Figure 8-5. This ghosted image helps you to see the size of your component and the direction it is facing. The reference point is represented by a small indicator that resembles a Standard Point at the location of the cursor.

If you are using Level 3 and do not see the ghosted image of the component as you are trying to place it, check the following items.

1. Make sure that COMPONENT DRAG (CG) is turned on. This toggle enables and disables the dragging of components during placement. Press ESC to cancel the COMPONENT PLACE command and select COMP DRAG from the COMPONENTS menu or type **CG** on the keyboard. You will get a message that tells you whether you have just turned it on or off. Make sure that it is on and try placing the component again. (For very complicated components, the ghosted image is often more trouble than it is worth, and in these cases you might want to turn COMPONENT DRAG off.)

2. Be certain that the component is not larger than the screen. If it is larger, you may need to ZOOM BACK (ZB) a few times until there is enough room for your component. (This should not happen with PLACESET, because if the table fits on the screen, so should the place setting.)

3. Check the primitives of the component. Components composed entirely of Curves, True Ellipses, and perfectly horizontal Lines cannot be displayed with a ghosted image, though you should still see the small point-like cursor at the component reference point.

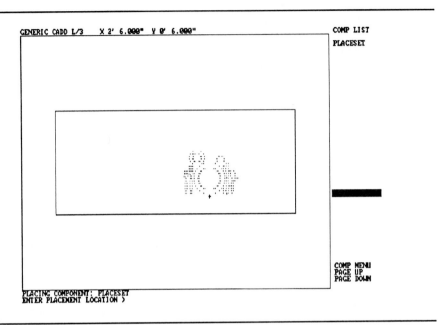

Figure 8-5. *Dragging PLACESET into place*

In the case of PLACESET, drag the component to a location at the edge of the table, as shown in Figure 8-6. Note that because of the location of the reference point, you can select a point on the table edge to place the component. When you get the component where you want it, press the first pointing device button to place it. It should appear in full lines rather than as a ghosted image as soon as you select the location. If DISPLAY REFERENCE POINTS is turned on, a reference point will appear at the reference point of the components.

Changing the Rotation The first component is placed in exactly the same size and facing in the same direction as when you first drew it because the component placement parameters, SCALE (CZ) and ROTATION (CR), were set at their default values of 1 and 0, respectively. A SCALE of 1 means the same size as the original, which is fine for now, because you want all of your place settings to be the same size.

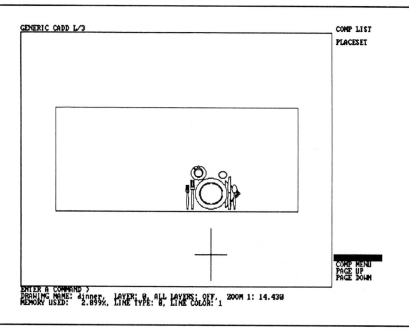

Figure 8-6. *The first PLACESET placed on the table*

If you want a component to face in a different direction (in this case facing toward the bottom of the screen), you must change the COMPONENT ROTATION before you place the component. This is done by selecting the ROTATION command on the COMPONENTS menu, or by typing **CR** on the keyboard. When you select this command, you are asked to type a number. To position a PLACESET on the right end of the table, select a rotation of 90 degrees by typing **90**. This rotation will apply to all components placed until you either change the COMPONENT ROTATION or define a new component. Whenever you define a new component with the COMPONENT CREATE (CC) command, both the ROTATION and SCALE parameters are set to their default values.

After changing the rotation, use the COMPONENT PLACE command to place another PLACESET component, or select it from the Component List. As you drag it on the screen, notice that it is dragged in its rotated position. This way you can tell before you place it whether you rotated it

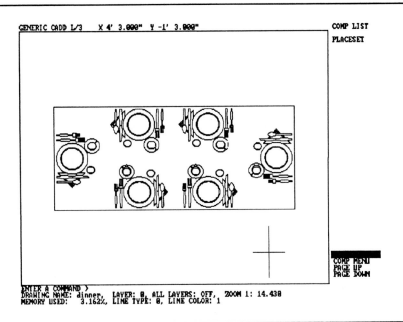

GENERIC CADD L/3   X 4' 3.000" Y -1' 3.000"   COMP LIST
                                                                 PLACESET

                                                                 COMP MENU
                                                                 PAGE UP
                                                                 PAGE DOWN

ENTER A COMMAND >
DRAWING NAME: dinner,   LAYER: 0, ALL LAYERS: OFF,   ZOOM 1: 14.438
MEMORY USED: 3.162%, LINE TYPE: 0, LINE COLOR: 1

Figure 8-7.   *The fully set table*

in the right direction or not. If not, press ESC, change the rotation, and try placing it again. After placing the rotated component at the end of the table, continue placing components until you have set the entire table, changing the rotation whenever necessary, according to Figure 8-7. You can get very accurate component placements if the GRID SIZE (GS) is set to the right value and you use SNAP TO GRID (SG). For the fully set table shown in the sample drawing a GRID SIZE of 3 was used.

The allowable values for a rotation are shown in the prompt. Components can be rotated in either positive (counterclockwise) or negative (clockwise) directions, up to 360 degrees either way. A rotation of – 90 is 1/4 turn clockwise and yields the same result as a 3/4 turn counterclockwise, or 270 degrees. If you type a number outside of the allowable range, you will not be allowed to continue. Illegal values will be accepted, but the *only* way to get out of the command at this point is to type a valid number. ESC is of no help, nor is ENTER or even CTRL-C. Note that rotation can be specified in fractions of degrees, such as 12.5 or – 5.75, as well as whole numbers.

Changing the Size   Like ROTATION, the SCALE parameter is set before a component is placed, and remains in effect for all components placed until the scale is changed or a new component is defined. The COMPONENT SCALE command actually consists of two separate parameters that control the horizontal or X scale and the vertical or Y scale of components that are placed into a drawing.

If you want to place a smaller version of the PLACESET component, you first need to change the COMPONENT SCALE parameters. To see how this works, select SCALE from the COMPONENTS menu. You are first asked for the X scale factor. Values larger than 1 create component placements larger than their original size; values smaller than 1 create smaller component placements.

To place components at half their original size, select a value of .5, and press ENTER. Next, you are asked for the Y scale factor, and the X scale factor that you just specified is shown as the default. (Generic CADD assumes that in most cases you want to enlarge or reduce your components equally in X and Y directions, so it gives you the value of X for the Y default.) To accept this default condition, simply press ENTER. If you want to scale your components differently in Y than in X, type another value before pressing ENTER. For illustrative purposes, just press ENTER now without typing a second value.

All values are allowable for scale factors, including negative numbers. A setting of – 1 for X and 1 for Y, for example, produces a mirror-image place setting, with all objects in the component on the opposite side from where they are currently. This is an easy way to produce a large number of variations from a single component by combining scale and rotation parameters.

After you have set the new smaller scale factors, place another PLACESET to see the result. The ghosted image that appears as you drag the component into place should be smaller than before. The ghosted image always reflects the current SCALE and ROTATION settings. Figure 8-8 shows an extra PLACESET inserted at the smaller size.

It is important to understand that only the component *placements* are being rotated and scaled as they are placed. Although the current values for COMPONENT ROTATION and COMPONENT SCALE are stored as part of the component placement entity in the database, no change whatsoever is made to the original *component definition* when these values

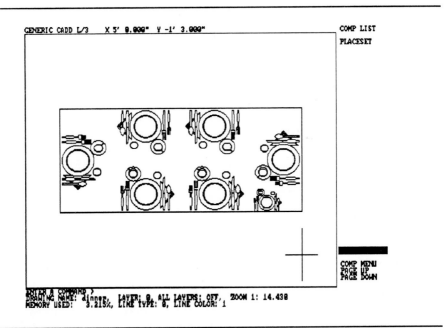

GENERIC CADD L/3   X 5' 0.000"   Y -1' 3.000"   COMP LIST
                                                                     PLACESET

                                                                     COMP MENU
                                                                     PAGE UP
                                                                     PAGE DOWN

ENTER A COMMAND)
DRAWING NAME: dinner, LAYER: 0, ALL LAYERS: OFF, ZOOM 1: 14.438
MEMORY USED: 3.215%, LINE TYPE: 0, LINE COLOR: 1

Figure 8-8.   *A half-sized PLACESET added to the table*

are changed. The original component is still exactly the same size and facing in the same direction as when you first drew it. This common reference is required to maintain the integrity and accuracy of the drawing. You can always get a component *exactly* like the one that you first drew by setting SCALE to 1 and ROTATION to 0.

A Circle Is a Circle, and an Arc Is an Arc   You may be surprised if you try to place the PLACESET component with different X and Y scale factors. In some cases, values of 2 for X and 1 for Y, for example, do produce a component that is twice as wide (but still the same height) as when you first drew it, but certain primitives do not "squash" or "stretch" due to the way that entities are stored in Generic CADD.

Because entities are always defined by their basic geometric properties and a number of definition points, their shapes always remain the same.

When you scale a component made of Lines, for instance, it does not matter how you "push" or "pull" on it; the Lines remain the same basic shape. If you stretch a square, it becomes a rectangle. If you rotate it, it becomes a diamond. In either case, the Lines themselves stay the same shape; they just get longer, shorter, or rotate.

You might think that if you stretch a Circle, you should get an ellipse. However, you will see that if you place a PLACESET with a scale factor of 2 for X and 1 for Y, this is not true: The Circles that represent the plate, saucer, and glass may get larger, or they may not; some may even get larger and some may stay the same size. Regardless, they always remain *round*—the basic geometric property of a Circle.

When you stretch or squash a CADD drawing or component, what you are really doing is pushing the definition points closer together or farther apart, and then reconstructing the drawing. Under these rules, you cannot make an Ellipse out of a Circle no matter how hard you try. If you had drawn the plate using a series of Curves, so that many definition points were located around the perimeter, you *could* stretch it, because as the points were pulled apart the shape of the Curve would change. That is the basic geometric nature of a Curve. In fact, this is such an important distinction that Generic Software sells a program as part of its utilities package for changing Circles and Arcs to Curves in case this is a problem for you.

But why do some Circles become larger and others stay the same size when the scale factor is 2 for X and 1 for Y? This has to do with the location of the definition point on the perimeter of the circle. If this definition point is to the right or left of the center, the point will be moved farther from the center and the circle will expand when the component is placed. If the point is directly above or below the center, however, the circle will stay exactly the same size, as the distance between the center and the point on the circle will stay the same. Points not directly above, below, right, or left of center will cause proportionate expansion of the circle when the component is placed with these scale factors.

The same basic facts are true for Arcs. Because Arcs are really circle segments, they do not change their shape to become ellipse segments when a component is stretched or squashed. How their size changes depends on the location of their definition points. Because Construction Ellipses are made of Arcs facing in four different directions, they will be subject to somewhat bizarre distortions if they are part of components that are placed with unequal X and Y scale factors.

Real Objects Versus Symbols

The place setting that you have drawn can be considered a *real* object, because it is a true scale representation of a real object. Later, you will be able to choose to print or plot it at any scale. Some objects that appear in drawings, however, do not represent real objects. These objects can be considered *symbols*. These include descriptive text or notes, drawing symbols such as North arrows, detail bugs, grid bubbles, dimension lines, arrows, text, and so on.

How big are these symbols, really? Most of the time, we think of the size of these symbols in relation to the paper on which they will be printed. With CAD, however, we must consider the size of these symbols relative to the real world objects with which they coexist. For example, if you want to include in your drawing a number to refer to a particular note or detail, you might think of drawing a 1/2-inch diameter circle with a 1/8-inch high letter in the middle of it. However, if you are drawing a house plan, and printing it at 1/4" = 1', a 1/2-inch circle will show up as little more than a dot. Conversely, if you are drawing an electrical circuit diagram to be printed at several times actual size, the 1/2-inch circle might be larger than the entire drawing.

One way to overcome this problem is to think of the symbols as part of the "real" object that you are drawing. In the house plan example, think of the circle as if it were painted on the floor, with a two-foot diameter. When the drawing is printed, this two-foot diameter circle will be scaled down to a very visible 1/2 inch. In the circuit drawing the circle might be drawn with a 1/8-inch diameter if the drawing is to be printed at four times its actual size.

The scale factors for the placement of components (and, as you will see later in this chapter, text) must be adjusted differently for symbols than for real objects. The general rule is to use actual dimensions for real objects, and to scale text or drawing symbology. This will become more obvious as you begin to work with text following this section on components.

One Component, One Entity, One Reference Point

If you try to use any of the OBJECT editing commands on a component, you will notice that the component is treated as one object. In PLACESET, for instance, you cannot erase a single plate without also erasing the silverware and other items in the component. The whole component placement is considered one entity. As noted previously, the only point that you need to capture for any of the WINDOW commands is the component's reference point. This makes components easy to work with when you need to select the entire object. You need not select every object when you want to move, copy, or otherwise edit a component.

Exploding a Component　　Sometimes, however, you may need to work with the individual entities that make up the component. Perhaps you need to replace the dinner knife on one of the guest's place settings with a steak knife. In this case, you need to edit a single component placement, but leave the others the same. You can select the EXPLODE command from the COMPONENT menu or type **CE** on the keyboard to replace any component placement with the entities that compose it.

When you select this command, a prompt asks you to point to the reference point of the component that you want to explode. When you select this point, the component is replaced with entities that can be edited individually. That particular component now acts exactly as if you drew it from scratch, without the COMPONENT PLACE command. In fact, from the point of view of Generic CADD, the component that you have just exploded is no longer a component placement. The placement entity is removed from the database and replaced with simple entities, which means that any commands that work specifically on components will no longer work on this part of the drawing. If the component contains other components, which is possible, the second level of components cannot be exploded unless you use the EXPLODE command on it as well.

When you explode components you also need to keep in mind their layer. The component placement is on the layer that is current when you place the component. However, the simple entities inside the component definition are located on the layers that were active when they were created. When the component is unexploded, the entire component is considered to be on one layer. When it is exploded, the individual entities return to the layers where they originated. If you explode a component and it vanishes from the screen, you are probably experiencing this phenomenon. Suppose that you define a component on layer 1, and then place it on layer 2. Meanwhile, you turn off layer 1 with LAYER HIDE (YH). You will still see the component on layer 2 as long as it is actually a component. If you explode it, it will return to layer 1, which is turned off, and it will disappear. If you turn layer 1 back on with LAYER DISPLAY (YD), you will see the entities again.

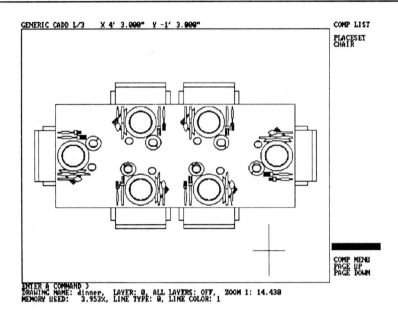

Figure 8-9. The table with chairs added

Placing Exploded Components   Most of the time, you will want components to be stored in the database as components, to save space and allow global component editing. However, if you find that you are placing components and then exploding them consistently, you may want to place them already exploded. This can be done using the IMAGE toggle on the COMPONENT menu, by typing two-character code CI on the keyboard.

When COMPONENT IMAGE is turned on, all components will be inserted in the drawing as if they had been exploded. In this mode, components are really just a quick way to copy entities in convenient groups. The inserted entities are not a component placement at all, but are in fact made up of copies of the simple entities that make up the original component definition. You can still use different scales and rotations, subject to the same limitations as true components.

Keep in mind that, as with components that you explode, components placed with IMAGE turned on are not treated as components at all by Generic CADD, and any editing command must now deal with each entity individually. If there are components inside the component definition, they will still be placed as true components.

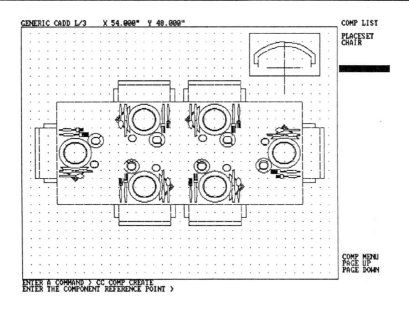

Figure 8-10. *Creating a new component, CHAIR2*

Manipulating Component Definitions

As noted earlier, component placements can be edited as individual entities with the OBJECT editing commands, or they can be edited with WINDOW commands if the component's reference point is captured in a window. Component placements are also subject to any of the LAYER commands that act on the layers on which they are placed. The definitions themselves, however, are not affected by these commands. Several commands on the COMPONENTS menu deal specifically with component definitions, one at a time or globally.

Replacing One Definition With Another One of the advantages of components is that their definitions can be swapped, allowing you to make global changes in your drawing to update it with new information or to try different ideas. Figure 8-9 shows the PLACESET table with six chairs that were added by creating a component called "CHAIR" placed at four different rotations. Suppose that you decide to use a different style chair. You can create a new component, as shown in Figure 8-10. This new component

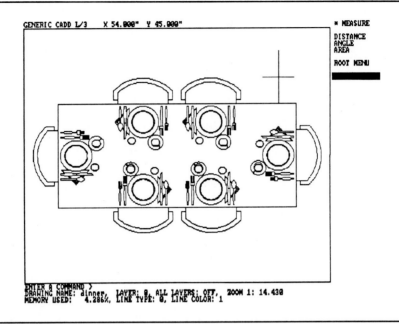

GENERIC CADD L/3   X 54.000"   Y 45.000"

* MEASURE

DISTANCE
ANGLE
AREA

ROOT MENU

ENTER A COMMAND >
DRAWING NAME: dinner,   LAYER: 0, ALL LAYERS: OFF,   ZOOM 1: 14.438
MEMORY USED: 4.286%, LINE TYPE: 0, LINE COLOR: 1

Figure 8-11.   *The table with new chairs*

can be created in a number of steps. First, place a CHAIR at a scale of 1 and a rotation of 0 and explode it. It is easiest if you place it on the GRID so that you can locate the former reference point easier. Then, edit the exploded chair to form the new round-back design. Once the new drawing is ready, use COMPONENT CREATE (CC) again to create a new component called CHAIR2. Make sure that you select the same reference point that you did when you made CHAIR. Finally, once the new component has been created, erase the temporary drawing of the new chair.

To swap chairs, use the REPLACE command on the COMPONENTS menu or type **CN** on the keyboard. You are prompted for the name of the component that you want replaced, CHAIR, and the name of the replacing component, CHAIR2. When you have supplied this information, CHAIR will be replaced with CHAIR2 in every placement. Rotation and scale will remain the same. Figure 8-11 shows the set table with the new chairs.

Note that the exploded components are not replaced, because, as discussed previously, these are no longer really components. The same is true for components that have been placed with COMPONENT IMAGE turned on. You can substitute the original chairs with another COMPONENT REPLACE (CN), specifying CHAIR2 as the component to replace and CHAIR as the replacing component.

Eliminating Components   Occasionally, you may need to remove components from the database. If you CREATE a component and never PLACE it, the definition will be lost. With your DINNER drawing, if you were to save the drawing after replacing CHAIR with CHAIR2 and then quit, the definition of CHAIR would be eliminated.

If you want to remove a component definition from the drawing without quitting, either to remove an unused component from the Component List or to erase all of the placements of a certain component, you may use the REMOVE command from the COMPONENT menu, or type **CX** on the keyboard. When you select this command, you are asked for a component name. Both the component definition and all placements (if any) of the specified component are eliminated from the drawing. A warning prompt verifies that you really want to do this.

If you want to remove a component from the current drawing but still be able to use it in another drawing, use the COMPONENT SAVE (CS) or COMPONENT DUMP (CD) commands to create a component file on a disk before using the COMPONENT REMOVE command (see Chapter 12).

Snapping Onto Internal Definition Points   Component placements have only one definition point, which is the reference point of the component. Therefore, the SNAP TO NEAREST POINT command normally can snap to only one point. The rest of the definition points are "hidden" in the definition. In Levels 2 and 3, however, the COMP SNAPS command, located on the COMPONENTS menu or accessed by typing **GC** on the keyboard, allows you to snap onto the definition points of the entities that make up the component definition.

The COMP SNAPS command is a toggle, so that it is either on or off. You don't have to select it every time you want to snap onto internal definition points. The abbreviation GC stands for "Ghost Components," meaning that the component placement acts as if it were made of individual entities *only for the purpose of snapping*. In every other respect, components still act like components whether COMP SNAPS is on or not.

COMP SNAPS is a global command, affecting *all* components and all snap commands. This means that if you have a lot of complicated components in your drawing, snapping will be slowed down noticeably. If you are not trying to snap to definition points in components, you should leave GC turned off and turn it on only when you need it. COMP SNAPS works with the rest of the snaps discussed in Chapter 10 as well as with SNAP TO NEAREST POINT.

Text

In many ways, Text Characters are very similar to Components. A number of placement parameters are set before you place the text, and a PLACE command actually inserts the text into the drawing. Each Text Character is a separate complex entity made up of simple entities that cannot be altered by normal editing commands.

There are more placement parameters for text than for Components, and unlike Components, many of these parameters will probably need to be changed before placing text. Text Characters cannot be exploded, nor can they be replaced one for another. However, numerous special editing commands work only on text, giving you a great deal of control over the text in your drawing. Most of the two-character TEXT commands start with the letter *T*.

Selecting the Type Style

The first parameter you will need to set is FONT. Each version of Generic CADD contains numerous fonts, which are listed in the back of the manual. Additional fonts are also available from Generic Software and from third-party vendors. In addition, you can create your own.

You can select and load a font with the FONT SELECT command on the TEXT menu, or by typing **FS** on the keyboard. When you choose FONT SELECT from the Level 3 TEXT menu, Generic CADD displays a menu of fonts from which you can choose. Otherwise, you are asked to type the name of a font. If the font exists, you will be asked if you want to load it now. Type **Y** to load the font. You might as well do this now; otherwise it will be loaded the first time you try to place a character anyway, and you will have to wait for the font to load. If you never use the FONT SELECT command, the MAIN font is considered the default and is loaded the first time you place a character. Later in this chapter, you will place some text on the DINNER drawing, so select the font you want and load it.

If the font cannot be found, you are asked if this is a new font. Usually, this is not the case unless you are trying to create your own font. If the font exists, but cannot be found, you may need to change the font PATH. In Level 3, this is done with the P3 command, and in Level 2 with GP. The default paths can also be changed in the CONFIG program if you find that you have to change the path every time you try to load a font.

After you have placed text using the current font, you may select and load another font and place characters using the new font. Only the font loaded last may be used, and loading several fonts in succession reduces the amount of space available in memory for your drawing. It is best not to load too many fonts in a single drawing session.

Setting the Text Color

Unlike simple entities, complex entities do not use the current line color. Components use the colors of the entities that make up the definition. Text uses a parameter called TEXT COLOR, selected by COLOR on the TEXT menu or by typing **TK** on the keyboard. If the video menu is on and you have more than one color option, you will see a special menu of color bars from which you can choose. Either use this menu or type a number between 0 and 255. The colors shown on the video menu repeat depending on your video card. All new text that you place will use this color, though it can be changed later with any of the CHANGE editing commands.

Setting the Text Size

The height of text is controlled by the SIZE command on the TEXT menu, or by typing **TZ** on the keyboard. The default value is one unit. Type a value representing the actual height of a typical uppercase letter. Unless you specify otherwise, this will also be the distance from the starting point of one letter to the next. The spacing between lines will be 1 1/4 times the text height. For one-inch-high text, for example, each new line of text is 1.25 inches apart, measured at the base of the text.

Unless you are designing a sign, text is usually considered a symbol, which means that you probably have some idea of how large you want it to be in the final print. If you are planning to print the drawing full size, you can use the actual height of the finished text for the TEXT SIZE. If the drawing will be printed at other than 1 to 1, you should size your text accordingly. For example, if you are working on a floor plan that will be printed at 1/4" = 1', text that you want to print at 1/4" high should be placed with a TEXT SIZE of one foot or 12 inches. Text that you want to print at 1/8" should be placed at 6 inches, and so on.

To add text to the back of your chairs in your DINNER drawing, try setting the TEXT SIZE to 2.5 inches for now. You may want to change it after you have tried placing some text.

Setting the Rotation

The default value for TEXT ROTATION is 0, which means that text will be placed along a horizontal line running from left to right, just like a typewriter. If you want to create text on some other angle (from top to bottom for instance), you can use the ROTATION command on the TEXT menu or type **TR** on the keyboard. Allowable values range from 360 to −360. As with component rotations, values such as − 90 and 270 have the same effect. A value of 90 produces text that runs up the screen from bottom to top, while − 90 or 270 yields text running downward. For the DINNER drawing, start with the TEXT ROTATION at the default value of zero to place the text horizontally on the first chair, and change it as required.

Setting the Width

The width of the Text Characters is the same as the height by default. If you want to make your characters narrower or wider, you can select the ASPECT command from the TEXT menu, or type **TA** on the keyboard. The value of the TEXT ASPECT is a multiplier of the TEXT SIZE. For instance, a TEXT ASPECT of 0.5 produces text that is half as wide as it is tall. A TEXT ASPECT of 2 produces text that is twice as wide as it is tall.

Although TEXT ASPECT controls the width of text, it does it only by association with the TEXT SIZE. The value of the TEXT ASPECT should not be thought of as the real width of the text, unless the TEXT SIZE is one. Allowable values range from 0.1 to 10, though reasonable values are usually between 0.5 and 2, unless you want some very unusual-looking characters. For the first test, leave TA set at the default of 1.

Setting the Slant

You can create an italic typeface out of any font by specifying a SLANT from the TEXT menu, also activated by typing **TS** on the keyboard. The TEXT SLANT is specified in degrees, and causes the characters to lean to the left or the right. Values between – 45 and + 45 degrees are valid, with negative values causing a lean to the left and positive values a lean to the right. The slant factor is applied to the characters before the TEXT ASPECT, so that if TA is less than one, the slant will appear to be less than what you have specified. Keep in mind that the characters are slanted first, and then widened or narrowed. Conversely, if the TEXT ASPECT is greater than one, the final slant will end up as more than the specified value. For the DINNER drawing example, set the SLANT at whatever you think will look good.

Placing the Text

After setting all the placement parameters, you can place text with the PLACE command from the TEXT menu or by typing **TP** on the keyboard. For a test, try placing some names on the chairs in the DINNER drawing.

Before you start typing, the TEXT PLACE command asks you to select the starting point—where the lower-left corner of the first character will be placed. Select a point on the screen, as shown in Figure 8-12. Because you should allow enough room for the text to appear, select a point at least one inch (the current TEXT SIZE) away from the table. After the starting point has been selected, a new type of cursor, the text cursor, will appear and you can start typing.

Begin by typing the word **MOM**. Each character appears in the preset font, color, size, aspect, rotation, and slant, at the location of the text cursor, as you type it. If you type an incorrect character, press BACKSPACE to remove it, and then type the correct character. When you get to the end of

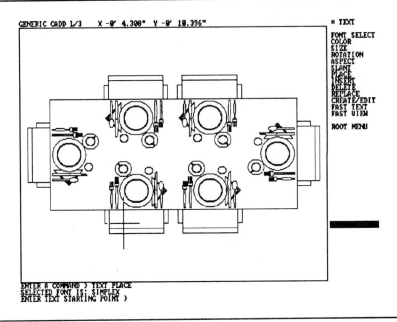

GENERIC CADD L/3   X -0' 4.300"   Y -0' 10.396"

* TEXT

FONT SELECT
COLOR
SIZE
ROTATION
ASPECT
SLANT
PLACE
INSERT
DELETE
REPLACE
CREATE/EDIT
FAST TEXT
FAST VIEW

ROOT MENU

ENTER A COMMAND > TEXT PLACE
SELECTED FONT IS: SIMPLEX
ENTER TEXT STARTING POINT >

Figure 8-12.   *Selecting a text starting point*

the text that you want to place, press ESC to end the TEXT PLACE
command. To place more text in another location, use another TEXT
PLACE (TP) command, and repeat the same procedure. To place some of
the names on the rest of the chairs, you will need to change the TEXT
ROTATION and TEXT ASPECT before placing the text. Figure 8-13 shows
text placed at different rotations and different aspects around the table.

More Than One Line   It is possible to type more than one line of text with
a single TEXT PLACE command. Simply press ENTER instead of ESC at the
end of a line of text, and the text cursor will move down one line (125% of
the text size), and back to a point directly below the first character of the
previous line. At this point you can simply continue typing. You can add
as many lines of text with one command as you like. If you would like to
skip a line, simply press ENTER twice at the end of a line of text.

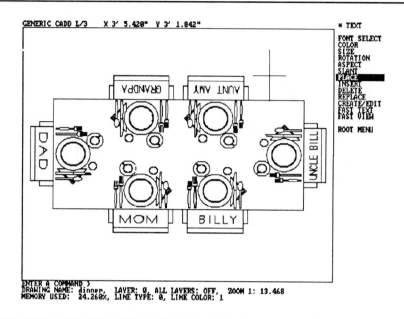

Figure 8-13.   *Text placed at various rotations and aspects*

Editing As You Type   As you are typing, you may notice a mistake that you made on a previous line. Rather than waiting until you have finished placing text and using an ERASE command to insert new text, Generic CADD allows you to do a limited amount of text editing as you go. Simply press the UP ARROW key on the numeric keypad or cursor control pad, and the text cursor will move up one line of text. The RIGHT, LEFT, and DOWN ARROW keys work in much the same way. Position your text cursor to the right of the error, and press BACKSPACE. The offending character will be removed. Another character is removed each time you press BACKSPACE. Once you have made the necessary deletion, simply type the new text into the space you have just cleared. If the error requires that you add characters to the line, you may have to move to the end of the line and BACKSPACE to the point of the error. When you have finished editing, use the arrow keys to return the cursor to the point where you left off typing and continue until you are done. When your last line of text is complete, press ESC.

Editing Text That Is Already Placed   Periodically you will need to correct or change text that has already been placed, and you are no longer in the TEXT PLACE command. Several commands allow you to replace, insert, and delete characters. While Generic CADD would hardly pass for a word processor, these editing commands do provide a great deal of control over the text in your drawings.

To replace one or more characters of existing text, use the REPLACE command on the TEXT menu, or type **TX** on the keyboard. You are asked to select the character to be replaced. Place the cursor near the lower-left corner of the character and use the SNAP TO NEAREST POINT option by typing **NP** on the keyboard or pressing the third button on the pointing device. Once the character has been selected, you can type a character to replace the existing one. You can replace a number of characters this way. Press ESC when you have finished. If you replace all the characters on a line, the command will be ended automatically.

Another useful editing method, particularly when you want to add text to an existing line, is the TEXT PLACE command. When asked for the starting point, snap onto the last character in the line. Press the RIGHT ARROW key once to move one space to right of the last character, and then BACKSPACE until you have deleted all the characters you want to replace. Now you can type as many new characters as you want without exiting the command.

To insert a single character between two existing characters, use the INSERT command on the TEXT menu, or type **TI** on the keyboard. When you select a location, preferably by snapping onto an existing character, all characters to the right (including the character selected) move one space to the right. You are then asked to insert the character. If you wish to insert more than one character, repeat the command by pressing SPACEBAR.

To delete a single character in the middle of a line of existing text, use the DELETE command from the TEXT menu, or type **TD** on the keyboard. Select a character by snapping onto it, and it will be removed. All characters on the same line to the right of the removed character slide one character to the left to fill the gap. To delete more than one character, simply repeat the command by pressing SPACEBAR, and pick another character to be deleted.

Note that in order to use any of the techniques for inserting or replacing text characters, the same font must be active as when the text was originally placed. Characters can only be inserted, replaced, or placed in the currently selected font.

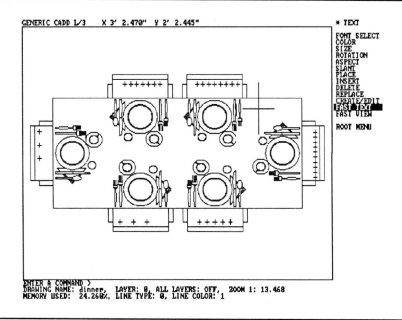

Figure 8-14. *Drawing redrawn with FAST TEXT turned on*

Large Amounts of Text   If you need to place large amounts of text, utility programs are available from both Generic Software and third-party vendors to import ASCII files into Generic CADD, so that you can use your word processor to create and edit the text before it is placed into your drawings.

Controlling Text Display

Text characters, relatively complicated entities, tend to display slowly on the screen, especially if there are many of them. If you use a great deal of text in your drawings, you may wish to speed up the display when you don't need to read the text. This is accomplished by using the FAST TEXT command, a toggle on the TEXT menu that can also be activated by typing **TF** on the keyboard. When FAST TEXT is off, the default condition, text displays normally, as you have seen. When FAST TEXT is turned on, text

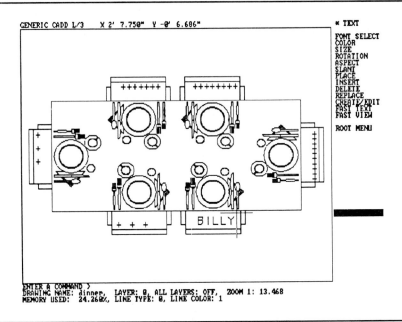

Figure 8-15.   *Using TEXT VIEW to "peek" at some text*

is replaced with STANDARD POINTS, one for each character, as shown in Figure 8-14. As the main purpose of the command is to save time, text is not redrawn immediately when you select it. Instead, the new status of FAST TEXT is considered the next time that the screen is redrawn when you use any of the ZOOM commands. If the text disappears entirely, it is probably because DISPLAY STANDARD POINTS (PS) is turned off. If you turn it on and execute REDRAW (RD), you should see the text as points. If more points seem to be displayed than the text characters they are supposed to represent, remember that spaces are also considered text characters; although they simply appear as blank spaces when FAST TEXT is off, they show up as standard points when FAST TEXT is on.

When you need to "peek" at a particular passage of text but do not want to turn on all the text, you can issue the TEXT VIEW command on the TEXT menu, or type **TV** on the keyboard. When you select this command, you are asked to place a window. Put the window around the standard points that represent the text that you want to see. The characters within the window will become visible again, as shown in Figure 8-15. This is a temporary condition, and the characters will revert to standard points on the next screen redraw.

Although text can be edited with the INSERT, REPLACE, and DELETE commands while FAST TEXT is on, the display will not act properly, even if you use TEXT VIEW first. If you want to edit text, it is best to turn off FAST TEXT first and then REDRAW (RD) the screen. The TEXT PLACE command always places visible text, even when FAST TEXT is on, so placing text in this manner presents no display problems because FAST TEXT is turned off automatically. After all, in many cases the only time that you actually need to see the text is while you are placing it.

Creating Your Own Fonts

The TEXT CREATE/EDIT command may be used for creating your own fonts, or for editing characters of existing fonts. If you intend to create your own font, make sure that you have used FONT SELECT to give the new font a name. If you are going to edit an existing font, make sure that you have a backup copy before you start.

When you use the CREATE/EDIT command from the TEXT menu, or type **TC** on the keyboard, you are asked for the character that you want to create or edit. Press the desired key. If you want an uppercase letter, make sure you have on CAPS LOCK or press SHIFT when you type the letter. All upper- and lowercase letters, numbers, and punctuation marks on the PC keyboard are available for creating or editing fonts.

After you have selected the character to be created or edited, a box appears in the lower-left corner of the screen as shown in Figure 8-16. If you are editing an existing font, the character that you have selected appears in the box. If you are creating a new font, the box will be empty. The box, one inch tall and one inch wide, is only used for reference when creating or editing characters; it is not considered part of the characters.

You may draw or edit characters using any simple entities and any of the OBJECT editing commands. Certain other commands may work, as well. However, you may not place any complex objects in the text character. Though the text character does not have to be entirely within the box, you should know how text placement works to ensure proper spacing for your font. Generally, you should place your characters in the left portion of the box, leaving room on the right for character spacing. Make uppercase characters the full height of the box. The lower-left corner of the box becomes the reference point for the text character, and the next character will be placed at the lower-right corner of the box. The fonts supplied with

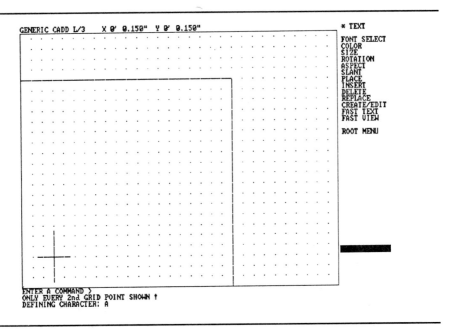

Figure 8-16.   *The one-inch-square text creation box*

Generic CADD are designed to use the first 3/4 inch, leaving the 1/4 inch farthest to the right for character spacing, and this seems to work well. Figure 8-17 shows a typical text character definition.

Certain lowercase letters, such as *g, j, p, q,* and *y* may actually need to extend below the bottom of the box. Use the PAN (PA) command on the ZOOMS menu to move the box to the middle of the screen. Very wide characters such as *W* and *M* may need to be wider than the imaginary 3/4-inch area. Of course, if you use more than 3/4 inch, you will get less space. Depending on the type of font you are creating, you may have to compromise to create the best characters within the available space. For best spacing, try to center the characters in the 3/4-inch area even if they extend a little beyond this.

When you have completed the character, select the CREATE/EDIT command or type **TC** again. You are asked if you want to save the font. If you have finished editing characters, type **Y** to save the new or edited font. If you want to edit more characters, you might not want to save every time you finish one. If you try to use undefined characters, you will see a

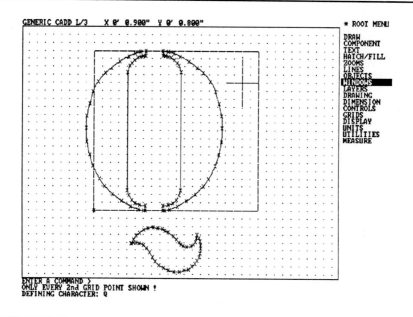

Figure 8-17. *A typical text character definition*

message that the character is not defined. You do not have to define the entire font in one drawing session, as the font file is updated every time you elect to save. If you want to return and add more characters to a partially completed font, use FONT SELECT to select and load the font, and then use TEXT CREATE/EDIT to add or edit the characters.

Notice that when you return to the normal drawing mode after leaving TEXT CREATE/EDIT, several drawing parameters have been changed. TEXT CREATE/EDIT changes the GRID SIZE, the status of SNAP TO GRID, and the ZOOM. You must change these manually when you return to normal mode.

Each of the 94 characters on the computer keyboard must be drawn individually if you are using TEXT CREATE/EDIT. If you are creating a complicated font, you may find this limiting. However, utility programs available from Generic Software and from third-party software developers speed up the process by allowing you to turn normal drawing into fonts, giving you the ability to COPY details from one character to another, and to put all of the characters side by side before you turn them into actual font characters.

Another Method There is a command on the WINDOWS menu for creating text characters as well. Again, you must have a font currently selected, preferably a *new* font. Draw your new characters, making them one inch tall. You can use any simple entities and any combination of editing commands. You can even copy one character to another location on your drawing and edit it to become another character. With this method, you can draw your characters and preview them on the screen before you make them into actual text characters. If you attempt to use hatches, fills, unexploded components, or actual placed text characters in your character drawings, these will be ignored when the character is defined.

After you have drawn characters that you want to add to the font, use the TEXT command on the WINDOWS menu, or type **WT** on the keyboard. You will be asked to place a window. Put a window around the drawing of the text character that you are trying to define, making sure that you get the entire character in the window. Once you have specified the window, you will be asked which character you want to define. If you are working on an uppercase letter, be sure to press SHIFT. If the character is already defined, you will be asked if you want to redefine it.

Finally, you will be asked for the lower-left corner of the character. This point will become the insertion point or reference point for the character, in the same way that the lower-left corner of the reference box in TEXT CREATE is used. Figure 8-18 illustrates the use of the WINDOW TEXT command.

When creating text characters using this method, be sure that the base height of the characters is 1 inch, and that your characters are not more than 1 inch wide. In fact, they should be a little narrower, so that there will be space between characters. Characters created in this way can have descenders or ascenders, as long as you make sure to capture these in the window, and place the lower-left corner at the correct point. Don't forget to make a space, by windowing a blank portion of the screen.

Hatches and Fills

Hatches and Fills, the two types of complex entities created on the fly, are used to fill a specified area with a selected pattern or solid color. The

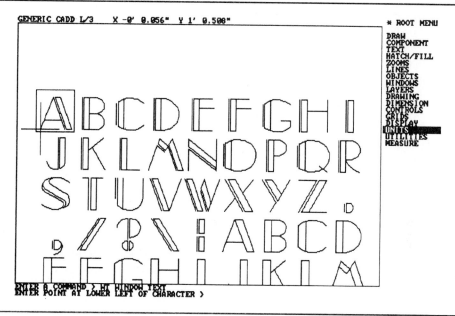

Figure 8-18. *Using WINDOW TEXT to define a character*

commands for working with Hatches and Fills, located on the
HATCH/FILL menu, are active only in Level 3 or Version 3.0 with Drafting
Enhancements-2. Like the other complex entities, Hatches and Fills are
created by specifying a number of placement parameters and then using
a placement command that uses these parameters.

The commands that create Hatches and Fills are so similar that fills
might be thought of as a special case of hatches. The pattern used for
hatching is selected from a number of patterns, while the pattern for fills
is simply a solid color. ROTATION and SCALE, two placement parameters
used for Hatches, do not make sense with fills; you cannot discern the angle
or the scale of a solid area of color.

Placement Parameters

Both Hatches and Fills have a COLOR placement parameter: for hatches
it is HATCH COLOR (HK); for fills it is FILL COLOR (FK). Notice that all
of the hatch two-character codes either start or end with *H*, and the fill

codes start or end with *F*. The remaining character is the same for both sets of commands where identical or similar functions are concerned. Both color commands bring up color bars on the video menu if the video menu is active. Colors are numbered from 0 to 255, and work just like any other color-setting commands.

As mentioned above, Hatches have a number of additional parameters. HATCH NAME on the HATCH /FILL menu, or typing **HN** on the keyboard, results in a prompt for the name of the hatch pattern that you want to use. Each hatch pattern, represented by a file on your disk with the extension .HCH, is illustrated in the back of the Generic CADD manual. The hatch files must be in the same directory as Generic CADD.

Another way to select the hatch pattern in Level 3 is from the HATCH LIST. When you select this item from the HATCH/FILL menu, you get a list of hatch patterns. Unlike the COMPONENT LIST, this list is "hardwired" into the menu and always appears regardless of where the hatch pattern files are stored. The first menu only shows a partial list, and you can see the rest by selecting LIST CONT... from the first list. Once you select a hatch pattern, choose HATCH/FILL to return to the HATCH/FILL menu. If you select more than one pattern, the last one that you pick will become the current hatch pattern.

The other parameters that differentiate HATCH from FILL, ROTATION and SCALE, apply to the hatch pattern definitions as they are shown in the Generic CADD manual. ROTATION (HR) allows hatches to be placed at an angle other than they were originally created. If you specify 0, which is the default, hatches will appear at the same angle shown in the back of the manual. Allowable rotations are between − 360 and + 360 degrees, and work the same way as Component and Text rotations. A HATCH ROTATION of 90, for instance, turns a hatch pattern on its side.

HATCH SCALE changes the distance between the lines that compose the hatch pattern. Although many of the hatch patterns are defined with one unit of space between lines, this is not true in all cases. Therefore, HATCH SCALE does not translate into HATCH SIZE. The SCALE is a factor that is applied to the size at which the hatch was originally created. These vary, and while in some cases the illustrations in the Generic CADD manual are printed at a HATCH SCALE of 1, others are not, so you will have to experiment a little to determine the spacing of the original definition. A scale factor of 0.5 produces hatches with twice as many lines, and a scale factor of 2 makes the lines twice as far apart.

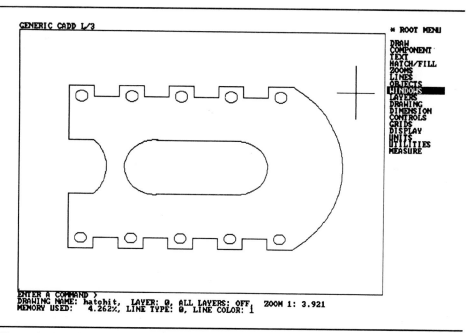

GENERIC CADD L/3

⋈ ROOT MENU

DRAW
COMPONENT
TEXT
HATCH/FILL
ZOOMS
LINES
OBJECTS
WINDOWS
LAYERS
DRAWING
DIMENSION
CONTROLS
GRIDS
DISPLAY
UNITS
UTILITIES
MEASURE

ENTER A COMMAND >
DRAWING NAME: hatchit,   LAYER: 0, ALL LAYERS: OFF,   ZOOM 1: 3.921
MEMORY USED: 4.262%, LINE TYPE: 0, LINE COLOR: 1

Figure 8-19. *An area that can be easily hatched or filled*

Placing Hatches and Fills

The commands for placing Hatch and Fill entities are functionally identical. There are three ways to place each entity type— WINDOW, OBJECT, and FITTED. The HATCH command codes are WH, OH, and FH, while the FILL codes are WF, OF, and FF. Each of these Hatch and Fill placement methods has its own rules.

Window Hatch and Fill   In order to use a WINDOW HATCH (WH) or WINDOW FILL (WF), the area *must* be enclosed by simple entities that connect end to end, as in RECTANGLE (RE), for example. A tic-tac-toe figure is a good example of a figure that you *cannot* hatch or fill with a window. Figure 8-19 shows an example of a figure that can be hatched or filled with a WINDOW.

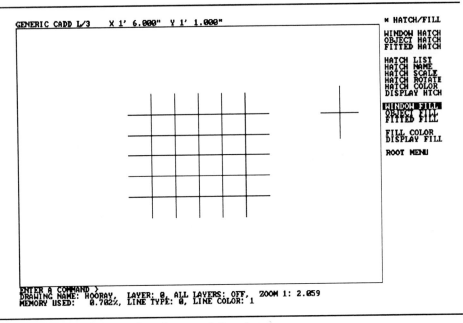

Figure 8-20. *A drawing that does not define closed areas*

The entities that can be used as hatch and fill boundaries include Lines, Arcs, and Circles. Rectangles, regular polygons, and construction ellipses can be hatched and filled, because they are made from these entities. Curves, Bezier Curves, and Ellipses cannot be used as hatch or fill boundaries. Even though Component placements cannot be hatched or filled, a HATCH or FILL may be part of a component definition, and the entities that make up a component placement may be hatched or filled if the component is exploded.

A WINDOW HATCH or FILL will attempt to use *all* of the valid entities that it finds in the window. This can lead to bizarre results if areas are not really enclosed. Figure 8-20 shows a group of lines that do not create enclosed areas. Figure 8-21 shows what would happen if you attempted a WINDOW FILL on this group of lines. On the other hand, the fact that WINDOW HATCH and FILL commands try to hatch all entities in a

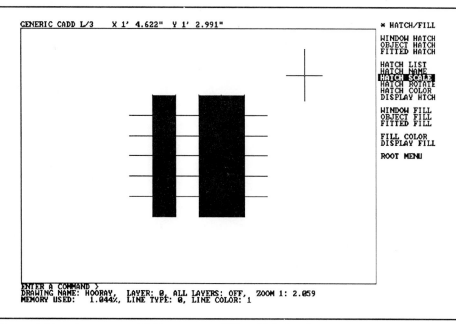

GENERIC CADD L/3   X 1' 4.622"   Y 1' 2.991"   * HATCH/FILL

WINDOW HATCH
OBJECT HATCH
FITTED HATCH

HATCH LIST
HATCH NAME
HATCH SCALE
HATCH ROTATE
HATCH COLOR
DISPLAY HTCH

WINDOW FILL
OBJECT FILL
FITTED FILL

FILL COLOR
DISPLAY FILL

ROOT MENU

ENTER A COMMAND >
DRAWING NAME: HOORAY,   LAYER: 0, ALL LAYERS: OFF,   ZOOM 1: 2.059
MEMORY USED: 1.044%, LINE TYPE: 0, LINE COLOR: 1

Figure 8-21.   *An unsuccessfull attempt at filling ill-defined areas*

window creates opportunities to fill or hatch some pretty unusual shapes which have enclosed entities inside each other, and other unusual configurations. Figure 8-22 shows a complex drawing with several enclosed areas inside each other that has been hatched at a fairly small scale. As you can see, the Hatch and Fill entities *start* when one boundary is encountered, and *stop* when they find another.

Object Hatch and Fill   The OBJECT HATCH (OH) and OBJECT FILL (OF) commands also require completely enclosed areas, but you are not constrained by a window. This technique requires a little more work on your part, but you can be much more selective about what you are hatching.

When you use either the OBJECT HATCH or OBJECT FILL command, you are asked to select the objects to hatch. Pick the objects that define the enclosed area in any order. Objects that are not selected will be ignored as

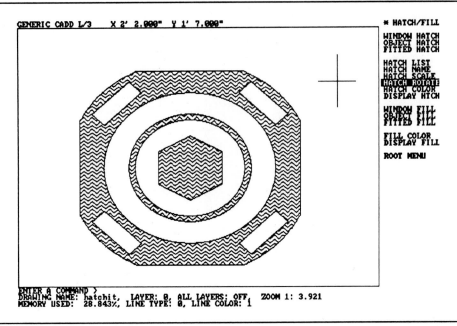

Figure 8-22. *A complex drawing with nested areas, hatched with WINDOW HATCH*

if they were not there. Figure 8-23 shows the same drawing as Figure 8-22 hatched with OBJECT HATCH, where only the perimeter was selected.

Fitted Hatch and Fitted Fill If you want to hatch or fill an area that is not properly described by existing simple entities, such as a tic-tac-toe drawing, you can use the FITTED HATCH (FH) or FITTED FILL (FF) command.

You are first asked to select the object to hatch or fill, just as with OBJECT HATCH and FILL. However, there are two differences between the FITTED and the OBJECT versions of hatch and fill. First, the entities that you pick for FITTED hatching and filling do not have to meet at the ends or corners. Second, the entities must be picked in order, working your way around the area to be hatched or filled until you get back to the beginning. Type **PU** or select a blank menu item to issue a PEN UP command when you have finished selecting entities; a new boundary will be created, and then the area will be hatched or filled.

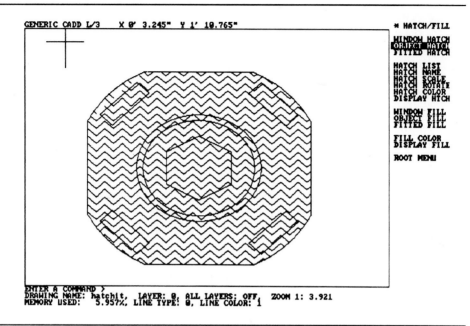

Figure 8-23.   *Hatching only the outer boundaries of the same drawing*

You cannot hatch or fill areas within other areas ("islands") with the FITTED commands because each entity must intersect the next entity. Also, only Lines and Arcs can be selected when you are using the FITTED commands. Circles—enclosed areas by definition —can be hatched or filled only with the OBJECT or WINDOW HATCH and FILL commands. FITTED HATCH and FILL commands require at least three entities to work.

Hatching and Filling Complicated Areas

Because the WINDOW HATCH (WH) and WINDOW FILL (WF) commands allow you to select many entities with one window, as opposed to tracing around entities, trying to make sure that you cover all of them, you should use these commands if at all possible.

The easiest way to ensure that you can use the WINDOW HATCH and FILL commands on complicated areas is to draw the boundary entities on a separate layer from the layers that contain the entities that you do not want to hatch or fill. Even if you have already drawn the complicated area, it can be easier and more useful for future editing to CHANGE (OG, WG, YG, DG) the boundary entities onto their own layer, make that layer the current layer with the LAYER CURRENT (YC) or LAYER SELECT (YS) command, turn off EDIT ALL LAYERS (AL), and then proceed to hatch or fill the area with a WINDOW.

Hatching the Bathroom Floor   The ROOM drawing that you created in Chapter 4 and edited in Chapter 5 is a good example of a reasonably complex area that would often require hatching. Suppose that you want to install 6-inch tiles on the floor. Before deciding on which technique to use, you should analyze several factors. First, at least two islands should not be hatched—the rectangle (four lines) and construction ellipse (four arcs) that define the toilet. This means that the floor cannot be hatched with the FITTED HATCH command, as islands are not allowed.

Second, the corners of the room are not accurately defined by lines that meet at their endpoints. Specifically, the places where the bathtub surround and the countertop hit the perimeter wall are a problem. These conditions cannot be properly hatched with OBJECT HATCH, which requires an accurately defined area. In addition, the doorway needs to be closed in order to define a hatchable area. Third, the entire drawing has been made on one layer, layer 0, which prohibits the use of the WINDOW HATCH command, because too many objects will be enclosed in the hatching area; in other words, the hatch will not go around the objects that you want it to miss.

These three factors indicate that the drawing must be changed in some way before it can be hatched. The most significant problems are the ill-defined corners and the open door. If these problems are corrected, you can use OBJECT HATCH. The simplest way to correct this situation is to erase the three lines that make up the inside left, right, and top interior walls, and replace these with shorter line segments. After erasing these two lines, as shown in Figure 8-24, set the GRID SIZE (GS) to 6 inches, turn on SNAP TO GRID (SG), and draw the new lines, starting in the lower-left corner, placing points at the lower-left edge of the counter, the upper-left corner of the room, the upper-right corner of the counter, the upper-left corner of the tub, the upper-right corner of the room, the lower-right corner of the tub, and finally, the lower-right corner of the room. You have now replaced the original three long lines with seven

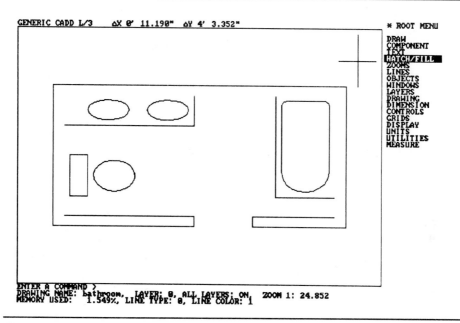

Figure 8-24. *The bathroom drawing with the too-long lines removed*

shorter ones. Finally, draw a line across the inside of the doorway to form an edge for the tile. Now that a defined area exists, you can use OBJECT HATCH (OH) to hatch this area.

1. Select the NET hatch from the Hatch List, and then set the HATCH SCALE (HZ) to 6. This produces a six-inch grid, because the NET pattern was originally defined with lines one inch apart.

2. To make sure that the tile pattern runs parallel to the walls, check to make sure that the HATCH ROTATION (HR) is set at 0.

3. When you use OBJECT HATCH (OH), start at one wall and work your way around the room, choosing only those entities that form the border of the floor. When you have gone around the room selecting every line segment on the perimeter, pick all of the entities which make up the toilet, making sure that you get all four lines of the rectangle and all four arcs of the construction ellipse.

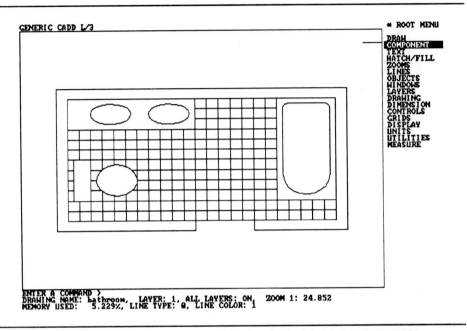

GENERIC CADD L/3

                                                                    ⋈ ROOT MENU
                                                                    DRAW
                                                                    COMPONENT
                                                                    TEXT
                                                                    HATCH/FILL
                                                                    ZOOMS
                                                                    LINES
                                                                    OBJECTS
                                                                    WINDOWS
                                                                    LAYERS
                                                                    DRAWING
                                                                    DIMENSION
                                                                    CONTROLS
                                                                    GRIDS
                                                                    DISPLAY
                                                                    UNITS
                                                                    UTILITIES
                                                                    MEASURE

ENTER A COMMAND 〉
DRAWING NAME: bathroom, LAYER: 1, ALL LAYERS: ON, ZOOM 1: 24.852
MEMORY USED: 5.229%, LINE TYPE: 0, LINE COLOR: 1

Figure 8-25.   *The bathroom floor successfully hatched with OBJECT HATCH*

4. Once you've selected all of the entities, type **PU** or pick a blank line from the video menu to issue PEN UP. If you've selected every line segment correctly, the floor should resemble the one shown in Figure 8-25.

Instead of selecting so many different entities and risk missing one or two (in which case you must erase the hatch with ERASE LAST (EL) and start over), you could use the easier WINDOW HATCH. In order to use WINDOW HATCH, it would be best if the hatchable entities were all on a separate layer. To try this technique, erase the hatch with ERASE LAST (EL), and then REDRAW (RD). Make sure that EDIT ALL LAYERS is on for now.

The easiest way to get these entities onto their own layer is with the WINDOW CHANGE (WG) command. Place a window around everything but the very outside wall. Your window should go right down the middle of the wall on all four sides. Don't worry that you are selecting too many

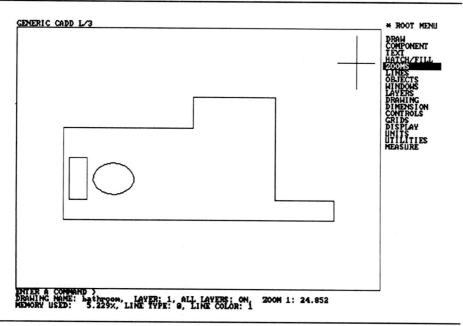

GENERIC CADD L/3

* ROOT MENU
DRAW
COMPONENT
TEXT
HATCH/FILL
ZOOMS
LINES
OBJECTS
WINDOWS
LAYERS
DRAWING
DIMENSION
CONTROLS
GRIDS
DISPLAY
UNITS
UTILITIES
MEASURE

ENTER A COMMAND >
DRAWING NAME: bathroom,   LAYER: 1, ALL LAYERS: ON,   ZOOM 1: 24.852
MEMORY USED: 5.229%, LINE TYPE: 0, LINE COLOR: 1

Figure 8-26.   *The boundary entities only displayed on layer 1*

objects. It's easier to put a few back with another window than to change each entity individually with the OBJECT CHANGE command. After you have placed the window, press ENTER for each prompt until you get to the one that asks you for the layer to "CHANGE TO." Type **1** (or the number of any unused layer) and press ENTER. At the end of the command, type **Y** to verify the CHANGE. At this point, make layer 1 the active layer with a LAYER CURRENT (YC) or LAYER SELECT (YS) command, and turn off the display of layer 0 with the LAYER HIDE (YD) command. REDRAW (RD) the screen to see the effect. Only the items that you changed to layer 1 should be visible. Use the WINDOW CHANGE (WG) and OBJECT CHANGE (OG) commands to put the rest of the entities that you don't want to use for hatch boundaries back onto layer 0. Each should vanish as you change it, because layer 0 is hidden. After a few commands, only the hatchable boundaries should remain, (see Figure 8-26). Once you have this on the screen, use the WINDOW HATCH command to hatch this area.

One big advantage of this technique is that you can **try** different patterns, scales, and rotations easily, without reselecting the same entities over and over. You can easily ERASE LAST (EL) to change a few parameters, and do another WINDOW HATCH. Once you have the correct hatch, turn the rest of the drawing back on with a LAYER DISPLAY (YD), entering a value of 256 to see the entire drawing. A redraw is automatic when you specify 256.

If you want to change the pattern later, simply go back to this layer, turn EDIT ALL LAYERS off, erase the existing hatch pattern (by putting a WINDOW ERASE window around its reference points), and hatch again.

If the available hatch patterns are not what you need, you can create others with a text editor or the utility program sold by Generic Software. The utility program is much easier. Hatch patterns may also become available in the near future from third-party developers.

In this chapter, you have seen how to combine existing entities to form Components, how to place Text into your drawing using any of a number of different Fonts, and how to Hatch and Fill portions of your drawing. You have seen that all of these complex entities are placed by first setting a number of specific placement parameters, and then using a placement command to put the complex entity into the drawing. Complex entities should be used in place of repetitive simple entities whenever possible: they provide a number of sophisticated features and techniques and save space in the database at the same time.

9 *Multiple Entities*

A number of entity placement commands fall between the simple entities (Line, Arc, Circle, and so on) and the complex entities (Component, Text, Hatch, and Fill). Each of these commands places into the drawing a number of simple entities simultaneously. Three of these commands were covered in Chapter 4: the RECTANGLE, REGULAR POLYGON, and CONSTRUCTION ELLIPSE commands. RECTANGLE and REGULAR POLYGON create multiple Lines, while CONSTRUCTION ELLIPSE creates four Arcs. In this chapter, you will be introduced to a few other commands that create more than one entity at the same time.

Early versions of Generic CADD, specifically 2.0 and earlier, included the simple entities Rectangle, Regular Polygon, and True Ellipse, but no Construction Ellipse. Rectangles and Regular Polygons are no longer used in Generic CADD. Version 3.0 automatically converted Rectangles and Regular Polygons to multiple straight lines when they were encountered, but Levels 1, 2, and 3 do not. If you want to call up these older drawing files in the CADD Levels, you will need to either first call them up and save them in 3.0, or update the files using *File Diagnostics,* available from Workshop 3D Software, a third-party vendor of utilities for Generic Software. See Appendix A for more information.

Bezier Curves

Generic CADD provides two ways of constructing a curve between a given set of points, the CURVE (CV) command (see Chapter 4), and the BEZIER CURVE (BV) command. The CURVE command creates one continuous *spline curve* through as many points as you select. The whole curve is one long entity, with a variable number of points. The BEZIER CURVE command creates individual *Bezier Curves,* one between the first two points, another between the second and third, and so on.

The entities created by the BEZIER CURVE command are quite different than those created by the CURVE command. While the CURVE command attempts to create as smooth a curve as possible through a variable number of points, a rather loosely defined task, each individual Bezier created by the BEZIER CURVE command is much more specifically defined. Although you only specify the endpoints of each, a single Bezier Curve is actually defined by four points—two endpoints and two *control points.* The locations of the control points are calculated automatically by Generic CADD, but can be changed later if you wish. (See Chapter 10 for discussion on editing Bezier Curves.) Bezier Curves are often used when you are not sure what shape you want because they are so easy to edit. The CURVE command is more useful when you are not likely to do much editing because Curves are much easier to place initially than the Bezier Curves. Bezier Curves take on the current Line parameters of COLOR (LK) and WIDTH (LW). Although they take the current LINE TYPE (LT) as part of their definition, neither Curves nor Bezier Curves are presently displayed or printed using line types. Like all entities, however, Bezier Curves are created on the current layer.

Figure 9-1 shows a single Bezier (though when you use the BEZIER CURVE command, you actually create a number of these entities). Notice that at each end, the Bezier is tangent to an imaginary line between the control point and the endpoint of the Bezier. This is how the curvature of the Bezier is determined.

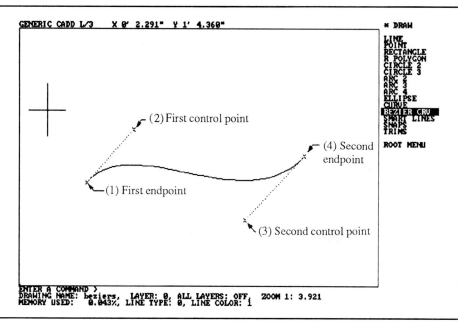

Figure 9-1.   *A single Bezier Curve*

Figure 9-2 shows two Beziers, created with a single BEZIER CURVE command. Notice that not only does each Bezier remain tangent to the imaginary line between control point and endpoint, but that the imaginary line between the second control point of the first Bezier and the first control point of the second Bezier passes through their shared endpoint. Because each Bezier is tangent to this imaginary line, the two Beziers flow together with no break in between, as if they were one curve. Again, this condition is established by the creation of multiple Beziers with a single BEZIER CURVE command. You need not line up the control points to make the curve smooth; it happens automatically.

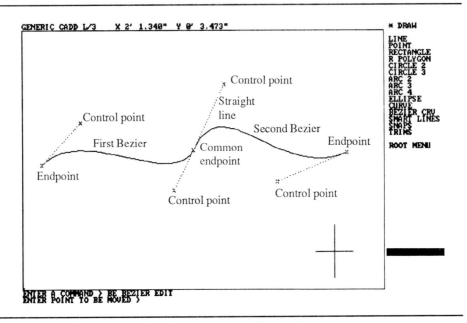

GENERIC CADD L/3   X 2' 1.340"   Y 0' 3.473"

* DRAW

LINE
POINT
RECTANGLE
R POLYGON
CIRCLE 2
CIRCLE 3
ARC 2
ARC 3
ARC 4
ELLIPSE
CURVE
BEZIER CRV
SMART LINES
SNAPS
TRIMS

ROOT MENU

Control point

Straight
line

Control point

First Bezier

Second Bezier

Endpoint

Common
endpoint

Endpoint

Control point

Control point

ENTER A COMMAND > BE BEZIER EDIT
ENTER POINT TO BE MOVED >

Figure 9-2.   *The relationship of two continuous Bezier Curves*

Placing Multiple Beziers

To place Bezier Curves, use the BEZIER command on the DRAW menu, or type **BV** on the keyboard. The prompts and placement of points function in a similar way to the CURVE command. When you are finished placing points, you type **PU** or pick a blank line from the video menu to issue the PEN UP.

The screen display for BEZIER CURVE is quite different from that for the CURVE command. Instead of placing temporary straight lines between curve points, the BEZIER CURVE command displays the individual Bezier entities as soon as it has enough information. Since Beziers that meet end-to-end influence each other, Generic CADD cannot actually calculate and draw the first Bezier until you have defined the endpoints of the second. This means that the first Bezier actually appears when you have placed the third point. Each subsequent point provides enough information to create another segment. When you get to the last point and type **PU** or pick a blank menu item, the last Bezier is placed.

The first control point of the first Bezier and the second control point of the last Bezier are arbitrarily placed by Generic CADD, using an internal algorithm. If you type **PU** after only two points, you produce only one Bezier. Since this is both the first and the last Bezier placed, there are no tangent Beziers to control the starting and ending directions. Both the first and second control points are arbitrarily placed by Generic CADD. You will be able to predict these locations after you have used the BEZIER CURVE command a few times.

Placing Single Beziers

At times you may want to place only one Bezier, but want to have more control over its shape than you do when you use BEZIER CURVE with only two points. An undocumented command (command code BW) intended specifically for placing a single Bezier lets you place not only the endpoints but the control points as well. This command is not on the video menu. The letter *W* does not stand for anything; it just happens to be the next letter in the alphabet after *V,* which is used for the multiple BEZIER CURVE command.

When you use the BW command, you are asked for four points in order: (1) the first endpoint, (2) the first control point, (3) the second control point, and (4) the second endpoint. By examining Figure 9-1 you can see how these four points define the single Bezier Curve. You do not have to type **PU** at the end because a single Bezier is always defined by these four points. After you have placed the four points, the Bezier will be drawn.

Editing Bezier Curves

As noted previously, one of the primary advantages of Bezier Curves is the ease with which they can be edited. The definition of a Bezier Curve includes two control points, which can be used to create the specific shapes that you are trying to draw.

Using MOVE POINT (MP) with Bezier Curves   When you use the MOVE POINT (MP) command, you are asked to select an entity. If the entity that you select is a Bezier Curve, placed either with a single or a multiple BEZIER command, dashed lines will appear between each endpoint and the control point that controls that end of the Bezier. When you select the point to be moved, you can specify either end of the dashed line. If RUBBER

BANDING (RB) is turned on, the Bezier will be stretched in various directions as you move the selected point. When you actually place the point, the Bezier will be redrawn.

If you use MOVE POINT to move the control point of a single Bezier in the middle of a string of Beziers, you will probably create a corner, where the Beziers are not tangent to one another.

Maintaining Tangent Bezier Curves   To keep all of the continuous Bezier Curves tangent to one another, you can use the BEZIER EDIT (BE) command. This command works just like MOVE POINT, except that you have to select *two* Bezier Curves before selecting the point that you want to move. If you try to select any other type of entity, the command will not work.

Once you have selected the two Beziers that you want to edit, dashed lines will be displayed at each end of both Beziers, as with MOVE POINT, and you will be asked to select a point to be edited. At the point where the two Beziers meet, two of the dashed lines may appear to be one straight line, but they are not. Choose one of the two control points at the end of one of the dashed lines that connect to the point where the two Beziers meet. As you move this point, *both* control points move to maintain the straight line between them. Both Bezier Curves will be rubber-banded as you move the point. The tangential relationship between the two Beziers will be preserved. Figure 9-3 illustrates how moving one point changes both Beziers.

Although the BEZIER EDIT command is intended for editing two Beziers that share a common endpoint, you can also select two Beziers that do not touch. Even if the two Beziers are not tangent when you start, they will be when you are done. If you first use BEZIER EDIT on two noncontinuous Beziers and then MOVE them together, the connection between them will be perfectly smooth.

Smart Lines

The SMART LINES commands on the DRAW menu provide a number of additional multiple entity placement commands. Like BEZIER CURVE, these commands place more than one simple or complex entity with a single command. These commands act more like complex entity commands

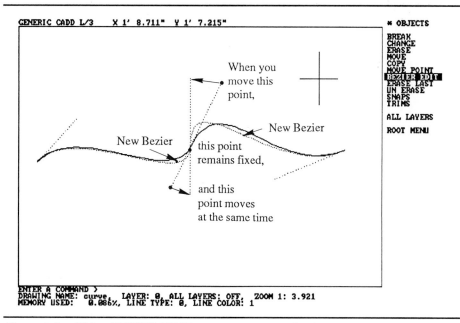

Figure 9-3. *Using BEZIER EDIT to move two control points*

than BEZIER CURVE, as they use placement parameters and placement commands.

Filleted Lines

You might say that the LINE command creates multiple entities, because you do not have to pick another LINE command to draw additional line segments. You can just keep selecting points, and more lines will be drawn until you select another command or press ESC. The multiple lines created automatically by the LINE command meet exactly at the corners, because the second point of one line becomes the first point of the next line.

This can be done automatically by using the AUTOFILLET command on the SMART LINES menu or typing **AF** on the keyboard. This mode of drawing lines works with another command, FILLET RADIUS (RF), which establishes the radius of an arc to be inserted at each new intersection as the lines are drawn.

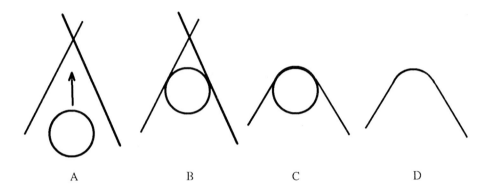

Figure 9-4.   *How two lines are filleted*

Once the FILLET RADIUS is set and AUTOFILLET is activated, you use the LINE command just as before, with only one difference. To end the command, you must press ESC or type **PU**. You won't notice any difference on the first line segment, but as soon as you place the second, an arc will be inserted tangent to the first and second lines, and the lines will be trimmed, as shown in Figure 9-4. Step A shows two lines and a circle of the specified fillet radius. Step B shows how the circle is placed tangent to the two lines. Steps C and D show how lines are trimmed at the tangent points, and the circle is trimmed to an arc to meet the endpoints of the lines exactly.

All the Lines and Arcs you have created take on the current Line parameters—color, type, width, and the current layer. If the angle between the lines or the length of the lines makes the insertion of a tangent arc impossible, you will get a simple trimmed intersection instead of a filleted corner. As a toggle, AUTOFILLET is turned off the same way that it was turned on, by typing **AF** or by selecting AUTOFILLET from the SMART LINES menu.

If AUTOFILLET is on and the FILLET RADIUS is set to 0, no arcs will appear between lines; in this case, you must press ESC or type **PU** to exit the LINE command. It is usually better to turn off AUTOFILLET when you do not want it instead of setting the FILLET RADIUS to 0. The FILLET RADIUS can be used without AUTOFILLET turned on, as you will see in Chapter 10.

Double Lines

The DOUBLE LINE command creates two lines at the same time. When you use DOUBLE LINE, you actually place two separate entities into the database for every pair of endpoints that you select. When using this command, you place two points, just as in drawing a normal line, but the two lines that are created are actually placed offset from an imaginary line between these two points, by distances specified by the DOUBLE WIDTH parameter.

Specifying the Distance Between Lines   First, you need to set the two DOUBLE WIDTH values that indicate the distance between the double lines—or, more accurately, the offsets from the imaginary line. The idea is quite simple: If you specify "1" for each value, the two lines will be two inches apart, each one inch from the imaginary center line. If you make one of the values 0, one of the lines will connect the two endpoints.

The only tricky part is which side of the imaginary line each line is drawn on. The rule is this: If you consider every line to be drawn from left to right, the first line always appears *above* the imaginary line if the DOUBLE WIDTH value is positive, and the second line will appear below. Negative values reverse the placement of the lines. Not every line in the drawing goes from left to right, of course, so you have to pretend that they do. In other words, if the second point is actually to the left of the first point, the first line will appear below these points, and the second above. If you turned the monitor upside down, the line *would* go from left to right, and the first line *would* be above the second. Another way to think of it is that if you consider all lines drawn from left to right to be clockwise around some imaginary center, the first line is always placed to the *outside,* and the second line to the *inside,* as shown here.

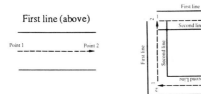

First line (above)

Point 1   Point 2

This conceptualization assumes that the values for DOUBLE WIDTH are both positive. If the DOUBLE WIDTH values are negative, simply reverse the line placements.

The DOUBLE WIDTH command is found on the SMART LINES menu (a submenu of the DRAW menu), or can be activated by typing **TH** on the keyboard. (TH stands for THickness or widTH, take your pick.) When you select it, you are shown the current value and asked to specify a new value. Type a number and press ENTER to set a new value, or simply press ENTER to leave the value the same. The default value of DOUBLE WIDTH can be set in the CONFIG program.

Drawing Double Lines   Once you have set the DOUBLE WIDTH variables, you are ready to draw DOUBLE LINES. Select DOUBLE LINE from the SMART LINES menu, or type **L2** on the keyboard. Just as in drawing a Straight Line, you are asked to specify endpoints. However, unlike the STRAIGHT LINE command, DOUBLE LINE does not return to the "ENTER A COMMAND >" prompt immediately after you select the second point; you can keep picking points after the first two. The intersections between subsequent pairs of double lines are automatically adjusted as each new set of double lines is added, shortening or lengthening each side as required. When you have finished placing double lines, press ESC, type **PU**, or select a blank line from the video menu.

Each line created using the DOUBLE LINE command is an individual entity. The two sides of the double line have no built-in relationship. In the database, these entities behave exactly as if you had drawn one line and then the other, with two separate line commands. The color, width and type of these LINES are controlled by the current settings of the variables on the LINES menu.

Automatically Filling Double Lines   A toggle on the SMART LINES menu allows you to fill the space between DOUBLE LINES. When this toggle, SOLIDFILL, is on, an enclosed area is created that can be filled. The fill itself is generated automatically.

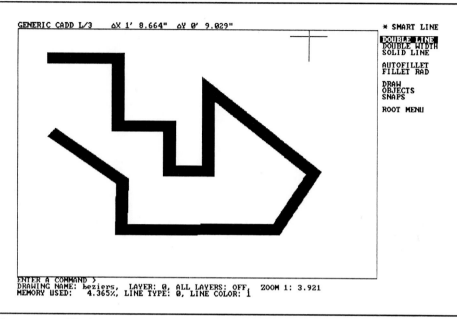

GENERIC CADD L/3   ΔX 1' 8.664"   ΔY 0' 9.029"   ＊ SMART LINE
                                                                                    DOUBLE LINE
                                                                                    DOUBLE WIDTH
                                                                                    SOLID LINE

                                                                                    AUTOFILLET
                                                                                    FILLET RAD

                                                                                    DRAW
                                                                                    OBJECTS
                                                                                    SNAPS

                                                                                    ROOT MENU

ENTER A COMMAND >
DRAWING NAME: beziers,   LAYER: 0, ALL LAYERS: OFF,   ZOOM 1: 3.921
MEMORY USED: 4.365%, LINE TYPE: 0, LINE COLOR: 1

Figure 9-5.   *The Line entities created by DOUBLE LINE with SOLID FILL turned on*

Instead of a simple double line, each new point selected after the first generates four lines to create a closed filled area. Figure 9-5 shows the creation of a Double Line with SOLID FILL turned on. The Fill entity is actually created when the *next* point beyond the double line is selected, or when you type **PU** or press *ESC*.

The lines created by solid filled DOUBLE LINES and the fill itself take on the current fill color instead of the usual line color. All of the entities will be located on the current layer using the current line width. The line type of all entities created will be 0.

Double Filleted Lines   If AUTOFILLETING (AF) is on when you use the DOUBLE LINE (L2) command, both lines will be filleted. The inside corner will use the specified FILLET RADIUS (RF), and the outside radius will be adjusted to remain parallel. If SOLID LINE is on as well, the areas bounded by the two arcs and the perpendicular connectors between the parallel lines will be filled as well. All entities will be in the current fill

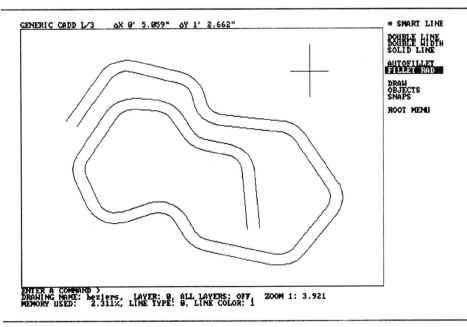

Figure 9-6. *Double filleted lines*

color, on the current layer. The Lines and Arcs will use the current line width, and line type will be ignored. See Figure 9-6 for an example of a drawing made with filleted double lines.

Double Line Tips   A standard method for using double lines is to set one of the DOUBLE WIDTH values to 0, usually the second one. This way, one of the lines will have as its endpoints the points that you specify when you place the DOUBLE LINE. The other side of the double line will be offset by the distance specified. This allows you to snap one side of the double line exactly onto either the grid or existing points in the drawing.

Double lines can also be used for offsetting a pair of lines from an existing object. This can be done by specifying one positive and one negative value for the DOUBLE WIDTH. Suppose that you want to draw a six-inch-thick wall ten feet above an existing wall. You could set your DOUBLE WIDTH values to 10′6″ and – 10′0″. If you then draw a double line by using SNAP TO NEAREST POINT on both ends of an existing wall, the first line will be drawn 10′6″ above the existing wall. The second line will be drawn –10′0″

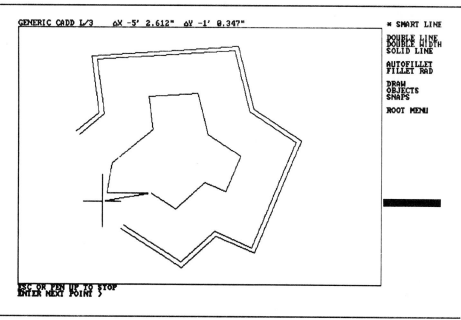

Figure 9-7. *Offsetting a double line with a negative and positive value*

below, or 10′0″ above, the existing wall. As a result, you end up with one line 10′ above and one line 10′ 6″ above the existing wall, which creates a six-inch wall ten feet above the existing wall. Figure 9-7 shows how you can create a double line five feet from an existing figure by tracing around the figure with DOUBLE WIDTH set at 5′6″ and − 5′0″.

You should note that you cannot issue another DOUBLE LINE command by pressing SPACEBAR, because the command ends with a PEN UP or an ESC. The PEN UP or ESC will be repeated if you press the SPACEBAR. You must either select it again from the video menu or type L2. Double lines take on the current LINE COLOR (LK), LINE WIDTH (LW), and LINE TYPE (LT), and are created on the CURRENT LAYER (YC). Double lines can be edited by any command that edits LINES.

In this chapter, you have seen that the number of entities actually created by the DRAW command varies. Some commands create a single simple entity, while others create either multiple simple entities or a combination of several simple and complex entities. The entities that are created by a given command are sometimes controlled by other mode- or parameter-setting commands.

It should be clear that there is not necessarily a direct relationship between the commands and the entities in all cases. Many of the commands that create multiple entities can be thought of more as "macro" or complex commands, which aid in the creation of simple shapes. As you will see in Chapter 15, you can invent your own menu items that act very much like these multiple-entity commands in order to create shapes that are not included with Generic CADD.

10 *Advanced Drawing and Editing Techniques*

The basic, general-purpose editing commands work with most entities, which can be selected in a number of different ways (see Chapter 4). These commands combine OBJECT (O), WINDOW (W), LAYER (Y), or DRAWING (D) with a desired action such as ERASE (E or X), ROTATE (R), or RE-SCALE (Z).

This chapter examines the more special-purpose editing commands and drawing techniques. These commands work only on a particular type of entity, or in a particular situation, in an unusual way, or to enhance the capabilities of other editing or drawing commands. Although these commands can be found on many menus, including the WINDOWS and DRAWING menus, most are listed on the SNAPS and TRIMS menus—both submenus of the DRAW menu and the OBJECTS menu.

Copying Around a Circle

The RADIAL COPY (RC) command on the WINDOWS menu in Level 3 copies objects in a circular pattern. As with any WINDOW command, the entities to be copied are selected by placing a window around them. Then you must specify a center point, the part of a circle (from 0 to 360 degrees) around which you want to copy the objects, and the total number of copies that you want, including the original.

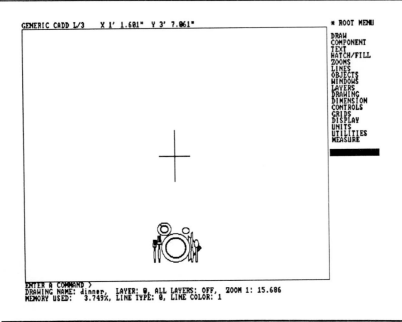

GENERIC CADD L/3   X 1' 1.601" Y 3' 7.061"

* ROOT MENU

DRAW
COMPONENT
TEXT
HATCH/FILL
ZOOMS
LINES
OBJECTS
WINDOWS
LAYERS
DRAWING
DIMENSION
CONTROLS
GRIDS
DISPLAY
UNITS
UTILITIES
MEASURE

ENTER A COMMAND >
DRAWING NAME: dinner, LAYER: 0, ALL LAYERS: OFF, ZOOM 1: 15.686
MEMORY USED: 3.749%, LINE TYPE: 0, LINE COLOR: 1

Figure 10-1.   *One PLACESET component ready to be radially copied*

Setting a Round Table

Try using RADIAL COPY on one of the place settings in the DINNER
drawing (see Chapter 8). To start, call up that drawing and ZOOM BACK
(ZB). Place a PLACESET component using COMPONENT PLACE or the
COMPONENT LIST, putting it into a blank area to the left or right of the
table, and then ZOOM UP (ZU) on the area around the new place setting.
For a screen center, pick a point above the PLACESET you just placed.
Your screen should resemble the one shown in Figure 10-1.

Select RADIAL COPY from the WINDOWS menu or type **RC** on the
keyboard. Place a window around the PLACESET component, keeping in
mind that you only need to enclose its reference point within the window.
Next, place the axis point directly above the PLACESET, maybe a few feet
away, as shown in Figure 10-2. When asked for the number of degrees to
span, type **360**, meaning a whole circle. Finally, type **6** for the total number

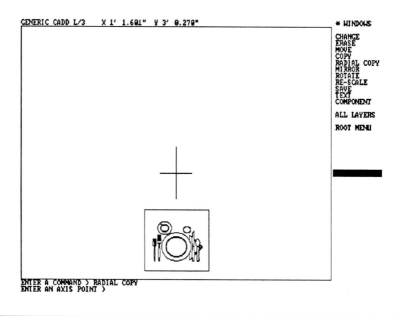

Figure 10-2. *Placing an axis point for RADIAL COPY*

of copies, including the original. The RADIAL COPY command will be executed, resulting in a drawing much like Figure 10-3.

Total Items Versus Number of Copies

Notice that the number specified works differently in the RADIAL COPY than it does in the WINDOW COPY command. In WINDOW COPY, you specify the number of *copies* that you want, *not including* the original. This means that if you have one object and you make one copy, you end up with two objects. This makes perfect sense when copying in a straight line, and specifying the distance between copies by a displacement, or two points. However, in the RADIAL COPY command, you specify the *total* number of objects, *including* the original. Therefore, you need to specify at least two objects in order for the command to work.

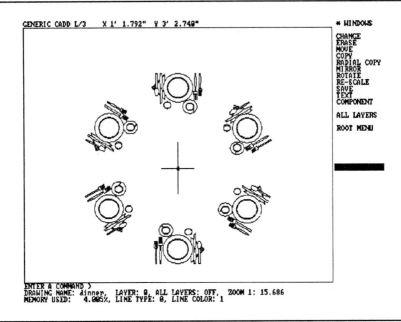

Figure 10-3.   *Six PLACESET components after the RADIAL COPY*

Although this procedure may seem awkward at first, it is much more convenient when working with objects copied around a circle. When you specify four objects, for example, you are probably thinking of one facing in each of four directions. Selecting six objects, as you have seen, places them 60 degrees apart. In general, the number that you specify for degrees is divided by the number of items to obtain the number of degrees between items. This is more intuitive than if you had to specify, say, seven copies when what you really want is an octagonal configuration.

Indicating the Direction

The direction of copying is the same as the standard method of measuring angles in Generic CADD. Positive angles indicate a counterclockwise

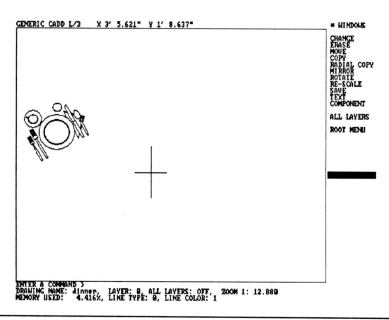

Figure 10-4. *One PLACESET ready for another RADIAL COPY*

direction, negative angles translate to clockwise. If you are copying around a whole circle, as in the previous example, it does not matter in which direction the copies are made. However, if you want less than 360 degrees, the direction of copying is very important.

To see the effect of the copying direction, place another PLACESET in a blank part of the drawing at a 30-degree COMPONENT ROTATION (CR). ZOOM or PAN until the PLACESET is to the left side of the screen, as in Figure 10-4. Issue RADIAL COPY (RC), place the window, select an axis point a few feet to the lower right of the PLACESET, and specify –60 degrees and four items. You should see four placesettings along an arc, as shown in Figure 10-5.

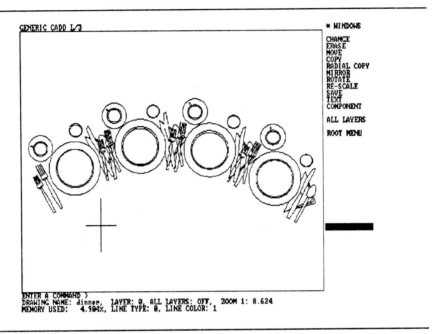

Figure 10-5. Four PLACESET *components along an arc*

Different Ideas

RADIAL COPY can also be used to copy an object on top of itself, by placing the axis point in the center, or near the center, of a simple object, as opposed to a certain distance away from the object. Figure 10-6 illustrates some of the possibilities.

RADIAL COPY can also place text along the periphery of arcs and circles. Simply place a single text character, use RADIAL COPY to replicate it, and then edit the copies with the TEXT REPLACE (TX) command. They will retain their placement and rotation.

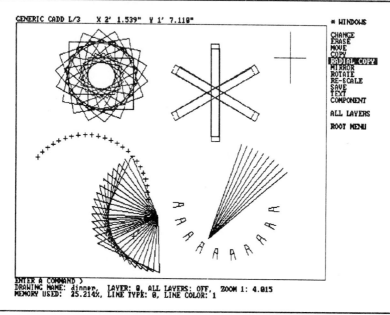

Figure 10-6. *A variety of effects that can be produced with the RADIAL COPY command*

Changing Your Point of Reference

As discussed in earlier chapters, everything in a CAD drawing is defined using a finite number of shapes, which are described by geometric properties and numeric values. In Generic CADD, as in most of the CAD programs, these numeric values are in the form of X and Y coordinates, which define objects in the drawing in relation to an origin, which is located at the coordinates 0,0.

It may become necessary, under certain conditions, to change the location of this point. This is done with the RE-ORIGIN command, found on the DRAWING menu in all versions of Generic CADD, and activated by typing **DO** on the keyboard. This command simply asks you to select a new origin point, and the point is changed.

A Warning

Use the RE-ORIGIN command with caution. Earlier versions of the Generic CADD manual included the warning: DO NOT USE THIS COMMAND. This was meant to keep you out of trouble. Changing the origin does not confuse Generic CADD or the computer in any way, but it just might confuse you instead.

When you RE-ORIGIN the drawing, not only are the X and Y coordinates of *every point* in the drawing changed, but so is the GRID, any NAMED VIEWS, and just about everything else. Two forms of manual entry, ORIGIN and BASEPOINT will respond differently after a DRAWING RE-ORIGIN than before. The coordinates of the BASEPOINT, of course, are relative to the origin.

Uses of the Origin

On the other hand, the command can be very useful. The simple fact that the GRID uses the origin for its first point makes it tempting to move the origin whenever you need to reference from a corner that is not currently on one of the grid points. Although there are other ways to accomplish this (for example, using MANUAL ENTRY RELATIVE (MR) or BASEPOINT (MB)), moving the origin is sometimes the best method. In fact, you may want to move the origin several times during a work session to take best advantage of the utility of the origin itself. For example, The Third Dimension, an add-on utility to create perspective drawings from Generic CADD drawing files, requires that you RE-ORIGIN the drawing to establish a focal point for the perspective. Once you have completed the drawing, moving the origin for this purpose has very little impact on the drawing itself.

Think of It As Moving the Entire Drawing   The DRAWING RE-ORIGIN command can be thought of as replacing the "drawing move" function, which does not exist. If it did, it would probably work just like WINDOW

MOVE: You would simply be asked for a reference point and a new location for it. In DRAWING RE-ORIGIN, the reference point is assumed to be 0,0, and you specify its new location. Of course, the new location of the origin is specified in terms of the coordinate system currently active when you issue the command.

To use the DRAWING RE-ORIGIN command, select RE-ORIGIN from the DRAWING menu, or type **DO** on the keyboard. When you are asked for the new origin, either select a point on the screen or type the coordinates of the desired point. If you are typing coordinates, make sure you know which manual entry mode you are using. It doesn't hurt to re-select MO, MR, or MB again, as all of the manual entry commands are one-way toggles—they always go on when you select them.

The DRAWING RE-ORIGIN command changes all of the definitions of every entity in the drawing to reflect the new origin location and automatically performs a ZOOM ALL. This arbitrary ZOOM ALL acts as a visual cue that you have significantly adjusted the drawing, and that you should be aware of a fresh starting point.

Making Use of Existing Geometric Properties

One of the advantages of CADD over hand drawing and other types of programs is its ability not only to remember data you have input, but to extrapolate additional information from this data. This is true with geometric properties as well as with numeric data.

You have already had the opportunity to use the SNAP TO NEAREST POINT function, which allows you to snap to an existing *definition point* of an object. This command lets you specify the exact endpoint of any line on the screen whenever Generic CADD asks you to specify a point. You simply type **NP** or press the third button on the pointing device when the cursor is close to the desired endpoint. Other definition points that can be found with the SNAP TO NEAREST POINT include the center of a circle, the endpoints of an arc, the axes points of an ellipse, the definition points of a curve, the control and endpoints of a Bezier Curve, the placement location of text characters, and the reference point of components.

Users of Levels 2 and 3 can take advantage of additional geometric properties. The SNAPS and TRIMS menus give you access to these properties, eliminating much of the tedious work of hand drawing, while at the same time allowing much greater precision.

The SNAPS Commands

The commands on the SNAPS menu modify the actions of many other commands to make them more accurate. For this reason, the SNAPS menu is accessible from a number of other menus, including the DRAW and OBJECT menus, where you will need them most often.

Like the SNAP TO NEAREST POINT command, the SNAPS commands help you to locate points whenever you are asked for them. Each provides a specific geometric function, as demonstrated by the examples on the following pages. The two-character codes for the SNAPS usually start with the letter *S,* followed by a letter indicating the type of snap. Two SNAPS do not follow this rule, the familiar SNAP TO NEAREST POINT, abbreviated NP, and SNAP TO NEAREST LINE, which is coded NL.

Another Nearest Point As you may have noticed, the SNAP TO NEAR-EST POINT is unlike any other Generic CADD command, in that it must be selected while you are positioning the cursor. This means that it cannot be selected from the video menu. While this makes the SNAP TO NEAR-EST POINT command extremely easy to use in most cases, it is somewhat inconsistent with the other SNAPS commands. The usual sequence for the SNAPS commands is to select a point after selecting the command.

On the SNAPS menu, the SNAP TO CLOSEST POINT command does exactly the same thing as SNAP TO NEAREST POINT but in this more common format. (The command is provided to make it easier to create macros on the video menu and through the use of batch files.) When you are ready to select a point, select CLOSE POINT from the SNAPS menu. You will be asked to select the point that you want to snap closest to. Position the cursor near the definition point that you want to snap onto, and use the first button on the pointing device to select the point. Just like SNAP TO NEAREST POINT, any construction point on any object can be found by the SNAP TO CLOSEST POINT command.

The only difference between these two commands is in the way that they are activated. CLOSEST POINT is done in three steps: selecting the command, positioning the cursor, and picking the point. NEAREST POINT requires just two steps: positioning the cursor and typing **NP** or pressing the third pointing device button. This second step simultaneously selects the command and the point.

How Near Is NEAR? These two SNAPS can find a point anywhere on the screen. If you draw a line in one corner, and then start another line and SNAP TO NEAREST POINT, you will always snap onto one of the endpoints, even if it is on the other side of the screen. The rest of the SNAPS, however, are not quite so generous. The specific location that you are trying to snap to must be within a certain distance of the point that you indicated with the cursor on the screen. This distance is specified using the TOLERANCE command, located on the CONTROLS menu, or activated by typing **TO** on the keyboard. The default is 0.25 (1/4 inch), but this can be changed with the CONFIG program. It can also be changed for the current session with the TOLERANCE command.

When you use the TOLERANCE command, you are asked to type a number up to a maximum of one inch. It is important to note that the tolerance is measured *on your video screen,* not in the units of the drawing. This means that if tolerance is set to 0.25, your cursor must be within 1/4 inch of the condition that you are looking for. This rule may be difficult to remember at first, because it is so different from all other Generic CADD operations, which are synchronized to the scale of the drawing. It makes sense, though, because if tolerance were measured to scale, it would be ruled by the current ZOOM: You would have to pick your points closer to where you wanted them when you were zoomed out, and would not need to be so precise when you were zoomed in closer. This would defeat the purpose of the tolerance, which is to remain fixed no matter how your drawing is displayed.

Tolerance also controls how close the cursor must be to an entity when you use any of the OBJECTS editing commands. With the MOVE POINT command, for example, the tolerance controls how close you have to be not only to select the object, but to move one of the definition points as well.

Snap to Anything in Sight Sometimes you are not looking for a specific point on an object, but just any point. You may simply want to make sure that the line that you are drawing actually touches another line. Selecting the NEAR LINE command on the SNAPS menu, or typing **NL** on the keyboard, assures this.

Simply select the NEAR LINE command or type **NL** whenever you are trying to make sure that the point you are selecting touches another object. When you are asked which object you want to snap near to, press the first button on the pointing device. The cursor will jump to the nearest object within the distance specified by the tolerance. It jumps in a straight line to the closest possible point on the object, so it is still important where you position the cursor.

NEAR LINE, like many of the other SNAPS, overrides the ORTHO MODE and the SNAP TO GRID toggles. Be careful when you use NEAR LINE and the rest of the SNAPS with the drawing controls, as you may not get the point you want. It is entirely possible to draw lines that are not exactly horizontal or vertical by using NEAR LINE even when ORTHO MODE is turned on.

Finding an Intersection   The remaining SNAPS look for even more specific geometric conditions. SNAP TO INTERSECTION, abbreviated as INTRSCT on the SNAPS menu and **SI** when typed on the keyboard, can find any intersection between Lines, Arcs, and Circles. The types of intersections that can be located are shown in Figure 10-7. These include intersections between a Line and another Line, a Line and an Arc, a Line and a Circle, an Arc and another Arc, an Arc and a Circle, and between a Circle and another Circle. You can also snap to Rectangles, Polygons, and Construction Ellipses because they are made from these three simple entities.

An intersection is defined as any place that the two entities cross. Therefore, there is an intersection defined if one entity is touching another entity, even where two lines simply share a common endpoint. Of course, these particular conditions could be located with the NEAREST POINT or CLOSEST POINT command, if you are sure that the endpoint of one object is exactly on the other object.

As with the rest of the SNAPS, this command can be selected whenever you are trying to place a point, whether you are executing a DRAW, OBJECT, or even a WINDOW command. The SNAPS can not only be used to locate definition points of entities, but also to indicate displacements for the MOVE and COPY commands, and other functions. Intersections between Curves, Beziers, and True Ellipses *cannot* be found.

Looking for a Midpoint   The SNAP TO MIDPOINT command can be used to find the midpoint of a Line. A Line is the only type of entity with which this command works. When you select MIDPNT from the SNAPS

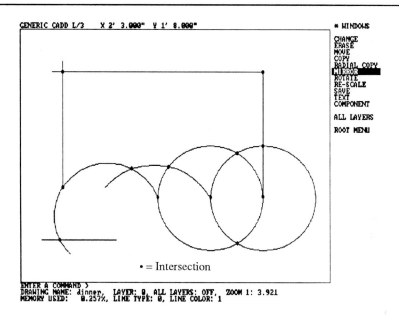

GENERIC CADD L/3   X 2' 3.000" Y 1' 8.000"

* WINDOWS

CHANGE
ERASE
MOVE
COPY
RADIAL COPY
MIRROR
ROTATE
RE-SCALE
SAVE
TEXT
COMPONENT

ALL LAYERS

ROOT MENU

• = Intersection

ENTER A COMMAND >
DRAWING NAME: dinner, LAYER: 0, ALL LAYERS: OFF, ZOOM 1: 3.921
MEMORY USED: 0.257%, LINE TYPE: 0, LINE COLOR: 1

Figure 10-7. *Various intersection conditions*

menu or type **SM** on the keyboard, you are asked to select the line for which you want the midpoint.

The *midpoint* of a line is defined as being halfway between the two endpoints. The SNAP TO MIDPOINT command can be especially handy when used with some of the editing commands. For example, Figure 10-8 shows the placement of a circle in the exact center of a rectangle. This can be done with one CIRCLE command, and then a MOVE command that uses SNAP TO MIDPOINT as the second point of a displacement.

Snapping Parallel to a Line, Circle, or Arc   CADD is tailor-made for certain geometric constructions, such as creating a line or arc parallel to an

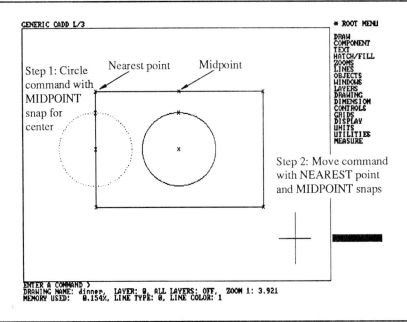

Figure 10-8. *Placing a circle in the center of a rectangle*

existing line, circle, or arc. Generic CADD offers two different ways to use this SNAP, depending on your circumstances.

SNAP PARALLEL may only be used in connection with the LINE, CIRCLE, and ARC commands, but may be used in many cases with various parts of these commands. To try out these commands, you will need a drawing similar to Figure 10-9 that includes lines, arcs, and circles.

With the LINE command, SNAP PARALLEL may be used when you are selecting either the first point or the second point. If you select PARALLEL from the SNAPS menu or type **SA** when you are asked for the *first* point, you are asked to select the original line to which you want the new line to be parallel. Then you are asked to specify an *offset distance,* which determines how far away from the original line the parallel line will be placed.

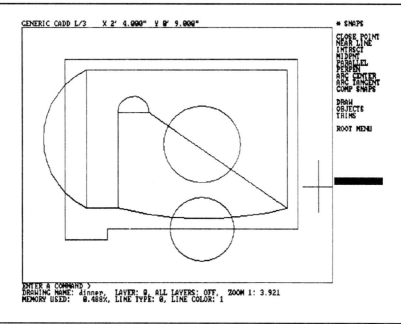

Figure 10-9. *A sample drawing for experimenting with SNAPS*

Type a number and press ENTER. You are then asked to place the first point and the second point. The new line will be constructed parallel to the selected line, as shown in Figure 10-10.

You may notice that Generic CADD sometimes puts the new line on the other side of the line from where you selected your new points. To correct this situation, simply specify a negative number for the offset. Generic CADD always puts the new line *above* the old one (see the discussion on the meaning of *above* in "Double Lines" in Chapter 9). In this case, left to right on the line is assumed to be from the first point given to the second *when the line was originally created.* Most of the time, you probably won't remember which direction you originally drew the line, so you may have to use trial and error.

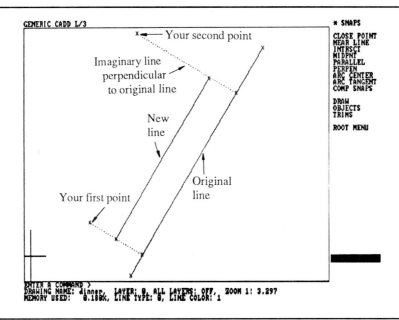

Figure 10-10.   *How endpoints are derived for parallel lines*

The other way to use the SNAP PARALLEL command for lines is to issue the SA command *after* placing the first point. This allows you to put one endpoint exactly where you want it, and on the side of the line where you want it. When you select PARALLEL after placing the first point, you are simply asked for the original line. After you have selected the line, place the second point. The point will be adjusted so that your line is parallel to the selected line, as shown in Figure 10-11.

When drawing a Line, you can only snap parallel to another Line. Though you can use an Arc or a Circle, the result has no meaning because there is no standard definition of what it means for a Line to be "parallel to an Arc or a Circle." You may find some occasion for these unorthodox uses, but they were not intended.

You can snap one Arc parallel to another Arc only by using the first method described above. The SNAP PARALLEL command only works when you select it before placing any of the points in the ARC 3 (A3) command. To create an Arc parallel to another Arc, use the SNAP PAR-

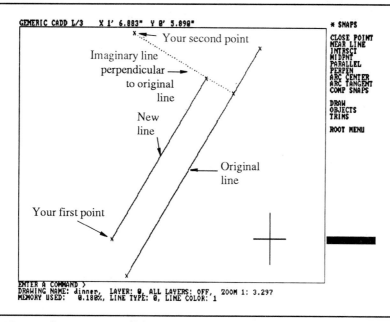

Figure 10-11. *Snapping parallel with one fixed point*

ALLEL command immediately after ARC 3. You are asked to specify the original Arc and the offset distance. With Arcs, a positive offset creates an Arc *outside,* or of greater radius than, the original Arc. Negative offsets create Arcs *inside* the reference Arc.

A Circle snapped parallel to another Circle creates a circle concentric with the original circle. Use the CIRCLE 2 (C2) command, and as with arcs, issue the SNAP PARALLEL (SA) command as soon as you are asked for the first point. You are asked for the reference circle and the offset. As with Arcs, positive offsets make circles bigger than the original, and negative offsets make smaller circles.

SNAP PARALLEL does not work with the ARC 2, ARC 4, or CIRCLE 3 command. Snapping one type of entity parallel to a different type of entity may have unusual results. Snapping an Arc parallel to a Circle creates a Circle, and snapping a Circle parallel to an Arc creates an Arc. The entity being snapped to overrides the command that you are using.

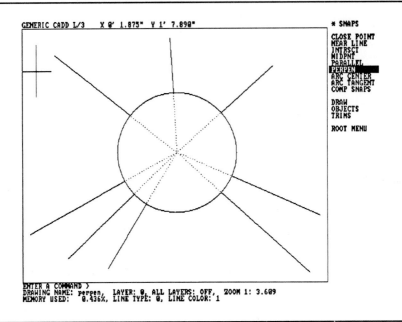

Figure 10-12.   *Several lines snapped perpendicular to a circle*

Snapping Perpendicular to a Line, Circle, or Arc   Another type of geometric construction that is simplified by Generic CADD Levels 2 and 3 is
a Line that meets another entity at a 90-degree angle. A Line can be
snapped perpendicular to another Line, a Circle, or an Arc. While a Line
cannot really meet a Circle or an Arc at 90 degrees unless the radius of the
Circle or Arc is infinite, a line *perpendicular* to a Circle or an Arc is defined
as a Line that radiates from the center of the Circle or Arc. Figure 10-12
shows several lines snapped perpendicular to a circle. The dotted lines
indicate imaginary extensions of the lines, which all meet at the center of
the circle.

The SNAP PERPENDICULAR command, abbreviated PERPEN on the
SNAPS menu and **SP** on the keyboard, can be used before selecting either
the first or the second endpoint of a line. If you select SNAP PERPENDIC-
ULAR before placing the first point, you are asked which entity you want
to snap perpendicular to, and you then place the second point, at which
time Generic CADD determines the first point and the Line is drawn. If
you place one point and then select the SNAP PERPENDICULAR com-

mand, you are simply asked which entity to snap to. Generic CADD locates the second point and the Line is drawn. In either case, you place one point and select one entity. Only the order is different.

Only Lines can be snapped perpendicular to these entities. Using SNAP PERPENDICULAR with other entities may be accepted by Generic CADD, but the results will most likely be nonsensical, as there are no geometric or mathematical definitions for the constructions.

Snapping to the Center of an Arc or Circle

Yet another geometric condition that can be located by a SNAP command is the center of an Arc or Circle. Actually, the center of a Circle can be located by a number of commands, because the center is one of the definition points of a circle. However, there is no definition point at the center of an Arc, so the SNAP TO ARC CENTER command comes in handy.

To snap to the center of an Arc, select ARC CENTER from the SNAPS menu or type **SN** on the keyboard. You are asked which Arc you want to snap to the center of, and the location of the center point is calculated by Generic CADD. You must pick a point near the Arc itself, not where you think its center is. The center point is a *calculated* piece of data, which does not exist until you select the Arc that determines its location.

You can use the SNAP TO ARC CENTER command, like the other SNAPS, whenever you are asked to specify a point. If you use it when you have the "ENTER A COMMAND >" prompt on the screen, you will start an automatic LINE command at the center of the selected Arc or Circle. If you select an entity that is not an Arc or a Circle, you simply get a message telling you that the center could not be located.

Snapping Tangent to an Arc or Circle

The final command that appears on the SNAPS menu, ARC TANGENT, provides an automated method for performing one of the more difficult geometric constructions in the hand drawing process, a Line tangent to an Arc or Circle. This Line touches the Arc or Circle at one point only and would, if extended, continue past the Arc or Circle without touching it again.

In trying to understand the meaning of *tangent,* it might help to think of the circle being tangent to the line, touching it ever so gently. For example, a billiard ball sitting on a table is tangent to the surface of the table, as it only touches at one point. A beach ball floating in water, however, is not tangent to the surface of the water, because part of the ball is below the water line.

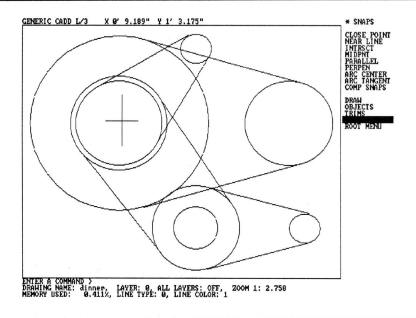

Figure 10-13. *Lines snapped tangent to several circles*

In any case, the ARC TANGENT (SX) command on the SNAPS menu allows you to construct a Line tangent to a given Arc or Circle. In fact, it is possible to draw a Line that is tangent to *two* Arcs or Circles by using the ARC TANGENT command at both endpoints of the line.

To draw a Line that is tangent to an Arc or Circle, start with a Line command, and place the first endpoint (the one that is not touching the Arc or Circle). When asked for the next point, use the ARC TANGENT (SX) command. You are asked to which Arc or Circle you want a tangent snapped. Pick one, and the Line is completed. If more than one tangent is possible, as with a Circle, Generic CADD will choose the tangent point closest to your first point.

To create a Line tangent to two Arcs or Circles, simply use the ARC TANGENT command before selecting each endpoint, choosing a different Arc or Circle for each snap. The drawing in Figure 10-13 shows several lines snapped tangent to several circles. You cannot reliably use ARC TANGENT to snap Arcs tangent to other Arcs, or Circles tangent to Arcs or Circles. If you want to try it, use ARC TANGENT on the second point of a three-point Arc or Circle, and you may get a relatively good approximation if the conditions are right.

Snapping to Components   All of the items on the SNAPS menu will work on placed components, if COMPONENT SNAPS (GC) is turned on. For detailed discussion on COMPONENT SNAPS, see Chapter 8. If COMPONENT SNAPS is off, the only point on a component placement that you can snap to is the reference points. Use SNAP TO NEAREST POINT or SNAP TO CLOSEST POINT to snap to the reference points.

The TRIMS Commands

Another way of editing existing entities is through the use of the TRIM commands. Not all of the entities that you select when using the TRIM commands are modified. These commands modify existing entities depending on their relationship to other entities.

Unlike the SNAPS commands, the TRIMS commands stand alone; that is, they may be used only at the "ENTER A COMMAND >" prompt, not in the middle of other commands. For the most part, they can be considered an extension of the OBJECT edit commands and are found only in Levels 2 and 3.

Trimming Lines and Arcs   The first command on the TRIMS menu is the TRIM command itself, typed **RM** (for tRiM) on the keyboard. Lines and Arcs can be trimmed to other Lines and Arcs, or to Circles. *Trimming* essentially means removing a portion of a Line or Arc that currently extends beyond another intersecting Line, Arc, or Circle.

To trim a Line or an Arc, select TRIM from the TRIMS menu or type **RM**. You are asked to choose the Line or Arc you want to trim. Make sure that the point that you use to select it is *on the side that you want to keep.* Next, you are asked for the entity to trim to. Select this boundary entity, and the first entity will be trimmed back to meet it.

The point at which the two entities meet is calculated very precisely, not according to the available screen resolution. Even if you ZOOM UP (ZU) or ZOOM WINDOW (ZW) several times, you will see that the trim is very accurate. In fact, the Line or Arc to be trimmed does not actually have to intersect the other entity. When you trim an entity to another that it does not intersect, an imaginary extension of the second entity is used to trim the first one. If the imaginary extension does not intersect the entity to be

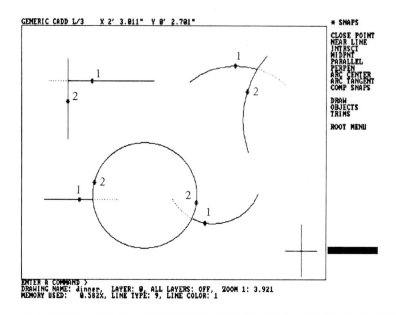

Figure 10-14.   *Examples of trimmable conditions*

trimmed, as might happen in the case of an Arc, the entity will not be trimmed.

When trimming to Arcs and Circles keep in mind that there are sometimes two possible intersection locations, and that the entity will be trimmed to the one closest to the point that you use to select the first entity.

Figure 10-14 illustrates some examples of trimmable conditions. The numbers indicate the order of selecting points, and the dotted lines indicate the portion that will be trimmed off.

Extending Lines and Arcs   The opposite of the TRIM command is the EXTEND command, also found on the TRIMS menu, and activated by typing **XT** (for eXTend) on the keyboard. As its name implies, the EXTEND command stretches or extends one entity to meet another. Lines and Arcs can be extended to meet other Lines, Arcs, or Circles.

You can use the EXTEND command whenever you have a Line or an Arc that does not quite meet another Line, Arc, or Circle. Select EXTEND from the TRIMS menu or type **XT**, and you are asked to select the entity to extend. After you select the entity, you are asked which entity you want to extend to. Once you select the second entity, the first entity will be extended.

As with the TRIM command, you can use the EXTEND command to extend a Line to an imaginary extension of the boundary entity. If the entity to be extended does not meet either the actual boundary entity or its imaginary extension, the entity will not be trimmed.

When you are working only with Lines, TRIM and EXTEND are interchangeable. TRIM will automatically extend a Line if necessary, and EXTEND will trim it. This is very convenient for editing, as you can TRIM and EXTEND several Lines by issuing either command, selecting two entities, pressing the SPACEBAR, selecting two more entities, and so on.

If Arcs or Circles are involved, either as the entity to be trimmed or extended or as the boundary entity, you have to be more precise because there is likely to be more than one intersection point between entities. TRIM will always cut off part of the entity selected, and EXTEND will always add to it.

Manually Filleting Lines and Arcs   Two Lines can be trimmed simultaneously, or an Arc can be inserted between two Lines or two Arcs with the FILLET command. Arcs are inserted in a similar manner to the AUTO-FILLET command (see Chapter 9), except that it is done *after* the Lines are drawn, instead of *while* they are being drawn. FILLET RADIUS (FR), the same command that establishes the radius of the arc inserted by AUTO-FILLET, also sets the radius for the FILLET command.

When used on two Lines, the FILLET command inserts an Arc of the specified radius, and trims or extends the two lines as required to meet the exact endpoint of the Arc. If the radius is too large for the Arc to be inserted between the two Lines, the fillet will not be done. The radius cannot, by definition, be too small. In fact, if the radius specified by the FILLET RADIUS (FR) command is zero, the two lines are simply extended or trimmed as required until they meet. No Arc is added at all. Filleting with radius zero is an excellent method of trimming or extending two lines at the same time. Parallel lines cannot be filleted.

The color, line type, line width, and layer of the inserted Arc are derived from the *second* Line selected if either entity is a Line. In other words, if you fillet a blue line to a red line, you will get a red arc. In addition, the first line will turn red. When you have finished with a fillet, all three entities are located on the same layer, and are the same color, line type,

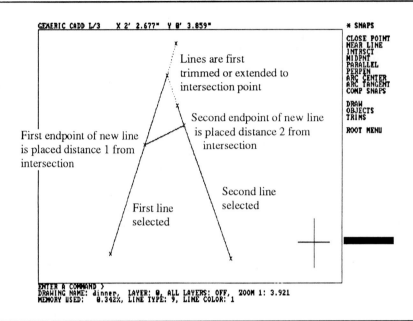

Figure 10-15. *How a line is inserted by the CHAMFER command*

and line width. This means that if the two lines are different in any of these attributes, it makes a difference which entity you pick first.

When one or both of the entities to fillet is an Arc, the same thing happens, except that the entities are not trimmed. *You* will have to trim or extend them, as required, with the TRIM or EXTEND command. It does no good, therefore, to try to FILLET two Arcs with a FILLET RADIUS of zero. Unlike Lines, which will eventually meet as long as they are not parallel, it is possible that the FILLET RADIUS can be too small when filleting Arcs. In this case, the fillet will not be done.

The Arc inserted by the FILLET command when both of the filleted entities are arcs takes on the current color, line type, line width, and layer, rather than taking on the attributes of either of the selected entities. The filleted entities are not changed in any way.

To fillet two Lines, two Arcs, or a Line to an Arc, first set the radius using the FILLET RADIUS (FR) command. Then select FILLET from the TRIMS menu or type **FL** on the keyboard. You are asked to select a point on one object to be filleted, and then the other. As soon as you have selected the second entity, the fillet will occur.

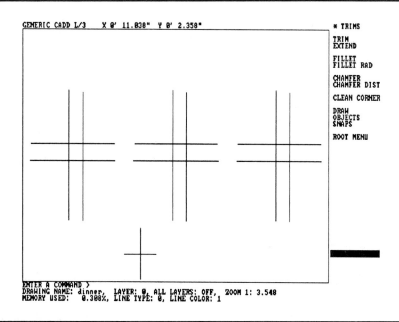

Figure 10-16.   *Three intersecting sets of parallel lines*

Chamfering Lines   The CHAMFER command, found on the TRIMS menu and typed **CH** on the keyboard, is similar in many ways to the FILLET command. Instead of inserting an Arc, the CHAMFER command inserts a Line near the intersection of two selected Lines. Arcs cannot be chamfered. CHAMFER works with a control variable, similar to FILLET RADIUS, called CHAMFER DISTANCES. This command, shortened to CHAMFER DIST on the TRIMS menu and typed **CA** on the keyboard, sets the distances from the intersection at which the endpoints of the new line will be placed. Two values need to be supplied: one for the endpoint on the first line selected, and one for the endpoint on the second line.

   Figure 10-15 shows the relationship between two lines, their intersection point, and the chamfer distances. As with the FILLET command, the two lines are trimmed or extended as required to meet the endpoints of the new line exactly. Note that the chamfer distances are actually measured from the intersection of the two lines selected, not from their original endpoints. The color, line type, line width, and layer of the inserted line are derived from the *first* Line selected, which is the opposite of how the

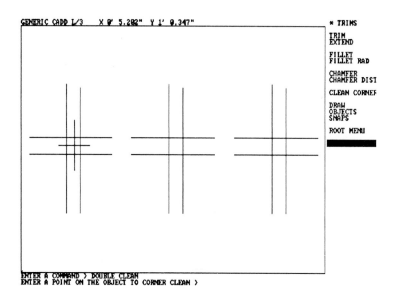

Figure 10-17. *Picking a point inside the intersection*

FILLET command works. The second Line selected is also changed to conform to these parameters. If either of the values specified by CHAMFER DISTANCES is zero, the CHAMFER command will act just like a FILLET radius zero, except for the way that the entity attributes are handled.

Filleting Four Lines at the Same Time   Levels 2 and 3 include the CLEAN CORNER command, which is found on the TRIMS menu and is activated by typing the two-character code **KT**, standing for "Korner Trim." In Level 2, this command works exactly like a fillet with FILLET RADIUS set to zero. The main advantage is that if you are also filleting entities with another radius, you don't have to keep changing the FILLET RADIUS to zero and back again. Just use CLEAN CORNER instead.

However, in Level 3, the CLEAN CORNER command is significantly different, and much more powerful. It works with intersecting pairs of parallel lines, a condition shown three times in Figure 10-16. These pairs of lines could have been created at any time with the LINE command or with the DOUBLE LINE (L2) command; as long as each is a separate Line entity, and not part of a component placement or hatch pattern, the CLEAN CORNER command can be used. The Lines do not have to intersect at right angles, nor do the individual pairs have to be exactly parallel. As long as one pair extends beyond the other pair, so that there are true intersections between every set of lines, this command can be used.

To use the CLEAN CORNER command, select CLEAN CORNER from the TRIMS menu or type **KT** on the keyboard. You will be asked to "ENTER A POINT ON THE OBJECT TO CORNER CLEAN >," which is not an accurate prompt. In fact, what you want to pick is a point *inside* the intersection of the two sets of lines, as shown in Figure 10-17. The second prompt asks you to "ENTER A POINT OUTSIDE CORNER >," which is another ambiguous request because three different places are possible, each producing different results.

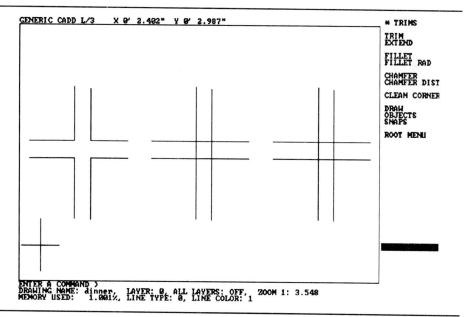

Figure 10-18. *A four-way trimmed intersection*

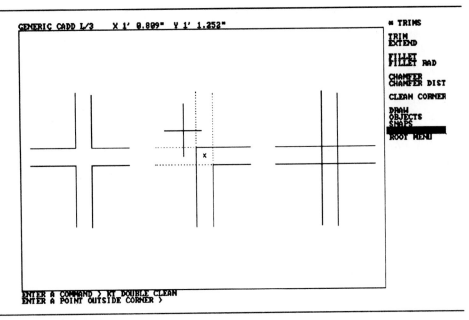

Figure 10-19. *Picking a point to create a corner*

1. If you pick a point inside the intersection, all four lines are broken and trimmed, as shown in the drawing on the extreme left of Figure 10-18. If the four lines have different colors, line types, line widths, or layers, Generic CADD will assign the attributes of one of the lines to all of them.

2. If you choose a point outside the intersection between two perpendicular lines, as shown in Figure 10-19, the lines are trimmed so that the opposite corner remains. The selected point should be located within the corner established by the perpendicular lines, not beyond the length of either.

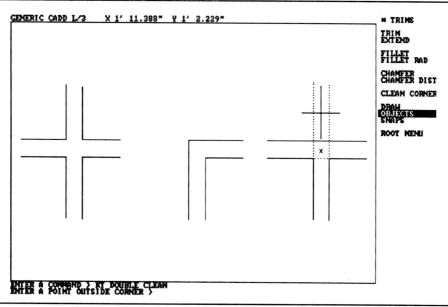

Figure 10-20. *Picking a point to create a "T"*

3. If you select a point outside the intersection but between two of the parallel lines, that set of lines is trimmed off, and the remaining lines form a "T" figure, as shown in the far-right drawing in Figure 10-20. Again, if your second point is beyond the endpoint of either line, the command probably will not work. This is one reason that you must have a true intersection condition in order to use the CLEAN CORNER command.

This chapter contains all of the basic and advanced Generic CADD drawing and editing commands. The commands in this chapter can enhance your ability to create accurate drawings more quickly and to edit existing drawings more accurately. The SNAPS and TRIMS commands are particularly effective for difficult or time-consuming geometric constructions.

11 *Dimensioning*

Generic CADD's dimensioning features include the automatic dimensioning of distances and angles. These capabilities are found only in Levels 2 and 3, follow their own rules in many ways, and can almost be thought of as a separate program inside Generic CADD. However, the dimensioning commands also have several similarities to some of the commands previously discussed.

Dimensioning has many things in common with multiple entity commands (see Chapter 9), in that the commands that place dimensions into the drawing actually create several entities at the same time: Lines, arcs, and circles are used to draw the dimension lines, extension lines, and arrowheads and Text Characters are placed to indicate distances and angles.

Dimensioning also has several characteristics in common with complex entities (see Chapter 8). A number of special parameter-setting commands determine the way that dimensions are placed, much like the text placement parameters influence the placement of text, and the component placement parameters control the way that components are placed.

Like text, dimensioning has its own color-setting command but goes one step further with its own layer parameter. In fact, almost everything about dimensioning is controllable by a parameter-setting command. So many parameters can be set that they have their own menu instead of being on the same menu with the dimension placement commands.

The SNAP commands are usually used to snap on to existing objects to maintain accuracy while dimensioning.

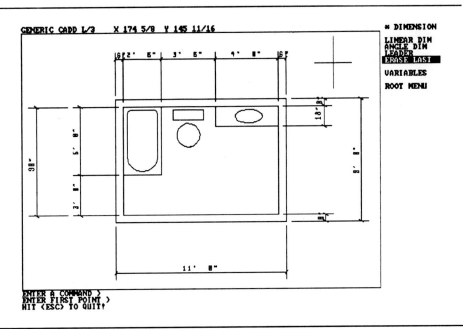

Figure 11-1.   *A dimensioned drawing*

When you select DIMENSION from the ROOT menu, you will get the DIMENSION menu, which contains the placement commands and the word "VARIABLES." This latter menu item takes you to the menu of dimensioning variables, or parameters. These 16 parameter-setting commands are organized in groups and have related names. At the end of this menu is a command to return you to the DIMENSION menu. When you place dimensions, you often go back and forth between these two menus.

Creating a Dimensioning Style

The VARIABLES menu contains all of the commands necessary to define a dimensioning *style*. These variables control the layer, color, lengths of

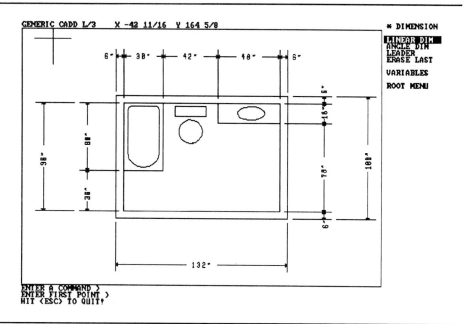

Figure 11-2. *A drawing dimensioned in a different style*

various parts of the dimensions, kind of arrowheads used, the placement of text and so on. Figures 11-1 and 11-2 show two typical styles of *linear dimensioning.*

If you always use the same style of dimensions, you can set the default values for all of these variables in the CONFIG program. Several of the variables may depend on the scale of the final printed drawing, so these may vary from drawing to drawing, even if you always use the same style.

Each dimensioning VARIABLE command either controls one particular aspect of dimensioning or works together with one or more of the other variables to create specific dimensioning styles. Although these commands are listed on the video menu according to frequency of use, they are examined in this chapter in an order more closely approximating how you might set them to create a particular style.

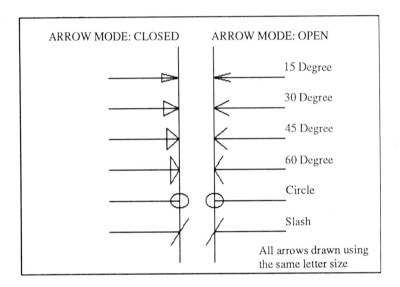

Figure 11-3.   *Generic CADD's arrowheads*

The Arrow Variables

The type of arrowhead is controlled by two commands, ARROW TYPE and ARROW MODE. Between these two commands, ten different arrowheads are available, as shown in Figure 11-3.

The ARROW TYPE Command   The ARROW TYPE command, typed **AT** on the keyboard, gives you a choice of six different arrowhead styles. Four are arrows, one is a circle, and one is a slash. The ARROW TYPE (AT) gives you a list of the six arrow types available. Choose one by typing the number shown next to it and pressing ENTER. The arrow type that you select will be used for all dimensions placed until you use this command again.

Arrow Mode (Closed or Open)   This variable provides four additional choices by adding a closing line to the back of the arrowheads. When you choose ARROW MODE from the VARIABLES menu or type **AW** on the keyboard, you toggle ARROW MODE on or off, depending on its current status. A message in the prompt area informs you of your selection with the message "ARROW CLOSED IS ON" or "ARROW CLOSED IS OFF." If you select ARROW TYPE 5 (circle) or 6 (slash), ARROW MODE still toggles on and off, but has no effect on the way that arrowheads are drawn unless you switch to another type.

The Letter Variables

To distinguish them from the normal text functions and parameters, the text characters that are placed as part of the dimensioning commands are called *letters*. The commands for the variables that control these letters start with the word "LETTER" on the menu, and their codes start with the letter *L* on the keyboard.

Letter Font   The font used for dimension letters is controlled by the LETTER FONT command on the VARIABLES menu, or **LF** on the keyboard. LETTER FONT is selected and loaded in exactly the same way as FONT SELECT determines the font for normal text placement, except that the available fonts are not listed on the video menu, so you must type the font name.

The letter font is used only by the dimensioning commands and must be loaded separately from the text font. The fonts that you can select must be on the disk somewhere, and the DOS path for finding these fonts should be specified in the CONFIG program. See Chapter 8 for more information on fonts.

Letter (and Arrow) Size   The size of the characters that compose the dimensioning text is controlled by the LETTER SIZE variable, typed **LH** on the keyboard, standing for Letter Height. Because there is no LETTER ASPECT command and TEXT ASPECT does not apply to dimensioning text, LETTER SIZE also controls the width of the letters placed by the dimensioning commands. To set LETTER SIZE, you type a value indicating the size of the letters you want in your dimensions.

The LETTER SIZE variable also controls the size of the arrowheads that are placed by the dimensioning commands. For the first four arrow types (four different angles of arrowheads), each angled line of the arrowhead is half the length of the letter size. If your letter size is 1, your dimensioning text will be one inch high, and your arrowheads will be 1/2 inch long. If you use circles instead of arrowheads, the diameter of the circle will be half the letter size. The length of slashes is the same length as the letter size.

Letter Placement Location   Various drawing disciplines prefer various locations for the dimensioning text. The LETTER PLACEMENT variable, typed **LP** on the keyboard, controls whether the text is placed "ABOVE" the dimension line or "IN" it. Most architectural applications use the former, while many other drawing disciplines require the latter.

If text is placed within the dimension line (the IN option), the line is broken to allow the text. An extra space of 1/2 LETTER SIZE is inserted at each end of the text, and the text is centered within the line, both horizontally and vertically. If text is placed above the dimension line, the dimension line is continuous from one arrowhead to the other, with the dimension text placed 1/2 LETTER SIZE above the line.

Letter Direction   The direction, or rotation, of the text created by the dimensioning commands is selected using LETTER DIR on the VARI-ABLE menu or by typing **LR** on the keyboard. You have two choices: HORIZONTAL and ALIGNED.

If LETTER DIRECTION is set to ALIGNED, text is rotated so that it is parallel to the dimension line, either above or within the line. With LETTER DIRECTION set to ALIGNED, text rotations are *normalized* between 0 and 90 degrees in either positive or negative directions. If the dimension line is at more than a 90-degree angle, the rotation of the text is converted to an angle that aligns with the dimension line, so that the text appears right side up. Figure 11-4 shows various text rotations for different aligned conditions. Notice that the text is never upside-down. When the drawing must be turned to read the text, it is always turned clockwise no more than 90 degrees.

If you select HORIZONTAL, all dimension text is placed at rotation zero, regardless of the angle of the dimension line. Since the LETTER PLACE-MENT mode does not apply in the same way if text is always horizontal, the role of the PLACEMENT variable is reduced to deciding simply whether the dimension line will be broken. When LETTER DIRECTION is set to HORIZONTAL, text is always centered on the dimension line. The line is broken if LETTER PLACEMENT is set to IN, and it is left whole if LETTER PLACEMENT is ABOVE. In most instances, you will want to set LETTER PLACEMENT to IN so that the dimension text and the dimension line will not run into each other.

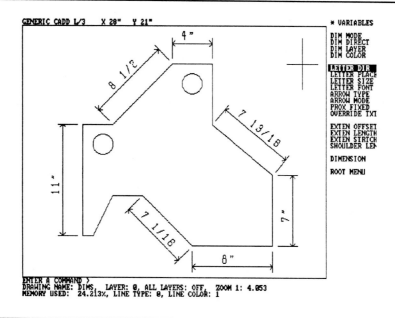

Figure 11-4. *Text aligned at various dimension directions*

You must set these two variables in the order that they are shown on the video menu. LETTER DIRECTION should be set first and then LETTER PLACEMENT, especially if you want to use aligned text above the dimension line, a very common style. If you first set LETTER PLACEMENT to ABOVE, and then change LETTER DIRECTION to ALIGNED, Generic CADD will change LETTER PLACEMENT to IN automatically. If you really want ABOVE, you must select it again. The moral is, always check the LETTER PLACEMENT variable after changing LETTER DIRECTION to make sure that it is still set the way that you think it is.

Override Text   Normally, Generic CADD generates the dimension text automatically, based on the actual distance between the points that you select when you are dimensioning. Both the type of units and their level of precision are set by the commands on the UNITS menu, discussed in Chapter 3.

In some cases, however, you may want to type your own dimension text, which you can do with the OVERRIDE TEXT toggle, activated by the characters OT on the keyboard. If OVERRIDE TEXT is off, dimension text is added automatically by Generic CADD; if it is on, you are asked to type the text when you use the dimensioning commands.

Dimensioning Attributes

Dimensioning is controlled by its own attribute-setting commands. Current line color, text color, line type, line width, and layer do not apply. All entities produced by the dimensioning commands use line type 0 and line width 0, but you can adjust these defaults using any of the CHANGE commands. Color and layer are controlled by two of the dimensioning VARIABLES.

The DIMENSION LAYER Command   All entities created by the dimensioning commands fall on the layer specified by the DIM LAYER command on the VARIABLES menu or by typing **UL**. Just like the LAYER CURRENT (YC) or LAYER SELECT (YS) command, you are simply asked to type a number and press ENTER.

Note that you can put dimensions on layers other than the current layer through the use of this command. This may be confusing at first if you try to edit the dimensions: To edit a dimension, you must either turn EDIT ALL LAYERS (AL) on, or make the dimensioning layer the current layer. It is often a good idea to have EDIT ALL LAYERS on while dimensioning anyway, so that you can snap to the objects in the drawing, even though they may be located on a variety of layers.

The ability to turn ALL LAYERS EDIT off and dimension objects on a particular layer can help to prevent snapping onto other objects by mistake. Specifically, you cannot snap onto other dimensions that may be close to the selected objects. This technique will be demonstrated under "Linear Dimensions" and "Angular Dimensions."

The DIMENSION COLOR Command   All entities, both text and simple entities, are created using the DIMENSION COLOR command instead of the normal LINE COLOR and TEXT COLOR commands. The dimension color is set by selecting the DIM COLOR command from the VARIABLES menu or by typing **SK** on the keyboard. As usual, if the video menu is turned on and more than two colors are available, you may select color bars

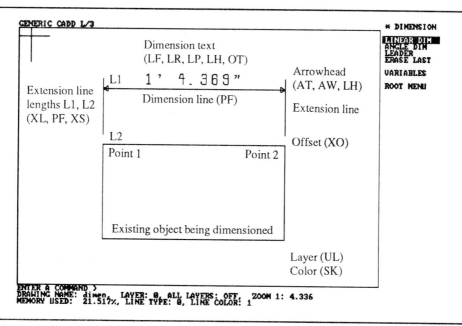

Figure 11-5. *The parts of a typical dimension*

from the menu or type a number between 0 and 255. Numbers that represent colors unavailable on your video card will repeat to fill out the list.

Extension Line Control

Extension lines are created by the dimensioning commands to indicate the points to which you are dimensioning. Figure 11-5 shows the various parts of a typical dimension. Several dimensioning variables control the way that the extension lines are used in your dimensions, including the distance from the lines to the object, the lengths of the extension lines, and whether the lengths of the lines are fixed or variable. A related variable controls the location of the dimension line, a factor that affects the length of the extension lines.

Extension Offset   You may not want the extension lines to start right at the object you are dimensioning. Graphic clarity usually mandates leaving some space around the dimensioned objects. The amount of space between the object and the extension lines is controlled by the EXTENSION OFFSET variable, shortened to EXTEN OFFSET on the VARIABLE menu and typed **XO** on the keyboard. A minimum value of 0 produces extension lines that touch the object. The value specified cannot be negative. If you attempt to supply a negative value, you will not be allowed to exit the EXTENSION OFFSET command until you have corrected the situation.

Extension Length   The default length of extension lines is set by the EXTENSION LENGTH command, found directly below OFFSET on the VARIABLE menu or activated by typing **XL** on the keyboard. As shown in Figure 11-5, two values determine the total extension line length: the distance from the dimension line to the outside end of the extension line (L1), and the distance from the offset end of the extension line to the dimension line (L2).

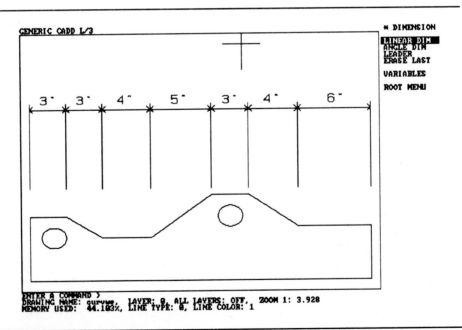

Figure 11-6.   *Dimensioning with EXTENSION STRETCH turned off*

When you use the EXTENSION LENGTH command, you are asked for both of these values, first L1 and then L2. The first of these values (outside length) is always used, but the second (inside length) may or may not be used, depending on the settings of some of the variables to follow. The values specified by this command must be positive numbers.

Extension Stretch The EXTENSION STRETCH toggle controls how strictly the EXTENSION OFFSET and EXTENSION LENGTH values are followed. If EXTENSION STRETCH is off, the value specified for the inside length of the extension lines is always used. This means that the OFFSET will be enlarged in some cases, as shown in Figure 11-6. In this example, the first dimension was created, then each subsequent dimension line location was snapped to the end of the previous one with the NEAREST POINT snap. All of the extension lines are the same length, as they are not allowed to stretch. If EXTENSION STRETCH is on, the OFFSET is fixed and the extension lines are stretched, as shown in Figure 11-7, also created by snapping subsequent dimension lines onto the previous ones. In either case, if the two points specified for the dimension are not the same

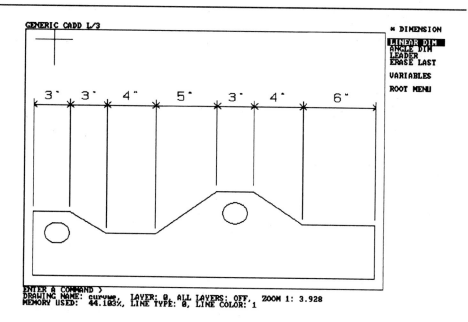

Figure 11-7. *Dimensioning with EXTENSION STRETCH turned on*

distance from the dimension line, the shorter of the two extension lines will use the actual EXTENSION LENGTH value.

Dimension Line Proximity Fixed   When the PROXIMITY FIXED toggle is on, the location of dimension lines is determined by the EXTENSION LENGTH and OFFSET variables. The distance between the dimension line and the object being dimensioned will be the total of the OFFSET and the second length value, measured at the end of the dimension line that is closest to the object.

If PROX FIXED, as it is called on the VARIABLES menu, is off, you are asked to locate the dimension line yourself. With PROXIMITY FIXED, (typed **PF** on the keyboard) turned off, EXTENSION OFFSET is still used, as is the first value of EXTENSION LENGTH (outside length). The inside length of the extension lines is determined by where you place the dimension line.

Dimensioning Scale

Dimensions fall into the category of CADD items defined as *symbols* (see Chapter 8). As with all symbols, the size of dimensions on the printed sheet is more important than their size in the drawing. However, you do have to put them into the drawing next to the objects that you are dimensioning, so the issue of scale arises. As with other symbols, the values that specify size must be adjusted, usually enlarged, so that they can be scaled, usually downward, when the drawing is printed or plotted.

This is done by multiplying the desired distances and lengths by a scale factor that is the inverse of the scale factor to be applied at printing time. For instance, if you are dimensioning an architectural drawing that will be plotted at 1/4" = 1′, the actual scale factor is 1/48 of real size, or 1:48. Therefore, all of the values for the dimensioning variable must be scaled up by a factor of 48. To get a 1/8" EXTENSION OFFSET, for example, you must use a value of 6" (1/8 × 48). When the drawing is printed, 6" represented at 1/4" = 1′ will appear as 1/8".

Once you have established a style with the VARIABLE commands, the variables that do not involve scale (the toggles, arrowhead selection, and so on) can be permanently set with the CONFIG program. You might want to put the values for 1:1, or the sizes that they will actually be printed at, into the scalable variables to remind yourself of these values. If you like, the scalable values could be stored in either batch files or menu items in

Generic CADD Level 3. Turn to Chapter 15 for more on this type of customization.

Linear Dimensions

The examples so far have dealt with the most common form of dimensioning, linear dimensions. Once you have set the style variables, you place the dimensions with the LINEAR DIMENSION command. While using this command, you will change two additional variables, DIMENSION MODE and DIMENSION DIRECTION.

In general, you place a dimension by selecting LINEAR DIM from the DIMENSIONS menu or by typing **LX** on the keyboard. You are asked for two points, which indicate the distance to be dimensioned. Usually, you will use SNAP TO NEAREST POINT or another of the SNAPS commands to locate these two points. Next, whether PROXIMITY FIXED is on or off, you are asked for the location of the dimension line. If PROX FIXED is off, the dimension line will pass through the point indicated. If PROX FIXED is on, your point will simply indicate which direction the extension lines should extend from the first two points selected. If OVERRIDE TEXT is on, you will be asked to type the dimension text. Finally, if the text does not fit in the available space, you are asked to specify a location, which will determine the lower-left corner of the first character, just as if you were placing text with the TEXT PLACE command. If there is room, Generic CADD places the text automatically. After the first dimension, another dimension command is started automatically. When you have finished placing dimensions, press ESC.

If you have DISPLAY CONSTRUCTION POINTS turned on, you may notice that construction points are not displayed while you are placing dimensions. If construction points were shown, it would be more difficult to see the dimensions as you were creating them. After a REDRAW (RD) or any zoom command, the construction points will be shown as usual.

Dimension Direction

Between any two points, three possible distances can be dimensioned: the actual shortest distance between the two points, the horizontal distance, and the vertical distance, all of which are illustrated in Figure 11-8. The

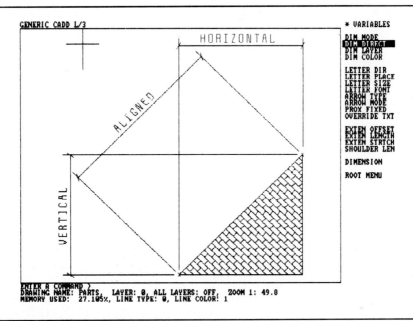

Figure 11-8.   *Various dimension directions*

distance you are actually dimensioning when you pick two points is determined by the DIMENSION DIRECTION command. To set the direction, select DIM DIRECT from the VARIABLES menu, or type **UD** on the keyboard. You are given three choices, ALIGNED (shortest distance), HORIZONTAL, and VERTICAL. Select one by typing the number shown next to its name, and press ENTER. As you can see, you will probably need to use this variable often while adding dimensions to your drawings. In fact, if you are adventurous, you might want to move this and the next variable onto the DIMENSIONS menu from the VARIABLES menu, using the techniques discussed in Chapter 15, so you do not have to switch to the VARIABLES menu to change them.

Dimension Mode

Another variable that you may need to change often is the DIMENSION MODE command, which controls all dimension commands after the first one. (The first LINEAR DIMENSION always works in the same way. The difference shows up in subsequent dimensions done with the same command, before pressing ESC.) The three available MODES, INDIVIDUAL, PARTITIONED, and CUMULATIVE, are selected by using the DIM MODE command on the VARIABLES menu or by typing **UM** on the keyboard. You will get a numbered list of these possibilities. Type one, followed by ENTER.

If DIMENSION MODE is set to INDIVIDUAL, you are asked for two more points, a dimension location, and so on. This process continues until you press ESC. This mode is called "INDIVIDUAL" because you specify separate first and second points for each dimension that you create.

If DIMENSION MODE is set to PARTITIONED or CUMULATIVE, you are asked only for the second point for each dimension because the first point of the new dimension is taken from the last dimension. In the PARTITIONED mode, the second point of the first dimension becomes the first point of the second dimension; the second point of the second dimension becomes the first point of the third; and so on. All of the dimension lines connect end on end, as shown in Figure 11-9.

In the CUMULATIVE mode, the *first* point of dimensions are shared, so that the first point of the first dimension is also the first point of the second dimension, and the third, and so on. Each subsequent dimension line is separated from the preceding line by the distance of the total EXTENSION LENGTH. The extension lines themselves stack up end on end at the first dimensioning point.

You can see that you might change the DIMENSION MODE variable quite often. It is important to note that once you press ESC to end the LINEAR DIMENSION command, you are always asked for a new first point the next time you start a new dimension, no matter which dimensioning mode you used previously.

Oops!

With so many variables to set, it is possible that you will not achieve the correct result on the first few tries. You will probably have to try out various

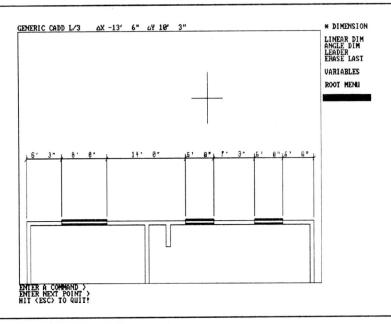

Figure 11-9. *Partitioned dimensioning*

combinations until you find a style you like by trial and error. Use the ROOM plan, for example, or another existing drawing. Once you have called up the drawing and set the dimensioning variables, use LINEAR DIM (LX) on the DIMENSIONS menu. If your first dimension does not turn out exactly the way you want it, press ESC to end the LINEAR DIMENSION command and use ERASE LAST DIMENSION, called ERASE LAST on the DIMENSIONS menu and typed **ED** on the keyboard. (Notice that, even though the menu name is the same, this command is not exactly the same as ERASE LAST (EL) on the OBJECTS menu, in that it erases more than one item at a time, specifically the lines, arrows, and letters of the last dimension.)

To erase the last dimension, you must use the ED command before adding any other entities or editing any objects. Once you have erased it, reset the variables using the VARIABLES menu, and try again. You can repeat this process as many times as you like. ERASE LAST always erases the *last* dimension added, whether it was the only dimension placed in one

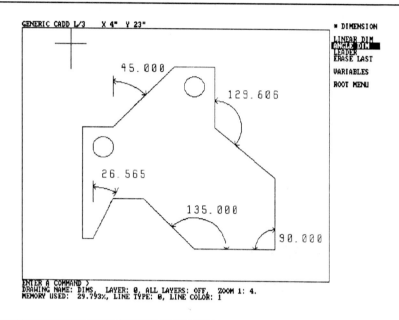

Figure 11-10.   *Angular dimensions*

command, or the last in a series of PARTITIONED or CUMULATIVE dimensions.

Angular Dimensions

Angular dimensions, such as the ones shown in Figure 11-10, use many of the variables that you have already set. The extension offset, lengths, and stretch variables apply, as do the color, layer, font, and arrow parameters. The letter direction and placement variables do not apply, because the text is always horizontal and you position it yourself. Neither can the proximity be fixed, for the same reason. DIMENSION MODE applies to angular dimensions, but DIMENSION DIRECTION does not.

The First Angular Dimension

In general, an angular dimension is placed by selecting ANGLE DIM from the DIMENSION menu or by typing **AX** on the keyboard. You are asked first for a center point—the point where the lines that form the angle intersect. If the two lines do not actually meet at this point, use the SNAP INTERSECT (SI) command to locate the center. Next, you are asked for a POINT ON THE FIRST RADIUS, which is simply a point on the first line. Use SNAP TO NEAREST POINT if there is an endpoint nearby; otherwise use SNAP NEAR to get a point on the object. Do the same when you are asked for a POINT ON THE NEXT RADIUS.

You need not worry about the location of the dimension line or the text when you are selecting these points; they simply determine the lines of the angle that you want to dimension. These points must, however, be selected in a counterclockwise direction, as that will determine the angle to be dimensioned. If you choose them in clockwise order, the dimension line (actually, an arc) will appear on the opposite side of the lines from where you intended. Instead of 90 degrees, for example, you will get 270.

Once you have selected these two lines, you are asked for the locations of the dimension arc and the dimensioning text. The "location of the dimension" is a point through which the arc will pass. Arrowheads are added to the ends of this arc according to the ARROW TYPE (AT) and ARROW MODE (AW) parameters. The "location of the dimension text" specifies the lower-left corner of the first character of the text. The text is formatted according to the UNITS that are currently active.

The text for angular dimensions always contains three characters, or, more closely, character spaces, before the decimal point. If the angle is smaller than a three-digit number, one or two spaces are added in front of the text, which is why the text does not appear right at the point you select in all cases. If you turn on FAST TEXT (TF), you will see standard points at the spaces.

Subsequent Angular Dimensions

The DIMENSIONING MODE affects angular dimensions in the same way that it does linear dimensions. If DIM MODE is INDIVIDUAL, you are asked for a new center and two lines to dimension. If the current MODE is PARTITIONED, you are asked for a new second line, as the second line from the previous angular dimension becomes the first line for the current dimension, and the dimension arcs automatically align end on end. If

CUMULATIVE is the active MODE, each new dimension uses the same first line, and each dimensioning arc is placed the total extension length from the preceding arc. In all MODES, you still place the text yourself. When you are done placing angular dimensions, or want to start with another first point or a new MODE, press ESC.

Leaders

The LEADER command lets you draw an arrow at the end of a line, usually at an angle, with a short horizontal line at one end, called the *shoulder*. *Leaders,* which are often used to draw arrows from notes to parts of the drawing, as shown in Figure 11-11, are often placed at the same time as dimensions. The leader is made entirely of lines, unless you are using circles for arrowheads, all created on the DIMENSION LAYER (UL) and

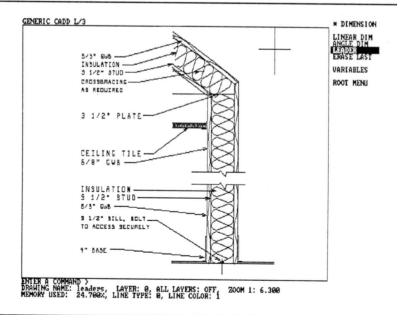

Figure 11-11. *A typical use of Leaders*

using the DIMENSION COLOR (SK). The current ARROW TYPE (AT) and ARROW MODE (AW) are used as well. The other dimensioning variables have no effect on the LEADER command.

The SHOULDER LENGTH Command

The SHOULDER LENGTH command specifies the length of the horizontal segment attached to the arrow line of the leader. Like all of the numeric dimensioning variables, the scale at which the drawing will eventually be printed or plotted should be considered when setting the SHOULDER LENGTH.

To set the SHOULDER LENGTH, select SHOULDER LEN on the VARIABLES menu or type **LL** on the keyboard. You are shown the current value and asked to type a new one. Unlike many of the other variables, you can set the SHOULDER LENGTH to zero, if you like. Like all of the other dimensioning variables, SHOULDER LENGTH can be fixed using the CONFIG program so you do not have to reset it every time you start a drawing.

Drawing the Leader

When you are ready to draw a leader, select LEADER from the DIMEN-SION menu or type **LE** on the keyboard. You are asked for the starting point. Leaders start with the shoulder and end with the arrow, so if you are using a leader to connect notes with parts of your drawing, your first point should be near the beginning or end of your text, wherever you want the leader to start. Next, you are asked for a direction for the shoulder. Select a point to the left or right of the first point to indicate the direction of the shoulder. If you are using the leader with text, move the cursor *away* from the text to specify this point. Finally, you are asked for the end of the leader (the end with the arrow), which should be placed at or near the corresponding object.

Once you have specified these three points, the leader is drawn. A horizontal line segment starts at the first point and ends at a horizontal distance equal to the SHOULDER LENGTH in the direction selected. A second line connects the end of the shoulder to the third point, where your selected arrowhead is drawn. Note that neither construction points nor rubber banding works while drawing leaders, so you have to remember where you put your first point to visualize the leader before it appears. As with the rest of the dimension commands, leaders do not take on the current line type and line width, but can be changed to any layer, color, line type or line width with any of the CHANGE commands.

Many facets of dimensioning can be automated in Level 3 through the use of BATCH commands or custom menus. Therefore, dimensioning is discussed in Chapter 15 as one of the important ways to customize Generic CADD.

12 *File Storage and Retrieval*

One of the most important functions of any computer program is to store and retrieve information to and from disks. This information is stored in *files*. Because Generic CADD stores several different kinds of information it uses several different types of files.

On MS-DOS systems, files are named with up to eight characters, which can be followed by a period and up to three optional characters, called the *filename extension*. As discussed in Chapter 3, Generic CADD uses these three optional characters to identify the type of files stored.

Drawings are stored in files with the extension .DWG, components in files with the extension .CMP, and fonts in files with the extension .FNT. Additionally, Level 3's hatch patterns are stored in .HCH files, and batch files are stored in .TXT files. All versions store images in .GX2 files. The CADD program files use a variety of file extensions. For more information on working with files, see Chapter 3.

The commands that save and retrieve information from files usually appear on the menus associated with the type of information being saved or retrieved and share the first letter of their two-character codes with the rest of the commands on that menu. In general, Generic CADD uses the term "LOAD" as part of the name for commands that retrieve information, assigning the letter *L* to the second character of the two-letter command, and the term "SAVE" for saving information on the disk, using an *S* as the second character in the two-character commands.

Default Paths

Whenever you need to load or save a file, Generic CADD needs to know where to find or put that file. In MS-DOS terminology, the location on disk where you want to store a file is known as the *path*. In the CONFIG program, you can set up default paths for the locations of drawing files, component files, and font files. If you want to load or save information from different default paths, you can reset the paths once you are in Generic CADD.

The commands for changing default paths are different for each level of Generic CADD. Level 1 and Level 2 use the CHANGE PATHS (GP) command for changing all three paths, while Level 3 has a separate command for each of the three different file types: DRAWING PATH (P1), COMPONENT PATH (P2), and FONT PATH (P3).

The CHANGE PATHS Command

To change any or all of the paths in Generic CADD Level 1 or Level 2, select CHANGE PATHS from the UTILITIES menu, or type **GP** on the keyboard. You are shown the current path setup for the DRAWING, COMPONENT, and FONT paths, and asked to type the new one. You should respond by typing the disk drive designator (**A:**, **B:**, **C:**, and so on) and the name of the directory where you want to keep the specified type of file. If Generic CADD is stored on the same disk drive, you do not have to type it. Chapter 3 contains more information on specifying paths.

If you do not want to change any of the paths for any of the three file types, simply press ENTER when shown the current path. The current path settings will be used for the current drawing session only, or until they are changed. Once you exit Generic CADD, the paths return to the defaults that have been set with the CONFIG program. If you want to change the default paths permanently, use CONFIG.

The Individual Path Commands

In Generic CADD Level 3, the individual path commands are found on the CONTROLS menu. Like the CHANGE PATHS command in Levels 1 and 2, these commands change the paths only for the current drawing session.

The DRAWING PATH Command Drawing files are stored in the default drawing path. These files are typically saved when you quit Generic CADD and loaded when you first start Generic CADD and are asked for the name of a drawing.

To change the drawing path, select DWG PATH from the CONTROLS menu or type **P1** on the keyboard. You are shown the name of the current path and asked to type a new one. Unlike many commands, including the CHANGE PATHS command in Levels 1 and 2, if you press ENTER you do not necessarily keep the current path. Instead, the path is set to CURRENT GENERIC CADD DIRECTORY, or the same path as the program itself. Essentially, this is *no* path, as Generic CADD simply uses filenames instead of full pathnames. This works just fine as long as you do not have too many drawing files. Once you have more than a few drawing files, however, it makes sense to keep them in your Generic CADD directory in their own subdirectory. You may want to divide them even further—by job, by drawing type, or by some other organizing scheme.

The current drawing path will be used with all commands that load or save drawings, including such commands as QUIT (QU), DRAWING SAVE (DS), DRAWING LOAD (DL), LAYER SAVE (YS), LAYER LOAD (YL), and WINDOW SAVE (WS).

The COMPONENT PATH Command Component files contain indi-vidual components that can be loaded and used in your drawings. These components may be of your own creation, they may be purchased from Generic Software or third-party sources, or they might come from your consultants, clients, colleagues, or friends. In any case, Generic CADD expects to find them in the default component path, which is set in the CONFIG program.

If you want to load or save components to or from anywhere but the default path, you can use the COMPONENT PATH command to temporarily change the default component path. This command, found on the CONTROLS menu, is abbreviated CMP PATH or can be issued by typing **P2** on the keyboard. The component path is declared in the same way as the drawing path, with the same result when you simply press ENTER instead of typing a pathname. Among the commands that use the component path are COMPONENT LOAD (CL) and COMPONENT SAVE (CS), COMPONENT PLACE (CP) (with which you place a component that has not yet been loaded), and COMPONENT DUMP (CD) (which saves all of the components in a drawing file as component files).

If you use few components, you might keep your components in the Generic CADD directory. On the other hand, if you make extensive use of use the P2 command whenever you need access to a different type of component. For more information on components, see Chapter 6.

The Font Path   Fonts are stored in the default font path, each font in its own file with the extension .FNT. When you use text of any kind, you must have a currently active font, found in the current font directory. Several fonts come with all versions of Generic CADD; you can buy more from Generic Software and third-party developers, and you can make your own, either with Generic CADD or with a pair of font-making utilities available as part of Generic UTILITIES.

To change the current font directory, select FNT PATH from the CONTROLS menu or type **P3** on the keyboard. As with the other path commands, you will be shown the current font path and asked to type a new one. If your fonts are stored in the same directory as Generic CADD, simply press ENTER. If you have elected to keep your fonts elsewhere, type the name of the path.

The current font path is used by two commands, FONT SELECT (FS), which determines and loads the font to be used by the text commands, and LETTER FONT (LF), the command that selects and loads the font to be used by the dimensioning commands.

Paths for Other Files

Files other than drawing, component, and font use the Generic CADD directory as their default directory. There is no command for setting a different path for these files. However, some of these files may be accessed from different directories. Hatch patterns (.HCH files) *must* be in the Generic CADD directory, but batch (.TXT) and image (.GX2) files may be loaded and saved to and from *any* disk or directory simply by typing the complete pathname as the filename whenever these files are used.

Storing Information

Generic CADD provides a wide range of methods for saving information. Not only can various types of information be saved in a variety of file formats, but the same type of information can often be saved in a number of ways.

Saving Drawing Files

Drawing files are probably the best method for storing Generic CADD data. Everything that Generic CADD knows about the drawing is saved in a drawing file. All geometric relationships are preserved, and all numeric data is accurately recorded. Several commands are available for the storage of these files.

The QUIT Command The most common time to save your drawing file is when you exit Generic CADD. Whenever you issue a QUIT (QU) command, you are asked if you want to save your drawing. A default name (which includes the default path, if any) is suggested, based on the name that you specified when you loaded the drawing. If you simply press ENTER, the drawing is saved in this file, but you may instead type a new name to be used for saving the file. If you simply type a filename, the drawing will be saved in the default drawing directory. If you want to save the drawing in a different directory without changing the default path, you must type the entire pathname along with the filename. If the path is on the same disk as Generic CADD, you can skip the disk drive letter.

Once you have selected a filename, Generic CADD checks to see if the file already exists on the disk. If it does not, the file is automatically saved. If a file by the specified name already exists, Generic CADD warns you that the file exists and asks if you want to "Rename" or "Overwrite" the file. If you elect to overwrite the file, the new drawing simply replaces it. If you select the Rename option, Generic CADD renames the original file using the same eight-character filename but changes the three-letter extension from .DWG to .BAK. The new drawing file is then saved, using the same name with the extension .DWG. This option allows you to keep backup files that are previous versions of your current drawing files.

Finally, after the drawing file has been saved, you are asked if you want to quit or continue. If you type **Q** to quit, you are returned to DOS; if you type **C** to continue, you return to the "ENTER A COMMAND >" prompt, where you may continue your Generic CADD drawing session.

If for any reason Generic CADD cannot save your file, a brief message informs you that the file has not been saved. Possible reasons include a path that does not exist or a full or damaged disk. Generic CADD does not refuse to save a file simply because you used more than eight characters in a filename. Instead, it just chops off the extra characters and saves the file using the first eight characters as the filename.

The DRAWING SAVE Command   The DRAWING SAVE command on the DRAWING menu is intended specifically for saving drawing files. This command operates in the same manner as QUIT, with two exceptions: (1) It does not ask you if you want to save the drawing, as it is assumed that is why you issued this command, and (2) it does not ask you if you want to quit or continue at the end of the command but instead returns you to the "ENTER A COMMAND >" prompt as soon as the save is complete.

The DRAWING SAVE command, activated by SAVE on the DRAWING menu or by typing **DS** on the keyboard, is used when it is more convenient to save the drawing in the middle of a drawing session than when you are exiting Generic CADD. Of course, unless you override the current path by typing a pathname as part of the filename, the drawing file is saved in the default drawing directory.

The LAYER SAVE Command   The LAYER SAVE command lets you save one layer of your drawing to an individual file on the disk. The resulting drawing file will include only the entities on the selected layer. All attributes of the entities on the selected layer are preserved when the layer is saved, and the only data lost are the entities that are not on the selected layer.

The LAYER SAVE command is selected by choosing SAVE from the LAYERS menu, or by typing **YS** on the keyboard. Generic CADD first asks for the layer you want to save and then reverts to the same process that is used for DRAWING SAVE, showing you the name of the file to be saved, and allowing you to type a new name if you desire. It is usually a good idea to select a new name in order to avoid overwriting the original drawing file.

Once again, if the file exists, you are warned of this fact and asked whether you want to rename the file as a backup or to simply overwrite it. If there are no entities on the selected layer, Generic CADD tells you that, and the command is automatically aborted even before you are asked for a filename.

Once a layer has been saved as a drawing file, it can be called up and edited just like any other drawing file. Saving layers from an existing drawing is sometimes a good way to create a new drawing out of an old one. Generic CADD does not presently offer a way to save *multiple* layers into a *single* file, but several techniques can accomplish the same goal through a number of saves and loads; each LAYER SAVE command saves just one layer.

The WINDOW SAVE Command   Another way to save a portion of your drawing is with the WINDOW SAVE command, which allows you to save the portion in a specified file by placing a window around it. The WINDOW SAVE command is often useful for breaking up a large drawing into smaller, more manageable files or for saving a portion of one drawing that will be later added to another drawing file, especially when the scaling, rotating, and repeatability features of a component are not required.

When you select SAVE from the WINDOWS menu or type **WS** on the keyboard, you are asked to place a window. Put a window around the part of the drawing that you want to save. Remember that if EDIT ALL LAYERS is off, you will only surround the objects on the current layer, even though other objects may appear to be in the window. If you want to make sure that you save everything in the window, turn on EDIT ALL LAYERS (AL). You can do this even after you have started the WINDOW SAVE command.

After you have placed the window, Generic CADD checks to see if you are actually saving anything, aborts the command if you are not, and asks you for a filename if you are. You will probably not want to save the portion under the current filename, unless you are attempting to edit the current drawing by saving a portion of it to a file and erasing the rest. If this is the case, remember not to save the current file when you quit.

The file saved with the WINDOW SAVE command is a drawing file just like any other. (Generic CADD makes no distinction as to how a drawing file was created.) This file can be loaded when you enter CADD and can be used in the same way that you use any other drawing file.

Saving Component Files

When you first create a component, it resides within the drawing file in which it was created. In this form, it cannot be used unless this drawing file is loaded. In order to make a component accessible to other drawing files, the component must be in a file by itself. Component files are slightly different from drawing files and are designated by the extension .CMP for this reason. Although you cannot directly call up a component file as if it were a drawing file, you can use a component that is saved in its own file while another drawing file is loaded. Generic CADD includes two commands for saving components into files.

The COMPONENT SAVE Command   Individual components within a drawing can be saved to disk files with the COMPONENT SAVE command, which allows you to choose the component you want to save and to specify a filename for it.

To save a single component, select SAVE from the COMPONENT menu or type **CS** on the keyboard. You are first asked for the name of the component to be saved. You must type the name of the component exactly as you typed it when you first created it. If you have forgotten the names of components that you have created, use the COMP LIST command on the COMPONENT menu to view them. You cannot do this in the middle of the COMPONENT SAVE command, so press ESC if you need to cancel the current command. Otherwise, type the name and press ENTER. If the component exists, you are next asked for the name of the file in which you want to save it. Generic CADD offers a default name composed of the current component path plus the first eight characters of the component name. You do not need to add the extension .CMP. If this name is satisfactory, just press ENTER. If you want to save the component using a different name or a different path, type that name and press ENTER.

Note that when you later load the component into another drawing file, you must use the *component name* rather than the filename to place the component. If possible, it is a good idea to use the same name for both the component and the file to avoid confusion. It is awkward to load a component using the filename and see it on the Component List under a different component name.

Keep in mind that although component names can have up to 12 characters, DOS filenames can only have 8. Interestingly, the four characters beyond the eighth are not lost when the component is saved. If you have a component called "ELEPHANTEARS," which contains 12 characters, Generic CADD saves it in a file called ELEPHANT.CMP by default. However, when you later load the component ELEPHANT into another drawing file, it appears on the Component List as "ELEPHANTEARS," and you must use this name to place the component after the first time.

The COMPONENT DUMP Command   To save all of the components in a drawing file with one command, use the COMPONENT DUMP command. This command simply goes through the components one-by-one, proposing filenames for each and saving them to the default component directory.

To save all the components, select COMP DUMP from the COMPONENT menu or type **CD** on the keyboard. One-by-one, filenames—the first eight characters of the name of the component being saved—are shown. No other prompt appears. The only way that you can tell which component is being saved is by the filename. To accept the default, simply press ENTER as each filename is shown. If you want to save a component under a different filename, you can override the default by typing this name when the default is shown. Otherwise, repeatedly pressing ENTER saves one component after the other until you are done.

When Generic CADD finds that one of your new component names already exists on the disk, it asks if you want to overwrite or rename the old file. If you rename it, the extension of the original file is changed from .CMP to .BAK. Be careful: Once the extension has been changed, it is difficult to distinguish component files from drawing files.

Saving Batch Files

Since drawing files are stored in a format that cannot be accessed by other programs, Generic CADD Level 3 provides a method for saving files in ASCII format. This makes it possible to access the information in your drawing files with other software, including any word processor that can read ASCII files. The format and use of batch files are covered in Chapters 15 and 16.

To save your drawing in batch file format, use SAVE BATCH on the UTILITIES menu or type **SB** on the keyboard. Generic CADD proposes the same name as the current drawing name for the batch filename, with the extension .TXT instead of .DWG. If you want to use a different name, you may type it at this point. If you do not type an extension, .TXT is added automatically. If you do not want the extension .TXT, you can type your own three-character extension as part of the filename. To get no extension at all, type a period at the end of the filename.

The batch file will be saved in the Generic CADD directory; if a file with the same name already exists, you are asked if you want to overwrite or rename the existing version. If you rename, the old batch file becomes a .BAK file.

Saving Image Files

Generic CADD is capable of capturing screen images on some graphics cards. *Screen images* are simply a record of how the dots on the screen are currently displayed. Screen images are similar to the type used by painting programs: No actual CADD data is saved, only pixel locations.

All Levels of Generic CADD are capable of saving screen images, and screen images created in one Level are loadable in any other Level, as well as being compatible with Generic's Presentation software package, which includes a painting program and a "slide show" presentation program that both utilize screen images.

To save a screen image, select IMAGE SAVE from the UTILITIES menu or type **IS** on the keyboard. You are asked for an image filename; no default name is supplied. Type a name up to eight characters long with no extension; the extension .GX2 is added automatically. If you type your own extension, the image file will not be saved. Also, if you simply press ENTER instead of typing a filename, the image file will not be saved.

Once you have entered a valid image filename, you are asked whether or not you want to save the full screen. If you are saving the image for use with Generic CADD, type **N**, and only the drawing area, including the border, will be saved. If you are saving for use with Generic Paint or Present, you will probably want to type **Y** and save the entire screen. The use of image files is discussed in Chapters 15 and 16.

If your video driver cannot create image files, you will see the message "IMAGES ARE NOT SUPPORTED." If you have a standard video card, such as CGA, EGA, or Hercules mono, and you are getting this message, you are probably using the small video drivers supplied with Generic CADD instead of the large drivers. On your distribution disk, you will find that there are two sets of drivers, and you may need to copy one of the large drivers from the distribution disk to your Generic CADD directory and reconfigure Generic CADD using the CONFIG program to take advantage of the larger driver. The large drivers are so named because, in fact, they take up more memory, leaving slightly less space for your drawing. If you consistently do very large drawings and do not use images, you should probably keep the smaller driver installed.

Retrieving Information

Generic CADD has almost as many ways to retrieve information as to store it. For each type of file, one or more commands allow you to load files, producing a variety of results.

Generic CADD can only load files that strictly follow Generic's file formats. This means that the files must have been created by Generic CADD or by another program that produces Generic CADD files; or, in the case of batch files, the files must strictly follow the rules established for this file format.

Loading Drawing Files

In addition to loading or creating drawings at the beginning of each drawing session, you can also load drawings after you have started up Generic CADD. Loading one drawing file into another allows you to move information from one drawing to another. Several options are available for doing this.

The DRAWING LOAD Command The DRAWING LOAD command loads an existing drawing file into Generic CADD whether or not you already have a drawing loaded. In theory, you can load as many drawing files as you like, as long as there is enough room in your computer's memory.

When you select LOAD from the DRAWING menu or type **DL** on the keyboard, you are asked for the name of the drawing file to load, and you are shown the current default drawing path. If the file that you want to load is in the default directory, simply type the name of the file. You do not need to include the extension .DWG. If you want to load a drawing from a different directory, you must type the pathname as well.

If the drawing file cannot be found in the default or specified path, you get a message stating that the file cannot be found. If the file is found, you are asked if you want to "RENAME THE WORKING DRAWING." If you do, the name is changed to the name of the file that you are currently loading, or another name of your choice. The rename function is typically used when you load one drawing into another and want to rename the current resulting drawing with a third name. As a result, when you save the current drawing, you end up with a third file that is a combination of the two that you loaded. If you choose not to rename, the default drawing name stays the same as when you first started CADD.

Finally, you are asked for an "INSERT ORIGIN" for the file that you are loading. You can select a point with the cursor, or type its coordinates. The origin of the second drawing is placed at this point. The rest of the drawing follows accordingly as illustrated in Figure 12-1. If you would like to load the new drawing at the origin of the old drawing, so that the coordinate systems of the two drawings are aligned, simply press ENTER.

When you load one drawing into another at other than the origin of the first drawing, the second drawing essentially goes through a DRAWING RE-ORIGIN. All of the points in all of the entities in the second drawing are adjusted by an amount equal to the distance between the origins of the two drawings. This allows you to load two drawings into a single drawing

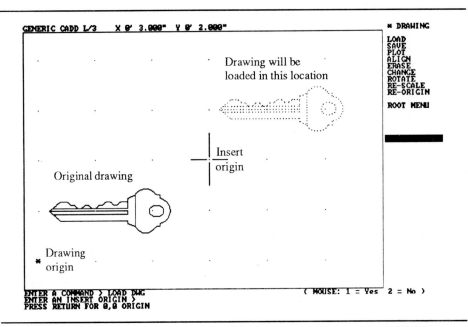

Figure 12-1.   *Loading a drawing into itself demonstrates the use of the INSERT*
                   ORIGIN

file without having them overlap, even if both were created at the same place in the drawing.

All of the components in the second drawing are loaded into the original drawing and will appear on the Component List. If there is a conflict in component definitions, as when you have different components with the same name in different files, the component definitions in the drawing will take precedence over the component definitions in the file being loaded. All instances of the component in the loaded drawing will appear as placements of the currently defined component of the same name.

Other than the RE-ORIGIN that the loaded drawing file goes through, and the possibility of conflicting component definitions, all other data in the drawing is preserved. Geometric relationships remain intact, and all entities keep their original colors, line types, line widths, and layers. Whenever a new drawing is loaded, Generic CADD automatically performs a ZOOM ALL, so that you can see the results of the load before continuing.

The LAYER LOAD Command   A special form of the DRAWING LOAD command allows you to load an entire drawing file onto a single layer of the current drawing. The principle feature of the LAYER LOAD command as opposed to DRAWING LOAD is that as the drawing file is loaded, all entities are relocated to one selected layer rather than on several. All other characteristics remain intact.

When you select LOAD from the LAYERS menu or type **YL** on the keyboard, you are asked for a layer number between 0 and 255. After specifying the layer number, you are asked for the drawing name and for an INSERT ORIGIN. (You are not asked if you want to rename the working drawing.) The drawing is loaded, the new entities are re-origined if necessary, and CADD executes a ZOOM ALL.

Note that a LAYER LOAD does not load a *single* layer from another drawing file but rather *an entire drawing.* If you want to load just a single layer from another drawing file, you must first go to that drawing file and use LAYER SAVE to create a separate file that you can load into another drawing file.

Loading Components

If you have saved components from any of your drawing files, or if you have purchased component libraries from Generic Software or third-party vendors, you can load these components into your current drawing file and place them with the COMPONENT PLACE command. These component files can either be loaded before you place components, or as you are placing them.

The COMPONENT LOAD Command   If you want to preload components before you place them, use the COMPONENT LOAD command. You might want to do this so that they will first appear on the Component List, where you can select them with the menu cursor. Another reason for preloading components is to move your components from several directories to one directory. You can change the COMPONENT PATH (P2), and then load the components in one directory, and then change paths again and load some more, until you have loaded all the components that you will be using. If you tried to use them without loading them first, you would need to make sure that your component path was set properly each time you used a new component.

To load a component definition, use LOAD on the COMPONENTS menu or the two-letter command **CL** on the keyboard. You are asked for the filename of the component that you want to load, and shown the current component path. Remember that the filename contains a maximum of eight characters, but the component name might have as many as twelve. Also, if the original filename is different from the component name, the name that appears on the Component List may be different from the name of the file that you just loaded.

If you try to load a component that has the same name as one that already exists in the drawing file, the new definition is ignored. Once the component has been successfully loaded, it can be placed with either the COMPONENT LIST command or the COMPONENT PLACE command.

The COMPONENT PLACE Command If you attempt to use COMPONENT PLACE to place a component that has not yet been defined or loaded, Generic CADD searches the default component directory for a file that has the same name as the component you are placing and then loads the component automatically if it is found. Otherwise, you get a message that the component cannot be found. After the component has been loaded, it appears on the Component List and can be placed in the normal way.

Loading Batch Files

Level 3 has the capability of loading ASCII files that contain commands and numeric data arranged according to the strict rules of the batch format. This format and the various uses of batch files are discussed in Chapters 15 and 16.

To load a batch file, select LOAD BATCH from the UTILITIES menu or type **LB** on the keyboard. You are asked for the batch filename, which is assumed to be in the Generic CADD directory. If it is not, you must type the pathname along with the filename so that Generic CADD can find the batch file. If the batch file is found, the commands in the batch file are executed one-by-one, just as if you were typing them by hand. Almost any Generic CADD command can be executed from a batch file.

When you save a drawing in batch file format, all of the commands and numeric input required to create that drawing are saved. If you start with a new drawing and load a batch file that has previously been saved from another drawing, the drawing is created step-by-step at top speed. This produces a kind of "magic": If you barely touch the keys and wiggle your fingers very quickly, you can amaze your friends with your "proficiency" with Generic CADD.

Loading Image Files

Image files that have been saved on a disk, either from the current drawing or from another drawing, can be loaded onto the screen. To load correctly, the image must have been saved using the same video driver that you are currently using, and you must currently be using one of the large drivers. For example, you can not load an image that has been created using a Hercules card if you are currently using an EGA.

Image files created by Generic PAINT (part of Generic's Presentation package) must be converted with PaintConvert before they can be loaded onto the Generic CADD screen. Convert .GX2 to .GX2, even though this seems a bit strange. PaintConvert will know what to do. (See Chapter 16 for more information on .GX2 files.)

Keep in mind that when you load an image file, you are not loading entities, only an *image* of those entities. If you perform a REDRAW or any sort of zoom after loading an image, the image quickly disappears. Possible uses for images are discussed in Chapters 15 and 16.

To load an image, select IMAGE LOAD from the UTILITIES menu or type **IL** on the keyboard. You are asked for the image filename, which is assumed to be in the Generic CADD directory unless you specify otherwise by typing the complete pathname. If the image is found and is compatible with your current video driver, it is loaded onto the screen, temporarily obscuring your drawing.

Be very careful drawing and editing while an image is on the screen. If you use an erase command, for example, you will not see what you have erased until the next time you redraw or zoom.

13 *Printing Your Drawings*

Until now, you have had the luxury of the expansive Generic CADD drawing area. This imaginary space can hold objects of almost any size without reducing them or losing any detail, always with room to spare all around. When it comes time to print the drawing, however, you must deal with more constraining physical limitations.

Printing and plotting, the two methods for producing paper output in Generic CADD, differ in use, but have several common principles, all concerning the translation of your drawing data from an infinite electronic workspace to a finite sheet of paper. Printing and plotting differ primarily in the technical aspects of the two different processes. Printers work with individual dots, much like a high-resolution video display; plotters use pens to draw continuous lines from one point to another.

Basic Concepts

Although the technical aspects of printing and plotting differ, and the commands vary depending on the Level of Generic CADD, both processes must deal with three issues: (1) the size of the paper on which the drawing is placed, (2) the *scale* at which the drawing is reproduced, and (3) the location of the drawing on the paper.

How Big Is the Sheet?

Whether you are printing or plotting, Generic CADD must know the space available for the drawing. Although Generic CADD calls this measure "sheet size," what it really means is the *printable* area on a sheet. If you are printing with a dot matrix printer on an individual 8 1/2" × 11" sheet, for example, it is not likely that your printer can print all the way to the edge of the paper. A more reasonable specification for "sheet size" would be 8" × 10," which leaves 1/4 inch on the sides, and 1/2 inch on the top and bottom. Dot matrix printers generally have the most trouble printing near the bottom of an individual sheet because the paper tends to slip out of the roller. If you use continuous feed paper, on the other hand, you can probably specify 8" × 10 1/2" or even 8 1/2" × 11" if you position the paper very carefully.

Plotters usually do not plot all the way to the edge of the sheet either. Your plotter probably leaves an unprintable margin all the way around the sheet, sometimes varying at the four edges. Some plotters need as much as one full inch of margin. A typical sheet size specification for a 24" × 36" sheet might be 22" × 34".

You can use less than the printable area, of course, simply by specifying a smaller sheet size. This is especially useful for printers when you want the drawing much smaller than the physical sheet. Since blank lines take just as long to print as lines with drawing information on them, you can avoid printing a lot of blank lines and save time by specifying a sheet size which is closer to the size that the actual printed output will take up. This can be done with plotters as well. Although plotters do not spend extra time on blank areas as do printers, you might want to plot only half a sheet and use the other half for another drawing.

If you are unsure of the allowable sheet size for your output device, you can find it in the device manual. In your plotter manual, look for the *hard clip limit,* and subtract these dimensions from the paper size. The easiest way to test the printable area is to create a drawing of a rectangle that is the actual size of the paper, with the lower-left corner of the rectangle at the origin. When you plot this drawing at full size, you will then be able to measure how close the drawing was actually plotted to the edges of the sheet. See Figure 13-1 for an illustration of this technique.

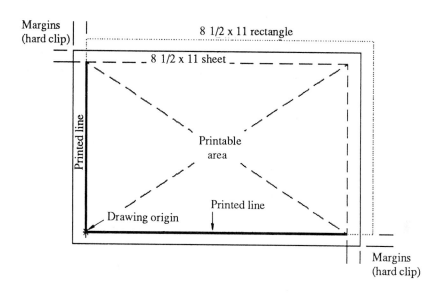

Figure 13-1. *A rectangle plotted onto a sheet of the same size*

Reduce or Enlarge the Drawing?

Generic CADD can store drawings that are very small or very large, but you will probably have to reduce or enlarge your drawing to fit it on a piece of paper. You cannot print building floor plans at full size, for example, because no plotter is big enough and the drawing would be unmanageable anyway: You would need a room larger than the building itself to examine the drawings. At the other end of the scale, integrated circuit layouts plotted at full size would probably appear as a black blob on paper: The individual entities in the drawing might be smaller than a single dot on your printer or the width of the pen on your plotter.

For these reasons, you must either specify a *print* or *plot scale* or let Generic CADD choose one for you. In the printing and plotting programs, a scale is simply a factor by which the drawing is reduced. It is specified as part of a ratio, 1:*x*, where *x* is the scale. If the scale supplied is 2, for example, the ratio of printed output to actual CADD data is 1:2, or one-half real size. Another way to think of it is that one unit on the paper represents two units in the drawing. If you want to double the size of the drawing, you would supply a scale of 0.5, meaning that one unit on the paper represents one half of a unit in your actual drawing.

If your drawing is the right size to fit on a sheet of paper, you can specify a scale of 1. If you do not know what scale will fit, you can ask the printing or plotting program to calculate it for you.

Where on the Paper?

Because the data in the CADD drawing is based on an X and Y coordinates system, the drawing contains an origin where the coordinates are 0,0. To determine where on the sheet to print your drawing, Generic CADD uses the location of this origin. If you are letting Generic CADD scale the drawing, the location of the origin is not important, because Generic CADD will calculate this point, too. However, if you are specifying the scale, you must also tell Generic CADD where to place the origin.

If the origin of your drawing is at the lower-left corner and you specify a plot or print origin of 0,0, your drawing is placed in the lower-left corner of the paper. However, if the drawing origin is somewhere else, you may need to specify another origin so that the entire drawing is positioned on the paper the way you want it.

Strangely enough, Generic CADD's print or plot origin is specified in the real scale of your drawing, not the reduced size of the actual sheet of paper. Thus, if you are trying to print a 20" × 20" box on a 10" × 10" sheet of paper at a scale of 1:2 (reduced to half real size), you would have to specify a plot origin of 10,10 if the actual drawing origin was in the middle of the 20" × 20" box. At half real size, the box would be placed up 5 inches and to the right 5 inches, where it would fit exactly. Therefore, when you specify the plot origin you are actually telling Generic CADD where on the sheet, in the scale of the drawing, you want the drawing origin to be placed.

Fortunately, Generic CADD provides a visual method for positioning the drawing on the sheet—moving a box representing the sheet over the drawing until it fits the way you want it (see "Display Plot" later in this chapter).

Printing

Using these basic ideas, Generic CADD provides two different methods for printing your drawings on dot matrix devices, including laser printers. In Levels 1 and 2, printing is built in through the use of the PLOT command on the DRAWING menu, accessed by typing **DP** on the keyboard. Level 3 users can plot their drawings by using the separate program, DotPlot, available separately or bundled with Generic CADD. Note that both methods use the terms *print* and *plot* interchangeably, even though what you are actually doing is printing.

Loading the Drawing

If you are printing directly from Generic CADD Level 1 or 2, call up Generic CADD and load the drawing in the usual way.

If you are using DotPlot, you will need to get out of Generic CADD. QUIT (QU) and save your drawing and call up DotPlot by moving to your DotPlot directory or inserting your DotPlot disk, and type **DOTPLOT** at the DOS prompt. Users of Level 3 version 1.07 or later can move directly into DotPlot without leaving CADD by typing **QD** on the keyboard. Choose LOAD A DRAWING from the DotPlot menu and specify the drawing that you want to load. If the drawing is not in the current drawing path, you may need to go first to the option that configures DotPlot and change the default paths.

Once you have the drawing loaded, select the option to SELECT DISPLAY AND VIEW OPTIONS, or go directly to PLOT DRAWING if you want to plot the entire drawing.

Before plotting, you may turn off layers that you don't want to plot, toggle on and off the display of standard points, hatches, and fills, and select FAST TEXT if you wish. These can be done from Generic CADD or from the drawing screen that you get under SELECT DISPLAY AND VIEW OPTIONS in DotPlot. You can also zoom in to a particular part of the drawing if you want to print only part of the drawing.

When you are ready to print the drawing, select PLOT from the DRAWING menu if you are in Generic CADD or in the drawing screen mode of DotPlot, or select PLOT DRAWING in DotPlot. You are asked several questions at this point.

Specifying Paper Size

As discussed above, specify the area on the paper available for printed output. Width is first, then length. Generic CADD or DotPlot offers default sizes based on your printer configuration. Use the *actual* area, not the size that the paper would be if you enlarged it to the size of the drawing. For most printers, the maximum width is 13.6 inches. You can specify greater widths, but you will probably get blank lines on your printed output. The length is limited only to the actual length of the paper; however, to save time and paper, you probably do not want to overestimate by too much or a great deal of blank space will appear at both the top and bottom of the drawing.

Selecting Plot Type

The PLOT TYPE prompts are intended to find out whether you or Generic CADD are going to specify the scale of the print and what part of the drawing you want to print.

Three alternatives are offered: Current View, Full Drawing, and User Scale. Only the last of these options asks *you* for the scale; under the first two options, Generic CADD supplies the scale.

Current View   Under this option, Generic CADD or DotPlot fits the current display screen to the paper as closely as possible. This means that if you have some space around the screen drawing, you will get space around the printed drawing. If you are zoomed in to a small portion of the drawing, so that the lines in the drawing are chopped off at the edges of the screen, the print will turn out the same way.

In most cases, your screen is horizontal, and your paper is vertical. To deal with this situation, Generic CADD centers the image on the paper and rotates the drawing 90 degrees to make it as large as possible on the sheet, printing more at either the top and bottom or the two sides to adjust the proportions of the screen to the proportions of the sheet of paper. If you want to avoid this adjustment, simply supply a width and length for the paper size that are closer to the actual proportions of the drawing area on the screen.

Full Drawing   This plot type option asks Generic CADD or DotPlot to make the drawing fit the paper. The drawing is printed exactly as wide or as tall as you have specified for the sheet size. Unless the drawing is exactly the same proportion as the sheet size, some blank space is added in the direction that does not fit exactly. As with the Current View option, the drawing is turned 90 degrees if necessary to print it as large as possible. No further questions are asked regarding scale, rotation, or origin, as these are decided by the program.

User Scale This plot type option lets you decide the scale, rotation, and origin. If you select this option, you are asked for three specifications before printing begins: (1) the plot scale, as discussed earlier, specified as a ratio of 1 to the number that you type; (2) whether to rotate the drawing 90 degrees (if your drawing is horizontal and your sheet vertical, answer "Yes" by typing **Y**; otherwise type **N**); and (3) the location for the plot origin (if you are not sure, accept the default of 0,0 and see what happens).

Previewing the Plot

After selecting the plot type and specifying the scale, rotation, and origin, you can preview the plot on the screen before sending it to the printer. This is usually a good idea, especially if you have specified the parameters rather than Generic CADD. The drawing is shown on the screen surrounded by a box indicating the borders of the paper. Make sure the portion of the drawing you want printed is within the border. If it does not turn out the way that you expected, you can cancel the plot and try resetting the scale, rotation, and origin.

Printing the Drawing

After the preview, or if you decline the opportunity to preview, you are asked if you want to print the drawing using the specified parameters. If so, type **Y** and wait for the results. If not, type **N** and try it again.

Printing large drawing files can take some time, as the printing program examines the entire drawing file to determine how it is going to resolve the lines, circles, arcs, and so on into dots. Generic CADD cannot just print them on the paper in the order that you drew them as it does when generating the video display, because most printers only advance the paper in one direction, or accept information one line at a time. For this reason, each line, printed or blank, requires many, many calculations. Your printer will probably pause several times during printing while more calculations are done. If you are printing a large drawing file, you might do other tasks while the drawing is being printed. Extremely large drawing files are best printed at the end of the day when you do not need the computer for other functions.

Plotting

Plotting is done with the PLOT command on the DRAWING menu in Generic CADD Level 3, or with the PenPlot utility, available separately for users of Levels 1 and 2. The two methods are very similar except for the way that the program and the drawing are loaded.

Loading the Drawing

If you are using Generic CADD Level 3, simply start up Generic CADD as usual and load the drawing that you want to plot. If you are using PenPlot, load this program from the directory where it is stored by typing **PEN-PLOT** at the DOS prompt, and load the drawing with the LOAD DRAW-ING option. As with DotPlot, you may have to use the configure option to set up the default drawing path.

Preparing the Drawing for Plotting

In Generic CADD, turn on or off layers and set the display toggles so that the drawing on the screen is the drawing that you want to plot. If you are plotting only a portion of the drawing, zoom in on that portion. In PenPlot, the SELECT DISPLAY AND VIEW option does the same thing. Most of the DISPLAY and ZOOM menus are available from this option.

Setting the Plotting Parameters

When you select the PLOT command from the DRAWING menu or type **DP** on the keyboard, you get a menu of plotting parameters that can be set before you plot the drawing. This same menu is available from PenPlot by selecting PLOT DRAWING from the main PenPlot menu. Items are selected from this menu by typing their numbers.

Select Paper Size   When you choose this option (discussed earlier in "How Big Is the Sheet?"), the currently selected or default size is shown. You will get a menu of standard sizes for the currently configured plotter. One of these options will be for a user-defined paper size. If you select this option, you are asked for the length and width of the paper.

Select Paper Origin   If you are not sure of the origin or are letting Generic CADD scale the drawing, leave the paper origin at 0,0, representing the lower-left corner of a horizontal sheet. Your origin will be overridden if Generic CADD or PenPlot scales the drawing.

Select Scale   This option allows you to enlarge or reduce the drawing to fit on the sheet. The value that you specify, expressed as a ratio 1:*x*, as discussed above, will be used only if you select the SPECIFY PLOT SCALE option of the PLOT VIEW parameter elsewhere on the PLOT menu. If Generic CADD scales the drawing, it changes this value so that you can see the scale it has calculated.

Select Plot Options   A number of more specific plotting options concerning the pen speed, pen width, number of pens, pen sorting, and layer-by-layer plotting are also available from this menu. If you select this option, you are shown a menu of these items, any of which can be changed by typing its corresponding number and supplying a new value.

Check your plotter manual to see if *pen speed* applies to your plotter. If the speed of your plotter is adjustable, the number you supply is fed straight to the plotter. The allowable values vary from plotter to plotter.

Pen width is used for creating line widths and for filling solid areas. If you want solid areas to be completely filled, use a pen width that is slightly smaller than the width of the pen tip, so that each pass of the pen slightly overlaps the one before it. For faster plots, or if the composition of filled areas is not that important to you, use a larger number.

The *number of pens* determines whether or not pens can be automatically swapped and which pens to assign to which colors. If the number that appears for this item is 1, you can either change pens manually or plot the entire drawing with the same pen. If the number is greater than 1, color 1 is assigned to pen 1, color 2 to pen 2, and so on, until the number of pens is exhausted, at which point the pen numbers start over while the color numbers continue. For example, if you specify four pens, colors 1 to 4 will be plotted with pens 1 to 4; color 5 will be plotted with pen 1; color 6 with pen 2; and so on. With many plotters, you do not have to use all available

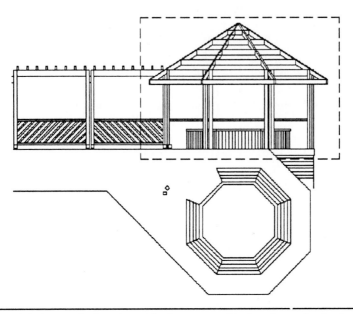

Figure 13-2.   *A sample drawing with the current display shown by the dashed rectangle*

pens. If you specify two pens on a one-pen plotter, for instance, manual pen-swapping is disabled, and Generic CADD simply thinks that it can use pens 1 and 2 for all plotting. Because your plotter actually has only one pen, this pen will be used. If you want to enable manual swapping on a multipen plotter, simply tell Generic CADD to use only one pen, and you will be allowed to change it when a new pen is needed.

Pen sorting by color is a toggle that determines whether entities are plotted in the order that you drew them, or color-by-color. If PEN SORT is on, entities are sorted by color and plotted one color at a time. This option is especially useful if you are using a single-pen plotter and changing pens yourself because you only have to change pens once for each color. Otherwise, you would be asked to change pens every time a different color entity is encountered.

Plotting by layer allows you to plot one layer at a time, without having to go back to the drawing and turn off the rest of the layers. If PLOT LAYER is off, all layers currently not hidden are plotted. If you select PLOT LAYER, you are asked for the number of the layer that you want to plot. This number is then shown as the current layer to be plotted. To plot

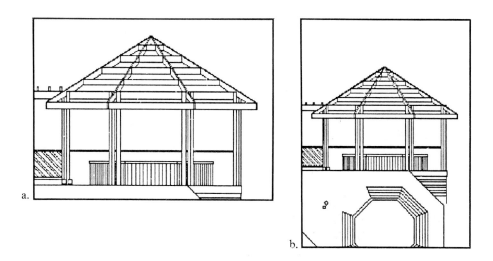

Figure 13-3. *The CURRENT VIEW fitted to (a) a horizontal sheet, and (b) a vertical sheet*

another layer, you must select this option twice. The first time, it returns to PLOT LAYER OFF status; when you select it again, you choose a new layer.

The final option on the PLOT OPTIONS menu is RETURN TO PLOT MENU.

Select Plot View   This option lets you decide how the drawing is scaled to the sheet. You can let Generic CADD or PenPlot do it, or you can select your own scale.

If you choose Current View, the plot of the drawing will resemble the last screen display of the drawing as closely as possible (scaled and rotated, if necessary, to fit on the sheet). Figure 13-2 is an example of a drawing display that you might want to print. If the proportions of the screen and the paper are different, some additional drawing entities not currently on the screen may be shown to either the top and bottom or to the right and left sides. Figures 13-3 shows how the sample drawing would be printed on a horizontal and vertical sheet.

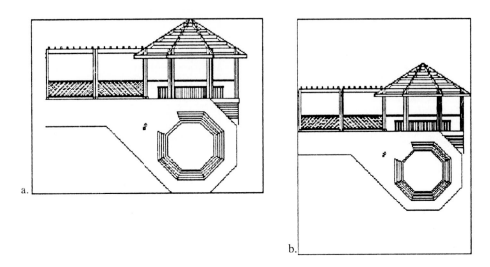

Figure 13-4.   *The FULL DRAWING fitted to (a) a horizontal sheet, and (b) a vertical sheet*

If you choose Fit Full Drawing, the entire drawing is scaled to fit the area allowed by the paper size. In the direction that the proportions of the drawing are closer to the proportions of the paper, the drawing will go all the way to the edges of the specified area. In the other direction, equal space may be added to each side. Figure 13-4 illustrates how the full sample drawing would be drawn on horizontal and vertical sheets.

If you want to use the scale that you have specified for the PLOT SCALE option, you must select SPECIFY PLOT SCALE for the plot view. If you select this option, you are asked if you want to rotate the drawing 90 degrees on the paper. If the drawing is not oriented in the same direction as the sheet, type **Y** to answer in the affirmative; otherwise, type **N**. Remember, your PLOT SCALE *will not be used* unless you select this option.

Display Plot   This option not only gives you a preview of how the drawing will be plotted (as in the PREVIEW option of Levels 1 and 2 and DotPlot), but also lets you change three of the plotting parameters as you are previewing the plot.

First, you are asked if you want a fast redraw. If you select FAST REDRAW, you are shown a dotted rectangle with diagonal lines through it that indicate the extent of your drawing. The dotted rectangle is overlaid by a solid rectangle indicating the boundaries of the sheet. If you simply want to see if the drawing fits on the sheet, this is good enough. If you decide against FAST REDRAW, your drawing is displayed on the screen in the normal fashion, overlaid with the solid rectangle indicating the boundaries of the printed sheet. If you are trying to be more precise about your placement, this might be required.

After you have made a decision regarding FAST REDRAW, your drawing is displayed either in detail or as a dotted rectangle surrounded by the sheet boundary, and you are asked to verify that the scale is satisfactory. If it is not, type **N**; you will be asked for a new scale, and the display will be adjusted. You can repeat this process as many times as necessary to fit the drawing on the sheet.

Once the scale is adjusted, you have another opportunity to rotate the drawing 90 degrees. Whichever you decide, the drawing will be redrawn, and you will move on to the next question.

Finally, with the aid of seeing the drawing on the screen as it will appear on paper, you can adjust the PLOT ORIGIN. You are asked if the location of the origin is correct. If not, you can move the paper-boundary box around on the drawing until it is in the right place. Some versions of Level 3 and PenPlot ask you to place the lower-left corner of the sheet; others let you drag the entire sheet border over the top of the drawing. In either case, use the first pointing device button to select the new location. The display is then adjusted, and you are asked again if the placement of the origin is OK. As with scale, you can repeat this process as many times as necessary. It may take several tries, especially if the drawing and the sheet were not well-coordinated on the first try, because you can move the sheet just a short distance each time. When the origin is in the right place, type **Y** and then ENTER to return to the PLOT menu.

Plot Drawing   This item begins actual communication with the plotter. If you have specified only one pen, you are asked if you want to change pens manually for each color. If you type **N**, the entire drawing will be plotted with one pen. If you answer **Y**, you are asked for a new pen each time a new color is encountered. Several messages at the bottom of the screen keep you informed of which pen is currently plotting, and how many points have been processed.

If you want to abort the plot for any reason, press ESC. The plotter pauses and you are given the opportunity to abort or to continue plotting. (If you need to put more ink in a pen, for example, you might press ESC and then continue plotting once you have filled the pen.)

When the plot is done, you are returned to the PLOT menu, where you can change the parameters and do another plot if you like.

Plot Files   The final option on the PLOT menu allows the plot program to import and export *plot files.* These files are in a special format that can be understood by your plotter.

If you want to save a plot file instead of sending the current plot to the plotter, use the first option, and specify the name of the file to which the plot should be sent. Use a valid DOS filename. If you do not specify a path, the plot file is saved in the Generic CADD or PenPlot directory.

If a plot file is currently specified, the PLOT DRAWING option on the main PLOT menu sends its output to this file instead of the plotter. You can either copy this file to the plotter at some later time, or use the IMPORT PLOTTER COMMAND FILE option to combine this plot file into the plotting of another drawing. Plot files are assigned the extension .DPF by Generic CADD.

If you would like to combine an existing plot file into the plot of your current drawing, use the second option on the PLOT FILES menu. Again, type the name of the file, including the pathname if it is different from the Generic CADD directory. This file is sent to the plotter when you use the PLOT DRAWING option from the main PLOT menu before current drawing is plotted.

The IMPORT PLOTTER COMMAND FILE option essentially has two uses. The first occurs when your plotter needs to be sent an *initialization string* before plotting actually begins. For example, your plotter may not be supported by Generic CADD but can be made to emulate a supported plotter by putting the proper commands into an ASCII file and sending them to the plotter. The second, more common use is for printing title blocks or borders on certain drawing sheets, but not every drawing that you are going to plot. You can plot the title block or border *once,* using the PLOT FILE option. Later, when you plot your drawing, specify this file to be imported. In this way, a title block and border will be printed onto each sheet that you plot.

14 *Using a Digitizer*

As one of the peripheral devices that can be used with Generic CADD, the digitizer is somewhat unique. Within Level 3, digitizer commands are found on the SELECT A POINTING DEVICE menu of the CONFIG program, but digitizers are different in a number of ways from the other pointing devices—mice, track balls, and the keyboard cursor keys—because digitizers provide several functions in addition to simply pointing to areas on the screen.

The Digitizer As a Pointing Device

Pointing devices typically send information back to the program regarding their movement and their direction of movement. When you move a mouse to the right, for example, a series of electrical impulses is translated by Generic CADD into "I'm moving to the right." When you stop moving the mouse, it sends a signal roughly saying "I'm not moving." In this way, the mouse controls the position of the cursor by telling Generic CADD that you have moved it, and Generic CADD responds by moving the cursor. A mouse cannot "sense" and so cannot communicate to Generic CADD the fact that you have picked it up and moved it to another part of the desktop. This means that you do not need a lot of desk space to use a mouse, because you can move it farther than the physical room that is available by rolling it, picking it up, and rolling it again, much like a friction toy.

The same principles apply to track balls or roller balls, which are really sort of upside-down mice. The signals that they send to Generic CADD translate into messages such as "nothing is happening here," or "I'm being rolled to the left." Like a mouse, the track ball does not care *how* you move it—that is, with one long continuous motion or in short strokes.

The keyboard cursor keys send very simple messages: "Up," "Left," "Down," and so on. If you do not press them, no message is sent.

Digitizers send a very different type of information back to Generic CADD. Physically, a digitizer usually consists of a rectangular flat box called a *tablet,* which contains a grid of very tightly spaced wires that are all connected to a central circuit. Attached to this tablet, usually by a wire, but sometimes by a radio signal, is a device that resembles a mouse or a pen. This device is positioned over the tablet and sends a signal indicating not which direction it is moving, but *where it is on the tablet.* This information is sent in the form of X and Y coordinates that are related to the grid of wires inside the tablet.

As a pointing device, therefore, there is a very straightforward relationship between the location of the digitizer *puck* (as the mouselike pointer is often called) on the tablet and the position of the cursor on the screen. It is as if you simply tipped the screen down onto the desk and can now drag the cursor around. When the puck is at the top of the tablet, the cursor is at the top of the screen; when you move the puck to the bottom of the tablet, the cursor moves to the bottom of the screen. Unlike the mouse, the puck sends a signal indicating its *position.* It does little good, therefore, to lift the puck in an attempt to move the cursor. As soon as the puck is lifted a half-inch or so (the active distance varies depending on the digitizer), the signal becomes too weak for Generic CADD to detect its location, and the cursor remains where it is.

If you go back and forth between using a mouse and a digitizer with Generic CADD, you will probably need to adjust mentally each time you switch: though the physical feeling of the mouse and the digitizer puck are very similar, the action on the screen is very different.

Selecting the Active Area

If you have a large digitizer, you may want to set it up to use only a small portion of the actual surface (called the *active area*) for screen pointing. This will save you from making sweeping arm movements across the tablet surface just to get to the other side of the screen. This can be done with the ACTIVE AREA command on the UTILITIES menu, or by typing **PM** on the keyboard. If Generic CADD is not currently configured for a digitizer, nothing will happen.

The active area has approximately the same proportions as the screen. After the active area has been set, the boundaries of this area become *mapped* to the boundaries of the screen, and locations outside this area cannot be used for pointing.

If your digitizer is attached and properly configured, you are asked to *digitize* the lower-left corner of the active area. Digitizing means using the digitizer puck to select a point on the digitizer. In this case, point to the lower-left corner of the area that you want to use for pointing. If your digitizer has a pen, simply position the point of the pen over this point. If you are using a puck, position the cross hairs of the puck over this point. The cross hairs are usually found on a transparent extension of the puck so that you can see a drawing or digitizer overlay placed on the digitizer. In some cases, the active area might be outlined on a sheet that you place over the digitizer. If so, select the lower-left corner of this area.

Once you have positioned the pen or puck, select the point by pressing the first button on the puck, or by pressing down on the pen. Digitizer pens have an internal button that is activated when you apply downward pressure. If you are using a digitizer pen, you should hold the pen as vertically as possible, while still maintaining a comfortable position. When the pen is held at a slant, the point may move when you press down on it, hampering accuracy.

When selecting this point, do not worry about the location of the cursor on the screen; in fact, the cursor may move right off the edge of the screen. You are not selecting a normal X-Y coordinate with this point, but an actual physical location on the digitizer, and the screen cursor is not involved.

After selecting the lower-left corner of the active area, you are asked to digitize the upper-right corner. (Only two points are required, as the active area is assumed to be a rectangle with sides parallel to the edges of the digitizer.) Once you have digitized the upper-right corner of the active area, the relationship between the screen coordinates and the digitizer coordinates is readjusted to match the new specification. Screen pointing can occur only in the new active area, and the rest of the digitizer may be used for other purposes, such as digitizer menus, as you will see later in this chapter.

Using the Digitizer to Trace Drawings

Because digitizers have their own internal coordinate systems and the actual position of the digitizer pen or puck is relayed back to Generic CADD, a digitizer can be used to trace a paper drawing into Generic CADD.

You must carefully follow several steps to ensure successful tracing. First, the drawing should be taped securely to the digitizer. If the drawing has many horizontal or vertical lines, they should be aligned closely with the edges of the digitizer. If the drawing does not fit on the digitizer, you must reduce it or trace it in sections. When digitizing in sections, you must be especially careful to align the drawing horizontally on the digitizer. You might want to draw a large grid over the drawing so that you can align these grid lines with the edges of the digitizer whenever you move the drawing.

Aligning Paper and Electronic Drawings

In order to trace the drawing accurately, Generic CADD needs to establish a relationship between the units of the paper drawing and the units in Generic CADD. When you select points on the digitizer, these are interpreted as actual X and Y coordinates by Generic CADD. To translate the digitizer coordinate system into Generic CADD's units of measurement, several commands are provided.

The Trace Scale   The TRACE SCALE command on the CONTROLS menu provides one means of translating digitizer units into real units. This command can also be accessed by typing **RZ** on the keyboard and is activated automatically when you use the DRAWING ALIGN (DA) command, covered later in this chapter.

The trace scale sets up a simple ratio between the paper drawing and your drawing. If the paper drawing is drawn at full size, the TRACE SCALE should be set to 1, meaning that one unit on the digitizer is the same as one unit in your drawing. If the paper drawing is at one-half full size, the TRACE SCALE should be set to 2, meaning that one unit on the digitizer equals two units in your drawing. Since your CADD drawing uses real scale, the relationship between the scale of your drawing and the paper drawing is the same as the relationship between the paper drawing and the real object. If the paper drawing is scaled at 1/4" = 1' 0" (a typical architectural scale), the trace scale is calculated by determining the relationship between the drawing and the real object. In this case, the real object is 48 times the size of the drawing, so TRACE SCALE should be set to 48.

If you do not know the proper trace scale, use the DRAWING ALIGN command (see "A General-Purpose Alternative" later in this chapter).

Enabling Tracing Mode   Tracing a drawing on the digitizer is very different from simply moving the cursor on the screen. When you are using the digitizer for pointing, a relationship is set up between the digitizer active area and the current video screen. When you are tracing, the relationship is between the entire digitizer and the actual coordinates of the drawing. These drawing coordinates may or may not be the same as what is currently displayed on the screen.

To map the digitizer coordinates to the actual drawing coordinates (instead of the current screen coordinates), you must activate TRACE MODE by selecting it from the CONTROLS menu, by typing **TM** on the keyboard, or by using the DRAWING ALIGN command, which activates TRACE MODE automatically.

If you need to return to pointing mode for any reason, use the TRACE MODE (TM) toggle again. Each time you select it, it reverses its status from TRACE MODE ON to TRACE MODE OFF or vice versa. You might want to turn off TRACE MODE temporarily in order to select a menu item, or to add something to the drawing that does not appear on the paper drawing. Just remember to go back to TRACE MODE before you start tracing again.

A General-Purpose Alternative   The ALIGN command on the DRAWING menu (DA on the keyboard) is designed to get you going when you first start tracing a drawing. It combines the functions of the TRACE SCALE and TRACE MODE commands and adds a little extra.

When you use the DRAWING ALIGN command, you will first go through a series of steps that are similar to TRACE SCALE. The current TRACE SCALE is shown, which is assumed to be one to one unless you have previously specified otherwise. You are asked if this is the right scale, and if not, asked if you know the scale. If you do, you can type it, just like with TRACE SCALE. If you use this option, TRACE MODE is not selected automatically.

If you don't know the scale, or if the drawing might not be exactly straight on the digitizer, you can specify the tracing scale by digitizing two points instead. Basically, this process gives coordinate values to two points on the drawing, so that Generic CADD can figure out the scale. In addition, it allows Generic CADD to make an internal adjustment for any rotation in case the drawing isn't aligned exactly horizontally on the digitizer tablet.

When you say that you don't know the scale, you will be asked to select a point on the screen using the **NP** command. Generic CADD assumes that you have a line already in the drawing that represents a line on the paper and wants you to select one of the endpoints. If you have such a line, you can use the third button on the pointing device to select it, or type **NP** on the keyboard when your cursor is near the point. Once you have selected the point on the screen, you will be asked to digitize the point on the tablet. Position the point of the digitizer stylus or the cross hairs of the digitizer puck over the point that you want to select and press the first button on the puck or press down on the stylus. This process will be repeated for a second point. Once you have given two points, a scale and rotation will be calculated, and you will be asked if they are right. If so, TRACE MODE will be selected automatically using these values. If not, you will be asked to digitize two more points to try again.

Notice that Generic CADD requires that you have a line in the drawing so that you can match it up with a line on the paper. However, sometimes you don't have such a line, or want to specify your points by another means. You can type the coordinates of the two points if you like, instead of picking them with the NP command, as long as you currently have at least one line in the database. Even a line that you have drawn and erased will do. If you want to type coordinates instead of picking points, simply type them as usual, separated by a comma, using any units format, and ignore the prompt that tells you to use NP. After typing the coordinates, you will be asked in the first and second cases to digitize the same point on the tablet. Select the point whose coordinates you have just typed.

Remember that unless you type the scale yourself, TRACE MODE is enabled automatically when you do DRAWING ALIGN, so remember to turn it off by typing **TM** if you want to use the digitizer for normal screen pointing.

Typically, you can use DRAWING ALIGN to set up your tracing scale and to turn on TRACE MODE at the beginning of a drawing session and then use TRACE SCALE and TRACE MODE when you need to change either of these parameters.

Tracing

Tracing drawings is similar to other ways of drawing in Generic CADD, except in the selection of points. You still use the basic DRAW commands to create simple entities, which take on the characteristics set by the current LINE parameters. Accuracy is still controllable by the GRID SIZE (GS) and SNAP TO GRID (SG) commands, as well as by the ORTHO MODE (OR) toggle. In fact, these drawing aids can help you to create a Generic CADD drawing that is more accurate than the one you are tracing.

You may encounter some difficulty editing a drawing in TRACE MODE, because the screen does not necessarily show an exact replica of what you are tracing. If this is the case, you can issue ZOOM WINDOW (ZW) with TRACE MODE active, and place the window by pointing to the area of the paper drawing that you want to have displayed on the screen.

To understand the tracing process, you must remember that you are working with three different manifestations of the drawing at one time. You are pointing to (1) scaled coordinates on a paper drawing that are being converted to (2) real scale in the Generic CADD drawing, and these, in turn, are being reconverted to (3) the arbitrary units of the screen display, which depend on how much of the drawing is currently displayed. Of these, usually only the units in the Generic CADD drawing file are scaled at 1:1, the actual size of the object.

Tracing Versus Drawing

Be wary of the urge to use tracing as a general-purpose input mechanism for Generic CADD. Even though it is possible to create accurate drawings by tracing, in many cases it is faster and more accurate to create them from scratch without tracing.

Digitizing works best when accuracy is not crucial, or when you know that you will be editing the drawing extensively later anyway, checking and adjusting the accuracy as you edit. The real key is to analyze the drawing task and determine whether tracing is really appropriate for it. Digitizing is an excellent technique for transferring topological drawings to Generic CADD, for example, or for tracing the basic shape of certain products. If, on the other hand, you are the manufacturer of the product, you probably want to create the shape using manual entry of relative coordinates—the most accurate of all data input techniques—rather than tracing a designer's sketch. It really depends on the application, and what will be done with the finished drawing.

Using the Digitizer
to Select Commands

The third use of a digitizer is to select commands. Just as commands can be selected by positioning the menu cursor on the video menu, they can also be selected by pointing to a specific area of the digitizer tablet. These areas are often identified by a *digitizer overlay,* which contains either the names of the commands or icons (pictures) representing the desired functions. An example of such an overlay is shown in Figure 14-1.

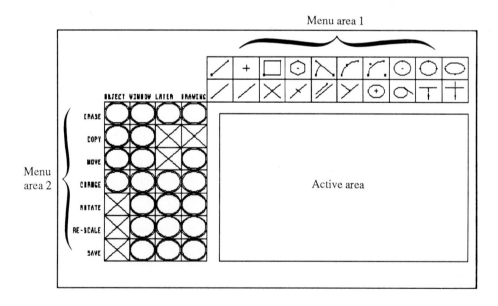

Figure 14-1.   *A sample digitizer menu overlay*

As with tracing drawings, several steps are required to use digitizer-driven commands. First, you must obtain a digitizer overlay. If you want to try the one shown in Figure 14-1, you can draw it in Generic CADD and then plot or print it at a scale that fits your digitizer, or you can xerographically or photographically enlarge this one.

A Menu File

The second necessary item is an ASCII file that contains, in order, the commands that you wish to execute from the digitizer overlay. This ASCII file is called the *digitizer menu file* (for detailed discussion, see Chapter 15). If you want to try the sample digitizer menu, type the following, using any text editor or word processor that is capable of producing ASCII files.

```
m01r01c01,LI;
m01r01c02,PO;
m01r01c03,RE;
m01r01c04,RP;
m01r01c05,A2;
m01r01c06,A3;
m01r01c07,A4;
m01r01c08,C2;
m01r01c09,C3;
m01r01c10,EP;
m01r02c01,SC;
m01r02c02,NL;
m01r02c03,SI;
m01r02c04,SM;
m01r02c05,SA;
m01r02c06,SX;
m01r02c07,SN;
m01r02c08,ST;
m01r02c09,XT;
m01r02c10,RM;
m02r01c01,OE;
m02r01c02,WE;
m02r01c03,YX;
m02r01c04,DX;
m02r02c01,OC;
m02r02c02,WC;
m02r02c03,PU;
```

```
m02r02c04,PU;
m02r03c01,OM;
m02r03c02,WM;
m02r03c03,PU;
m02r03c04,DO;
m02r04c01,OG;
m02r04c02,WG;
m02r04c03,YG;
m02r04c04,DG;
m02r05c01,PU;
m02r05c02,WR;
m02r05c03,YR;
m02r05c04,DR;
m02r06c01,PU;
m02r06c02,WZ;
m02r06c03,YZ;
m02r06c04,DZ;
m02r07c01,PU;
m02r07c02,WS;
m02r07c03,YS;
m02r07c04,DS;
```

Some terms used by various programs to produce these files include PRINT TO A FILE, SAVE AS TEXT FILE, and NONDOCUMENT FILE. Be careful not to add any extra spaces, either at the end of lines or between lines, that are not shown in the listing. Name this file **DIGIT.MNU,** and you will be ready to try the sample digitizer menu.

Configuring for the Tablet Menu

You will notice that the digitizer overlay is divided into three rectangular areas. Two of these areas are used for commands, and the third, blank area becomes the active area for screen pointing. The active area is set up once you are in Generic CADD, as you have seen. The menu areas must be assigned with the CONFIG program.

From the DOS prompt, start up the CONFIG program by typing **CONFIG** and pressing ENTER. Press ENTER again to get past the configuration display screen and the main configuration menu will be displayed. Select the item OTHER OPTIONS, and then SET MOUSE AND DIGITIZER OPTIONS. From this menu select PLACE DIGITIZER MENU ON DIGI-

TIZER. You are asked which menu you want to place. (Although the sample menu has only two menu areas, you can have up to 10 areas at one time.) Start with number 1. You are asked to *digitize* the lower-left and upper-right corners of menu area 1, and then to indicate the number of horizontal boxes (columns) and vertical boxes (rows) of commands in each area. Type a number for each. The sample menu contains 10 horizontal boxes and two vertical boxes in the first menu area.

Repeat the PLACE DIGITIZER MENU ON DIGITIZER option for the second area. This area contains four horizontal and seven vertical boxes.

If you want Generic CADD to start automatically with the tablet menu instead of the normal video menu, select the DISPLAY VIDEO MENU toggle to turn it off, and select the DIGITIZER MENU toggle to turn it on. Thereafter, when you start up Generic CADD, DIGIT.MNU will be loaded instead of LEVEL3.MNU, and the video menu will not be displayed. Instead, you will be ready to use the digitizer menu.

Loading the Digitizer Menu

If you have not configured Generic CADD to load the digitizer menu automatically, you will need to load it by selecting LOAD DIG MENU on the UTILITIES menu, or by typing **LD** on the keyboard. Because you have started up Generic CADD with the video menu active, you are warned that loading a digitizer menu erases the video menu, and you are given a chance to change your mind. If you elect to continue, you are asked for the name of a menu file. Type **DIGIT**, and press ENTER. The menu is assumed to be in the Generic CADD directory unless you specify a pathname. If there is such a file with the extension .MNU, it will be loaded.

The first command in the menu file is located in the upper left of digitizer menu number 1. The next command will be in the box immediately to the right of the first box, and so on, until the end of the row of boxes (in this case, 10 commands). The eleventh command in your menu will be placed in the first box in the second row of digitizer menu number 1, and so on, until all the boxes in menu area 1 are exhausted. Because the first menu area has 20 boxes, the 21st command in the menu file is mapped to the upper-left-corner box of digitizer menu area 2, and the remaining commands appear from left to right to the end of the row, and then on to the next row. You can see this relationship clearly if you compare the sample menu overlay with the menu file listing.

Using the Digitizer Menu

To select a command from the digitizer menu, position the point of the digitizer pen or the cross hairs of the digitizer puck within the box that contains the desired command and press the first button on the puck or press downwards on the pen. Note that this button is different from the button that you use for selecting items from the video menu. The digitizer uses the first button both for selecting digitizer menu items and for pointing on the screen, to allow the use of single-button pens. When you select a command in this manner, it is activated exactly as if you had selected it from the video menu or typed its two-character code.

Because you need to go back and forth between choosing commands and selecting points on the screen, and because these tasks are both accomplished with the same button on the digitizer puck, there is a potential conflict between the two functions. Initially, Generic CADD assumes that you want to use the entire digitizer for pointing on the screen. When you have two digitizer menu areas enabled, these areas are made unavailable for screen pointing; that is, you form two "blind" screen areas where points cannot be selected. If you attempt to select points within these areas, you will get commands from the digitizer menu instead.

To solve this problem, you must reset the portion of the digitizer that is used for screen pointing using the ACTIVE AREA (PM) command discussed earlier in this chapter. When you are asked for the lower-left corner, select the lower-left corner of the large blank box on the digitizer overlay, and select the upper-right corner of this same box for the next point. Once you have done this, the screen pointing area is reassigned to this box, and the conflict between pointing to the screen and selecting commands is resolved.

Activating More Digitizer Menus

When you first load Generic CADD and a digitizer menu, either automatically or with the LOAD DIG MENU (LD) command, all the commands from that menu are loaded and are active simultaneously, as long as the digitizer menu areas do not overlap. If they do overlap, the command that appears earlier in the digitizer menu file will supercede any that appear further down in the file.

For example, if you configure menu areas 1 and 2 to be in the same location on the digitizer, each containing 10 boxes, only the first 10 commands in the menu file are active; the second 10 are hiding "under" the first 10. In order to activate the second group of 10, you must use the SELECT DMENU command on the UTILITIES menu, or type **SD** on the keyboard.

This command asks if you want to enable all digitizer menus. You might want to do this if you had previously disabled some and want to return to the default conditions; otherwise, type **N**. You are then asked to type the number of the menu that you wish to enable. You must type a number between 1 and 10 and press ENTER. You can enable as many menus as you like with a single command. When you are finished specifying the menus that you want to enable, press ESC to end the command.

Note that *unselected menus* become automatically *disabled*. Therefore, if you select menu number 2 and press ESC, the commands in menu 2 (command lines 21-48 in the menu file) will be available instead of the commands in menu 1 (command lines 1-20). Once again, if you enable menus that overlap, the commands that appear near the top of the menu file supercede those further down. The ability to turn on and off menu areas gives you access to several at one time without using up the entire tablet.

Switching Digitizer Menus

In some cases, the default menu, DIGIT, might not contain the appropriate commands for your application. If you want to load another digitizer menu *in place of* DIGIT.MNU, you must unload, or delete, the current menu with the MENU DELETE command on the UTILITIES menu, or with the **VX** command on the keyboard. Any video or digitizer menu that is currently loaded will be eliminated, so that you can load a different one. Until another menu is loaded, you will, however, have no menu whatsoever, video or digitizer. To load another digitizer menu, type **LD** to activate the LOAD DIG MENU command.

Loading More Commands

On the other hand, you might start with a small DIGIT.MNU file and then want to add more commands. If DIGIT.MNU has just 20 commands in it, for example, and you load another digitizer menu with another 20 commands, these commands are numbered 21 to 40 and are assigned to the next available set of boxes.

Chapter 15 contains more specific instructions on customizing Generic CADD by creating your own digitizer and video menus to take advantage of these functions.

15 *Customizing Generic CADD*

Generic CADD can be customized for your specific applications using various methods. You can configure for your specific hardware combinations, configure many of the parameters and toggles by using the CONFIG program, and write your own custom menus, which may include complex macro commands consisting of Generic CADD commands, values, and your own input of points and values.

Custom Configurations

Now that you have had a chance to try all Generic CADD commands, you probably have a better idea of how you want to set up the configuration of toggles and parameters. As you gain more experience with Generic CADD, work with more drawing files, or upgrade your equipment, you might occasionally want to change your configuration. This is a normal part of customizing Generic CADD to suit your hardware and your own style of working.

Multiple Configurations

You may have different needs for configuration settings depending on the type of drawing that you are doing and colleagues who might also be using the computer.

Another reason for needing more than one configuration is if you use more than one video display, pointing device, or plotter with the same computer. You might, for instance, be running Generic CADD on a laptop with a built-in display that uses a different video driver and a different screen aspect ratio when you plug in an RGB monitor. Or perhaps you have several computers that normally use mice but share the use of a digitizer, which is moved from machine to machine whenever it is needed for tracing.

Generic CADD stores the information that is entered in the CONFIG program in a file called CONFIG.FIL. This file is updated whenever you make a change in any part of the configuration. When Generic CADD starts up, it looks in this file for information on how you want the various parameters and toggles set.

You can take advantage of this external storage by creating several versions of this file. For example, if you work on a laptop computer, you might configure Generic CADD to work with one of the graphics alternatives and test it to make sure that it is what you want. Select the proper video driver, set the color selections, and adjust the aspect ratio. Make sure that all of the other configuration options are appropriate for your needs.

Once you are satisfied with the current configuration, copy CONFIG.FIL to another file, substituting a mnemonic extension, such as CONFIG.LAP. This is done at the DOS prompt, by typing **COPY CONFIG.FIL CON-FIG.LAP** and pressing ENTER. You now have two copies of the configuration file for Generic CADD running on the laptop screen.

Now, go back to the CONFIG program and configure for the RGB monitor. Select the appropriate video driver (it is different from the one you are using with the laptop screen), adjust the screen ratio, set the default colors, and make any other changes for the RGB monitor. When you exit CONFIG, a new CONFIG.FIL will be created. Don't worry about overwriting the laptop configuration because it is now in CONFIG.LAP. Test the configuration on the RGB monitor and make any necessary adjustments on the CONFIG program. Then, copy *this* new version of CONFIG.FIL to a new file, such as CONFIG.RGB. At the DOS prompt, type **COPY CONFIG.FIL CONFIG.RGB** and press ENTER. You will now have three separate configurations, each in its own file.

At this point, whenever you want to use the laptop screen, instead of going to CONFIG and resetting parameters, just type **COPY CONFIG.LAP CONFIG.FIL** at the DOS prompt before running Generic CADD. Similarly, to run CADD on the RGB monitor, type **COPY CONFIG.RGB CONFIG.FIL** before starting Generic CADD.

You can now go back and forth between the laptop screen and the RGB monitor much more easily. You can streamline the procedure even further. If you have a text editor or a word processor that creates ASCII files, you can create DOS batch files that copy these files for you. Start a file called LAP.BAT with the following:

```
COPY CONFIG.LAP CONFIG.FIL
CADD
```

Make a second file called RGB.BAT that contains the lines

```
COPY CONFIG.RGB CONFIG.FIL
CADD
```

With these two files, you can start up Generic CADD to run on the laptop screen simply by typing **LAP** and pressing ENTER. You can also start CADD on the RGB monitor by typing **RGB** and pressing ENTER. If you do not want CADD to start up right away when you switch configurations, just leave out the line that contains the word "CADD" in both files.

This technique can be used for various purposes. Even if your equipment stays the same, you might store configurations for different path setups, for different styles of dimensioning, or for metric instead of English units. Typing **METRIC** is much faster than loading CONFIG and trying to remember which parameters you must change.

Illegal Parameters

The allowable range for some parameters is limited, such as the limit of color variables to a range between 0 and 255. The reason for this limitation is that only one byte is used for the storage of this data in the drawing file, and values outside this range cannot be stored in a single byte. There is physically no way to handle values outside this allowable range.

In other cases, however, the reason for limiting the possible values is to "protect" you from errors. An example is the EXTENSION LENGTH variable in dimensioning. Generic CADD insists that you supply a positive number for the first XL variable. If you try to give a value of zero, which would mean no extension beyond the dimension line, this value is *not* accepted, even though you will be asked for the second extension length (which *can* be zero). After this second value has been accepted, Generic CADD will notice that the first value is illegal and will automatically start the command over again. The only way out of the command at this point is to supply a valid value; that is, a positive number. If you try to get around this barrier by setting the first extension length to zero in CONFIG, you will find that you are similarly locked out. There is, however, a way to draw dimensions in which the extension lines do not extend beyond the dimension line.

If you examine CONFIG.FIL with a text editor or word processor that handles ASCII files (it would be a good idea to make a backup copy first), you will find that it is annotated so that you can understand the meaning of many of the variables. You will find two lines near the end of the file that are labeled "EXTENSION LINE LENGTH ABOVE" and "EXTENSION LINE LENGTH BELOW." Simply change the value of the one labeled ABOVE to 0.00000.

Be careful not to change the location of any characters when you are editing CONFIG.FIL: Leave the decimal point in the same place and the same number of zeros after the decimal point. This procedure is not always required, but it is good practice, especially when you are trying to "fool" Generic CADD.

If you save the file this way and then use Generic CADD, you will find that the default value of the first extension length is in fact zero. When you use linear dimensioning, you will get no extension line beyond the dimension line. Don't use the EXTENSION LENGTH command though! If you do, Generic CADD will notice that the first length is zero and will not let you continue until you give a positive value.

Most of the numeric dimensioning values are similarly limited. The allowable values will work for most situations, but you might find some that are a bit too limiting. Almost all of the values can be set to illegal values by editing CONFIG.FIL, and these values will be used. It is a good idea to test the function that you have modified before trying it on an important drawing file, however, as certain illegal values will cause trouble. You cannot have a negative grid size, for example, and some changes that you make to CONFIG.FIL may render Generic CADD unbootable. If you alter CONFIG.FIL in a way that makes it unusable, you must either copy it from your backup or go back to the CONFIG program and reconfigure a new, valid CONFIG.FIL.

Another function that can only be accomplished by editing CONFIG.FIL is clearing digitizer menu areas (see Chapter 14). If you have positioned digitizer menu areas using CONFIG, the locations of these digitizer menus are saved in CONFIG.FIL. The locations are represented by four rows of ten numbers each, which represent two points (four numbers) for each of the ten digitizer menu areas, just above the line containing the name of the pointing device. If you wish to clear the digitizer, so that these digitizer menus are no longer positioned anywhere, you must change all 40 numbers to zero.

You will more likely want to move menu areas, rather than clear them, but if your application requires clearing them, the best you can do without editing CONFIG.FIL is to assign each to a very small area on the perimeter of the digitizer.

In general, if you think a parameter is unreasonably constrained, check to see if you can set it in CONFIG. If you can, you might be able to change the parameter by editing CONFIG.FIL. If you are a programmer, you might even write a program to set some of these CONFIG.FIL values for you. Perhaps one will become available through a third-party source.

Custom Menus

Like CONFIG.FIL, the Generic CADD video and digitizer menus are stored in ASCII files, which can be created or modified with many text editors and word processors. You can customize Generic CADD to perform your specific tasks by editing the existing menu or by creating your own.

Menu Items

The standard video menu files are called LEVEL1.MNU for Level 1, LEVEL2.MNU for Level 2, and LEVEL3.MNU for Generic CADD Level 3. Each line in each of these files represents one command on the video menu. Lines without text appear as blank lines on the video menu, and lines marked with an asterisk, such as * ROOT MENU, usually indicate movement from one part of the video menu to another.

In all of the versions of Generic CADD, the first item in the video menu file is the name of a command as it appears on the video menu. This is followed by a comma, and then the command(s) that are to be executed when this menu item is selected. The line ends with a semicolon. A typical menu item is

LINE,LI;

In this menu item, only the word "LINE" appears on the menu. Whenever you select this word from the video menu, the command LI is issued. The command operates exactly as if you had typed the LI command yourself, except that these two letters do not appear on the screen. In fact, this is the key to how the video command works: It simply types the letters that appear after the comma for you, whenever you select the word that appears before the comma. You can use as many characters as you like for the command name, but only 12 characters fit on the menu.

Multiple Commands

In Level 3, commands can be combined after the comma. Multiple commands must be separated by a comma. A command in Level 3 looks like this:

NEW VIDEO,VX,VL;

This command, which appears as NEW VIDEO on the menu, erases the current video menu (VX) and loads a new one (LV). At this point, the menu item runs out of information, but since the command requires additional information, you are asked for the name of the video menu to be loaded.

Commands That Supply Information

In addition to combining commands, Level 3 also allows you to supply the answers to prompts as part of your menu. In the previous example, the command could be modified to load a particular menu. Suppose that you wanted to load a menu that has been designed specifically for drawing floor plans, called PLAN.MNU. The command to load this might be

PLAN MENU,VX,VL,PLAN;

This menu item would erase the current video menu and load a new one, just like the previous example. However, instead of asking you for the name of the menu, Generic CADD would continue to read the menu item, find the word PLAN, and load this menu.

You can see that in order to write menu items that automatically respond to prompts, you must have a good idea of what the prompts are going to be. A logical procedure is to go through the process that you want to automate in Generic CADD, writing down all of the answers to all of the prompts. Many commands include "Yes" or "No" questions, which must be answered by typing **Y** or **N**. For example, a command to change all entities on layer 0 to layer 1, using a DRAWING CHANGE command, would be the following:

MOVE 0 TO 1,DG,,,,,0,,,,1,Y;

The series of commas is interpreted by Generic CADD as ENTER. In this example, the command simply presses ENTER for the entity type to be changed, the existing line type, line width, and line color. It then types a 0 for the existing layer. ENTER is typed again for the new line type, line width, and line color, and 1 is typed for the new layer. Finally, since the command asks you for confirmation, the letter *Y* is typed to execute and end the command.

Commands That Allow Interactive User Input

Level 3 also allows you to create a menu item that pauses in the middle of a command and lets you supply the required information, either by selecting a point or typing a value.

In these instances, an "at" sign (@) is used to prompt you for a point, and a tilde (~) is used to ask for a single value. For example, a command for drawing a one-inch-radius circle anywhere on the drawing would be constructed as follows:

1"CIRCLE,C2,@,MR,1,0;

This command, appearing as 1"CIRCLE on the menu, would first issue a C2 command (shown on the standard video menu as CIRCLE 2). Then, due to the @ symbol, it would ask you to select the first point—the center of the circle. After you select this point, an MR command (MANUAL ENTRY RELATIVE) would be issued, followed by the second point of the circle, which is 1,0 or one inch directly to the right of the last point that you entered, the center of the circle. For this menu item you would only have to select one point, the center.

To illustrate user input of single values, as opposed to points, consider a command that allows you to set the current line color, line type, line width, and layer all at the same time:

CURRENTS,LK,~,LT,~,LW,~,YC;

The tilde following the LINE COLOR (LK) command allows you to type a number, after which you move on to the LINE TYPE (LT) command and type another number, and so on. Note that a special character for user input is not required on the last command, as the menu item has run out of data, and you will have to supply anything beyond the semicolon anyway.

You can combine commands that require user input and those that do not into a single menu item. For example, you could create a command to set the grid size and the origin simultaneously, and also make sure that manual entry is set to origin, so that the grid can be aligned with any point in the drawing, from which coordinates can be typed:

NEWGRID,GS,~,DO,@,MO;

If you need to put an ESCAPE into a menu item, you can use the two-character command ES, which only works when used in a menu. An ESCAPE might be used when you want to execute only part of a command. For example, you could insert an ESCAPE in the MEASURE DISTANCE (MD) command that measures a single distance and then returns to the "ENTER A COMMAND >" prompt:

ONE DIST,MD,@,@,ES;

After the MD command is issued, it will pause twice for point input, and then an ESCAPE stops the command. Many commands can be ended with either the ES or the PU (PENUP) code.

Digitizer Menus

All of the preceding rules apply to digitizer menus as well as video menus. Because the text before the first comma is essentially only a command label, you might number the commands instead of naming them, so that you can remember which box they are activated by. You could indicate the menu area, column, and row numbers in only nine characters per item:

```
M01R01C01,LI;
M01R01C02,PO;
M01R01C03,C2;
```

These items would not mean much if you saw them on a video menu, but they might help you use the commands on a digitizer menu. If your digitizer menu is small enough that you can remember which box each command is in, you might use the same names that are on your video menu. For more detailed discussion on digitizer menus, see Chapter 14.

Video Submenus

Unlike digitizer menus, on which numerous commands may be displayed at one time, video menus must be divided into smaller groups that will fit on one area of the screen. These *submenus* are generally activated from a master menu. In the standard Generic CADD menus, the first group of commands in the menu file is called the ROOT menu, which is a list of the available submenus, and each submenu has an entry that returns you to the ROOT menu. Though this is a fairly typical organization, you may organize your menus however you like.

To divide a menu into submenus, a pair of menu items is created: one that allows you to jump ahead to the desired submenu, and another to identify the submenu. To activate a submenu called EDIT, for example, you might have an item on your initial menu like the following:

```
EDIT,**
```

When you select this item, Generic CADD looks for an item somewhere in the menu that starts with an asterisk and has the same text:

```
* EDIT
```

This entry would normally be followed by a number of commands that fit into this category. Usually following these items is an item to get you out of this menu. A simple two-screen menu for drawing and editing objects might look something like this:

```
* DRAW

LINE,LI;
POINT,PO;
ARC,A3;
CIRCLE,C2;
ELLIPSE,EP;
CURVE,CV;

EDIT,**

*   EDIT

ERASE,OE;
MOVE,OM;
COPY,OG;
BREAK,OB;
CHANGE,OG;

QUIT,Y,,Q;

DRAW,**
```

This is a relatively simple menu, but it illustrates how one menu can call another one. When you first load this menu, only the first part, the * DRAW section, is displayed, due to the * EDIT line, which Generic CADD recognizes as a separate screen. When you select EDIT from the DRAW menu, the EDIT commands appear; when you select DRAW from the EDIT menu, the DRAW commands appear. Note that the QUIT command is on the EDIT menu, and automatically elects to save the drawing, assumes that the default name is acceptable, and then escapes to DOS by typing **Q**. This command will not make it to the end of the prompts if the file already exists, because you must type **O** or **R** to get beyond this point, and neither of these letters is included in this command.

Loading a Video Menu

There are two ways to load a video menu for use with Generic CADD. If you have elected to display the video menu in the CONFIG program, Generic CADD automatically loads LEVEL1.MNU, LEVEL2.MNU, or LEVEL3.MNU, depending on the version you are using. If you name your menu file LEVEL3.MNU, it will be loaded instead of the standard menu when you start up Level 3. You should probably rename the standard menu before naming your menu LEVEL3.MNU. STANDARD.MNU might be a good name.

The other means of loading a video menu is from within CADD after you have already loaded LEVEL3.MNU. In this case, you can either load the new menu at the end of the current menu, or you may erase the current menu and replace it with the new one. If you exceed the maximum length of video menus, about 5120 characters (5K), the last few submenus in your file will not be active. In these cases, you will need to break your menu into separate files, and erase one before loading another.

To erase the current menu, use the MENU DELETE command on the UTILITIES menu or type **VX** on the keyboard. The menu is cleared. Now you can load the new menu with the LOAD VID MENU command, also on the UTILITIES menu, or type **LV** on the keyboard. You are asked for the name of the menu to load. Type the name of your menu. Level 3 users can use the NEW VID MENU command, which is really a macro command that performs the same function as the NEW MENU example, discussed earlier in the chapter, by combining the VX and LV commands.

If you do not want to erase the current menu first, simply use the LV command to load the new menu. Some versions of Level 3 require that you turn off the video menu with the VM command before loading another video menu. The LV command automatically turns the menu display back on. If you do not turn off the menu display before loading a new menu, some versions of Level 3 think that you are using a digitizer, and ask if you really want to erase the digitizer menu. If you are using Level 1 or 2, you do not have to worry about turning off the display.

When you add a new video menu to an existing one, the submenus may not be accessible from your ROOT menu. To use the newly loaded menus, use the PG UP and PG DN keys, which flip through one menu screen at a time. If you construct your own menu system, you can put references on your ROOT menu that activate submenus, which may or may not be loaded, depending on what you have done previously.

If you call a submenu that does not exist, nothing happens. If two submenus have the same name, you will only be able to use the first one, as Generic CADD always looks for submenus by starting at the beginning of the file and searching downward.

You can create commands with the same name, as long as you can tell them apart. Notice that the standard menu includes several SAVE and LOAD commands, but you can tell them apart because they are on different submenus. You can even include commands with the same name on the same submenu if you like. These can activate either the same or different command codes. The following submenu uses command lines with different names that do the same thing, and commands with the same name that do slightly different things:

```
* NOTES

FIRST,FS,DECO,Y,TA,0.75,TS,15,TK,12;
TIME,FS,DECO,Y,TA,0.75,TS,15,TK,12;
==========,PU;
 LARGE,TZ,1,YC,12,TP;
    -,TZ,0.875,YC,12,TP;
    -,TZ,0.75,YC,12,TP;
    -,TZ,0.625,YC,12,TP;
    -,TZ,0.5,YC,12,TP;
    -,TZ,0.375,YC,12,TP;
    -,TZ,0.25,YC,12,TP;
  SMALL,TZ,0.125,YC,12,TP;
==========,PU;
HORIZONTAL,TR,0;
VERTICAL,TR,90;

ROOT MENU,**
```

Note that this menu would work only in Level 3, because it contains multiple commands and values. This menu would appear on the screen as the following.

```
* NOTES

FIRST
TIME
==========
  LARGE
      –
      –
      –
      –
      –
      –
  SMALL
==========
HORIZONTAL
VERTICAL

ROOT MENU
```

Note the flexibility that you have in breaking up the menu into groups by introducing nonfunctional commands or blank spaces. In this menu, the items are arranged in the order that they might normally be used. The first time that you use text, you would select *either* FIRST or TIME. These items have been allocated two lines so that you will be more likely to notice them when you go to the NOTES menu. Both menu items perform exactly the same tasks: select and load the font DECO, and specify the text aspect, slant, and color.

The group of menu items ranging from LARGE to SMALL all do the same thing except for creating a different size text. Each then goes on to set the layer, makes sure that your notes are always on layer 12, and finally starts a text placement.

This combination of commands eliminates the need for you to decide on which font to use and how to set the text parameters to match every time. The commands also eliminate the need for you to worry about colors and layers when working with text. You have built into the menu the answers to all of these questions. Six of the text placement commands begin with the same text—a dash preceded by several spaces—but you can tell which is which by the way that they are arranged. Generic CADD doesn't care what you call these commands, as all it does with the text is to show it on the screen. The next two commands allow you to change back and forth between horizontal and vertical text. The last menu item takes you back to the ROOT menu.

Unsupported Commands

You may find that certain commands cannot be run completely from a menu item. For example, when drawing an ellipse, you are always asked if you want a True or Construction Ellipse. You answer this question by typing a **T** or a **C**. However, you cannot type this letter from the video menu. The following command would *not* work:

T ELLIPSE,EP,@,@,@,@,T;

The ELLIPSE command could be activated, and each of the four user inputs would work, but the *T* at the end of the command would not be accepted until after you are prompted for True or Construction. After you type a **T**, the Ellipse would be drawn, and *then* the *T* in the menu would be read; you would be "stuck" in the middle of a two-letter command starting with *T*. You must either type another letter or press ESC in order to continue.

Another command that cannot be fully automated is the REGULAR POLYGON command. *You* must always type the number of sides on the Polygon.

CHANGE commands are somewhat finicky. These commands allow you to insert extra commas to skip over prompts that can be anwered by ENTER, but they get stuck when you try to include user input by using a tilde.

Long Menu Items

Each line of a Level 3 menu file can be up to 80 characters long. This is true for both video and digitizer menus. Characters beyond the eightieth are simply ignored. Though 80 characters are enough for most commands, you may occasionally want to use longer macros.

To write commands longer than 80 characters, you must use batch files with the menu. The actual commands that you want to execute would be stored in a separate ASCII file with the extension .TXT, and the item on the menu would use a LOAD BATCH (LB) command to activate this batch file. Batch files can include pauses for user input as well as data required by command prompts.

Suppose, for example, that you want to create (1) a menu item that would load several components from a special directory and (2) a menu designed for automated placement of these components. Your menu item for such a task might look like this:

```
FURNITURE,LB,FURN;
```

The batch file associated with this menu item would be called FURN.TXT, and should be in the same directory as Generic CADD. It might look like the following:

```
P2,\CADD\CMP\FURN\;
CL,CHAIR;
CL,TABLE;
CL,DESK;
CL,LAMP;
CL,BED;
CL,COUCH;
CL,LOVESEAT;
CL,DRESSER;
P2,\CADD\CMP\;
LV,FURN;
CZ,1,1;
```

Note that the batch file returns the component path to the normal component directory after loading the furniture components from their own directory. This batch also makes sure that the component scale is returned to the default value of 1, as the furniture will probably be inserted at real scale. Rotation of the furniture will likely be controlled by the furniture placement menu, called FURN.MNU, which might look something like the following.

```
• FURNITURE

facing:,PU;
--------,PU;
 RIGHT,CR,0;
   LEFT,CR,180;
      UP,CR,90;
 DOWN,CR,270;
 OTHER,CR;
========,PU;
CHAIR,CP,CHAIR;
TABLE,CP,TABLE;
DESK,CP,DESK;
LAMP,CP,LAMP;
BED,CP,BED;
COUCH,CP,COUCH;
LOVESEAT,CP,LOVESEAT;
DRESSER,CP,DRESSER;

ROOT MENU,••
```

This menu allows you to select one of four preset directions (component rotations) or specify your own, and then place any of the furniture components, which are preloaded if this menu is accessible. If you are placing more than one component using the same direction, you would not need to select a direction each time. As usual, the last item allows you to return to the ROOT menu.

Batch files can be called from digitizer menus as well, and as you can see from this example, menus can be used to activate each other, so that all of your commands need not be in a single menu file.

Including Images to Illustrate Menus

The previous example included a menu item on one menu that loaded a batch file, which, in turn, loaded components and another menu. In the example, .CMP files, .MNU files, and .TXT files were used. To this, you could add one more file type, .GX2, which would allow you to illustrate the menu as well.

First, you must create the .GX2 file. Place each component in a drawing, title it with the name of the component, and indicate the reference point somehow. If you have DISPLAY REFERENCE POINTS turned on, the

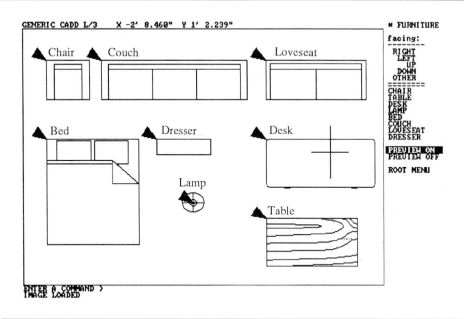

Figure 15-1. *An image for use with the FURNITURE menu*

actual reference points will show. Figure 15-1 shows what this screen might look like. To create a .GX2 file from this screen, use the IMAGE SAVE (IS) command on the UTILITIES menu, and call this image "FURN," to match the batch and menu files.

To use this image file, add the following lines to the FURN.MNU file:

```
PREVIEW ON,IL,FURN;
PREVIEW OFF,RD;
```

The first of these lines loads the image file so that you can see each component, and the location of its reference point. The second line erases the image from the screen by issuing a REDRAW command, which returns your drawing to the screen.

Image previews can also be useful for font selection, hatch pattern selection, or any situation when a picture is helpful. Digitizer menus can call image files in exactly the same way.

Some Useful Menu Macros

The best way to write your own menus is to keep track of the tasks that you do in Generic CADD on a continual basis and try to automate these functions. The type of drawings and procedures that you do the most should influence which macros you create.

Here are some menu macros that you may find useful, or you may want to modify them to suit your own requirements. They may also give you some ideas on how to write your own.

Wall Intersections   Figure 15-2 shows a plan that has been drawn with double lines (L2). The manual technique for cleaning up the intersections between the interior and the exterior walls requires that you break the double line of the interior wall, and then either TRIM or FILLET the two new corners to make sure that they were true intersections.

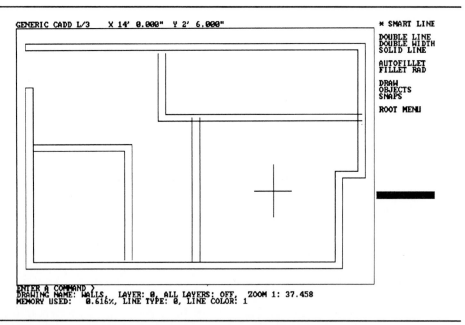

Figure 15-2.   *A drawing with unbroken intersections of double lines*

All of this manual work can be accomplished with four macros, which correspond to the direction of the intersections, as follows:

⋆ WALL T's

ABOVE,OB,@,MR,0,0,0,0,BP,0,0,MB,RF,0,FL,–9,0,–3,9,FL,9,0,3,9;
BELOW,OB,@,MR,0,0,0,0,BP,0,0,MB,RF,0,FL,–9,0,–3,–9,FL,9,0,3,–9;
RIGHT,OB,@,MR,0,0,0,0,BP,0,0,MB,RF,0,FL,0,9,9,3,FL,0,–9,9,–3;
　LEFT,OB,@,MR,0,0,0,0,BP,0,0,MB,RF,0,FL,0,9,-9,3,FL,0,–9,–9,–3;

ROOT MENU,⋆⋆

The title of each menu item indicates on which side of the continuous wall the butting wall intersects. The point that is picked at the beginning of the command is a point on the continuous wall, on the side where the butting wall intersects, between the two sides of the butting wall. Note that because fillets are used, the butting wall doesn't have to exactly touch the continuous wall; it can miss or overlap by as much as 9 inches.

If you are using an EGA card or another graphics card that supports the extended ASCII character set, you can even use special characters to illustrate the items on the menu. The following menu items are self-explanatory:

⋆ T's

　,OB,@,MR,0,0,0,0,BP,0,0,MB,RF,0,FL,–9,0,–3,9,FL,9,0,3,9;
　,OB,@,MR,0,0,0,0,BP,0,0,MB,RF,0,FL,–9,0,–3,-9,FL,9,0,3,–9;
　,OB,@,MR,0,0,0,0,BP,0,0,MB,RF,0,FL,0,9,9,3,FL,0,–9,9,–3;
　,OB,@,MR,0,0,0,0,BP,0,0,MB,RF,0,FL,0,9,–9,3,FL,0,–9,–9,–3;

Some new techniques are introduced with these macros. One of these is the use of the BASEPOINT (BP) to mark a point so that you can specify coordinates relative to this point later in the menu command. In this case the basepoint is located at the point that you first selected by positioning it at 0,0 using manual entry mode. After this point on the continuous wall has been located and broken, all further points are specified relative to the basepoint by using the MANUAL ENTRY BASEPOINT (MB) command. This allows you to make sure that you are getting the lines that you want, regardless of the width of the wall. Figure 15-3 illustrates a typical use of this macro command.

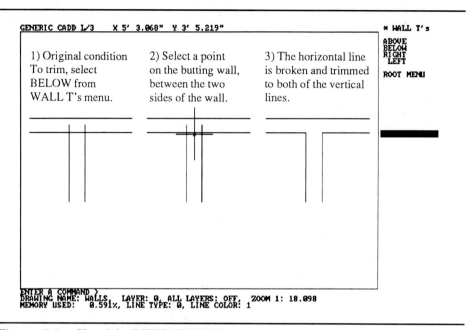

Figure 15-3. *Use of the INTERSECTION macros*

Another technique introduced by this macro is one of generalization. You may not know exactly where the lines are going to be located, but you can estimate the thickness of a wall to be between 4 inches and 24 inches. The points specified by the FILLET command are overestimated, in recognition of the fact that a line will probably be found somewhere in the vicinity of the point specified, and will usually be the line that you want. This command will work in most instances, except those in which another wall or an opening in either wall is nearby.

In general, this macro will save quite a bit of time in the editing process. Special cases will still require editing "by hand." What's more, these macros can be revised to work with any type of drawing that makes use of double lines that need to be trimmed at butting intersections. Simply change the values to coordinate with your typical spacings.

Openings in Double Lines These macros are especially useful for putting doorways and windows in walls, but like the previous example, they can be modified for other applications. Simply adjust the values used here.

The technique used is to add a line at each end of the opening, and then to break the original lines. Note that these particular macros work only for walls that are six inches thick.

horizontal:

30",MR,NL,@,0,6,PU,30,0,0,–6,OB,–15,0,15,0,–30,0,OB,15,6,15,0,–30,0;
36",MR,NL,@,0,6,PU,36,0,0,–6,OB,–18,0,18,0,–36,0,OB,18,6,18,0,–36,0;
42",MR,NL,@,0,6,PU,42,0,0,–6,OB,–21,0,21,0,–42,0,OB,21,6,21,0,–42,0;

vertical:

30",MR,NL,@,–6,0,PU,0,30,6,0,OB,0,–15,0,15,0,–30,OB,–6,15,0,–15,0,30;
36",MR,NL,@,–6,0,PU,0,36,6,0,OB,0,–18,0,18,0,–36,OB,–6,18,0,–18,0,36;
42",MR,NL,@,–6,0,PU,0,42,6,0,OB,0,–21,0,21,0,–42,OB,–6,21,0,–21,0,42;

ROOT MENU,**

Note that the opening in the horizontal walls is created to the right of the selected point, which must be on the lower of the two lines, and the opening in the vertical walls is created above the point selected, which must be on the line farthest to the right of the wall. If these assumptions will not always be true, you must write additional macros to cover these cases. Figure 15-4 illustrates the use of the OPENING macro.

Note that MANUAL ENTRY RELATIVE is turned on right away, so that everything can be specified from the first point that you show, which selects the first line to break.

Setting Variables Several variables in Generic CADD depend on the scale at which the drawing is plotted. These include Text Size, Component Scale, and many of the Dimensioning Variables.

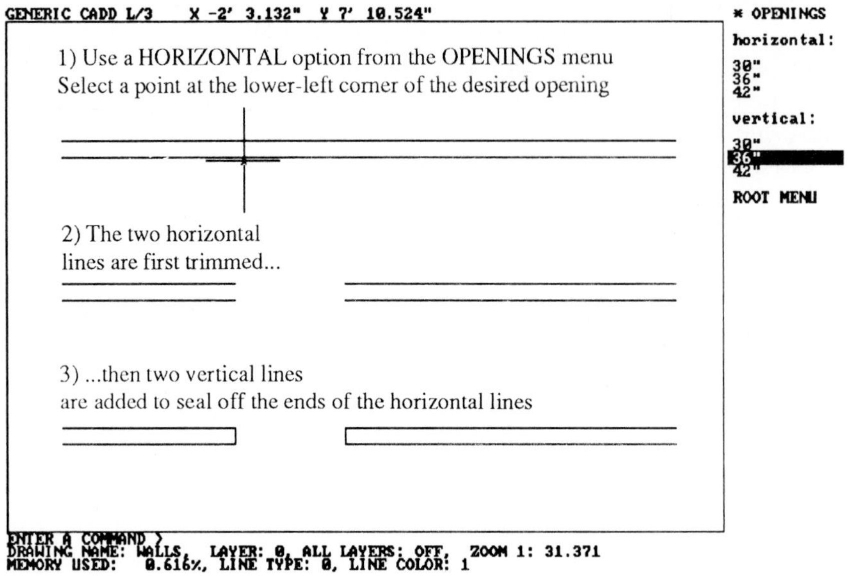

```
GENERIC CADD L/3    X -2' 3.132"  Y 7' 10.524"                    * OPENINGS
                                                                 horizontal:
    1) Use a HORIZONTAL option from the OPENINGS menu           30"
    Select a point at the lower-left corner of the desired opening  36"
                                                                 42"

                            |                                   vertical:
    ─────────────────────────────────────────────────          30"
    ─────────────────────────────────────────────────          36"
                            |                                   42"
                            |                                   ROOT MENU

    2) The two horizontal
    lines are first trimmed...

    ─────────────────          ─────────────────


    3) ...then two vertical lines
    are added to seal off the ends of the horizontal lines

    ┌─────────────────┐        ┌─────────────────────────┐


ENTER A COMMAND >
DRAWING NAME: WALLS,  LAYER: 0, ALL LAYERS: OFF,  ZOOM 1: 31.371
MEMORY USED:   0.616%, LINE TYPE: 0, LINE COLOR: 1
```

Figure 15-4. *Use of the OPENING macros*

The following menu items set these values by selecting a scale from the menu:

* SCALE

1/8"=1',TZ,12,CZ,96,96,LH,8,XO,6,XL,12,48,LL,18;
1/4"=1',TZ,6,CZ,48,48,LH,4,XO,3,XL,6,24,LL,9;
3/4"=1',TZ,2,CZ,16,16,LH,1.5,XO,1,XL,2,8,LL,3;
1-1/2"=1',TZ,1,CZ,8,8,LH,.75,XO,.5,XL,1,4,LL,1.5;

ROOT MENU,**

These items make certain assumptions about the text size and the dimensioning values that you want to use. They also assume that you will be inserting components that are *symbols* rather than real objects. Of course, you can modify these menu items to use whatever values suit your drawing requirements or scales. The important point is that you only have to remember to set the scale once, instead of variable by variable. Similar macros could be written to set other variables.

Macro Tricks

You can automate almost any drawing task with Generic CADD Level 3's macro programming capabilities. Some tasks may require that you use a combination of menu macros, batch files, user input of points, user input of single values, and various forms of manual entry that allow you to keep track of where you are at any given time.

One of the limitations of Generic's macro function, however, is the lack of variables. A few pseudo-variables are available: the Origin, the Basepoint, and the last point entered, because you can specify future points in reference to any of these. If used carefully, these points can help you overcome some interesting programming difficulties, as seen in the wall-intersection examples. Consider the macro on the following page. It creates the house shape shown in Figure 15-5 from one user-selected point.

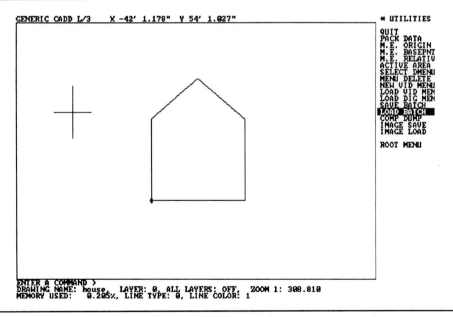

Figure 15-5. *A house shape that can be created with a macro command*

```
LS,200',200';
ZL;
MO;
RE,0,0,@;
MR;
BP,0,0;
MB;
LI,0,0,-100',100';
BP,SC,-100',0;
LI,0,0,MR,100',100',MB;
RF,0;
BP,SM,1,0;
OE,0,0;
TO,1.0;
BP,SI,0,100';
TO,0.25;
FL,1,-1,-1,-1;
```

This batch file will automatically start up a RECTANGLE command, fixing the first point at the origin. You will be asked for the second point. The rest of the drawing will be done automatically. This particular version of the batch macro will work on almost any rectangle that is roughly the size of a house. If you have ABSOLUTE COORDINATES turned on before you load this batch, you will be able to see the size of the rectangle. Alternatively, you can simply type the width and height of the rectangle at the first prompt.

You can create another version of this macro that will work at almost any scale by "cheating" on the TOLERANCE command. Leave out the first

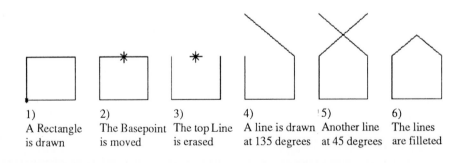

1)	2)	3)	4)	5)	6)
A Rectangle is drawn	The Basepoint is moved	The top Line is erased	A line is drawn at 135 degrees	Another line at 45 degrees	The lines are filleted

Figure 15-6.　*A slow-motion replay of the HOUSE batch macro*

few lines that set the Limits, and do the Zoom Limits, and eliminate the lines that change the Tolerance. These commands are trying to make sure that the SNAP INTERSECTION command will actually work by specifying as large a tolerance as Generic CADD will allow. However, you can get an even larger tolerance if you edit CONFIG.FIL.

Near the top of CONFIG.FIL, you will find a line that looks like this:

```
1.0000  0.2500              { GRID SIZE, TOLERANCE }
```

Don't worry if your version says GRIG SIZE instead of GRID SIZE; just change the second value to a much larger value, such as the full height of your screen, say 9 inches. This line should now look like this:

```
1.0000  9.0000              { GRID SIZE, TOLERANCE }
```

Save the file, start up Generic CADD again, and zoom to whatever size screen you want to draw the house shape in. Make sure that the origin is near the lower-left corner of the screen, and that there is room for the entire house shape. Load the batch file, and select the upper-right corner of the rectangle. This macro will now work almost every time, as long as the upper-right corner of the rectangle that you draw is below the centerline of the screen. This needs to be the case so that the intersection of the "roof" lines will occur on screen. With your expanded tolerance, Generic CADD should be able to find an intersection *anywhere,* as long as it is on the screen. Figure 15-6 illustrates the use of this batch macro.

If Generic CADD's macro capabilities are not powerful enough to automate your drawing procedures, you may be able to combine Generic CADD's menu or batch capabilities with other software, as discussed in the next chapter.

16 *Communicating with Other Programs*

Because Generic CADD creates and reads several types of disk files, it can communicate with other software that is also capable of creating or reading these files.

Regardless of file type, Generic CADD can send information to the disk, where it can be interpreted by other programs, and it can read information from the disk, allowing other programs a channel into Generic CADD.

Communication Through Drawing Files

Generic CADD's most natural form of communication is through drawing files. Any drawing created in any version of Generic CADD using any hardware combination can be read and processed by any other version of Generic CADD, even if the hardware configuration is different. Levels 1 and 2 cannot interpret everything in a Level 3 drawing, such as Hatches and Fills, but for the most part, two-way communication is possible.

Sending Drawing Data to Other Software

In addition to communication between different computers running Generic CADD, drawing files can be used to send information to and from other Generic Software. Generic DotPlot, PenPlot, and DeskConvert are all capable of reading Generic CADD drawing files and performing functions with them. DotPlot and PenPlot print drawings on printers and plotters, respectively, for users of Generic CADD versions that do not contain these functions. DeskConvert creates files in publishing formats from Generic CADD drawing files, and prints to PostScript devices, allowing Generic CADD drawing files to be used together with a wide variety of desktop publishing software.

Data Input Through Drawing Files

Several Generic Software programs can create Generic CADD drawing files, so that information developed in other programs may be loaded into Generic CADD. Both Generic CADD Solid Modeling and 3D Drafting create 2D drawing files from 3D viewpoints that are readable by any version of Generic CADD. Once exported from the 3D programs and imported into Generic CADD, these viewpoints become fixed, of course, and can be edited as you would any other drawing created in Generic CADD.

Only a few other programs can create Generic CADD drawing files, as the format and rules for drawing files are not generally available to other software developers. This may change in the future, allowing other software to send data directly into Generic CADD.

Two-Way Communication

Generic IGES and AutoConvert read and write Generic CADD drawing files, allowing other CAD programs to communicate with Generic CADD. Any program that creates either .DXF or IGES files can send drawing information to Generic CADD through the use of these programs.

A number of utility programs are available, both as part of Generic's UTILITIES package and from third-party software developers, that perform specific functions on Generic CADD drawing files, leaving them in drawing file format so that they can be reloaded into Generic CADD with the revisions.

Communication Through Batch Files

Generic CADD drawing files are stored in a special compact format that is difficult for other software to access. For this reason and others, batch files are provided as an access route, both in and out of Generic CADD, in the much simpler form of ASCII files.

Batch files are actually just a list of all of the commands and values that are required to create a given drawing file. When you save a batch file from a drawing, you are actually saving a list of the commands and values required to create *that* drawing; when you load a batch file, a drawing is created from these commands and values.

Data Extraction

Because a batch file contains all of the commands and values required to create a drawing, other software can use the file to extract this information. The other software can then change, analyze, or use this information as necessary.

As a simple example, every time a certain component is used in a drawing file, the batch file saved from that drawing file includes a CP (Component Place) command, followed by the name of the component. External software could be written that would read the batch file and count the number of various components for cost analysis, inventory, parts ordering, or other purposes.

Many other types of information can be extracted from batch files. Square footages of Filled or Hatched areas can be derived, character placements can be accumulated into an even simpler ASCII text file, and so on. The data that can be extracted from a batch file is limited only by the amount of information put into the drawing file, and sometimes you can extract more than you imagined possible.

Data Input Through Batch Files

Chapter 15 explained how you can create your own batch files to automate certain drawing tasks, using a text editor or word processor. Batch files can also be created by other software. Many third-party products on the market perform automated drawing tasks or transfer drawing information to Generic CADD through the use of batch files. Batch files are popular for this task because their format is well documented, and ASCII files are much easier to create than Generic CADD drawing files.

Additionally, you can use different types of software to create intelligent batch files for automating many drawing tasks. Spreadsheet and database programs, for example, can manipulate text and numeric data, process and sort this data, and provide user-formatted output.

Creating a Drawing with a Spreadsheet Program   Spreadsheet software programs can help you create drawings automatically by manipulating numeric data through the use of formulas and by combining text and numeric data. These capabilities make spreadsheets excellent vehicles for the automation of drawing procedures. For example, you might need to make several drawings that vary only in dimension or in the number of times a certain part appears. Often, these variable dimensions or numbers can be derived from a few simple parameters.

Figure 16-1 is an example of a drawing that can be created by a spreadsheet program. The parameters for this drawing of a column are the height and width of the base; the height of the column shaft and its width at top and bottom; and the height and width of the column capitol. From this information, the drawing can be made.

To create a spreadsheet program to draw the column, place titles for these parameters and sample values into the first two columns of a spreadsheet program. In the following example, assume that the spreadsheet columns are labeled with letters and the rows are numbered. The following might be your list of parameters:

	A	B
01	BASE HEIGHT	36
02	BASE WIDTH	18
03		
04	SHAFT HEIGHT	72
05	SHAFT WIDTH at BOTTOM	12
06	SHAFT WIDTH at TOP	9
07		
08	CAPITOL HEIGHT	15
09	CAPITAL WIDTH	12

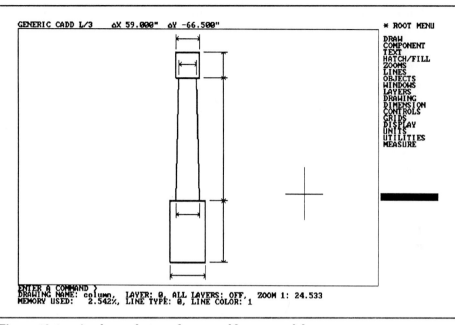

Figure 16-1. *A column that can be created by a spreadsheet*

After you have created this part of the spreadsheet, make a sketch of a typical column and imagine how you would go about drawing it from the information available.

The base is easy. Suppose that you were to start at the Drawing Basepoint. (This will later allow you to place the Basepoint wherever you want the column to be drawn, and then load the batch file to run this macro.) The first step in this automated macro then would be to set manual entry to Basepoint, using the MB command. Next, you would simply draw a rectangle that uses the Basepoint as its lower-left corner and the base width and height as its upper-right corner. If you were writing the batch file to make this drawing instead of with this spreadsheet, the commands so far would be as follows:

```
MB;
RE,0,0,18,36;
```

But what happens if you decide to change the width or height of the base? When you write the automated macro, you should use references to the parameters in the spreadsheet instead of the actual numbers that appear there. Therefore, since the height and width of the base appear in column B, rows 01 and 02, you should replace the height and width in the RECTANGLE command with B01 and B02 (or use whatever column and row references your spreadsheet uses). At this point, your batch file would look like this:

```
MB;
RE,0,0,B02,B01;
```

Of course, Generic CADD will not be able to understand the B01 and B02 values, but you can get the spreadsheet to take care of this, by putting these commands and values into some additional columns:

```
    C   D  E F  G H   I  J   K

01  MB                       ;
02  RE, 0.0 , 0.0 ,  B02 ,  B01 ;
```

By putting in B02 and B01 as *formulas* rather than absolute values, the values in H01 and H02 should change whenever you change the values in B01 and B02.

The next task is to draw the shaft. It is a good idea to move the Basepoint to the top middle of the base as a better reference point for the shaft, as shown in Figure 16-2. Specify a new Basepoint that is one-half the base width to the right of the current Basepoint, and above the current Basepoint by the full height of the base. The following command would do the trick:

```
BP,B02/2,B01;
```

With the new Basepoint in place, the right side of the column could be described as follows:

```
LI,B05/2,0,B06/2,B04;
```

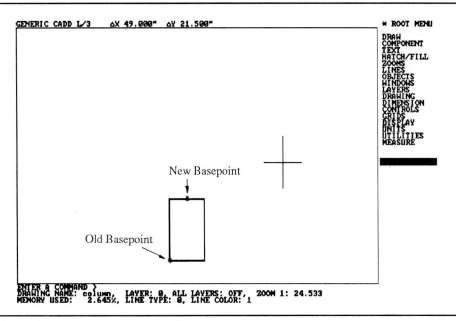

Figure 16-2. *The column base with the new Basepoint*

This would draw a Line (LI) starting half the bottom column width (B05/2,0) away from the center of the top of the base (the Basepoint) to a point half the top column width (B06/2) to the right and the column shaft height (B04) above the same point. The line at the left side of the column can be similarly described, but with negative X values:

LI,–B05/2,0,–B06/2,B04;

At this point, the column would resemble the one shown in Figure 16-3. These three lines could then be added to the spreadsheet:

	C	D	E F		G	H		I	J	K
03	BP		, B02/2	,	B01					;
04	LI,	B05/2	, 0.0	,	B06/2		,		B04	;
05	LI,	–B05/2	, 0.0	,		–B06/2	,		B04	;

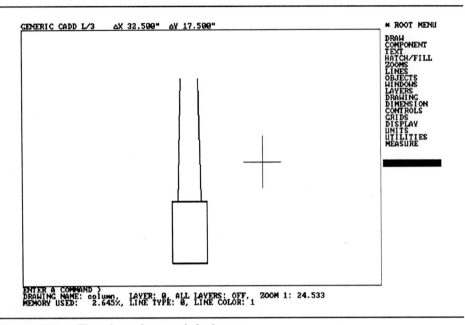

Figure 16-3. *The column base and shaft*

The Basepoint would move once again—to the center of the column top, or even better, to the left corner of the column capitol. This location is one-half the capitol width to the left and the full column shaft height above where it is now, or

BP,–B08/2,B04;

The column capitol can now be drawn quite easily with a single REC-TANGLE command:

RE,0,0,B09,B08;

With these last two commands, columns C through K of your spread-sheet will now look like the following.

	C	D	E	F	G	H	I	J	K
01	MB				;				
02	RE,	0.0	,	0.0	,	B02	,	B01	;
03	BP		,	B02/2	,	B01			;
04	LI,	B05/2	,	0.0	,	B06/2	,	B04	;
05	LI,	−B05/2	,	0.0	,	−B06/2	,	B04	;
06	BP		,	−B08/2	,	B04			;
07	RE,	0.0	,	0.0	,	B09	,	B08	;

Now, any time that you change any of the parameters in column B, the batch file, stored in columns C through K, will change to reflect these changes. Set the values in column B to what you want, and save the spreadsheet in the usual way.

To create the actual batch file that Generic CADD will use to draw the column, save columns C through K only to an ASCII file called COL-UMN.TXT. How this is done varies among different spreadsheets. Many have an option to *print to a file,* or to *export to an ASCII file.* Before doing this, make sure that column K is *right-justified*—that is, the semicolons are flush to the right edge of the column. Spaces at the ends of the lines may cause the batch to work improperly in Generic CADD.

If your spreadsheet program does not save ASCII files with the extension .TXT, you may have to rename the file with the DOS RENAME command. For example, if your spreadsheet automatically gives ASCII files the extension .PRN, you must rename the ASCII file so that Generic CADD can load it as a batch:

```
REN COLUMN.PRN COLUMN.TXT
```

Once you have saved the spreadsheet in the normal way and columns C through K as an ASCII file, exit to DOS and start up Generic CADD again. Select a line color, layer, and whatever drawing parameters you want to preset. Next, place the Basepoint at the lower-left corner of where you want the column to be drawn. Use the BP command and select a point. Finally, load the batch with the LB command, and type the name of the batch file, **COLUMN**. The column described in the spreadsheet will be drawn.

To create more columns of varying shapes, you can simply edit column B of the spreadsheet, resave columns C through K as an ASCII file, and load them into Generic CADD with the LOAD BATCH command. Figure

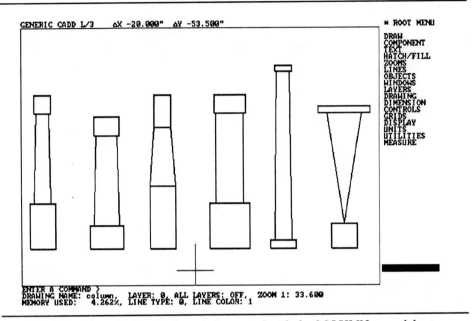

Figure 16-4. *Several columns that can be created with the COLUMN spreadsheet macro*

16-4 shows the variety of columns that can be created with this simple spreadsheet macro program.

You can add additional parameters, such as the total number of columns, the distance between them, and the colors and layers of each part of the column. Number and spacing could be added by introducing two new parameters:

	A	B
11	NUMBER OF COLUMNS	6
12	COLUMN SPACING	60

The additional columns could be created with a WINDOW COPY command, which uses the previous parameters to figure out how large to make the window, and the new parameters for the copy number and distance, as in the following.

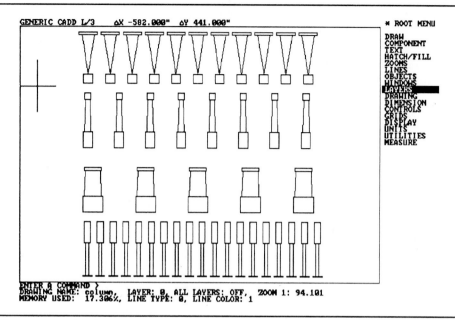

Figure 16-5. *Different column types and spacings that can be produced with the expanded spreadsheet macro*

```
MR;
WC,B02/2,0,-(B09+B02+B02/2),(B01+B04+B08),0,0,B12,0,B11;
```

The WINDOW COPY macro looks complicated, but it is really just combining the various heights and widths to make sure that the window is big enough. The final five values indicate the displacement and number of copies. If you insert these formulas into the spreadsheet, you can produce a great variety of multiple-column combinations, as shown in Figure 16-5.

Communication Through Image Files

The image files produced by the Generic CADD SAVE IMAGE command can be transferred to other programs, and images created by other software can be loaded into Generic CADD. These files have the extension .GX2.

Image files are less compatible between various hardware configurations and programs than drawing files because they contain specific pixel locations, colors, and so on, which may be defined differently on different hardware.

Sharing Images in CADD

In general, .GX2 files created by any version of Generic CADD using a particular type of graphics card can be loaded by other versions of Generic CADD as long as the same type of graphics card is in use. You can load a Level 3 image made on an EGA card into Level 1 running on an EGA card, for example. However, you cannot load a Level 3 image made on a Hercules monochrome card into any version of Generic CADD running on an EGA card, or vice versa.

Keep in mind that when images from one drawing or copy of Generic CADD are loaded into another, no actual CADD data is transferred, only the image on the screen. This image will be wiped clean the next time that the screen is redrawn.

Transferring Images to and from Generic Presentation

Image (.GX2) files are also used by several other Generic products, including Generic Present and Generic Paint, both part of Generic's Presentation software package.

These files are compatible with Generic CADD .GX2 files, but are in a different format, which must be changed before a transfer can take place in certain directions. The same rules apply regarding the hardware in use when the files were made, except that Generic Paint can display CGA images on an EGA card.

Generic CADD .GX2 to Generic Paint   You can load .GX2 files created by any version of Generic CADD into Generic Paint. When these files are loaded, they are automatically changed to Paint's preferred format, so that they do not have to be converted each time that you use them in Paint. However, once Paint converts and saves them in the new format, they can no longer be loaded directly back into Generic CADD. If you want to use the same image in CADD and Paint, it is a good idea to load the CADD

.GX2 file into Paint, and then use the Save As... option to save it using a different name, so the original CADD version is preserved.

Generic CADD .GX2 to Generic Present   Generic Present has no built-in conversion capabilities, so CADD .GX2 files must be converted to the Paint/Present format before they can be used in Present. There are two ways to accomplish this goal. A conversion program, called PaintConvert (PCON) is provided for this purpose with Generic Presentation. Use this program, and specify .GX2 for both the input and output file types. PaintConvert checks the current format of the .GX2 file and converts it to the opposite format. In this case, your CADD .GX2 files are converted to Paint/Present .GX2 files, so you will be able to use them in Generic Present. The second method is simply to load the image file into Generic Paint and save it in the converted format. This method is usually quite a bit faster.

Generic Paint or Present .GX2 to Generic CADD   Generic CADD also has no conversion functions, so Paint/Present .GX2 files must be converted before they can be used in Generic CADD. Use the PaintConvert utility, once again specifying .GX2 for both input and output file formats. Paint-Convert will recognize the Paint/Present format file and convert it to CADD format.

Communication With Other Software

You can convert .GX2 files to a number of other formats with PaintConvert, and vice versa. Among the supported formats are PC Paintbrush's .PCX, GEM's .IMG, and Generic 3D's .IMG files. By selecting the appropriate input and output formats, you can convert any of these formats for use in Generic CADD, or you can convert Generic CADD .GX2 files into any of these formats.

If you have converted another format into .GX2, you may find that it still doesn't load into Generic CADD. This is because it was converted into Paint/Present .GX2 format instead of CADD .GX2 format. If you convert it again, this time from .GX2 to .GX2, the file may become loadable.

A Related Software

Numerous programs interface with Generic CADD, including Generic Software products that perform specific additional functions, third-party software that has been designed to add capabilities to Generic CADD, symbols libraries developed by other users, and software that creates Generic CADD drawing or batch files as its output. This appendix briefly describes these programs and how they can be used to increase the productivity of Generic CADD.

Software That Works with Generic CADD Drawing Files

Many Generic Software products are designed to perform additional functions using Generic CADD drawing files. These include printing and plotting utilities, conversion programs, and utility software.

Program:	DotPlot
Published by:	Generic Software, Inc., Bothell, Washington.
Function:	Prints Generic CADD drawing files on laser and dot-matrix printers.

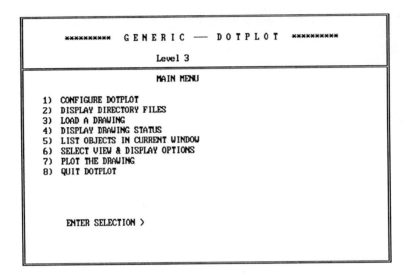

Figure A-1. *The DotPlot main menu*

Description: Provides printing capabilities for users of Generic CADD Level 3 similar to those provided in Levels 1 and 2. Over 100 dot matrix printers plus Hewlett-Packard LaserJet printer and compatibles are supported at various resolutions, at user-selectable scales and sheet sizes. In some cases, the program is bundled with Level 3 and accessible through the XD command. Figure A-1 shows the DotPlot main menu.

Program: PenPlot

Published by: Generic Software, Inc., Bothell, Washington.

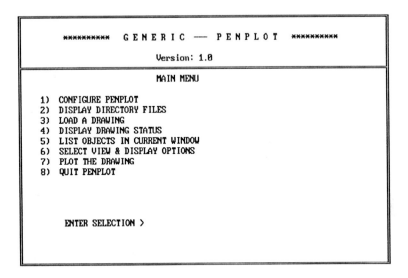

Figure A-2.   *The PenPlot main menu*

Function: Plots Generic CADD drawing files on a wide variety of plotters.

Description: Provides plotting capabilities for users of Generic CADD Levels 1 and 2 similar to those provided in Level 3. Most popular plotters, including all Hewlett-Packard and Houston Instruments plotters are supported. Includes pen sorting, plotting by layers, and plotting to a file. Multiple drawings can be loaded and plotted simultaneously, or portions of individual drawings can be plotted. Figure A-2 shows the PenPlot main menu.

Program: **AutoConvert**

Published by:	Generic Software, Inc., Bothell, Washington.
Function:	Two-way translation between Generic CADD drawing files and .DXF format ASCII files.
Description:	Allows Generic CADD drawing files to be sent to a program that accepts .DXF format files (a Drawing Exchange Format file popularized by AutoDesk, Inc. and supported by many CAD and CAD-related utility programs). The program also converts .DXF files to Generic CADD drawing format so that drawings made in other CAD programs supporting the .DXF format may be loaded into Generic CADD. In addition to allowing file transfer between Generic CADD and other CAD programs, AutoConvert allows Generic CADD users to take advantage of numerous programs that have been designed to perform functions on .DXF files. Figure A-3 shows the AutoConvert main menu.

Program: **Generic IGES**

Published by:	Generic Software, Inc., Bothell, Washington.
Function:	Two-way tranlation between Generic CADD drawing files and IGES format files.
Description:	Allows CAD data to be transferred to and from any program that reads and writes IGES (Initial Graphics Exchange Standard) files. Generic IGES converts Generic CADD drawing files to IGES format, and IGES format files to Generic CADD drawing files. It allows

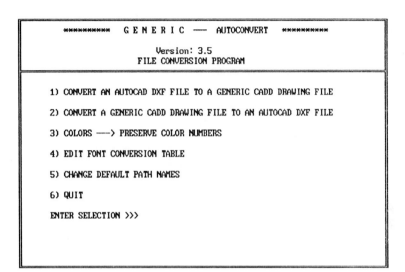

Figure A-3.   *The AutoConvert menu*

Generic CADD users to share drawing information with
many mainframe CAD programs. Figure A-4 shows the
IGES main menu.

Product: **Generic Utilities**

Published by: Generic Software, Inc., Bothell, Washington.

Function: A grab bag of utilities for Generic CADD users.

```
GENERIC IGES V2.0
(C) Copyright 1987 The Data Exchange Company.
The Data Exchange Company.
Version 2.0 (07/28/87)


Generic IGES Main Menu

  0. Exit to DOS
  1. Translate a single Generic file to IGES
  2. Translate a batch of Generic files to IGES
  3. Translate a single IGES file to Generic
  4. Translate a batch of IGES files to Generic
  5. Edit IGES file
  9. Configure Generic IGES


Enter Option:
```

Figure A-4.   *The Generic IGES menu*

Description: Includes a number of individual programs including:

■ Utilities for converting output files from other software into Generic CADD drawing files. HPGL, DMPL, and Lotus .PIC formats are supported, allowing users to bring output from spreadsheets, scheduling programs, and business graphics packages into Generic CADD.

■ A program for creating your own hatch patterns.

■ A program for turning ASCII text files into drawing files; especially useful when adding large amounts of text to drawings.

■ Two font utilities, one for making a Generic font from a drawing file of components, and one for turning a font into a drawing file of components so that they may be exploded, manipulated, and made into a font again.

■ A program for turning arcs and circles into curves so that they may be scaled differently in two directions.

■ A drawing analyzer/editor for finding and fixing minor bugs in Generic CADD drawing files.

Product: **The Third Dimension**

Published by: Workshop 3D Software, Inc., Seattle, Washington.

Function: Creates 3D views from Generic CADD drawings.

Description: A Wireframe extrusion program that projects orthographic, perspective, and stereo drawings from 2D Generic CADD drawing files. 3D heights and thicknesses are stored in the layers and colors used to create a single 2D drawing from which the projections are made, and a focal point is selected in Generic CADD by moving the drawing origin.

The program allows the user to select any viewpoint from which to project the 3D view. Output is to another Generic CADD drawing file, which is called up, edited, and printed or plotted like any other drawing. Multiple views can be created from a single 2D drawing. Users with EGA or better color resolution can view the drawings in stereo on the screen. Figure A-5 shows a Generic CADD drawing created with The Third Dimension.

Program: **File Diagnostics**

Published by: Workshop 3D Software, Inc., Seattle, Washington.

Function: Views and edits drawings files in text mode.

Description: Originally designed to correct file errors in Generic CADD drawing files, this program allows you to edit your drawing file by calling up each entity individually.

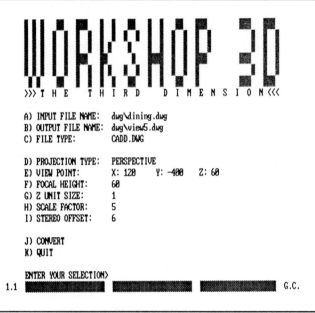

Figure A-5. *A drawing made with The Third Dimension*

Entity type, point data, layer, color, line type, line width, and any other pertinent data can be edited. Includes functions to search for specific entity types or data, and a cut-and-paste buffer for moving data around in drawing files, or even from one file to another.

Automated features enable any user to fix certain drawing problems, and manual editing features give advanced users even more flexibility. Figure A-6 shows the File Diagnostics editing screen.

Program: **Font Swapper**

Published by: Workshop 3D Software, Inc., Seattle, Washington.

```
FILE DIAGNOSTICS      >>> E D I T O R <<<           WORKSHOP 3D

DRAWING NAME: \CADD\LEVEL3\DWG\KEY.DWG    117 RECORDS IN BUFFER

RECORD NO: 13            ENTITY RECORD            OPTIONS:

ENTITY: LINE                             KEEP          * F1
                                         DELETE        * F2
LAYER:      0
COLOR:      1                            CUT           * F3
LINETYPE:   0                            PASTE         * F4
THICKNESS:  0
                                         SEARCH          F5
EXTRA:      0                            EDIT            F6

DATA:       2                            FAST FORWARD    F7
                                         REWIND          F8

                                         FOCUS           F9
                                         DISPLAY MODE    F10


       ENTER YOUR SELECTION>                (ESC) TO QUIT
  1.00 ▓▓▓▓▓▓▓▓▓▓▓▓▓  ▓▓▓▓▓▓▓▓▓▓▓▓▓▓▓  ▓▓▓▓▓▓▓▓▓▓▓▓▓ G.C.
```

Figure A-6.   *The editor menu from File Diagnostics*

Function:	Replaces font characters with characters from other fonts.
Description:	Up to six fonts may be swapped at once, for any six of the same or different fonts. It allows users to create drawings using one font and later switch to a different font. Any valid fonts may be swapped, including original Generic CADD fonts and add-on fonts libraries available from Generic CADD or other developers. Figure A-7 shows the Font Swapper menu.
Program:	**Font Development Kit**
Published by:	Workshop 3D Software, Inc., Seattle, Washington.

A) INPUT FILE NAME: OLDFONTS.DWG
B) OUTPUT FILE NAME: NEWFONTS.DWG
C) PATH FOR FONTS: C:\CONVERT\

D) EDIT   COMPLEX B E C O M E S: SIMPLEX
   FONT   DECO B E C O M E S: SIMPLEX
   TABLE   MAIN B E C O M E S: MAIN
             SIMPLEX B E C O M E S: DECO
                TEXT B E C O M E S: TEXT
              UNCIAL B E C O M E S: SIMPLEX

E) SWAP FONTS
F) QUIT

ENTER YOUR SELECTION>

Figure A-7.   *The Font Swapper menu*

Function: Creates and disassembles fonts.

Description: Two programs allow users to create fonts from drawing files containing components that have been properly named and placed, and to turn a font into a drawing file containing component placements. Used together, these two programs allow the user to make and edit fonts with all characters on the screen at one time, borrowing details from one character to make another.

Used independently, the font disassembler allows users to turn font characters into components so that they can be exploded and manipulated like any other part of a drawing file.

These same programs are sold as part of Generic Utilities, packaged individually. Figure A-8 shows the Font Maker menu.

A) DRAWING FILE NAME: DRAWING.DWG
B) FONT FILE NAME: FONT.FNT

C) CREATE FONT
D) QUIT

ENTER YOUR SELECTION>
1.01 ▓▓▓▓▓▓▓▓▓▓▓▓ ▓▓▓▓▓▓▓▓▓▓▓▓▓ ▓▓▓▓▓▓▓▓▓▓▓ G.C.

Figure A-8.   *The Font Maker menu*

Program: **Curve Maker**

Published by: Workshop 3D Software, Inc., Seattle, Washington.

Function: Turns arcs and circles into curves.

Description: A conversion program that turns arcs and circles in a selected drawing file into curves, with a user-selected number of points. Because Generic CADD arcs and circles remain arcs and circles even when stretched or squashed, curves are often preferable for use in drawings, components, and fonts when the proportions will probably need to be changed.

A) INPUT FILE NAME: OLDFILE.DWG
B) OUTPUT FILE NAME: NEWFILE.DWG

C) ARC POINTS: 20

D) CONVERT
E) QUIT

ENTER YOUR SELECTION>
1.0   G.C.

Figure A-9.   *The Curve Maker menu*

This same program is sold as part of Generic Utilities, packaged individually. Figure A-9 shows the Curve Maker menu.

Libraries for Use with Generic CADD

Certain packages contain predrawn symbols for use with Generic CADD, including component libraries and font libraries.

Product: Symbols Libraries

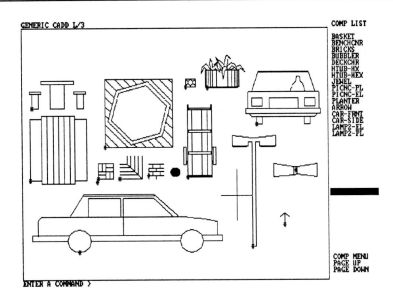

Figure A-10. *Some of the symbols in Generic's Symbols Libraries*

Published by: Generic Software, Inc., Bothell, Washington.

Function: Components for use with Generic CADD.

Description: Over 25 individual packages are available, each containing from 50 to 500 components organized by application, such as Residential and Commercial Furnishings, Industrial Pipe Fittings, Landscape Architecture, and Electronic Symbols I-V. Each symbols library includes an illustrated manual and placement menus, and works with all versions of Generic CADD. Figure A-10 illustrates some of the available symbols.

Product: **Type Fonts-I and Type Fonts-II**

ABCDEFGHIJKLMNOPQRSTUVWXYZ
ABCDEFGHIJKLMNOPQRSTUVWXYZ
ABCDEFGHIJKLMNOPQRSTUVWXYZ
ABCEDFGHIJKLMNOPQRSTUVWXYZ
ABCDEFGHIJKLMNOPQRSTUVWXYZ
ABCDEFGHIJKLMNOPQRSTUVWXYZ

Figure A-11. *Some of the fonts in Type Fonts I and II*

Published by: Generic Software, Inc., Bothell, Washington.

Function: Fonts for use with Generic CADD.

Description: Each package includes a number of fonts that can be used with any version of Generic CADD. Figure A-11 shows some of the available fonts.

Product: Font Pak 1 and Font Pak 2

Published by: Workshop 3D Software, Inc., Seattle, Washington.

Function: Fonts for use with Generic CADD.

ABCDEFGHIJKLMNOPQRSTUVWXYZ

ABCDEFGHIJKLMNOPQRSTUVWXYZ

Abcdefghijklmnopqrstuvwxyz

ABCDEFGHIJKLMNOPQRSTUVWXYZ

ABCDEFGHIJKLMNOPQRSTUVWXYZ

ABCDEFGHIJKLMNOPQRSTUVWXYZ

Figure A-12.   *The fonts in Font Pak 1*

Description: Each package includes a number of fonts that can be used with any version of Generic CADD. Figure A-12 shows some of the available fonts.

Programs That Are Interfaced with Generic CADD

Many programs are designed to work with Generic CADD, even though they do not operate on Generic CADD drawing files. These programs either produce Generic CADD drawing files or batch files as an output format or make use of other aspects of Generic CADD.

Product: **Generic 3D Solids Modeling**

Published by: Generic Software, Inc., Bothell, Washington.

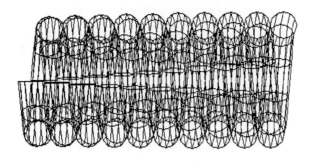

ADD   UTIL DEL   LINE MOD   SET   MOVE SEL   DRAW DISP

Figure A-13. *Generic 3D Solids Modeling*

Function: Full-featured 3D solid modeling program.

Description: This Generic product includes an option to save draw-
                   ings to Generic CADD drawing file format, allowing
                   users to send drawings made in 3D Solids to any version
                   of Generic CADD for the addition of text, dimensions,
                   hatching, and so on. Figure A-13 shows Generic 3D
                   Solids in action.

Product: **Generic 3D Drafting**

Published by: Generic Software, Inc., Bothell, Washington.

Function: 3D drawing program.

Description: Includes an option to save drawings to Generic CADD
                   drawing file format, allowing users of 3D Drafting to
                   send drawings to Generic CADD for printing, plotting,

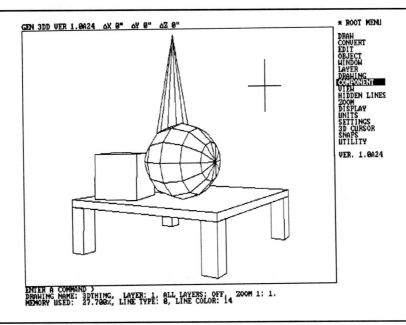

Figure A-14. *Generic 3D Drafting*

or additional editing. Figure A-14 shows the 3D Drafting screen.

Program:	**PaintConvert** (part of Presentation software)
Published by:	Generic Software, Inc., Bothell, Washington.
Function:	Two-way translation between Generic CADD image files and various pixel formats used by painting programs.
Description:	Allows Generic CADD image files (.GX2 format) to be converted to PC Paintbrush .PCX file format, GEM .IMG file format, and Generic 3D Solids .IMG format.

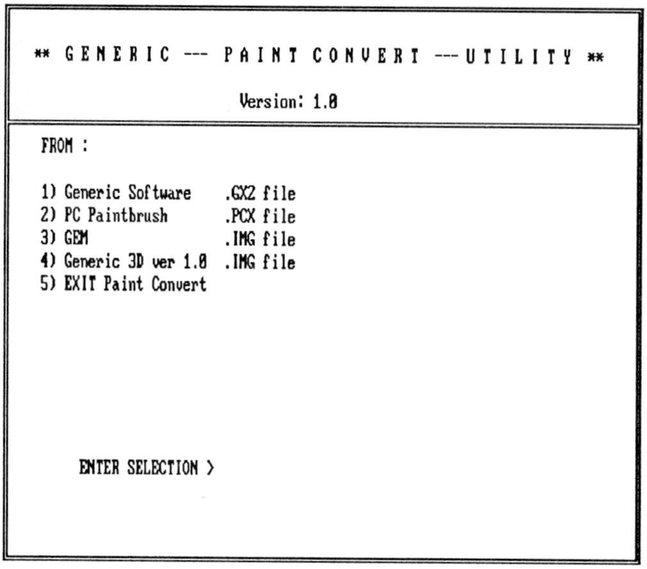

```
 ┌─────────────────────────────────────────────────┐
 │                                                   │
 │   ** G E N E R I C --- P A I N T  C O N V E R T  --- U T I L I T Y **
 │                                                   │
 │                    Version: 1.0                   │
 ├───────────────────────────────────────────────────┤
 │  FROM :                                           │
 │                                                   │
 │  1) Generic Software    .GX2 file                 │
 │  2) PC Paintbrush       .PCX file                 │
 │  3) GEM                 .IMG file                 │
 │  4) Generic 3D ver 1.0  .IMG file                 │
 │  5) EXIT Paint Convert                            │
 │                                                   │
 │                                                   │
 │                                                   │
 │                                                   │
 │       ENTER SELECTION >                           │
 │                                                   │
 │                                                   │
 └─────────────────────────────────────────────────┘
```

Figure A-15.   *The PaintCovert menu*

These files contain only screen display information, which is suffcient for use with the various programs that use these file formats. Many desktop publishing programs also accept files in one or more of these popular pixel formats. Figure A-15 shows the PaintConvert menu.

With this general-purpose utility, any of the file formats can be converted to any other; that is, GEM .IMG files may be converted directly to PC Paintbrush .PCX format without going through Generic's .GX2. It also provides the ability to translate Generic Paint .GX2 files to CADD .GX2 files and vice versa.

Program:	**CadText**

Published by:	Workshop 3D Software, Inc., Seattle, Washington.

Function:	Imports ASCII files into Generic CADD.

Description: Allows an ASCII file to be read into memory before Generic CADD is loaded, and then dumped when you are ready to place the text. The user typically selects a font and sets the text parameters before dumping the file. The TEXT PLACE command is used, and when you are asked to type the text, the file is imported by pressing a hotkey combination.

In reality, this program is really a large (up to 15K) keyboard buffer, which can be used to import keystrokes into almost any program. The author has used this program to automate processes in other CAD software, and even to make batch files work in Levels 1 and 2.

Program:	**Turbo-Fast Plan**

Published by:	Island Software, Coronado, California.

Function:	Automates the drawing of rooms and keeps track of multiple rooms in a separate database.

Description: This program creates Generic CADD batch files through an interface that prompts you for dimensions of rooms. Data, including square footages and volumes, are stored so that the rooms can be edited and re-created.

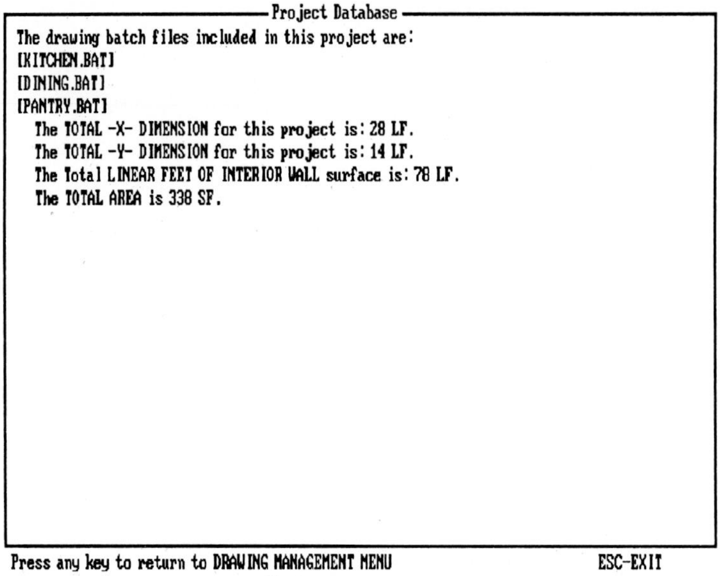

```
┌──────────────────────── Project Database ────────────────────────┐
│ The drawing batch files included in this project are:            │
│ [KITCHEN.BAT]                                                    │
│ [DINING.BAT]                                                     │
│ [PANTRY.BAT]                                                     │
│    The TOTAL -X- DIMENSION for this project is: 28 LF.           │
│    The TOTAL -Y- DIMENSION for this project is: 14 LF.           │
│    The Total LINEAR FEET OF INTERIOR WALL surface is: 78 LF.     │
│    The TOTAL AREA is 338 SF.                                     │
│                                                                  │
│                                                                  │
│                                                                  │
│                                                                  │
│                                                                  │
│                                                                  │
│                                                                  │
│                                                                  │
└──────────────────────────────────────────────────────────────────┘
 Press any key to return to DRAWING MANAGEMENT MENU        ESC-EXIT
```

Figure A-16.   *A Turbo-Fast Plan screen*

Turbo-Fast Plan is intended to automate the drawing of rooms in architectural floor plans but can be used for any application that includes rectangles; the rectangles can be created on various layers, in selected colors, line types, and line widths. Figure A-16 shows a database screen from Turbo-Fast Plan.

Product: **Pro-Lines**

Published by: Vacanti Yacht Design, Renton, Washington.

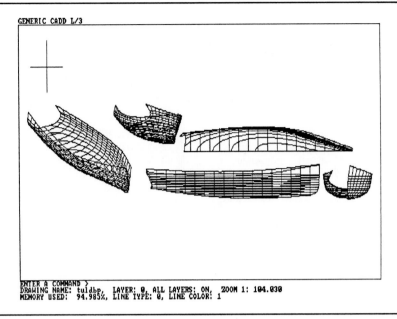

Figure A-17.   *A Pro-Lines drawing in Generic CADD*

Function: Computer-aided hull design.

Description: Parameter-driven program with graphic interface pro-
                     duces Generic CADD batch files as one of its output
                     options, allowing users to send drawings to Generic
                     CADD Level 3 for additional editing, plotting, and so on.
                     Figure A-17 shows a Pro-Lines drawing that has been
                     imported into Generic CADD.

Product: **Generic Estimator**

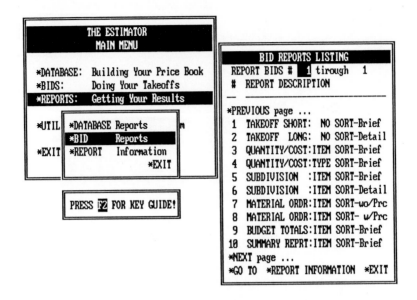

Figure A-18. *A menu from the Generic Estimator*

Published by: Generic Software, Inc., Bothell, Washington.

Function: Construction estimating.

Description: A stand-alone estimating program that produces cost estimates from a database of unit prices. Quantities, linear measurements, and area calculations can be taken off from a Generic CADD drawing loaded simultaneously. Makes use of the ESTIMATE BOUNDARY (EB) and ESTIMATE COMPONENT (EC) commands in Generic CADD Level 3 and includes a multitasking program to allow switching back and forth between Generic CADD and Generic Estimator with data transfer. Figure A-18 shows a Generic Estimator menu screen.

B Command Summary

This summary lists the commands in the order that they appear on the Generic CADD Level 3 menu. (They are arranged differently on the Level 1 and Level 2 menus.) Each listing has five elements: (1) the name of the command, (2) its two-character code, (3) the chapter in this book where a description of the command can be found, (4) the Level(s) in which the command is supported, and (5) the function of the command, or the command "type." Technically, Generic CADD makes no distinction between command "types," but certain "families" of commands can be identified and defined.

The CREATE ENTITY Commands

These commands are used for placing new objects into the drawing. Some of these commands create one entity at a time (SINGLE); others create several new entities simultaneously (MULTIPLE).

The PARAMETER Commands

These commands preset certain information that is used by other commands. This information is in some cases a number (VALUE), such as scale or rotation. In other cases it takes the form of an integer between 0 and 255 (RANGE) or one of several possibilities (CHOICE). Certain parameter

417

commands specify a particular way of doing something (SETTING). Still others ask for a text string (STRING) such as a filename or path.

The TOGGLE Commands

Toggles create conditions that are either on or off. Some of the toggle commands can be issued while another command is active (for example, TRANSPARENT).

The COMMAND MODIFIER Commands

These transparent commands modify the actions of other commands. They are generally issued after the main command, while the main command is asking for certain information. These commands generally qualify the information that you are providing.

The EDIT OBJECTS Commands

These commands change existing entities. They include commands that erase, copy, move, and otherwise modify either one (SINGLE) entity or many (MULTIPLE).

The DATABASE MODIFIER Commands

Some information stored in the drawing file (database) is not shown on the screen and does not appear on a print. This information can be component and character definitions, named views, and other information that helps to define the drawing without being explicitly shown. Commands that modify this type of information fit into this catagory.

The FILE INPUT/OUTPUT Commands

These commands send information to, or retrieve information from, a disk.

The MENU ACTION Commands

This type of command does not affect the drawing file or the drawing screen, but merely causes something to happen on the video menu, which allows you to select an action to take place in the drawing.

The PLACE COMPLEX OBJECTS Commands

These commands, similar to the CREATE ENTITY commands, place "defined" objects, rather than individual entities. The defined objects only appear in the database (drawing file) once and are placed in various locations by reference only.

The DISPLAY MODIFIER Commands

This group of commands changes the way that the drawing appears on the screen without actually changing the drawing itself. An editing command, for instance, actually makes the drawing larger, but a display modifier only makes it *appear* larger.

The PROGRAM MODIFIER Commands

Because Generic CADD is a configurable, customizable program, it has certain commands that specify how the program works. These commands control such program aspects as use of the video and digitizer menus.

The INQUIRY Commands

This type of command asks Generic CADD to obtain and display certain information, such as distances, angles, and areas, as well as drawing status information, layer usage, disk directories, and so on.

MENU COMMAND	CODE	CHAP	LEVEL	TYPE
DRAW				
STRAIGHT LINE	LI	4	1,2,3	CREATE SINGLE ENTITY
POINT	PO	4	1,2,3	CREATE SINGLE ENTITY
RECTANGLE	RE	4	1,2,3	CREATE MULTIPLE ENTITIES
REGULAR POLYGON	RP	4	1,2,3	CREATE MULTIPLE ENTITIES
2-POINT CIRCLE	C2	4	1,2,3	CREATE SINGLE ENTITY
3-POINT CIRCLE	C3	4	1,2,3	CREATE SINGLE ENTITY
2-POINT ARC	A2	4	1,2,3	CREATE SINGLE ENTITY
3-POINT ARC	A3	4	1,2,3	CREATE SINGLE ENTITY
4-POINT ARC	A4	4	1,2,3	CREATE SINGLE ENTITY
ELLIPSE	EP	4	1,2,3	CREATE SINGLE/MULTIPLE ENTITIES
CURVE	CV	4	1,2,3	CREATE SINGLE ENTITY
BEZIER CURVE	BV	9	3	CREATE SINGLE/MULTIPLE ENTITIES
SINGLE BEZIER	BW	9	3	CREATE SINGLE ENTITY
PEN UP	PU	4	1,2,3	COMMAND MODIFIER
SMART LINES				
DOUBLE LINE	L2	9	3	CREATE MULTIPLE ENTITIES
DOUBLE WIDTH	TH	9	3	PARAMETER (VALUE)
SOLID LINES	SO	9	3	TOGGLE
AUTOFILLET	AF	9	3	TOGGLE
FILLET RADIUS	RF	9	2,3	PARAMETER (VALUE)
SNAPS				
SNAP CLOSE	SC	10	1,2,3	COMMAND MODIFIER
NEAREST LINE	NL	10	2,3	COMMAND MODIFIER
INTERSECTION	SI	10	2,3	COMMAND MODIFIER
MIDPOINT	SM	10	2,3	COMMAND MODIFIER
PERPENDICULAR	SP	10	2,3	COMMAND MODIFIER
PARALLEL	SA	10	2,3	COMMAND MODIFIER
CENTER	SN	10	2,3	COMMAND MODIFIER
TANGENT	SX	10	2,3	COMMAND MODIFIER
NEAREST POINT	NP	4	1,2,3	COMMAND MODIFIER
COMPONENT SNAPS	GC	10	1,2,3	TOGGLE

MENU COMMAND	CODE	CHAP	LEVEL	TYPE
TRIMS				
TRIM	RM	10	2,3	EDIT SINGLE OBJECT
EXTEND	XT	10	2,3	EDIT SINGLE OBJECT
FILLET	FL	10	2,3	EDIT MULTIPLE OBJECTS
FILLET RADIUS	RF	10	2,3	PARAMETER (VALUE)
CHAMFER	CH	10	2,3	EDIT MULTIPLE OBJECTS
CHAMFER DISTANCES	CA	10	2,3	PARAMETER (VALUE)
CLEAN CORNER[1]	KT	10	2,3	EDIT MULTIPLE OBJECTS
COMPONENT				
PLACE	CP	8	1,2,3	PLACE COMPLEX ENTITY
IMAGE	CI	8	1,2,3	CREATE MULTIPLE ENTITIES
EXPLODE	CE	8	1,2,3	DATABASE MODIFIER
REPLACE	CN	8	1,2,3	DATABASE MODIFIER
REMOVE	CX	8	1,2,3	EDIT SINGLE OBJECT
LOAD	CL	12	1,2,3	FILE I/O
SAVE	CS	12	1,2,3	FILE I/O
CREATE	CC	8	1,2,3	DATABASE MODIFIER
SCALE	CZ	8	1,2,3	PARAMETER (VALUE)
ROTATION	CR	8	1,2,3	PARAMETER (VALUE)
DUMP	CD	12	1,2,3	FILE I/O
SNAPS	GC	8	1,2,3	TOGGLE
DRAG	CG	8	3	TOGGLE
LIST		8	1,2,3	MENU ACTION
LIST ON/OFF	CO	8	1,2,3	TOGGLE
TEXT				
FONT SELECT	FS	8	1,2,3	DATABASE MODIFIER
COLOR	TK	8	1,2,3	PARAMETER (RANGE)
SIZE	TZ	8	1,2,3	PARAMETER (VALUE)
ROTATION	TR	8	1,2,3	PARAMETER (VALUE)
ASPECT	TA	8	1,2,3	PARAMETER (VALUE)
SLANT	TS	8	1,2,3	PARAMETER (VALUE)
PLACE	TP	8	1,2,3	PLACE COMPLEX ENTITY
INSERT	TI	8	1,2,3	PLACE COMPLEX ENTITY
DELETE	TD	8	1,2,3	OBJECT EDIT
REPLACE	TR	8	1,2,3	DATABASE MODIFIER

MENU COMMAND	CODE	CHAP	LEVEL	TYPE
CREATE/EDIT	TC	8	1,2,3	DATABASE MODIFIER
FAST TEXT	TF	8	1,2,3	TOGGLE
TEXT VIEW	TV	8	1,2,3	DISPLAY MODIFIER

HATCH / FILL

MENU COMMAND	CODE	CHAP	LEVEL	TYPE
HATCH COLOR	HK	8	3	PARAMETER (RANGE)
HATCH NAME	HN	8	3	PARAMETER (CHOICE)
HATCH ROTATION	HR	8	3	PARAMETER (VALUE)
HATCH SCALE	HZ	8	3	PARAMETER (VALUE)
WINDOW HATCH	WH	8	3	PLACE COMPLEX ENTITY
OBJECT HATCH	OH	8	3	PLACE COMPLEX ENTITY
FITTED HATCH	FH	8	3	PLACE COMPLEX ENTITY
FILL COLOR	FK	8	3	PARAMETER (RANGE)
WINDOW FILL	WF	8	3	PLACE COMPLEX ENTITY
OBJECT FILL	OF	8	3	PLACE COMPLEX ENTITY
FITTED FILL	FF	8	3	PLACE COMPLEX ENTITY

ZOOMS

MENU COMMAND	CODE	CHAP	LEVEL	TYPE
ALL	ZA	4	1,2,3	DISPLAY MODIFIER
LIMITS	ZL	3	1,2,3	DISPLAY MODIFIER
WINDOW	ZW	6	1,2,3	DISPLAY MODIFIER
VALUE	ZM	6	1,2,3	DISPLAY MODIFIER
VIEW	ZV	6	3	DISPLAY MODIFIER
PREVIOUS	ZP	6	1,2,3	DISPLAY MODIFIER
UP	ZU	4	1,2,3	DISPLAY MODIFIER
BACK	ZB	4	1,2,3	DISPLAY MODIFIER
PAN	PA	6	1,2,3	DISPLAY MODIFIER
REDRAW	RD	6	1,2,3	DISPLAY MODIFIER
BACKWARDS	BR	6	1,2,3	TOGGLE
NAME VIEW	NV	6	3	DATABASE MODIFIER

LINES

MENU COMMAND	CODE	CHAP	LEVEL	TYPE
LINE COLOR	LK	3	1,2,3	PARAMETER (RANGE)
LINE TYPE	LT	3	1,2,3	PARAMETER (RANGE)
LINE WIDTH	LW	3	1,2,3	PARAMETER (RANGE)
LINE SCALE	LZ	3	1,2,3	PARAMETER (VALUE)

MENU COMMAND	CODE	CHAP	LEVEL	TYPE

OBJECTS

MENU COMMAND	CODE	CHAP	LEVEL	TYPE
BREAK	OB	5	1,2,3	EDIT/CREATE SINGLE ENTITY
CHANGE	OG	5	1,2,3	EDIT SINGLE ENTITY
ERASE	OE	4	1,2,3	EDIT SINGLE ENTITY
MOVE	OM	5	1,2,3	EDIT SINGLE ENTITY
COPY	OC	5	1,2,3	CREATE SINGLE/MULTIPLE ENTITIES
MOVE POINT	MP	5	1,2,3	EDIT SINGLE ENTITY
ERASE LAST	EL	5	1,2,3	EDIT SINGLE ENTITY
BEZIER EDIT	BE	5	3	EDIT MULTIPLE ENTITIES
UNERASE	UE	5	2,3	DATABASE MODIFIER

WINDOWS

MENU COMMAND	CODE	CHAP	LEVEL	TYPE
CHANGE	WG	5	1,2,3	EDIT MULTIPLE ENTITIES
ERASE	WE	5	1,2,3	EDIT MULTIPLE ENTITIES
MOVE	WM	5	1,2,3	EDIT MULTIPLE ENTITIES
COPY	WC	5	1,2,3	CREATE MULTIPLE ENTITIES
RADIAL COPY	RC	5	3	CREATE MULTIPLE ENTITIES
MIRROR	WI	5	1,2,3	EDIT MULTIPLE ENTITIES
ROTATE	WR	5	1,2,3	EDIT MULTIPLE ENTITIES
RE-SCALE	WZ	5	1,2,3	EDIT MULTIPLE ENTITIES
SAVE	WS	12	3	FILE I/O
TEXT	WT	5	3	DATABASE MODIFIER
COMPONENT	CC	5	1,2,3	DATABASE MODIFIER

LAYERS

MENU COMMAND	CODE	CHAP	LEVEL	TYPE
CURRENT	YC	3	1,2,3	PARAMETER (RANGE)
DISPLAY	YD	6	1,2,3	PARAMETER (RANGE)
HIDE	YH	6	1,2,3	PARAMETER (RANGE)
ERASE	YX	5	3	EDIT MULTIPLE OBJECTS
CHANGE	YG	5	3	EDIT MULTIPLE OBJECTS
ROTATE	YR	5	3	EDIT MULTIPLE OBJECTS
RE-SCALE	YZ	5	3	EDIT MULTIPLE OBJECTS
LOAD	YL	12	3	FILE I/O
SAVE	YS	12	3	FILE I/O
ALL LAYERS EDIT	AL	3	1,2,3	TOGGLE (TRANSPARENT)

MENU COMMAND	CODE	CHAP	LEVEL	TYPE

DRAWING

MENU COMMAND	CODE	CHAP	LEVEL	TYPE
LOAD	DL	12	1,2,3	FILE I/O
SAVE	DS	5	1,2,3	FILE I/O
PLOT	DP	5	1,2,3	FILE I/O
ALIGN	DA	14	3	PARAMETER (SETTING)
ERASE	DX	4	1,2,3	EDIT MULTIPLE OBJECTS
CHANGE	DG	5	3	EDIT MULTIPLE OBJECTS
ROTATE	DR	5	3	EDIT MULTIPLE OBJECTS
RE-SCALE	DZ	5	3	EDIT MULTIPLE OBJECTS
RE-ORIGIN	DO	12	1,2,3	EDIT MULTIPLE OBJECTS

DIMENSION

MENU COMMAND	CODE	CHAP	LEVEL	TYPE
MODE	UM	11	2,3	PARAMETER (CHOICE)
DIRECTION	UD	11	2,3	PARAMETER (CHOICE)
LAYER	UL	11	2,3	PARAMETER (RANGE)
COLOR	SK	11	2,3	PARAMETER (RANGE)
LETTER DIRECTION	LR	11	2,3	PARAMETER (CHOICE)
LETTER PLACEMENT	LP	11	2,3	PARAMETER (CHOICE)
LETTER SIZE	LH	11	2,3	PARAMETER (VALUE)
LETTER FONT	LF	11	3	PARAMETER (CHOICE)
OVERRIDE TEXT	OT	11	2,3	TOGGLE
ARROW TYPE	AT	11	2,3	PARAMETER (CHOICE)
ARROW MODE	AW	11	2,3	TOGGLE
PROXIMITY FIXED	PF	11	2,3	TOGGLE
EXTENSION OFFSET	XO	11	2,3	PARAMETER (VALUE)
EXTENSION LENGTHS	XL	11	2,3	PARAMETER (VALUE)
EXTENSION STRETCH	XS	11	2,3	TOGGLE
SHOULDER LENGTH	LL	11	2,3	PARAMETER (VALUE)
LINEAR DIMENSION	LX	11	2,3	CREATE MULTIPLE ENTITIES
ANGLE DIMENSION	AX	11	2,3	CREATE MULTIPLE ENTITIES
LEADER	LE	11	2,3	CREATE MULTIPLE ENTITIES
ERASE LAST DIM	ED	11	2,3	EDIT MULTIPLE ENTITIES

MENU COMMAND	CODE	CHAP	LEVEL	TYPE

CONTROLS

MENU COMMAND	CODE	CHAP	LEVEL	TYPE
TOLERANCE	TO	10	1,2,3	PARAMETER (VALUE)
ALL LAYERS EDIT	AL	3	1,2,3	TOGGLE (TRANSPARENT)
ORTHO MODE[2]	OR,SO	4	1,2,3	TOGGLE (TRANSPARENT)
LIMITS	LS	3	1,2,3	PARAMETER (VALUES)
BASEPOINT	BP	3	1,2,3	PARAMETER (VALUES)
TRACE MODE	TM	14	3	TOGGLE
TRACE SCALE	RZ	14	3	PARAMETER (VALUE)
FAST TEXT	TF	6	1,2,3	TOGGLE
FAST ARCS	FA		1,2,3	TOGGLE
DRAWING PATH	P1	12	3	PARAMETER (STRING)
COMPONENT PATH	P2	12	3	PARAMETER (STRING)
FONT PATH	P3	12	3	PARAMETER (STRING)
CHANGE PATHS[3]	GP	12	2	PARAMETER (STRING)

GRIDS

MENU COMMAND	CODE	CHAP	LEVEL	TYPE
GRID SIZE	GS	3	1,2,3	PARAMETER (VALUE)
SNAP TO GRID	SG	3	1,2,3	TOGGLE (TRANSPARENT)
GRID ON/OFF	GR	3	1,2,3	TOGGLE (TRANSPARENT)

DISPLAY

MENU COMMAND	CODE	CHAP	LEVEL	TYPE
DISPLAY MENU	VM	6	1,2,3	TOGGLE
REFERENCE POINTS	PR	6	1,2,3	TOGGLE (TRANSPARENT)
CONSTRUCTION POINTS	PC	4	1,2,3	TOGGLE (TRANSPARENT)
STANDARD POINTS	PS	6	1,2,3	TOGGLE (TRANSPARENT)
ABSOLUTE COORDS	AC	3	1,2,3	TOGGLE (TRANSPARENT)
DELTA COORDS	DC	3	1,2,3	TOGGLE (TRANSPARENT)
POLAR COORDS	PT	3	1,2,3	TOGGLE
STATUS LINE	SL	7	1,2,3	TOGGLE
RUBBER BANDING	RB	4	1,2,3	TOGGLE
DISPLAY COLOR	DK	6	1,2,3	PARAMETER (RANGE)
CURSOR COLOR	CK	6	1,2,3	PARAMETER (RANGE)
CURSOR SIZE	CU	6	1,2,3	PARAMETER (VALUE)
REDRAW	RD	6	1,2,3	DISPLAY MODIFIER
FLIP SCREEN	SF	7	3	INQUIRY

MENU COMMAND	CODE	CHAP	LEVEL	TYPE

UNITS

MENU COMMAND	CODE	CHAP	LEVEL	TYPE
METERS	MT	3	1,2,3	PARAMETER (SETTING)
CENTIMETERS	TC	3	1,2,3	PARAMETER (SETTING)
MILLIMETERS	MM	3	1,2,3	PARAMETER (SETTING)
FEET	FT	3	1,2,3	PARAMETER (SETTING)
FEET & INCHES	FI	3	1,2,3	PARAMETER (SETTING)
INCHES	IN	3	1,2,3	PARAMETER (SETTING)
FRACTIONS	FR	3	1,2,3	PARAMETER (SETTING)
FRACTION VALUE	FV	3	1,2,3	PARAMETER (VALUE)
DECIMALS	DE	3	1,2,3	PARAMETER (SETTING)
DECIMAL VALUE	DV	3	1,2,3	PARAMETER (VALUE)
ARC MINUTES	AM	3	1,2,3	TOGGLE
ARC DEGREES	AD	3	1,2,3	TOGGLE

UTILITIES

MENU COMMAND	CODE	CHAP	LEVEL	TYPE
QUIT	QU	4	1,2,3	FILE I/O
PACK DATA	PD		1,2,3	DATABASE MODIFIER
M. E. ORIGIN	MO	3	1,2,3	PARAMETER (SETTING)
M. E. BASEPOINT	MB	3	1,2,3	PARAMETER (SETTING)
M. E. RELATIVE	MR	3	1,2,3	PARAMETER (SETTING)
ACTIVE AREA	PM	14	3	PARAMETER (SETTING)
SELECT DIG MENU	SD	14	3	PARAMETER (CHOICE)
CLEAR MENU	VX	14	1,2,3	PROGRAM MODIFIER
LOAD VIDEO MENU	LV	14	1,2,3	PROGRAM MODIFIER
LOAD DIG MENU	LD	14	3	PROGRAM MODIFIER
SAVE BATCH	SB	12	3	FILE I/O
LOAD BATCH	LB	12	3	FILE I/O
COMPONENT DUMP	CD	12	1,2,3	FILE I/O
IMAGE SAVE	IS	12	1,2,3	FILE I/O
IMAGE LOAD	IL	12	1,2,3	FILE I/O

MENU COMMAND	CODE	CHAP	LEVEL	TYPE

MEASURE

MENU COMMAND	CODE	CHAP	LEVEL	TYPE
DISTANCE	MD	7	1,2,3	INQUIRY
ANGLE	MA	7	1,2,3	INQUIRY
AREA	MV	7	1,2,3	INQUIRY

Notes

[1] The CLEAN CORNER (KT) command works differently in Level 2 and Level 3.

[2] The two-character code for ORTHO MODE is SO in Level 1 and OR in Levels 2 and 3.

[3] In Level 2, the CHANGE PATHS (GP) command changes all three paths. In Level 3, each path has its own command (P1, P2, and P3).

C Glossary

Some of the following definitions are specific to Generic CADD. The terms may have different meanings in other programs.

ABS   Abbreviation for Absolute.

Absolute   Coordinates that are measured from the origin, 0,0, and the coordinate system in which the definitions of entities are stored.

Arc   A portion of a circle. One of Generic CADD's basic entity types, defined by three points, two of which are the endpoints of the Arc.

Area   The amount of space contained within specific boundaries, measured in square feet, square inches, or other units.

ASCII   Acronym for American Standard Code for Information Exchange. Used to refer to a file format in which alphanumeric data is stored according to a predefined standard code. The term *ASCII file* is generally used to refer to text files that can be viewed with the TYPE command in DOS or edited with any simple text editor.

Aspect Ratio   The ratio between height and width. In Generic CADD, two aspect ratios are employed. The aspect ratio of the screen is calculated automatically when you specify the SCREEN RATIO values in the CONFIG program. The aspect ratio of text characters is specified using the TEXT ASPECT (TA) command.

AutoConvert   A Generic Software program for converting Generic CADD drawing files to and from .DXF (Drawing Exchange Format), a file format developed by AutoDesk, Inc., allowing transfer of data between different CADD programs.

Automate   To create and save a series of commands, known as a *macro*, for the purpose of speeding up the execution of repetitive drawing tasks.

Automatic Dimensioning   A group of commands that are used to create dimensions by selecting the endpoints of the line or angle that is to be dimensioned. See *Dimensioning*.

Backspace   To delete an unwanted character or space by positioning the cursor to the right of the character and pressing the BACKSPACE key. Used to correct typing errors when typing commands, specifying filenames, and so on.

.BAK   A file extension used to signify files that have been superceded by newer versions. BAK is a shortened form of BACKUP, used, if something goes wrong with the newer version of the file, to mitigate the amount of lost data by going back to this earlier version.

Basepoint   A user-defined position in the drawing, from which other locations can be referenced. X and Y coordinates can be specified *relative* to the Basepoint.

Bezier   A type of curve specified by four points: two endpoints and two *control points*. If the curve itself is thought of as a path between two endpoints, the two control points determine the angle at which the curve takes off as it leaves one endpoint to head toward the other.

Break   To separate a simple entity, such as a line or arc, into two parts. Normally, two points are specified, and the portion between them removed. Breaking a circle turns it into an arc.

Bug   An error in the way that software functions.

CAD   Acronym for Computer Aided Design. Widely used to refer to a specific class of computer programs that feature the creation, storage, display, and editing of accurate dimensional and geometric data, generally broken down into object primitives, such as Lines, Circles, Arcs, and so on.

CADD Acronym for Computer Aided Design and Drawing used by Generic Software as the name of its 2D drawing program.

Callouts Words or characters that identify parts of the drawing. Sometimes used with an arrow or other symbol to specify materials, refer to other drawings, and so on.

CGA An acronym for Color Graphics Adaptor. A hardware standard popularized by IBM to add color capabilities to its system of Personal Computers. The 320×200 color and 320×400 monochrome resolutions are generally considered marginally adequate for CAD purposes, and are not supported by many CAD programs. Generic CADD supports the CGA card and clones at only the higher monochrome resolution.

Chamfer A procedure by which a third line is constructed at specified distances from the intersection of two lines to form a flattened rather than a sharp corner.

Change Alters the properties (layer, color, line type, and line width) of an entity.

Character A single letter, numeral, or punctuation mark. All the characters of a particular style make up a font, and characters are always placed from the active font. Though several characters may be placed with a single command, each character placed is a separate entity in Generic CADD.

Circle One of Generic CADD's basic entity types, defined by the location of the centerpoint and one point on the perimeter.

.CMP The file extension used by Generic CADD to identify files in which component definitions are stored. See *Component*.

Color An attribute of objects drawn in Generic CADD. Color can be specified whether or not you are using a color monitor. Because colors are specified and stored by number, not name or actual hue, objects drawn using one color on one system may appear as a different color on another system that uses a different graphic standard.

.COM   A file extension for certain executable programs, which can be started by typing the name that appears to the left of the period.

Command   A single function that has a corresponding two-character keyboard code. Although the items on the video menu may appear to be commands, they simply *activate* commands. In Level 3, several commands may be activated from a single menu item.

Component   A portion of a drawing that has been *defined* to include certain entities, and given a name and *reference point*. Components, once defined, can be reused in a drawing, inserted at various rotations and scales, and saved to a disk file for use in other drawings.

CONFIG   The program that tells Generic CADD what kind of equipment you are using and sets a number of default parameters.

Configure   To use the CONFIG program to select equipment and set default parameters.

Construction Point   A definition point of an entity, such as the endpoint of a line, the center of a circle, and so on, displayed by a small *x* on the screen (if you choose). Temporary construction points are placed by certain editing commands as you select points on the screen.

Coordinates   The numeric values that identify the location of a point, specified as a horizontal distance X and a vertical distance Y, measured from a selected origin.

Copy   To duplicate a portion of the drawing without reconstructing it. Several commands vary in the method of selecting the objects to be copied, but all use prompts that ask you to select objects, and specify the displacement and direction, and the number of copies.

Cross Hair   Two lines that intersect at their midpoints, forming a cursor that can be moved around the screen.

Cursor   A graphic device on the screen used to aid in user input. Generic CADD makes use of several cursors. The *drawing cursor* is a cross hair that can be moved around the screen by the mouse, a digitizer puck, or the cursor control keys. Points are selected by pressing the first button on the mouse or digitizer puck, or by pressing the ENTER key on the keyboard.

The *menu cursor* appears as a solid block of color in the menu area when the video menu is in use. This block can be moved up and down with the mouse, digitizer puck, or the keyboard cursor keys, highlighting items on the video menu. These highlighted items can be selected by pressing the second button on the mouse, the digitizer puck, or the HOME key on the keyboard.

The *text cursor* appears on the screen as a horizontal line when you use the TEXT PLACE (TP) command. The line is the same length as the width of the character that you are about to place, as calculated by the combined values of the TEXT SIZE (TZ) and TEXT ASPECT (TA) commands. If the TEXT ROTATION (TR) is other than zero, the text cursor is rotated to the proper angle. This cursor is moved by typing a character, or by pressing the BACKSPACE key, the ENTER key, or any of the cursor control keys on the keyboard. It cannot be moved with the mouse or digitizer puck.

Database   Bits of information that have been grouped and organized in a particular way. A Generic CADD drawing file can be thought of as a database, because it stores information in a manner that can be retrieved or manipulated.

Default   A value, parameter, or situation that exists when you do not specifically select an alternative. In Generic CADD, many defaults can be established in the CONFIG program, rather than simply accepting those that are set when the program is first installed.

DeskConvert   A program published by Generic Software for converting Generic CADD drawing files to various file formats used in desktop publishing programs and PostScript devices, such as the Apple Laser Writer. In some bundled versions of Generic CADD Level 3, DeskConvert can by used by typing **XC** from within Generic CADD.

Desktop Publishing Software   Software used to combine and print text and graphic information in a single document. These programs generally offer a so-called "What You See Is What You Get" (WYSIWYG) graphic interface.

Digitizer   A hardware device, consisting of a tablet and a pen or puck, used for controlling the cursor and tracing drawings. Cursor control is through positional rather than directional information.

Digitizer Menu   A system for issuing commands to Generic CADD, consisting of a plastic or paper digitizer overlay with the names of the commands and an ASCII file containing the commands.

Digitizing   The process of tracing a drawing into a Generic CADD drawing file using a digitizer. Generic CADD commands are combined with points selected on the digitizer instead of the screen.

Dimensioning   A process in which lines, text, and arrows are added to a drawing to convey information about the distances or angles between points in the drawing.

DIR   A command that can be typed at the DOS prompt to display a list of files on the current disk or directory.

Directory   A subdivision of a disk, used to organize the information stored on a disk. Normally, Generic CADD is stored in its own directory, which may be further divided into directories for drawings, components, fonts, and so on. Also, the list of files that appears on the screen when you use the DIR command in DOS.

Disk   A device for storing files. *Floppy disks* are inserted and removed from a disk drive. *Hard disks* store more information and are permanently installed in your computer.

Displacement   The distance between two points, usually associated with an action of some type.

Distance   The shortest measurable length between two points. The distance between two points can be displayed with the MEASURE DISTANCE (MD) command.

Display   Another name for the video screen. Also used as a verb for showing information on the screen, as in "Display Hatches ON/OFF" or "Display Directory Files."

DOS   Acronym for Disk Operating System, which is a software program that coordinates the activities of the computer and its disk drives, allowing you to access files stored on disks. DOS is used to load Generic CADD and for a variety of file manipulating functions. DOS is normally started up automatically when you turn on your computer and must be running before Generic CADD will start.

DotPlot   A program published by Generic Software for printing drawing files on dot matrix printers. Not required for Levels 1 and 2, and bundled with some versions of Level 3. In bundled versions, DotPlot can be accessed from within Generic CADD by typing **XD.**

Drag   Moves something across the screen. Components can be dragged when they are placed if COMPONENT DRAG (CD) is on; components and text characters are dragged when you use the MOVE POINT (MP) command.

Drawing   A set of related entities stored in a single file in memory or on a disk. Comparable to a document in a word processing program.

.DWG   A file extension used by Generic CADD to identify drawing files. This extension is added automatically to all files that you save as drawing files from Generic CADD. Any file that is to be loaded as a drawing must have this extension.

.DXF   The file extension for an ASCII file format popularized by Auto-Desk for exchange of drawing information. Generic CADD files can be converted to and from .DXF files with AutoConvert.

Edit   To perform functions, such as erase, copy, move, change, rotate, and re-scale, on existing Generic CADD entities.

EGA   Acronym for Enhanced Graphics Adapter, a video standard developed by IBM and improved by many other manufacturers. Use of the EGA card requires an EGA-compatible monitor. The 16-color 640×350 resolution of the EGA standard is widely considered the minimum for professional use of CADD. Many EGA clones can be run at higher resolutions than the original IBM specification.

Ellipse   An oblong circular shape, geometrically derived from the angled section of a cone, and one of Generic CADD's basic entities. The ellipse is defined by the endpoints of its two axes, normally of different lengths (though both may be the same length, in which case the ellipse is a circle).

Endpoint   The terminating point of a Line, Arc, or Curve. Each of these entities has two endpoints, which define it.

Entity   A single object. *Simple entities* include Standard Points, Lines, Arcs, Circles, Ellipses, Curves, and Bezier Curves. *Complex entities* are portions of the drawing that are composed of simple entities, but are treated as one object. Text Characters, Components, Hatches, and Fills are all complex entities.

Erase   To remove entities from the drawing. Several commands offer methods for selecting the entities to be erased. Because erased entities are not immediately removed from the computer's memory, they can be restored in most cases with the UNERASE (UE) command.

.EXE   A file extension used to indicate executable program files, such as CADD and CONFIG. Programs that are located in files with .EXE extensions can usually be run by typing the first part of their name at the DOS prompt.

Extension   The three letters after the period in a filename. Extensions are optional but are often used to indicate the type of file. Extensions used in Generic CADD include .DWG for drawing files, .CMP for components, .FNT for fonts, .HCH for hatch patterns, .MNU for menu files, .TXT for batch files, .GX2 for image files, and a number of different extensions for various parts of the program.

Fast Arcs   A function that displays arcs as a selectable number of line segments instead of perfectly curved entities. This function can greatly speed up redraws.

Fast Text   A function that displays text characters as standard points instead of actual characters. This function can reduce redraw time, while still allowing you to see where text is placed in the drawing.

File   A collection of related information stored under a single name on a disk. Each drawing that you create is a file, each component that you save is a file, each font is in its own file, and so on. Filenames can be up to eight characters, plus an optional period and up to three characters called the file extension.

Fill   To "paint in" a closed area with solid color. Several commands allow you to specify the area and the color of the fill. The display of filled areas can be turned on and off with the DISPLAY FILLS (DF) command.

Fillet   An operation in which an arc of specified radius is inserted as close as possible to the intersection of two lines or arcs, tangent to each line or arc. When filleting lines to lines, the lines are trimmed or extended as required to make their endpoints meet the endpoints of the inserted arc.

Fillet Radius   The radius used by the FILLET and AUTO-FILLET commands. If the fillet radius is too large, filleting will not occur. A fillet radius of zero simply trims or extends two lines simultaneously.

Floppy Disk   A flat magnetic storage media that can be removed from the computer disk drive. Popular formats include 5 1/4" flexible disks and 3 1/2" disks in hard plastic sleeves. Floppy disks store from 360K to 1.4 MB of file data.

.FNT   An extension used by Generic CADD to identify font files. Font files are in a special format and must be created with Generic CADD or with special software designed for making fonts.

Font   A set of definitions for each character that can be typed on the computer keyboard. A font can include the upper- and lowercase alphabet, numerals, and punctuation marks. A font must be loaded with the FONT SELECT (FS) command before it can be used. Each version of Generic CADD includes several fonts, and additional fonts are available from Generic Software and third-party sources, or you can make your own.

Fraction Value   The largest denominator that you will allow to be used in a display of fractional data. The allowable values are in powers of 2, starting with 2, 4, 8, 16, and so on. The larger the specified denominator, the smaller the fractions that will be displayed.

Function Key   One of 10 or 12 keys on the PC keyboard that perform functions specific to the program being run. These keys are usually located either on the left or along the top of the keyboard and are marked F1, F2, F3, and so on. In Generic CADD, the CONFIG program can be used to assign a two-character command to each function key.

Graphics Card   The hardware device that runs the monitor. This card controls the resolution and number of available colors and is an add-on to the standard PC. Typical graphics cards that work well with Generic CADD include the Hercules monochrome graphics card for monochrome monitors, the CGA card for color monitors, and the EGA for enhanced color monitors. Generic CADD supports a large number of graphics cards by many different manufacturers. You use the CONFIG program to tell Generic CADD the name of your card.

Grid   A visual aid for estimating dimensions on the screen. In Generic CADD, the grid appears as a series of equally spaced dots. The spacing of these dots may be used to limit cursor movement to a specific interval.

.GX2   A file extension used by Generic CADD to identify image files (a record of the color of each pixel on the screen) created by Generic CADD or Generic Paint. .GX2 files made on one graphics card may only be loaded on another system using a compatible graphics card. .GX2 files made in Generic Paint must be converted with PaintConvert before they can be loaded into Generic CADD. Similarly, .GX2 files made in Generic CADD must be converted before they can be used by Generic Present. Generic CADD .GX2 files loaded and saved by Generic Paint are automatically converted for compatibility with Paint and Present, but must be reconverted before they can be loaded into Generic CADD again.

Hardware   The electronic and mechanical parts of the computer, such as circuit boards and chips, the disk drives, the monitor, the mouse or digitizer, the printer, and the plotter. The programs that make the hardware run are known as software. In the case of floppy disks, the disk itself is hardware, while the program stored on the disk is software.

Hatch   An operation in which continuous or dashed lines are drawn through a closed area at a regular interval in one or more directions. Often the spacing in the dashed lines is arranged so as to form special shapes or figures when combined with other similar lines.

Hatchable Area   An area that is bounded by lines and arcs that meet at their endpoints. Hatchable areas may be nested in such a way that a second enclosed area inside the first (as with a square inside a larger square) is considered to be an edge of the hatchable area and so excluded from hatching.

.HCH   A file extension used by Generic CADD to identify files that contain the definitions of hatch patterns.

Hierarchical   Organized in an outline or "tree" format. The Generic CADD video menu is said to be hierarchical because it contains a ROOT menu from which you select other menus, from which you select either commands or other menus. This implies greater detail at each sublevel of the menu.

   In Generic CADD, it is possible for the user to create hierarchical organizations of drawings and Component files, by having components within components, and drawings within drawings.

IGES   Acronym for Initial Graphics Exchange Standard, an ASCII format designed to allow the transfer of CAD data from one computer system to another. Generic IGES converts IGES format files into Generic CADD drawing files and vice versa, allowing Generic users to communicate with users of mainframe CAD systems and other programs that make use of the IGES format.

Image   A record of the colors of the pixels on the screen containing no actual CAD data but more like a "photograph" of the screen. Even when an image is loaded, the entities displayed in the image cannot be changed, as they do not really exist in the drawing.

.IMG   A file extension used by Generic 3D Solids to identify image (pixel) files. These files can be converted for compatibility with Generic CADD and Generic Paint and Present by using PaintConvert. The .IMG format is also used by certain products from GEM and other manufacturers and may or may not be compatible with Generic CADD through the use of PaintConvert.

Incrementation   To add a constant value repeatedly. In Generic CADD, the X and Y coordinates are incremented by the movement of the pointing device when SNAP TO GRID is turned on. If the Grid Size is 1, X and Y values increase or decrease by one unit every time the pointing device is moved a small amount.

Insert   To place a text character between two existing characters. When characters are inserted, the attributes of the character to the right are taken on, but the currently loaded font is used. In some other CAD programs, the term *insert* applies to the placement of components, hatches, or fills. Generic CADD uses the term *place* for this function.

Intersection   A point (including an endpoint) where two or more lines, arcs, or circles meet. *Imaginary intersections* exist at the point where entities would meet if they were extended.

Kilobyte (K)   A unit of measurement of computer data, consisting of 1024 bytes or characters. Each letter of the alphabet, numeral, and punctuation mark takes up a single byte. Numeric data is stored in a number of formats, using multiple bytes for the storage of each number.

Korner   A term specific to Generic CADD, as part of the KORNER TRIM command. A korner is defined as the point where two sets of parallel or near-parallel lines meet perpendicularly. Although the parallel and perpendicular aspects of the korner may vary from the mathematic ideal, the ideal that they must *completely* intersect for the command to work is inviolable. Each of the four lines must actually intersect both of the lines that are perpendicular to it.

Laser   A printer technology that involves a narrowly focused beam of light passing over a charged plate in order to create an image which is transferred to paper via carbon "toner" particles. Laser printers are currently capable of resolutions up to 300 dots per inch (dpi), much greater than most dot matrix printers.

   Three types of laser printers are supported by Generic CADD. Level 1, Level 2, and DotPlot print to Hewlett-Packard LaserJet, Canon laser printer, and compatible laser printers. DeskConvert prints on PostScript devices, such as the Apple Laser Writer series of printers.

Layer   A device for linking certain information together. In Generic CADD, 256 layers, numbered 0 to 255, are available. Each entity is created on the "current" layer, but can be changed to any other layer via several commands. Information may be displayed or hidden layer-by-layer, and editing may be done on either the current layer or all visible layers.

Library   A group of symbols. Generic Software sells symbols libraries that consist of 50 to 300 components, menus for placing these components, and a manual that illustrates these components. Symbols libraries are usually grouped by application or discipline, such as landscaping or plumbing.

Limits   An arbitrarily selected "boundary" for your drawing. The limits are measured relative to the objects that you are drawing, not the size of the paper on which you print. It is not unusual, therefore, to have limits in the hundreds of feet if you are doing building plans or elevations.

Line   In Generic CADD, the term is used in two ways. In the more specific use, a Line is a simple entity with two endpoints, created by the LINE command, the implied LINE command, or the RECTANGLE or REGULAR POLYGON command. In the general use, any entity is referred to as a line, as in the LINE WIDTH and LINE TYPE commands.

Line Type   An attribute of simple entities, the line type determines the pattern of dots and dashes of each entity. A continuous line is line type 0.

Line Type Scale   The line type scale determines the interval for repetition of the dash pattern in line types 11 through 19, in the units of the drawing. Line types 1 to 9 are not affected by the line type scale, and line types above 20 are scaled by the integer value of the line type number divided by 10 times the line type scale.

Load   To read a file from disk into the computer memory. Loading a drawing file causes the entities in the file to become part of the current drawing, and to be displayed on the screen. Loading a font or a component simply makes the definition or definitions in the file accessible by other commands. Loading a batch file causes the commands in the batch file to be executed. Loading a menu file makes the menu items in the file available from the video menu or digitizer, and loading an image displays the image on the screen.

Macro   A group of commands can be stored and executed with one action to automate certain drawing tasks. In Generic CADD Level 3, macros can be executed from either the video or digitizer menu, or from a batch file.

Menu   A list of commands or actions. In Generic CADD, a menu is kept in a file with the extension .MNU. This file contains the words that appear on the screen and the actions that are taken when these words are selected. Generic CADD menus can be entirely redefined by the user. The second button on the pointing device or the HOME key on the keyboard is used to select an item from the video menu after a menu bar has been placed over the desired item.

Midpoint   The point on a Line that is equidistant from each endpoint.

Mirror   To reflect a portion of the drawing across an imaginary plane, creating additional entities that are mirror images of the originals. In Generic CADD, entities can be reflected across either the horizontal or vertical axis.

.MNU   A file extension used by Generic CADD to identify a menu file. .MNU files contain the commands that are executed when certain items are selected from the video menu or boxes are selected from the digitizer menu. Menu files are in ASCII format and can be modified or created by the user.

Monochrome   A type of graphic system or monitor capable of displaying only one color, amber, green, or white on a black background. Generic CADD can assign color attributes to entities on a monochrome system, even though these attributes may not be displayed at the time the drawing is created.

Mouse   A device for controlling the cursor that moves back and forth on a desktop surface. An *optical mouse* rolls over a gridded surface and "sees" which direction it is moving. A *mechanical mouse* "feels" direction through wheels that turn as the mouse is moved. Many mice currently on the market are opto-mechanical combinations.

Move   In Generic CADD, an action that causes the coordinates of the definition points of an entity or entities to be displaced by a specified amount.

Object   Each identifiable entity in a Generic CADD drawing is sometimes called an object. Examples include Lines, Circles, Arcs, and other simple entities, as well as Text Characters, Components, and other complex entities.

Operating System   A program or set of programs that control the operation of your computer. In many ways, the operating systems acts as an interpreter or buffer between your computer and the application software, such as Generic CADD. Generic CADD requires an operating system of DOS 2.0 or later.

Ortho   Short for orthogonal, ortho is in Generic CADD a mode of operation in which cursor movement is restricted to vertical or horizontal.

Override   An action of certain commands that negates the action of other commands. For example, certain SNAPS commands can override both ORTHO MODE and SNAP TO GRID if the point in question does not meet the requirements of the current modes.

Overwrite   To replace one item with another, usually a file. This action occurs because you cannot have two files by the same name in the same directory. Whenever you attempt to save a file, Generic CADD checks to see if a file by the same name already exists. If it does, you are given the choice of overwriting the existing file, in which case it is replaced by the new file, or renaming the existing file, in which case its extension is changed to .BAK so that there is no conflict between the two filenames.

PaintConvert   A program published by Generic Software for converting files in various image formats to other formats, mostly for the purpose of compatibility and file transfer between various painting programs. Generic CADD .GX2 (image) files may be transferred to a variety of painting and publishing programs in this way.

Pan   To change the part of the drawing that is displayed on the screen by moving left, right, up, down, or diagonally. When panning, the scale of the drawing as it is displayed on the screen remains the same.

Parametric Programming   A technique whereby a drawing can be created by establishing a number of known geometric relationships between entities, and by allowing the distances, lengths, angles, and so on to vary. In Generic CADD, parametric programming may be accomplished through menu macros, batch files, and interfaces with other programs.

Partitioned   A mode or style of dimensioning in which two or more linear dimensions are created continuously, each starting where the previous one left off.

Pathname   The complete name of a file, which includes the disk drive letter, any directory or subdirectory in which the file may be stored, the filename, and the extension. A colon (:) follows the disk drive letter, backslashes (\) are used to separate directories, subdirectories, and filenames, and a period or decimal point (.) is used to separate the filename from the extension. The pathname for the drawing file HOUSE in the DWG subdirectory of the CADD directory on the C drive would be C:\CADD-\DWG\HOUSE.DWG.

PCON   The command that is typed at the DOS prompt to start the PaintConvert program.

.PCX   A file extension used by a number of software publishers to identify pixel images files. Many manufacturers follow a standard developed by Z-Soft for their PC-Paintbrush program, allowing direct transfer of files between these programs. Generic PaintConvert can convert several other formats to and from this version of the .PCX file format.

PenPlot   A program published by Generic Software for plotting drawing files on pen plotters. PenPlot can plot files created by any Generic Software product or any other program that produces Generic CADD drawing files, allowing Levels 1 and 2 users to plot their drawings. The functions available in PenPlot are almost identical to those found in the DRAWING PLOT command in Generic CADD Level 3.

Peripheral   A hardware device that attaches externally to a computer, other than the keyboard or monitor. Examples include printers, plotters, digitizers, and mice.

Perpendicular   The geometric relationship that exists when two lines intersect at a 90-degree angle. In Generic CADD, this definition is extended to lines that intersect circles and arcs in a similar way.

PGDN   A keyboard key normally used for cursor movement. In Generic CADD, the PGDN key moves the video menu forward one screen, an especially useful function when placing components from a Component List longer than one screen.

PGUP   A keyboard key normally used for cursor movement. In Generic CADD, the PGUP key moves the video menu back one screen, an especially useful function when placing components from a Component List longer than a single screen.

Pick   A term sometimes employed in CADD jargon to indicate the selection of a menu item or screen location by pressing a button on the mouse or digitizer puck. For example, the ARC4 command is so named not because you actually place four points on the arc but because four "picks" are required, each providing a different type of information.

Pixel   A single dot of light on the video monitor.

Plot   A form of hard copy output that is printed with moving pens rather than individual dots. The term *plot* is often used for both the process and the result. You can "plot a drawing," and the resulting drawing can be called a "plot."

Plotter   A hardware device that produces hard-copy output through the action of moving pens rather than by placing individual dots. Generic CADD Level 3 and PenPlot support plotters made by a number of different manufacturers.

Point   A single coordinate pair that has been selected for a particular purpose. Generic CADD employs three separate definitions and on-screen representations for Standard Points, Constructions Points, and Reference Points. Standard Points, placed into the drawing by the user, and usually intended to be printed as part of the drawing, are represented by short vertical and horizontal line segments that intersect at their midpoints. Construction Points, which can be displayed to indicate the definition points of entities and other locations, are shown as two short diagonally crossed lines. Reference Points, used to indicate the Origin and the insertion points of complex entities, are displayed as a combination of horizontal, vertical, and diagonal line segments, slightly longer than those that make up Construction Points.

Pointing Device   A hardware device, such as a mouse, digitizer, or track-ball, that is used for controlling the movement of the cursor, and for selecting points on the screen. The keyboard cursor keys may also be used as crude pointing devices. The extra buttons on a digitizer puck or multi-button mouse can each be assigned a two-character command in Generic CADD Level 3.

Polar Coordinates   An optional format for the display and input of rela-tive coordinates, in which a distance and angle from the last point entered is employed.

Polygon   See *Regular Polygon.*

Print   A form of hard-copy output that is created by placing a number of individual dots onto paper. The term *print* is often used for both the process and the result. You can "print a drawing," and the resulting drawing can be called a "print."

Printer   A hardware device that produces hard-copy output through the placement of characters or dots on paper. Generic CADD drawings can be printed on dot matrix or laser printers, which are supported by Generic CADD Levels 1 and 2 and DotPlot. A large variety of printers by many different manufacturers may be used, some at user-selectable resolutions.

Prompt   A line of text at the bottom of the Generic CADD screen that usually asks you for information. To respond to the prompt, you may be required to select a point or a menu item, type a value or a name, or answer a question by typing a number or a character.

Properties   Descriptive qualities of any Generic CADD drawing entity. The properties of any simple entity include its color, line type, line width, and layer. Complex entities have other properties as well. Text characters, for example, also have size, aspect ratio, slant, and rotation.

Puck   A device that is attached to a digitizer tablet for the purpose of pointing to and selecting locations on the tablet, often corresponding to locations on the screen or items on the digitizer menu, selected with the first and second buttons. The puck usually has additional buttons, each of which may be assigned a two-character command.

Quit   To exit Generic CADD. You have the option of saving or ignoring the work that you have been doing as you exit.

Radial Copy   To copy selected entities around an axis point a specified number of times, each time rotating the objects around the axis point by a specified angle.

RAM   Acronym for Random Access Memory, the type of computer memory in which both Generic CADD and your drawing are located as you are using Generic CADD. The 640K that can be addressed by DOS is memory of this type.

Redraw   To refresh the video display. This process "cleans up" any extra or missing lines that may be left over from a previous operation and recognizes any display toggles or changes that may have been set since the screen was last redrawn, such as layers that may have been displayed or hidden, the use of fast text, and other display variables.

Reference Point   The insertion point of a complex entity such as a component or hatch pattern. Visual display is optional and consists of four short line segments, a vertical, horizontal, and two diagonals, which meet at their centers to form an asterisk-like figure. A Reference Point is displayed at the drawing Origin when display of Reference Points is on.

Regular Polygon   A multisided figure with equal-length sides and equal angles between all sides. Although the REGULAR POLYGON command in Generic CADD asks only for a center point, a point on one of the vertices of the polygon, and the number of sides, a number of individual Line entities are actually created.

Relative   To be measured from the previously selected point. Coordinates may be displayed and data may be manually entered in relative mode if you wish.

REN   A DOS command for reassigning the name of a file. To rename the file HOUSE to MYHOUSE, for example, the command would be REN HOUSE.DWG MYHOUSE.DWG.

Rename   In Generic CADD, to replace the extension of a filename with the extension .BAK. Whenever you attempt to save a file, Generic CADD checks to see if a file by the same name already exists. If it does, you are given the choice of overwriting the existing file, in which case it is replaced by the new file, or renaming the existing file, in which case its extension is changed to .BAK so that there is no conflict between the two filenames.

Representational   The quality of conveying information about real situations. Generic CADD and CAD in general are said to be representational processes because real data and geometric relationships can be defined, stored, and re-created in a way that conveys true, accurate information.

Resolution   The number of dots available for representing information on the screen or printer. Video resolutions are generally expressed in terms of the entire screen (EGA resolution, for example, is 640 × 350), while printer resolutions are often expressed either in dots per inch (many laser printers operate at up to 300 dpi) or pins per character (most dot matrix printers offer either 9 or 24 pins).

Rubber Banding   A process in which an entity is continually redrawn on the screen as the cursor is moved to give the impression that it is stretching as it moves. Rubber banding is optional in Generic CADD and is used in a number of drawing and editing commands to increase visual feedback.

Save   To store information in a file on a disk. Generic CADD can save drawing files, font files, component files, batch files, and image files.

Scale   A parameter applied to a complex entity before it is placed that determines the final size of the entity. Each scalable type of complex entity has its own scale variable(s).

Snap   To place a point or locate the cursor based on existing points in the drawing, existing geometric relationships, or the spacing and origin of the grid. All versions of Generic CADD allow both grid and definition point snaps, while Levels 2 and 3 provide extended geometric references, such as intersections, midpoints, centers; parallel, perpendicular, and tangent relationships; and so on.

Software   Instructions that cause the computer to perform various functions. Software stored on a chip (known as the BIOS) tells the computer how to look on the disk drive for more software (the operating system) that issues prompts, receives commands, and loads and runs programs (application software such as Generic CADD).

Spline   A type of curve defined by a number of points or nodes. The curve created by Generic CADD's CURVE command is a spline curve that passes through the user-placed points.

Stretch   An editing operation or option in which certain definition points are moved while others remain in the same place, changing the shape of entities. In Generic CADD, lines may be stretched by using an option of the WINDOW MOVE command when one end of a line is selected within the window and the other is not.

Stylus   A pen-like pointing device that works with a digitizer tablet. The stylus is usually connected to the tablet by a wire and includes a single button that is depressed when the point of the stylus is pressed downward on the tablet. A second button is sometimes present on the side of the stylus, which may be depressed with a fingertip.

Symbol   A drawn representation of an object or concept. In this book, the term *symbol* is used to distinguish those items that are added to a drawing as reference rather than as a representation of the real object that you are drawing. Notes, dimensions, North arrows, titles, and so on are considered symbols.

Tablet   The flat portion of a digitizer on which you point with a puck or stylus. Most tablets contain a very fine grid of wires that detect the presence of the pointing device and relay coordinates to the computer. Often a printer overlay is taped to the tablet to identify various areas that may be used for pointing on the screen and for selecting menu items.

.TDG   An extension used by Generic Software to identify files that contain pointing device drivers, that communicate technical information about a variety of mice, digitizers, and track balls to Generic CADD.

Text   Predefined complex entities which are placed according to a number of predetermined parameters. The definitions of text characters come from a selected font file. Generic CADD contains a number of simple text editing commands for manipulating text characters.

Toggle   A command that changes a parameter from one state to another. Most toggles in Generic CADD are switched on and off by selecting the same toggle command.

.TPL   An extension used to identify files that contain plotter drivers, which communicate technical information about a variety of plotters to Generic CADD.

.TPR   An extension used to identify files that contain printer drivers, which communicate technical information about a variety of dot matrix and laser printers to Generic CADD.

Transferability   The quality of certain file types to be shared between various programs. Generic CADD drawing files are transferable among all Levels of Generic CADD in their native format, and transferable to other CADD programs through AutoConvert and Generic IGES, which create .DXF and IGES files, respectively. In addition, Generic CADD drawing and image files are transferable to a variety of painting and publishing formats through the use of Generic's PaintConvert and DeskConvert.

Unerase   A function for restoring to the screen and database entities that have been previously erased. Each UNERASE command restores the same number of entities that were erased by a corresponding ERASE command.

Units   In Generic CADD, a variety of measurement systems are available. English units may be expressed in feet, feet and inches, or just inches. In either feet and inches or inches, the basic unit of measurement is an inch. Partial inches may be expressed in either decimal or fractional format. Three different metric formats are also available: meters, centimeters, and millimeters. The number of places after the decimal point is user-selected. All of these unit systems are intended to allow you to draw whatever you are trying to draw in real units.

.VGD   An extension used to identify files that contain video drivers, which communicate technical information about a variety of video graphic cards to Generic CADD.

Video Menu   A list of commands that appears on the right side of the screen, from which you can select a desired action. The video menu is used by moving a menu cursor up and down with the pointing device or cursor keys and pressing the second button on the pointing device or the HOME key on the keyboard. The actual text of the video menu and the commands associated with each text item are stored in an ASCII file with the extension .MNU.

Viewport   A term used to describe the way that the video monitor functions as a device for displaying the CADD drawing. Often, only part of the drawing is displayed on the screen at any one time, as if you were seeing only a small portion of a larger drawing.

Window   A rectangular area described by placing two points on the screen with the cursor. The window is displayed as a visible box on the screen and is used for selecting items for editing, display, and other functions. Items are defined to be "in the window" only if all of their definition points fall within the rectangular area. Only the reference point of a complex entity need be captured, as this is the only definition point that it has.

Zoom   To change the portion of the drawing that is displayed on the video monitor. Most of the ZOOM commands also change the scale at which the drawing is displayed on the screen.

Trademarks

AutoCAD®	Autodesk, Inc.
AutoConvert™	Generic Software, Inc.
AutoDimensioning™	Generic Software, Inc.
CadText™	John Adams, Jr.
Curve Maker™	Workshop 3D Software, Inc.
DeskConvert™	Generic Software, Inc.
DotPlot™	Generic Software, Inc.
Drafting Enhancements 1™	Generic Software, Inc.
Drafting Enhancements 2™	Generic Software, Inc.
DXF™	Autodesk, Inc.
File Diagnostics™	Workshop 3D Software, Inc.
First CADD™	Generic Software, Inc.
Font Development Kit™	Workshop 3D Software, Inc.
Font Swapper™	Workshop 3D Software, Inc.
GEM®	Digital Research, Inc.
Generic 3•D™	Generic Software, Inc.
Generic 3D Drafting™	Generic Software, Inc
Generic CADD™	Generic Software, Inc.
Generic CADD™ Level 1	Generic Software, Inc.
Generic CADD™ Level 2	Generic Software, Inc.
Generic CADD™ Level 3	Generic Software, Inc.
Generic Estimator™	Generic Software, Inc.
Generic IGES™	Generic Software, Inc.
Generic Presentation™	Generic Software, Inc.
Hercules®	Hercules Computer Technology, Inc.
IBM®	International Business Machines Corporation
Logimouse®	Logitech, Inc.
Logitech™	Logitech, Inc.
MS-DOS®	Microsoft Corporation

PC Paintbrush™	Zsoft, Inc.
PenPlot™	Generic Software, Inc.
Plexiglas™	Rohm and Haas
PostScript®	Adobe Systems, Inc.
PROLINES™	Vacanti Yacht Design
The Third Dimension™	Workshop 3D Software, Inc.
Toshiba® 3100	Toshiba America, Inc.
Turbo-Fast Plan™	Island Software
WORKSHOP 3D®	Workshop 3D, Inc.

Index

The manuscript for this book was prepared and submitted to Osborne/McGraw-Hill in electronic form. The acquisitions editor for this project was Elizabeth Fisher, the technical reviewer was Ralph Ferrin, the project editor was Nancy Beckus, and production was by Kevin Shafer using Ventura Publisher.

Text design by Judy Wohlfrom, using New Century Schoolbook for text and Helvetica for display

Cover art by Bay Graphics Design Associates. Color separation by Colour Image. Cover supplier, Phoenix Color Corp. Screens produced with InSet from Inset Systems, Inc. Book printed and bound by R.R. Donnelley & Sons Company, Crawfordsville, Indiana.

You're important to us...

We'd like to know what you're interested in, what kinds of books you're looking for, and what you thought about this book in particular.

Please fill out the attached card and mail it in. We'll do our best to keep you informed about Osborne's newest books and special offers.

YES, SEND ME A FREE COLOR CATALOG
of all Osborne/McGraw-Hill computer books.

Name:_____ Title:_____

Company:_____

Address:_____

City:_____ State:_____ Zip:_____

I'M PARTICULARLY INTERESTED IN THE FOLLOWING(Check all that apply)

I use this software:
- ❏ Lotus 1-2-3
- ❏ Quattro
- ❏ dBASE
- ❏ WordPerfect
- ❏ Microsoft Word
- ❏ WordStar
- ❏ Others_____

I use this operating system:
- ❏ DOS
- ❏ OS/2
- ❏ UNIX
- ❏ Macintosh
- ❏ Others_____

I program in:
- ❏ C
- ❏ PASCAL
- ❏ BASIC
- ❏ Others_____

I chose this book because...
- ❏ Recognized author's name
- ❏ Osborne/McGraw-Hill's reputation
- ❏ Read book review
- ❏ Read Osborne catalog
- ❏ Saw advertisement in _____
- ❏ Found while browsing in store
- ❏ Found/recommended in library
- ❏ Required textbook
- ❏ Price
- ❏ Other_____

I rate this book:
❏ Excellent   ❏ Good   ❏ Poor

Comments_____
_____

Topics I would like to see covered in future books by Osborne/McGraw-Hill

include:_____
_____

ISBN# **499-5**

BUSINESS REPLY MAIL

First Class   Permit NO. 3111 Berkeley, CA

Postage will be paid by addressee

OsborneMcGraw-Hill

2600 Tenth Street
Berkeley, California 94710–9938